MW00582144

Oracle Press™

OCP Building Internet Applications I & II Exam Guide

Oracle Press™

OCP Building Internet Applications I & II Exam Guide

Christopher Allen

Osborne/**McGraw-Hill**

New York Chicago San Francisco
Lisbon London Madrid Mexico City Milan
New Delhi San Juan Seoul Singapore Sydney Toronto

Osborne/**McGraw-Hill**
2600 Tenth Street
Berkeley, California 94710
U.S.A.

To arrange bulk purchase discounts for sales promotions, premiums, or fund-raisers, please contact Osborne/**McGraw-Hill** at the above address. For information on translations or book distributors outside the U.S.A., please see the International Contact Information page immediately following the index of this book.

OCP Building Internet Applications I & II Exam Guide

1234567890 FGR FGR 01987654321
Book p/n 0-07-219334-4 and CD p/n 0-07-219335-2
parts of
ISBN 0-07-219333-6

Publisher
Brandon A. Nordin

Vice President & Associate Publisher
Scott Rogers

Acquisitions Editor
Jeremy Judson

Project Editor
Janet Walden

Acquisitions Coordinators
Jessica Wilson and Athena Honore

Technical Editor
Christian Bauwens

Project Manager
Jenn Tust

Composition & Indexing
MacAllister Publishing Services, LLC

Series Design
Jani Beckwith

Cover Design
Damore Johann

This book was composed with QuarkXPress™.

For Grace

About the Author

Christopher Allen has been a database professional for over 20 years and has provided computer consulting services for clients such as IBM, Dell, Microsoft, Universal Studios, the California Institute of Technology, and the Department of Justice. He has programmed hundreds of customer applications and has taught more than a thousand computer classes for professionals.

Allen is an Oracle Certified Professional DBA and OCP Internet Developer. He is the author of *PL/SQL 101*, co-author of the *OCP Financial Applications Consultant Exam Guide*, and co-author of the *OCP Application Developer Exam Guide*.

OracleCertified Professional

About the Oracle Certification Exams

Oracle Corporation is very committed to helping professionals learn how to use the inherently complicated products they sell. Oracle's Education division produces a wide variety of quality courses, along with a growing battery of exams designed to recognize those who have both "book learning" about Oracle products and plenty of hands-on experience with those products. Although these exams do not guarantee that someone who is certified is an expert, they do guarantee that the person is not an amateur.

The response to the Oracle Certified Professional (OCP) programs has been impressive. In a study performed by International Data Corporation, most of the companies said the increased effectiveness of OCP-certified professionals resulted in savings that paid for the certification in less than nine months! Not surprisingly, when OCP professionals were surveyed, 97 percent said they benefited from becoming certified. These benefits include increased knowledge, of course, but professionals have also gained other, less tangible benefits such as getting in the door for a more fulfilling job, being given more complicated (and more visible) projects at their current job, and gaining concrete leverage for increased pay. OCP-certified professionals also receive the right to use the OCP logo.

Requirements for Certification

This may sound strange, but each exam in the Oracle Applications Developer Release 6/6*i* certification track has a different passing score. That's because Oracle Education changes the exams frequently, but they want the level of skill necessary to pass them to remain constant. So when they change an exam, they carefully gauge the difficulty of the new questions compared to the old ones, and if the questions are more difficult, they let you answer fewer of them correctly and still pass. If the questions are easier, you must give a correct answer on more of them in order to pass. They've been doing this for several years, so the number of questions on each exam, as well as the number you have to answer correctly, is a little different for each exam. The following table shows the current requirements in the Oracle Applications Developer Release 6/6*i* certification track. By the time you take your exams, the figures could be slightly different than those in the table, but the overall point is the same: you must answer 60 to 70 percent of the questions correctly in order to pass an exam. Because of this, it makes sense to wait to schedule each exam until you are consistently scoring at least 85 percent on the related practice exams in this book. If you have the time, it will also help if you invest a few months into application development before taking your exams.

Exam Number	Exam Title	Number of Questions	Minimum Correct Answers to Pass	Passing Percentage
1Z0-001	Introduction to Oracle: SQL and PL/SQL	57	39	68%
1Z0-101	Develop PL/SQL Program Units	57	39	68%
1Z0-131	Build Internet Applications I	60	38	63%
1Z0-132	Build Internet Applications II	60	36	60%

If you take an exam and do not pass, you have to wait 30 days before you can take it again. You may repeat an exam three times in a 12-month period.

Recertification

As Oracle products are upgraded, the exams must also be upgraded. When Oracle Education releases a modified exam track for a new software version, they notify people who have been certified in the earlier version of the software. The prior certification remains valid for six more months. During that time you can become certified in the new version of the product by taking a New Features exam that covers the features added in the new release of the software.

Exam Format

The OCP exams are administered by Sylvan Prometric, an independent professional testing company with over 800 locations worldwide. Because the exams are computer based, they can be scheduled at your convenience—you don't have to go at a specific predetermined time. You only need call Sylvan, identify what exam you want to take, select the location you want, and identify when you want to go. Generally, you will take the exam in a room with a few computers in it; you will be assigned a computer and you will take your exam individually. Another person may or may not be in the room at the same time, and if a person is in the room, the chances are good he or she is taking some other exam. The exams consist of 60 to 90 questions; you have 90 minutes to answer them. The questions are either multiple choice, or scenario based, in which you are presented with a problem, shown an image of an Oracle product, and asked to click on the areas of the product that you would use to solve the problem. While taking the exam, you can mark questions to come back to later for further review. Once you have finished, your exam will be graded on the spot.

Contents at a Glance

Contents

PART II
Preparing for OCP Exam 4: Build Internet Applications II

Preface

he Oracle Internet Application Developer certification track consists of four exams:

- Introduction to Oracle: SQL and PL/SQL
- Develop PL/SQL Program Units
- Build Internet Applications I
- Build Internet Applications II

The first two exams are the basis of numerous Oracle certifications, and they can be prepared for using a variety of SQL and PL/SQL books. (In fact, you can prepare for the first exam using the Oracle Press book *PL/SQL 101*, which I wrote. I don't mean to be self-serving in mentioning it—I really believe it's the best preparation available for the first exam.)

This book covers the last two exams, and it contains two units—one for each exam. Within each unit, you will find a number of chapters that teach the information you need to know to achieve a successful score on the related exam.

How Chapters Are Organized

The chapters in this book observe the following format:

Discussion Sections

Each subject covered in an exam will be addressed with a discussion section in this book. Each discussion section will be immediately followed by a brief set of questions that review the material just presented. The answers to these questions are not printed elsewhere in the book; the idea is that if you read the questions and don't know the answers, you have not absorbed the information just presented, and you should go back and reread it before you continue forward.

Chapter Summaries

Each chapter closes with a summary of the chapter's main points. In addition to helping drive home the important points after you have read the discussion sections, this compressed review is a powerful, efficient review tool to use before you take the exam. After you have gone through a unit in the book and have scheduled to take the related exam, I recommend that you reread the relevant summaries once a day for several days preceding the exam. This will keep the material fresh in your mind with very little time investment.

Two-Minute Drills

Following the chapter summary, the same information is presented in an even briefer format: as a series of bullet points called Two-Minute Drills. These are great to read over just before you go in to take your exam.

Chapter Questions and Answers

The final part of each chapter is a series of multiple-choice questions that emulate the questions you will encounter in the actual exam. After the questions, you will find the answers, along with an explanation of why the correct answer is correct and why the others choices are not. Answer these questions after reading the chapter. If you get 85 percent or more correct, proceed to the next chapter. If you don't, go back and read the chapter sections related to the questions you missed, and then wait a couple of days and answer the sample questions again.

Conventions Used in This Book

Bold text indicates text that you will type as shown. *Italics* are used to identify new terms the first time they are presented, as well as to emphasize key facts. Items that deserve special notice are set apart as Notes or Tips. They look like this:

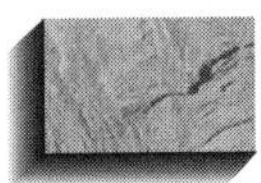

NOTE
Remember to do all the right things and to not do the things that aren't.

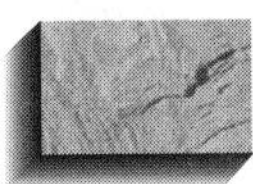

TIP
Never tie your shoelaces together before a hike.

How to Get the Most Out of This Book

You must do three things to get the most out of this book:

1. **Do.**
2. **The.**
3. **Exercises.**

The exercises take the "book learning," which is quickly forgotten, and put it into your hands, where it can be retained for a long, long time. Through the course of this book, you will go through the steps to create a variety of new forms for working with data. If you want to really maximize your learning and retention, do the exercises, and then do them *again* with an application of your own. Your application can be real or fanciful—it doesn't matter. The magical retention phenomenon called "transferring the knowledge" will happen either way.

The only exception to doing the exercises is if you are a seasoned Oracle Forms professional who has created numerous forms already. If this is the case, you can test out of a chapter by going directly to the questions at the end of the chapter, answering them, and checking your score. If you get 85 percent or more of the answers right, and you are pressed for time, it's worthwhile to consider skipping that chapter and proceeding to the next one, which you might test out of as well.

Acknowledgments

Once again I find myself privileged to be part of the distinguished Oracle Press collection. A tip of the hat to Brandon Nordin and Scott Rogers for guiding the Oracle Press line to make it the quality series that it is. I'm honored to be in such a company.

I would like to thank Jessica Wilson, Athena Honore, and Molly Applegate for stewarding this book through the production process so smoothly. In addition, Christian Bauwens did an exceptional job of technical editing, adding substantial polish to the finished product. And through it all, Jeremy Judson kept the rudder firmly pointed in the right direction.

Lastly, I thank my wife Grace, for more reasons that I can fit on this page.

Introduction

The market for professionals who understand how to install, modify, and manage Oracle Forms is exploding. The product is as easy to use as any point-and-click form generator, but much more robust than products designed strictly to run with PC-based databases.

Companies are clamoring for Oracle Forms consultants. As of this writing, the job-oriented Internet newsgroups contained 8,400 messages from people looking to hire Oracle Forms experts. The market for this skill set is strong.

But how does a company's hiring manager know who is hot and who is just hot air? Well, word of mouth is always helpful, but only if you trust the mouth you're listening to. Getting in the door can be a challenge. It helps to have something that makes you stand out. Putting the Oracle Certified Professional logo in your resume can certainly help. And once you are on the job, you have an advantage too. On-the-job training is great, but it tends to be spotty—you learn the things that the particular job calls for, filtered by whatever the people around you happen to already know. In contrast, studying for the OCP exams takes you into every area of Oracle Forms. It is extremely likely that you will learn things you can apply in your work—things you didn't even know were available. That helps make you an expert, and experts are noticed and rewarded in the workplace.

How Should You Prepare for the OCP Exams?

With dedication. You will get the most out of this process if you can set aside a certain amount of time each day (or, perhaps, each *work* day—let's be realistic) for study and practice. This enables you to build on recently acquired knowledge while it is still fresh. At the end of each chapter, take the sample exam. If you answer 85 percent or more of the questions correctly, proceed to the next chapter. If not, go back and reread the chapter, taking special care to answer the small collection of exercises that follow each subject point. If you follow this approach, you should do quite well on the sample exam at the end of the chapter. Continue this process, as regularly as possible, until you have completed one of the book's two units.

After you have successfully completed a unit, schedule your OCP exam with Sylvan Prometric. Then read through the Chapter Summaries and the Two-Minute Drills until the day you take the exam. On that day, wear comfortable clothing (nobody cares how you look there) and plan to arrive early, so that unforeseen delays don't ruffle your feathers. When it is time to take the exam, you will be seated in front of a PC at the testing center you've selected. The Prometric personnel will not let you take any books or notepaper in with you—they even ask that you turn off your pager so an accomplice can't page you with answers! (Remember, they're just doing their job.) They do provide some notepaper of their own, which you have to turn in after the exam (to be thrown away, not graded).

The computer-based exam starts by asking you to identify yourself. Then it offers to give you an introduction to how the testing software works. It's a good idea to go through this introduction, and it will not count against your time. When you do decide to start the actual test, you will be presented with the first question and the timer will start. Each screen contains a question, several potential answers (or a screen shot on which you will click), buttons to go to the next or prior question, and an option to mark that question for later review. If you read a question and are reasonably sure of the correct answer, select the answer and move on to the next question. If you are not sure, ponder the question for a bit of time—you have an average of a minute and a half per question—and if you don't know the answer after several moments, mark the question to be reviewed later and move on. After you have answered all the questions you know, you can return to the questions that stumped you earlier, and spend more time thinking about the answer to each. If you really don't know the answer to a question, then eliminate whatever answers you are sure are *incorrect* and guess from those that remain. A question left blank is considered incorrect, so you have nothing to lose by guessing an answer to a question you don't know.

After you are done with the exam, you will be shown an on-screen analysis of how you did. This is where you hoot and holler, congratulate yourself, and tell the Prometric administrator that he or she is your best friend. Or maybe it's where you introspectively ponder how you can study more effectively, and think about scheduling a repeat performance in 30 days. The on-screen analysis includes both an overall score and a subject-by-subject summary—the latter is handy if you have to take the exam again because it lets you know what areas need further review. This screen is also printed for you to take home with you.

Remember, you have taken two important steps already. First, you have decided what you want: OCP certification. Knowing what you want enables you to focus your attention and schedule your time accordingly. Second, you have acquired a trusty study guide to help you prepare. These steps reflect a level of commitment that will serve you well as you study. Keep that level of commitment high, do the work, and you will get the rewards.

Go for it!

Preparing for OCP Exam 3: Build Internet Applications I

CHAPTER 1

Introduction to Oracle Forms 6*i*

n this chapter, you will cover the following areas of Oracle Forms 6*i*:

- Overview of Oracle Forms 6*i*
- Introduction to Oracle Forms 6*i* tools
- Customizing your Oracle Forms 6*i* session

This unit covers materials that are tested in *OCP Exam 3, Build Internet Applications I*. The first section of this chapter gives a high-level overview of Oracle Forms 6*i*'s features, along with the benefits of using it. The next section provides a first look at the components that make up the Oracle Forms 6*i* package. The final section describes how you can tune the Oracle Forms 6*i* application so it more closely matches the way you like to work.

Overview of the Oracle Forms 6*i* Package

In this section, you will cover the following points about the Oracle Forms 6*i* package:

- Features and benefits of using Oracle Forms 6*i*
- Component groups in Oracle Forms 6*i*

Oracle Forms 6*i* is comprised of several powerful tools enabling developers to create robust, highly scalable applications more quickly than would be possible using a programming language such as C, Visual Basic, or Java. With it, developers can use tools (known as *Builders* in Oracle Forms 6*i*) to create the different parts of an application, such as forms, charts, queries, procedures, and database objects.

Features and Benefits of Using Oracle Forms 6*i*

Oracle Forms 6*i* is a sophisticated and, some might say, complicated program. That is true of any application designed to do as many things as Oracle Forms 6*i* does. Learning it well takes time, but that investment will be rewarded with a broad array of powerful, timesaving capabilities. Some of the benefits include enhanced productivity, the ability to design scalable applications, adherence to Oracle's standard of openness between applications, creation of reusable applications, Dynamic Visualization, and Web deployment of applications to take advantage of advances in Internet/Web technology.

Productivity

For individual developers, Oracle Forms 6*i* speeds application design by employing object orientation, rapid application design (RAD) techniques, a unified client-server architecture, and online computer-based training modules. It allows components to be reused and to be grouped into classes whose characteristics can be inherited by subclasses. You can use wizards to create application components quickly and easily. (*Wizards* are special interfaces that prompt you to specify values for certain components and then configure objects according to parameters you defined.) If you use Oracle's Designer 6*i* CASE tool, you can have Oracle Forms 6*i* base an application on a Designer 6*i* model. In addition, forms created in Oracle Forms 6*i* can interface with programs written in other languages (C, for instance) using the Open API. The Open API can also be used to create or modify form modules.

Scalability

Because Oracle Forms 6*i* is designed to accommodate a multitiered architecture, it has many features that help an application scale up to handle large quantities of data. On the database server side, it provides array data manipulation, such as array inserts and deletes. This feature can dramatically improve application performance by automatically sending inserts, updates, and deletes to the server in a batch without having to write complex optimization code. In addition, Oracle Forms 6*i* can base forms on data returned from server-based stored procedures, and, when a user updates data, an Oracle Forms 6*i* application can recompute subtotals on the client computer without having to run another server query. All of these features reduce network traffic, thereby increasing the number of users a given server can accommodate with reasonable performance. Oracle Forms 6*i* provides a simple drag-and-drop interface to specify whether an object runs on the client or the server.

Openness

Oracle Forms 6*i* provides a rich set of features for interacting with other applications. It accommodates OCX/ActiveX controls, Object Linking and Embedding (OLE), and Dynamic Data Exchange (DDE). In addition to its native Oracle database, Oracle Forms 6*i* can work with data stored in SQL Server, Sybase, Informix, Rdb, and DB/2, as well as any database accessible via ODBC or the Oracle Gateway. It can even work with data from multiple databases simultaneously.

In addition, numerous third-party companies have created interfaces between their products and Oracle Forms 6i. Available from members of the Open Tools Initiative, these interfaces allow Oracle Forms 6*i* to interact with CASE and modeling tools, configuration management (version control) tools, workflow engines, and transaction-processing (TP) monitors, among many others.

Usability

Oracle Forms 6*i* provides a variety of features enabling you to create applications that are extremely easy to use. You can build intuitive drag-and-drop user interfaces; incorporate image and sound files that are stored either within the database or as individual files; call dynamic link library (**.dll**) files to take advantage of platform-specific features within your applications; and incorporate animations, tooltips, and pop-up menus.

Visualization

With a sophisticated feature called *Dynamic Visualization*, Oracle Forms 6*i* enables you to create applications in which data and the graphics depicting the data can interact. This allows you to create features such as run-time chart editing, seamless Web reporting, graphical drill-down from overview to line-item detail, visual selection of data based on a graphical display, and conditional formatting of the display based on the content of the data within it.

Web Deployment

Oracle Forms 6*i* provides features enabling you to deploy your application on the Internet or an intranet with a minimum of effort. Data entry forms, graphics, and online reports can all use a Web browser as the "client" portion of the multitier model. This feature is built using Java, bringing with it the many benefits of platform independence. Using a Java-enabled browser, your application can run in any environment. This eliminates the need to learn a new language to create applications for different environments.

Exercises

1. **Name six important features of Oracle Forms 6*i*. Why are they important?**
2. **What form of server data manipulation is available in Oracle Forms 6*i*? What is the advantage of using it?**
3. **What is the benefit of using Java for database applications?**

Component Groups in Oracle Forms 6*i*

In situations where an application needs to be deployed in more than one language (written language, not computer language), the Translation Builder enables you to map text strings from one language to another. It then applies prior translation decisions to later versions of the application, thereby making subsequent translations easy to do.

Components for Development

The major front-end development components of Oracle Forms 6*i* are Forms and Graphics. These components provide the front-end capabilities of an application: inserting and querying data, and displaying information in graphical formats. Object management is accomplished using other Oracle Forms 6*i* components that allow manipulation of code and objects at the client and server level. Oracle Forms 6*i* supports three-tier architecture: the database server, an application server, and the client computer.

Oracle Forms 6*i* offers special features for back-end server development, as well as for Web deployment. For back-end development, Oracle Forms 6*i* offers the Query Builder, Procedure Builder, and Schema Builder. These tools are designed to speed up the nuts-and-bolts work needed to put the essential infrastructure of an application into place. Oracle Forms 6*i* handles Web transactions and publishing through its Web components as well. The Oracle Forms 6*i* Server allows applications to be accessed through any browser on the Web. The product's Graphics components also facilitate publishing data and reports on the Web.

Exercise

1. **What is the purpose of the Translation Builder?**

Introduction to Oracle Forms 6*i* Builder Tools

In this section, you will cover the following points about Oracle Forms 6*i* Builder tools:

- Builder tools for project management
- Builder tools for front-end development
- Builder tools for back-end development

When you install Oracle Forms 6*i*, you have the option to install some or all the components. The following tools are the major components in the Oracle Forms 6*i* package: Form Builder, Graphics Builder, Procedure Builder, Query Builder, Schema Builder, and Translation Builder. The various Builders in Oracle Forms 6*i* can be grouped into the categories of project management, front-end application management, and back-end application management. These components work together in a hierarchy that is depicted in Figure 1-1.

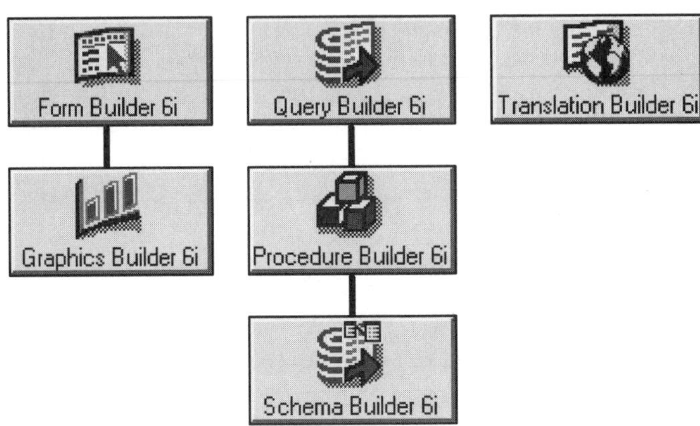

FIGURE 1-1. *Functional hierarchy of Oracle Forms 6*i *components*

Builder Tools for Project Management

For project management Oracle Forms 6*i* offers the Translation Builder. The Translation Builder provides the means for developers to translate an application's text into other languages and to store those translations in a repository to be used automatically when future versions of the application are translated. The Translation Editor performs the actual translation and manages the translation strings so future translations can be accomplished more quickly. Figure 1-2 displays an example screen from Translation Builder to aid your understanding.

Exercise

1. **What are the benefits of using the Translation Builder?**

Builder Tools for Front-End Development

To help you build your application's front-end interface, Oracle Forms 6*i* provides the Form Builder and Graphics Builder tools. The Form Builder simplifies the creation of data-entry screens (also known as *forms*). Forms are the applications that connect to a database, retrieve information requested by a user, present it in a layout specified by the form's designer, and allow the user to modify or add information. Form Builder enables you to build forms quickly and easily, working with a set of wizards to step you through various tasks. Figure 1-3 shows a sample screen from the Form Builder tool.

The Graphics Builder allows you to create interactive graphical displays of the data in a database. These graphics can then be embedded in forms and reports.

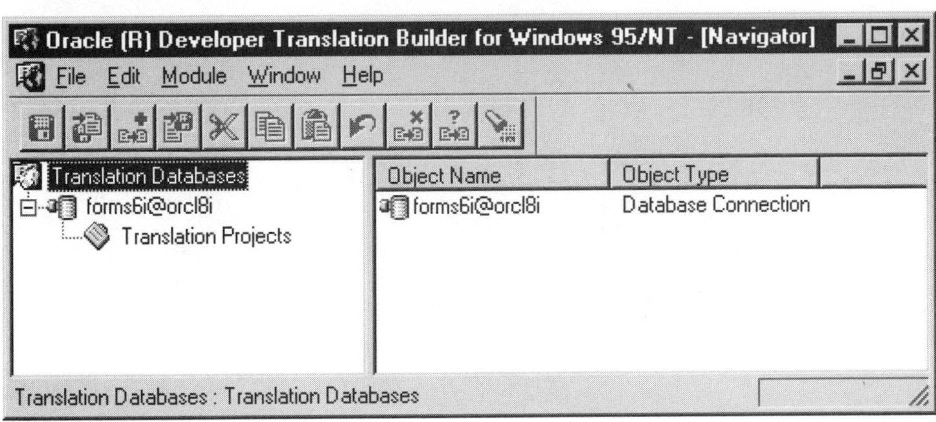

FIGURE 1-2. *Translation Builder example screen*

Graphics Builder provides a complete set of drawing and editing tools, along with a Chart Wizard to simplify the process of using the tools. Graphics created with Graphics Builder can be designed to change, based on user interaction at run time. The program also allows you to import and export a wide range of image formats. Figure 1-4 displays the Graphics Builder main screen.

Exercises

1. **What is a database's "front end"?**
2. **What Builder(s) would be used to create a data-entry screen? Add a pie chart to it?**

Builder Tools for Back-End Development

Back-end server development is a task covered by Oracle Forms 6*i* as well. Developing PL/SQL stored procedures, functions, and packages are not tasks that should be handled using flat files and SQL*Plus alone, as any seasoned developer who's struggled through it the hard way can attest. Instead, Oracle Forms 6*i* uses Procedure Builder to work on PL/SQL code for either client-side or server-side execution. It incorporates a broad set of features to aid in creating, testing, and debugging PL/SQL code in program units, libraries, and triggers. Figure 1-5 displays an example screen from Procedure Builder.

Schema Builder is a useful tool that allows you to define the tables, views, snapshots, synonyms, constraints, and relationships that will make up your

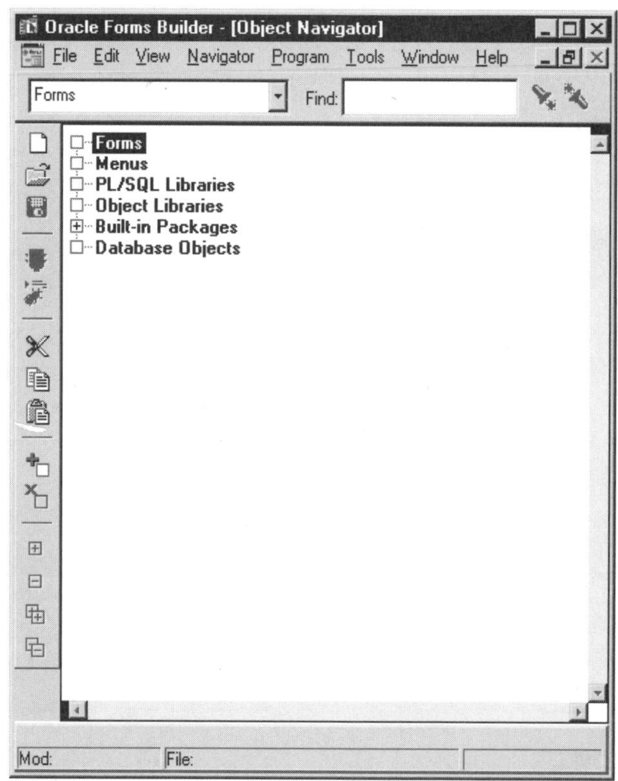

FIGURE 1-3. *Form Builder example screen*

database. It lets you visualize a database design, including the tables, columns, data types, and relationships, and then create the database objects to realize that design. This tool is useful to both developers and DBAs, in that it manages all aspects of Oracle database object creation and then displays all those components with ease. Figure 1-6 displays an example screen from Schema Builder.

One final aspect of back-end server development in Oracle Forms 6*i* is the creation of SQL statements. Building sophisticated forms and graphics can require writing complex SQL programs behind the scenes. Query Builder facilitates writing SQL code by providing a visual interface to the database objects being linked. Query Builder constructs SQL Data Manipulation Language (DML) queries that modify data in the database. Using this tool, you can design an efficient query based on its performance in several scenarios. Figure 1-7 displays a sample screen from the Query Builder tool.

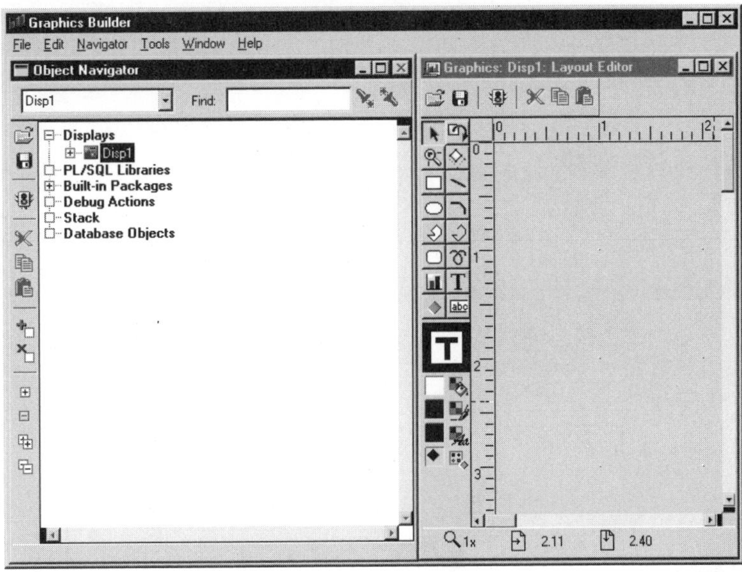

FIGURE 1-4. *Graphics Builder main screen*

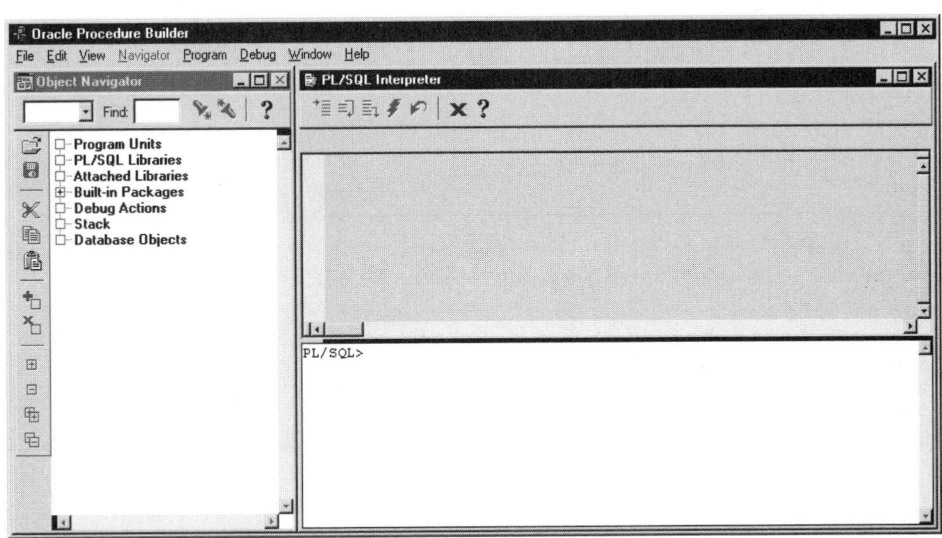

FIGURE 1-5. *Procedure Builder example screen*

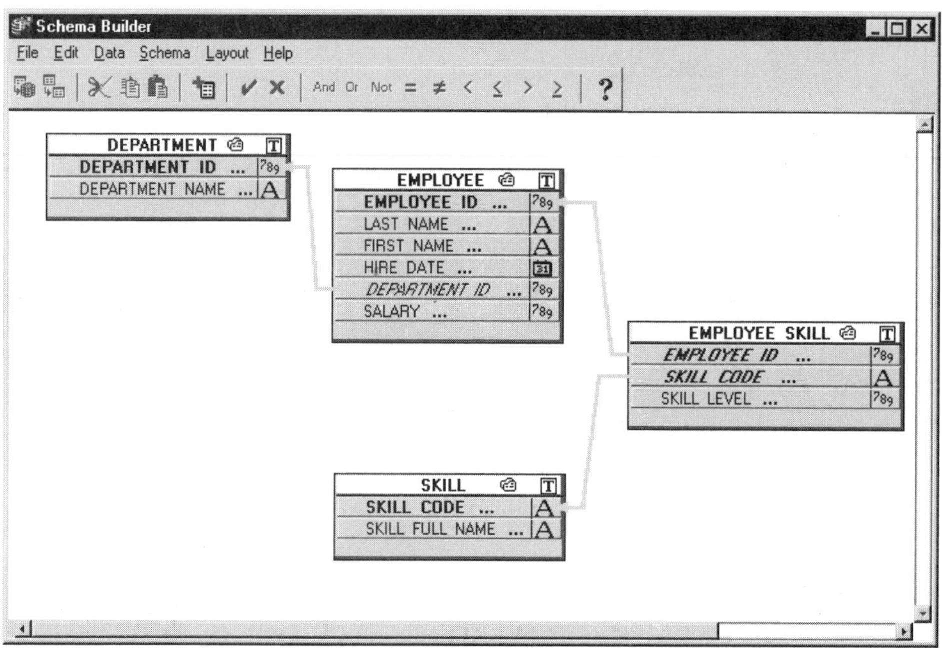

FIGURE 1-6. *Schema Builder example screen*

Exercises

1. **Identify and describe the components in the three broad divisions of the Oracle Forms 6*i* Builder set.**
2. **Which Oracle Forms 6*i* Builder can be used to add columns to an existing table? Put a new button on an existing form? Create a database trigger? Track common libraries and menus in forms?**

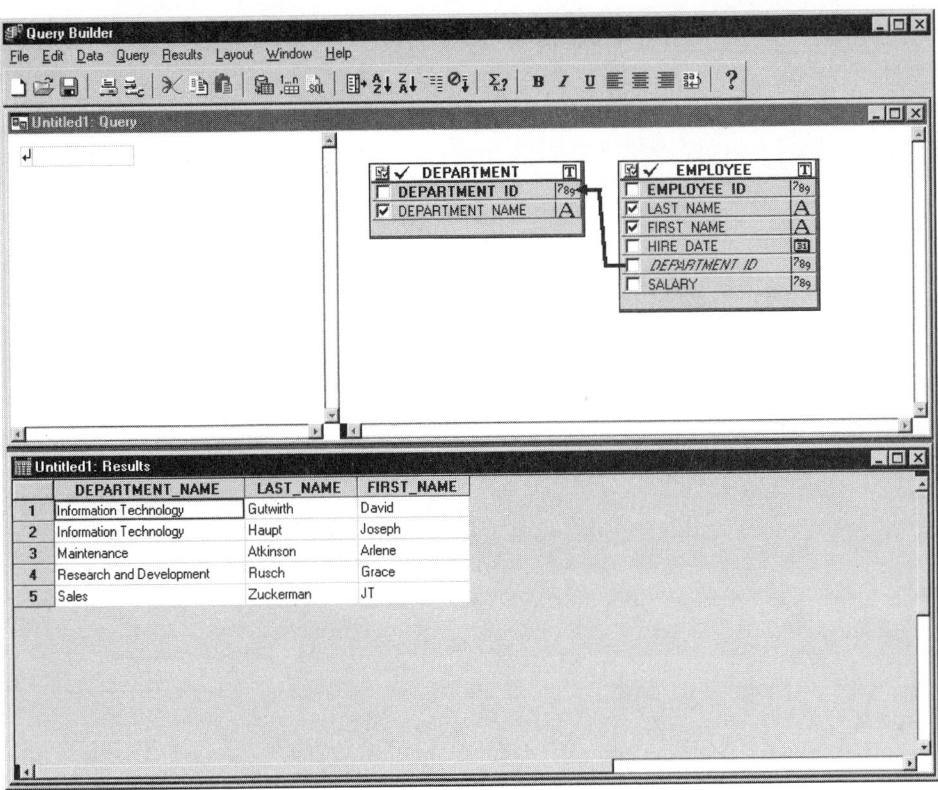

FIGURE 1-7. *Query Builder example screen*

Chapter Summary

This chapter provided an overview of the Oracle Forms 6*i* components. It began by introducing the features and benefits you can enjoy by using Oracle Forms 6*i*. These features include productivity resulting from an object-oriented rapid application design (RAD) environment. Your productivity also benefits from reusable components; a unified, multitiered architecture; component classes whose characteristics can be inherited by subclasses; and wizards to quickly guide you through many common tasks.

The next feature is the scalability that comes from being able to easily specify whether objects execute on the client or the server, as well as bandwidth-saving features such as array data manipulation for performing batch inserts, updates, and deletes without writing code. Scalability is also enhanced by the ability to base forms on server-run stored procedures, as well as the ability to recalculate aggregate values on the client without having to requery the server.

Another benefit of Oracle Forms 6*i* is the openness resulting from support for OXC/ActiveX controls, Object Linking and Embedding (OLE), and Dynamic Data Exchange (DDE) to interact with other programs. Adding to the openness of Oracle Forms 6*i* is its ability to work with data in many other databases, and its ability to interact with programs that provide CASE and modeling functions, configuration management (version control), and transaction-processing (TP) monitoring, written by companies in the Open Tools Initiative, whose products provide CASE and modeling functions, configuration management (version control), and transaction-processing (TP) monitoring.

The next benefit is the high degree of usability you can build into your Oracle Forms 6*i* applications. You can incorporate pop-up menus, tooltips, and animations to make your applications easier to use. You can build easy-to-understand drag-and-drop user interfaces, and you can have your applications include image and sound files, with the files being stored either within the database or as separate files. If your project prioritizes performance over portability, you can employ **.dll** files to access platform-specific features within your applications.

The next benefit is visualization, which enables you to create such handy features as run-time chart editing, graphical drill-down from overview to line-item detail, conditional formatting of a display based on its content, and visual selection of data based on a graphic display. Finally, Oracle Forms 6*i* provides Web deployment features enabling you to create Web-browser-based applications with minimal effort. Without having to learn Java, your applications can run in any environment in which a browser is available, including the Network Computing Architecture.

Next, you learned about the two groups of Oracle Forms 6*i* components: management components and development components. The management components consist of the Translation Builder. Translation Builder keeps track of text strings within your application that you translate from one language to another, and, when you have a future revision of that application to translate, Translation Builder automatically translates any strings that match those translated before. The development components include the Form Builder, Graphics Builder, Procedure Builder, Schema Builder, and Query Builder.

The last section covered Oracle Forms 6*i* Builders in more detail. This section divided the development components of Oracle Forms 6*i* into two subgroups: front-end development (items the user sees and interacts with) and back-end development (behind-the-scenes objects). Oracle Forms 6*i* expedites front-end development with its Form Builder and Graphics Builder. For the back end, Oracle Forms 6*i* helps you get work done quickly by offering the Procedure Builder, Schema Builder, and Query Builder.

Two-Minute Drill

- Oracle Forms 6*i* is a collection of several programs enabling developers to quickly produce database applications. Oracle Forms 6*i* enables developers to quickly produce database applications.
- In addition to increased productivity, Oracle Forms 6*i* also offers developers a high degree of scalability, openness, usability, visualization, and ease of Web deployment.
- The productivity of Oracle Forms 6*i* benefits comes from its object orientation, multitier architecture, and use of rapid application design (RAD) techniques. Oracle Forms 6*i* allows classing and subclassing of components; provides wizards to simplify common tasks; uses the Open API to interface with programs written in other languages; and can interface directly with Oracle's Designer 6*i* CASE tool, as well as with version-control systems and other applications.
- The scalability features of Oracle Forms 6*i* include the ability to identify whether an object runs on the client or the server simply by dragging and dropping it into the appropriate location within the interface. Oracle Forms 6*i* further promotes scalability with numerous features to reduce network traffic, such as array data manipulation, the ability to base forms on stored procedures running on the server, and the ability to recalculate aggregate values on the client without having to requery the server.
- Oracle Forms 6*i* provides a high degree of openness by making it easy to interact with non-Oracle databases, as well as with other applications. Several major database platforms are supported, as well as any database accessible via ODBC or the Oracle Gateway. To interact with other applications, you can employ OCX/ActiveX controls, OLE, and DDE.
- To promote usability within your applications, Oracle Forms 6*i* lets you include pop-up menus, tooltips, and animations in your interfaces; incorporate drag-and-drop functions; include image and sound files stored either as separate files or as objects within your database; and make calls to **.dll** files if you need to employ platform-specific features.
- The Dynamic Visualization feature of Oracle Forms 6*i* lets you include graphics in your applications and have the graphics interact with the data beneath them. This enables you to deploy features like graphical drill-down from overview to line-item detail; run-time chart editing; visual selection of data based on a graphic display; and conditional formatting of a display based on its data.

- Oracle Forms 6*i* enables you to produce forms and reports that run within any standard Web browser without having to learn another language or install a different run-time client for each client environment.
- Oracle Forms 6*i* programs can be divided into two main categories: management components and development components.
- Its development components include function-specific tools to create specific portions of your project. For front-end development, it offers the Form Builder and Graphics Builder. For back-end development, it provides the Procedure Builder, Schema Builder, and Query Builder.
- You can set preferences within most of the Oracle Forms 6*i* Builders to tailor their appearance and operation to suit your work style.

Chapter Questions

1. Which of the following are major features of Oracle Forms 6*i*? (Choose six.)

A. Graphical depiction of business processes

B. Ease of Web deployment

C. Centralized control over user access levels

D. Productivity

E. Openness

F. Wide acceptance by international standards committees

G. Usability

H. Radio buttons

I. Scalability

J. Visualization

2. What form of batch data manipulation is available in Oracle Forms 6*i*?

A. Bidirectional data links

B. ODBC

C. Array data manipulation

3. **What is the primary advantage of using the client data manipulation type referred to in question 2?**

   A. Minimal coding

   B. Reduced network traffic

   C. Web deployment

   D. Faster PL/SQL procedures

4. **What is the primary benefit of using Java in database applications?**

   A. More complete database functionality

   B. Can deploy on numerous platforms easily

   C. Cool addition to résumé

   D. Faster PL/SQL procedures

5. **What is the purpose of the Translation Builder?**

   A. To automatically translate your application into other languages

   B. To simplify conversion of data from one database format to another

   C. To ensure that forms are easy to understand

   D. To store earlier translations performed manually and applies them to subsequent translations

6. **Which statement most accurately describes what Oracle Forms 6*i* does if it finds a parameter with different settings in the Global Registry and the User Registry?**

   A. Prompts user to ask which setting to use

   B. Resets User Registry setting to match that in the Global Registry

   C. Uses the setting from the Global Registry

   D. Uses the setting from the User Registry

   E. Stops with an error message

7. **Which of the following are among the management components of Oracle Forms 6*i*?**

   A. Form Builder

   B. Procedure Builder

C. Query Builder

D. Schema Builder

E. Translation Builder

8. **Which of the following are not among the front-end components of Oracle Forms 6*i*? (Choose two.)**

   A. Form Builder

   B. Procedure Builder

   C. Graphics Builder

   D. Schema Builder

9. **Which of the following are among the back-end development components of Oracle Forms 6*i*? (Choose three.)**

   A. Form Builder

   B. Procedure Builder

   C. Graphics Builder

   D. Query Builder

   E. Schema Builder

   F. Translation Builder

10. **What Builders would be used to create an online report containing a pie chart?**

    A. Form Builder

    B. Procedure Builder

    C. Graphics Builder

    D. Query Builder

    E. Schema Builder

    F. Translation Builder

11. **Which of the following features enable Oracle Forms 6*i* applications to interact with various manufacturers' databases? (Choose two.)**

    A. ODBC

    B. OCX/ActiveX

C. OLE

D. Oracle Gateway

E. DDE

12. Which of the following features enable Oracle Forms 6*i* applications to interact with other programs? (Choose three.)

A. ODBC

B. OCX/ActiveX

C. OLE

D. Oracle Gateway

E. DDE

13. Which of the following Oracle Forms 6*i* features promote creating easy-to-use applications?

A. Pop-up menus

B. Tooltips

C. Animations

D. Drag-and-drop

14. What does the Dynamic Visualization feature in Oracle Forms 6*i* provide?

A. Graphical drill-down from overview to line-item detail

B. Run-time chart editing

C. Visual selection of data based on a graphic display

D. Conditional formatting of a display based on its data

15. Which Oracle Forms 6*i* builder enables you to add a column to an existing table?

A. Form Builder

B. Graphics Builder

C. Procedure Builder

D. Schema Builder

E. Query Builder

16. Which Oracle Forms 6*i* Builder enables you to view data in an existing table?

   A. Form Builder

   B. Graphics Builder

   C. Procedure Builder

   D. Schema Builder

   E. Query Builder

17. Which Oracle Forms 6*i* Builder enables you to automate repetitive tasks?

   A. Form Builder

   B. Graphics Builder

   C. Procedure Builder

   D. Schema Builder

   E. Query Builder

Answers to Chapter Questions

1. B, D, E, G, I, J. Ease of Web deployment, Productivity, Openness, Usability, Scalability, Visualization

Explanation Graphical depiction of business processes is a feature of Oracle Designer 6*i*, not Oracle Forms 6*i*. Centralized control over user access levels comes from the Oracle server Security Manager. The level of acceptance by international standards committees is not relevant, since you distribute Oracle Forms 6*i* applications in executable format, or design them to be used in Web browsers. And whereas radio buttons are certainly available as features within an Oracle Forms 6i form, it cannot be considered a major feature.

2. C. Array data manipulation

Explanation Bidirectional data links are not inherently batch-oriented. ODBC capabilities were present in earlier version of Oracle Forms 6*i*.

3. B. Reduced network traffic

Explanation By allowing you to specify that inserts, updates, and deletes should occur in batches rather than one record at a time, array data manipulation reduces the number of transactions necessary to affect large numbers of records, thereby reducing network traffic, which generally improves an application's performance.

4. B. Can deploy on numerous platforms easily

Explanation Platform independence is Java's main claim to fame.

5. D. Stores earlier translations performed manually and applies them to subsequent translations

Explanation The Translation Builder does not automatically translate your application. It stores the translations you create manually when converting your application's front end from one language to another. It then remembers and reapplies those translations automatically during subsequent translations. It does not convert database data or try to determine how easy your forms are to use.

6. D. Uses the setting from the User Registry

Explanation By definition, the Global Registry contains default settings that can be overridden by individual developers. When a setting is overridden, the overriding setting is stored in the individual's User Registry.

7. E. Translation Builder

Explanation The Translation Builder gives umbrella-like control over the language of text within modules created using the other Builders.

8. B, D. Procedure Builder, Schema Builder

Explanation The Oracle Forms 6*i* tools designed to create front-end components-components the user interacts with directly—are the Form Builder and the Graphics Builder.

9. B, D, E. Procedure Builder, Query Builder, and Schema Builder

Explanation The Oracle Forms 6*i* tools designed to create back-end components—components the user does not interact with directly—are the Procedure Builder, the Query Builder, and the Schema Builder.

10. A, C. Form Builder, Graphics Builder

Explanation An online report is essentially a form designed to display output. The Form Builder is going to be involved. The Graphics Builder is included as well, because the form is going to contain a pie chart.

11. A, D. ODBC, Oracle Gateway

Explanation Using the Open Database Connectivity (ODBC) protocol or the Oracle Gateway, you can build applications to use databases from many different manufacturers.

12. B, C, E. OCX/ActiveX, OLE, DDE

Explanation All three of these features are designed to link code or objects created by other programs into Oracle Forms 6*i* applications.

13. A, B, C, D. Pop-up menus, Tool tips, Animations, Drag-and-drop

Explanation All of these features promote creating applications that are easy to use.

14. A, B, C, D. Graphical drill-down from overview to line-item detail, Run-time chart editing, Visual selection of data based on a graphic display, Conditional formatting of a display based on its data

Explanation The ability to use graphics elements to control program operation offers all of the benefits listed.

15. D. Schema Builder

Explanation The Schema Builder's purpose is providing control over the structure of tables and related objects.

16. A, E. Form Builder, Query Builder

Explanation Forms Builder displays data when you run a form, and Query Builder displays data each time you tell it to execute a query.

17. C. Procedure Builder

Explanation Automating repetitive tasks falls into the realm of programming, and Procedure Builder helps you write PL/SQL programs.

CHAPTER 2

Form Builder

In this chapter, you will learn about the following facets of Form Builder:

- Working in the Form Builder environment
- Creating basic form modules
- Running a Form Builder application

In this chapter, you will get a thorough introduction to Form Builder. You will start by learning about the Form Builder environment, the main Form Builder components, and the main objects in a form module. Next, you will step through the basics of creating form modules, and learn the four steps involved in creating and using an Oracle Forms Developer 6*i* form. You will create a new form module, generate data blocks to use within the module to access database data, and create a basic form layout for viewing the data. After modifying the data blocks and form layout a bit, you will learn how to compile form modules. Once your sample application is compiled, you will run it using the Forms Runtime program. Next, you will be introduced to Form Builder file formats and their characteristics. With that under your belt, you will go on to create a relationship between two data blocks, and then modify your single-table form so it shows records from two tables synchronized in a master/detail relationship. In the final section, you will learn a variety of ways to run a Form Builder application, as well as how to filter the data retrieved into a Form Builder application. You will be shown timesaving techniques for inserting repetitive data, and you then will learn how to get detailed information about database errors in the Forms Runtime program.

The *OCP Exam 3* includes test questions in this subject area worth 12 percent of the final score.

Working in the Form Builder Environment

In this section, you will cover the following points about working in the Form Builder environment:

- Identifying the main Form Builder executables
- Identifying the main components of Form Builder
- Identifying the main objects in a Form module

It is time to move beyond theory and start learning about the nuts and bolts of building forms in Forms Developer 6*i*'s Form Builder. This section will begin by defining the main executable files that make up the Form Builder application. Next, you will learn about the main components that Form Builder makes available to you, and what each component does. Finally, you will take one of those components, the Form module, and get an understanding of the main objects within it.

Identifying the Main Form Builder Executables

As shown in Table 2-1, three executable programs make up the Form Builder application in Forms Developer 6*i*. All three are located in the **bin** directory beneath your Developer 6*i* software home directory.

Form Builder stores all settings for the forms you create in files with the extension **.fmb**. The Form Compiler program takes the **.fmb** file containing your Forms Builder application and compiles it so it can be run by the Forms Runtime program. This process compiles the PL/SQL code in your application's program units, producing an **.fmx** file as a result. The Forms Runtime program reads the **.fmx** file and runs your application. This entire process occurs automatically when you run your form from within Form Builder, as long as you leave the Build Before Running preference at its default setting of Yes. You can also compile your form at any time from within Form Builder by executing the Program | Compile menu command. (The File | Administration | Compile File menu command does the same thing, but does not offer incremental compilation.)

Program Name	Function	FileName	Reads File Type	Creates File Type
Form Builder	Development environment for creating Forms Developer 6*i* forms	**Ifbld60.exe**	N/A	**.fmb**
Form Compiler	Creates an executable **.fmx** file from an **.fmb** file	**Ifcmp60.exe**	**.fmb**	**.fmx**
Forms Runtime	Runs compiled Forms application **.fmx** files	**Ifrun60.exe**	**.fmx**	N/A

TABLE 2-1. *Form Builder Executables*

Exercises

1. **What are the Form Builder executables?**
2. **What does each Form Builder executable do?**

Identifying the Main Components of Form Builder

A Form Builder application contains several different types of components, each providing a unique kind of functionality. The individual components are called *modules*. The modules can be grouped into the following categories:

- **Form modules** Make up the bulk of most applications. It is within form modules that you define what data is presented to the user, how it is presented, and what the user can do with it. This is also where you define relationships, PL/SQL triggers, limits on the number of records fetched, and similar parameters.
- **Menu modules** Where you store information about custom menus you create for your application. In addition to storing the definitions and underlying code for menu and submenu items, a menu module keeps track of any libraries the menu uses, information about object grouping and classes/subclasses, help items associated with the menu, and visual attributes such as font name, size, weight, style, and spacing. Because a form's menus are stored in a Menu module, you can customize or replace the default menus and provide exactly the functionality your application requires.
- **PL/SQL Library modules** Contain the client-side procedures, packages, and functions that you write. Other modules within your application call these modules.
- **Object Library modules** Enable you to store objects your application uses and reuse them wherever you need them. This can speed development dramatically, as well as make it easier to enforce standards throughout your company or organization.

Exercises

1. **What are the four main components in Form Builder?**
2. **What default Form component can you modify or replace in order to tailor the functionality of a new application?**
3. **What are the benefits of using an Object Library?**

Identifying the Main Objects in a Form Module

Most users see a data-entry form as a single object. As a developer, you need to think about a form's contents not only in more detail, but also in a hierarchical structure. In Forms Developer 6*i*, a form module contains numerous large objects that, in turn, hold smaller objects. All of these form module objects come together into a single cohesive interface that lets the user interact with database data. What follows is a description of these objects, in the order of largest to smallest. Figure 2-1 shows a sample form and the object types within it.

Window Objects

The window is the outermost boundary for a form—an empty frame to hold objects. All of the visual objects in a Form Builder application are contained within two types of windows: *document* and *dialog*.

Document Windows Document windows are used for standard data-entry forms. If you are developing on a Windows platform, your application automatically has a special type of document window called a multiple document interface (MDI) window that serves as a parent window containing all the other document windows. The MDI window usually holds the main menu and toolbar of the application, as well. While the MDI window is not included in an application's list of windows, you can still maximize, minimize, and resize it via code. All other document windows—in other words, the ones you create—must fit within the confines of the MDI window. When users are in a document window, they can generally enter and query

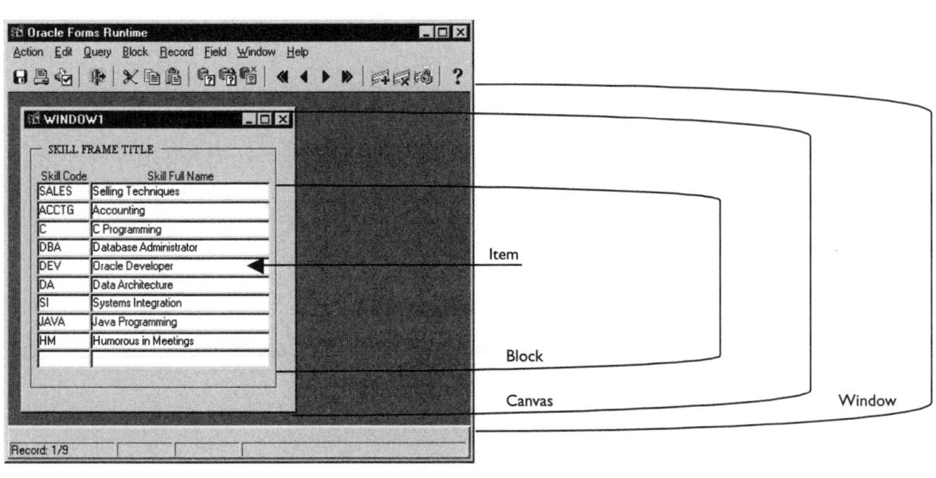

FIGURE 2-1. *Main objects in a form module*

data, move to other windows within the application, and interact with the application's menu and toolbar.

Dialog Windows Dialog windows are used for displaying messages to the user. When defining the properties of a dialog window, you can specify its size and position; whether or not it is *modal* (forcing users to respond to it before they can do anything else); whether the user can move, resize, maximize, minimize, or close it; and visual attributes such as colors, fill patterns, font name, size, weight, style, and spacing.

Canvas Objects

The visual backgrounds on which you place form objects are called *canvases,* and a window can contain one or more. There are four types of canvases: content, stacked, tab, and toolbar.

Content Canvases A content canvas is the essential background for any form window. Because of this, a content canvas is automatically placed in any new form layout you create. It is the default canvas type and occupies the entire window pane. A window only contains one content canvas at a time.

Stacked Canvases A stacked canvas resides on top of a content canvas, hiding a portion of the content canvas as it does so. The stacked canvas can look either similar to or different from the content canvas background, depending on the effect desired by the developer. You can use stacked canvases to make items seem to appear and disappear on the screen, based on criteria you specify. You can also use a stacked canvas to create scrolling subwindows within a window, and to display a single form header above multiple forms without having to lay the header out in each form, among other things. A window can contain numerous stacked canvases.

Tab Canvases A tab canvas is a multiple-page object that is familiar to users who have set options for practically any Windows object. It allows the user to move between multiple pages of related information simply by clicking intuitive *tabs* at the top of the pages. A tab canvas is most useful when you need to display a large quantity of related data while consuming relatively little screen space. A tab canvas resides on top of a content canvas, hiding a portion of the content canvas as it does so.

Toolbar Canvases Toolbar canvases are available in several flavors: horizontal, vertical, and MDI. A window can have one or more toolbars—even multiple horizontal or vertical toolbars—and you have programmatic control over which toolbars are visible at a given time, as well as over what items within each toolbar are visible. If you are developing within a Windows environment, you can also create toolbars for the MDI window.

Block Objects

In Forms Builder, a block is a logical container that holds form objects such as data items and control buttons. There are two types: *data* block and *control* block.

Data Blocks A data block creates a bridge between your form and the data in your database. It enables you to access data from a database table, database view, procedure, or transactional trigger. Form Builder automatically puts a *frame* around a data block. The frame is owned by the canvas it appears on, and you can use the frame not only to move the block on the layout, but also to select the block for modification.

Control Blocks A control block holds items that do not interact directly with your data, but instead exert control over the application itself. For instance, when you add buttons to a form, you place them within a control block.

Item Objects

The *items* are the individual objects on your forms with which your users interact. The most common item is a *text item*, which contains fields enabling your users to view, enter, and modify database data. There are also items to display read-only data (*chart item, display item,* and *image item*); to depict changeable data in a graphical representation (*check box, list item,* and *radio group*); to control the application (*button*); to manipulate audio objects (*sound item*); and to simplify the creation of user interfaces (*ActiveX control*).

Exercises

1. **When you create a new form layout, what type of object is always automatically on it?**
2. **What is the relationship between a window and a canvas?**
3. **What are the types of canvases, and what are the differences between them?**
4. **What is the relationship between a block and an item?**
5. **What are the different kinds of blocks?**

Creating Basic Form Modules

In this section, you will cover the following points about creating basic form modules:

- How to create a form module
- Using the Data Block Wizard to create and modify data blocks

- Creating and modifying layouts with the Layout Wizard
- Saving, compiling, and running a form module
- Form Builder file formats and their characteristics
- Creating data blocks with relationships
- Running a master/detail form module

When you want to create a new database form with Forms Developer 6*i*, you need to complete four steps. First, you create a new form module in Form Builder. Next, you create a data block to supply the new form module with data. After that, you create a form layout depicting the data block's items on one or more canvases. Finally, you save, compile, and run the module. In this section, you will go through all of these steps. Starting with a sample requirement for a one-table form, you will create a new form module, give it a data block, lay the data block's items out on a form canvas, and compile and run it in the Forms Runtime environment. You will then learn about the different file types that Form Builder produces when you generate form modules. Next, you will learn how to create relationships between data blocks. The section will wrap up by stepping you through the process of creating a form using a master/detail relationship.

Creating a Form Module

Creating a new form module is quite simple. The first step is to start the Form Builder application. (If you see the Welcome dialog box as shown in Figure 2-2, deselect the **Display at startup** option, then select the option labeled **Build a new form manually**

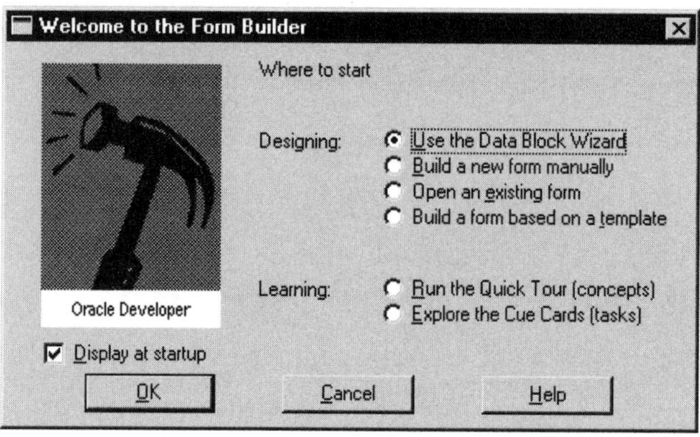

FIGURE 2-2. *Form Builder Welcome dialog*

and click the OK button.) You should see the Form Builder Object Navigator, with the Forms *node* open and a module showing, usually with the name MODULE1. If your Forms node does not have any modules, simply double-click the node name **Forms** to create one.

Your new form module can contain many types of objects: triggers, alerts, attached libraries, and so on. Notice that all of the object nodes have an empty square to the left of their names, except one: the Windows node has a plus sign to the left of its name. Click the plus sign to the left of the Windows node name, and you will see that a default window has automatically been created for your form module. A form module must have at least one window, so Form Builder created one for you.

Exercise

1. **When a new form module is created manually, what object does it automatically include?**

Using the Data Block Wizard to Create and Modify Data Blocks

In order to manipulate data, a form needs a data block to serve as a link between the form and the database or, more accurately, between the form and the data *source*, since a data block can be based not only on a table in a database, but also on a database view, procedure, or transactional trigger. The data block is the foundation for any standard data-entry form. Form Builder provides a Data Block Wizard to simplify the process of creating data blocks.

Before starting the Data Block Wizard, create the test tables used in this chapter. A listing of the SQL code to create and populate the test tables is shown in L 2-1. For your reference, an entity-relationship diagram for the test tables is shown in Figure 2-3. If you would rather not type in the SQL code, you can download it by going to www.oraclepressbooks.com or writing me at plsql101@yahoo.com.

L 2-1

```
-- Create tables
CREATE TABLE department (
     department_id          NUMBER(8,0)  PRIMARY KEY,
     department_name        VARCHAR2(25) NOT NULL
     )
;

CREATE TABLE employee (
     employee_id            NUMBER(8,0)  PRIMARY KEY,
     last_name              VARCHAR2(20) NOT NULL,
```

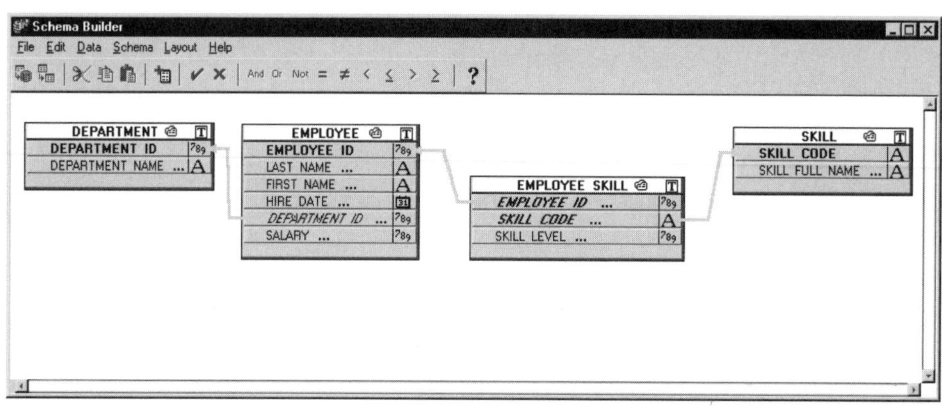

FIGURE 2-3. *Entity-relationship diagram for test tables*

```
     first_name          VARCHAR2(15) NOT NULL,
     hire_date           DATE         NOT NULL,
     department_id       NUMBER(8,0)  NOT NULL,
     salary              NUMBER(8,2)  NOT NULL
     )
;

CREATE TABLE skill (
     skill_code          VARCHAR2(8)  PRIMARY KEY,
     skill_full_name     VARCHAR2(30) NOT NULL
     )
;

CREATE TABLE employee_skill (
     employee_id         NUMBER(8,0) NOT NULL,
     skill_code          VARCHAR2(8) NOT NULL,
     skill_level         NUMBER(1,0) NOT NULL
                            CHECK (skill_level BETWEEN 1 AND 5)
     )
;

ALTER TABLE employee_skill
ADD PRIMARY KEY (employee_id, skill_code)
;

ALTER TABLE employee
ADD FOREIGN KEY (department_id) REFERENCES department
;
```

```
ALTER TABLE employee_skill
ADD FOREIGN KEY (employee_id) REFERENCES employee
;

ALTER TABLE employee_skill
ADD FOREIGN KEY (skill_code) REFERENCES skill
;

-- Populate tables
INSERT INTO department VALUES (1, 'Sales');
INSERT INTO department VALUES (2, 'Research and Development');
INSERT INTO department VALUES (3, 'Information Technology');
INSERT INTO department VALUES (4, 'Maintenance');

INSERT INTO employee VALUES (
     1001, 'Haupt', 'Joseph', '30-JUN-1972', 3, 65000);
INSERT INTO employee VALUES (
     1002, 'Avila', 'Arnold', '29-OCT-1988', 4, 50000);
INSERT INTO employee VALUES (
     1003, 'Gutwirth', 'David', '30-JUN-2002', 1, 75000);
INSERT INTO employee VALUES (
     1004, 'Rusch', 'Grace', '28-JUL-1999', 2, 80000);
INSERT INTO employee VALUES (
     1005, 'Zuckerman', 'John', '29-OCT-2001', 3, 95000);

INSERT INTO skill VALUES ('SALES', 'Selling Techniques');
INSERT INTO skill VALUES ('ACCTG', 'Accounting');
INSERT INTO skill VALUES ('C', 'C Programming');
INSERT INTO skill VALUES ('DBA', 'Database Administrator');
INSERT INTO skill VALUES ('DEV', 'Oracle Developer');
INSERT INTO skill VALUES ('DA', 'Data Architecture');
INSERT INTO skill VALUES ('SI', 'Systems Integration');
INSERT INTO skill VALUES ('JAVA', 'Java Programming');
INSERT INTO skill VALUES ('HM', 'Humorous in Meetings');

INSERT INTO employee_skill VALUES (1005, 'DEV', 5);
INSERT INTO employee_skill VALUES (1005, 'DBA', 4);
INSERT INTO employee_skill VALUES (1005, 'DA', 5);
INSERT INTO employee_skill VALUES (1004, 'DEV', 4);
INSERT INTO employee_skill VALUES (1004, 'DA', 2);
INSERT INTO employee_skill VALUES (1004, 'HM', 5);
INSERT INTO employee_skill VALUES (1002, 'SI', 5);
INSERT INTO employee_skill VALUES (1002, 'DA', 1);
INSERT INTO employee_skill VALUES (1001, 'SALES', 4);

COMMIT;
```

Creating a Data Block Using the Data Block Wizard

To start the Data Block Wizard, right-click on the Data Blocks node beneath your Form module, and select **Data Block Wizard** from the context menu that appears. You will be presented with the dialog box shown in Figure 2-4, asking whether to base the data block on a table, view, or stored procedure. Select the Table or View option and click the Next button.

In this dialog page, the Data Block Wizard asks what table or view you wish to use as a base for your data block. For this first exercise, you will create a data block based on the DEPARTMENT table. You can either type in the table's name and click the Refresh button to get a list of the table's columns, or you can click the Browse button, enter the user and database information provided by your system's database administrator (DBA), then select the DEPARTMENT table and click the OK button. Whichever approach you prefer, you end up with a dialog box filled in as shown in Figure 2-5. Press the button with the two right arrows on it to move all of the table's column names from the Available Columns area to the Database Items area of the dialog box. Then, click the Next button. This takes you to the Finish page, which is depicted in Figure 2-6. Select the option labeled Just Create The Data Block and click the Finish button.

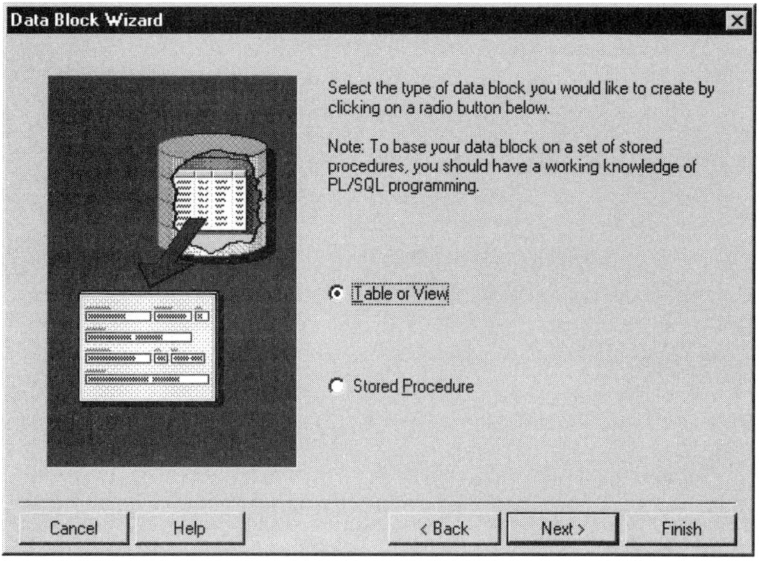

FIGURE 2-4. *Data Block Wizard data block type dialog*

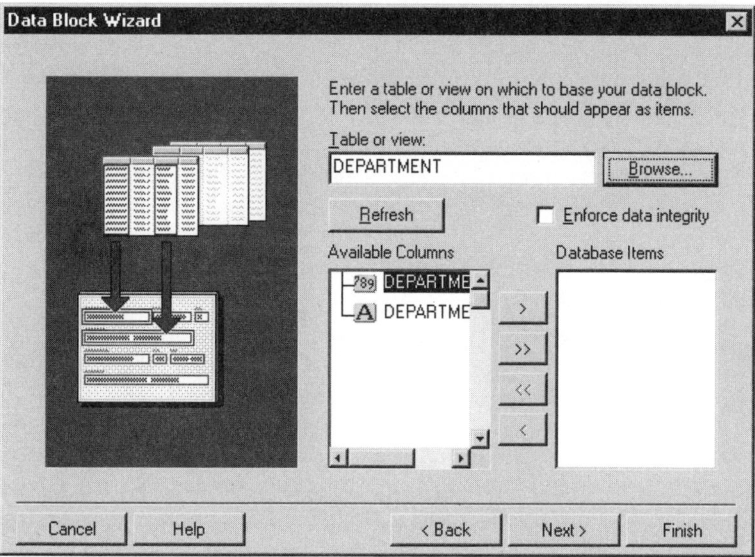

FIGURE 2-5. *Data Block Wizard Table page*

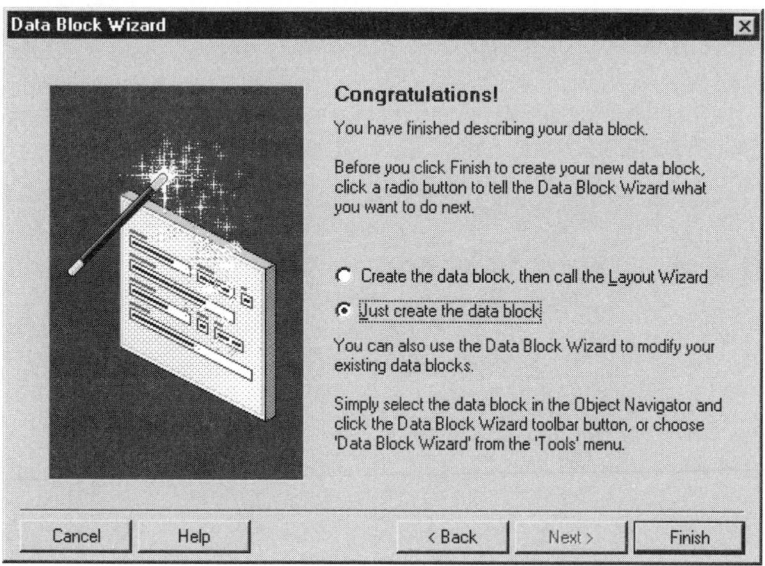

FIGURE 2-6. *Data Block Wizard Finish page*

Modifying a Data Block Using the Data Block Wizard

In addition to simplifying the creation of new data blocks, the Data Block Wizard can assist you in modifying existing data blocks. When used in this way, the Data Block Wizard offers the same options it did when you initially created the data block: control over the data source, selection of columns included, and the ability to generate relationships between data blocks. To change other data block parameters, you must open the data block's *property sheet* (that will be discussed in detail later).

You can start the Data Block Wizard on an existing data block in either of two ways. You can either right-click the data block's name and then choose Data Block Wizard from the context menu, or you can click the data block's name and then choose Tools | Data Block Wizard from the standard Form Builder menu. Once you have started the Data Block Wizard, you will see the familiar tabs to control the data block's type (table, view, or stored procedure) and columns. For instance, in the tab page labeled Table, you can use the arrows between the Available Columns and the Database Items areas to change which columns are included in the data block, or to change their column order. Once your changes are complete, you click the Finish button to exit the Data Block Wizard. Take a moment now to experiment with making changes to your data block using this wizard. When you are done, click the Cancel button to return to Form Builder.

Exercises

1. **If you wanted to modify the way in which a data block was sorted, would you be able to do it with the Data Block Wizard? If so, on what Wizard page?**
2. **What are the two methods for starting the Data Block Wizard on an existing data block?**

Creating and Modifying Layouts Using the Layout Wizard

The Layout Wizard is the Form Builder tool for creating and modifying forms quickly. It works by asking you a series of questions and then generating a basic form that fulfills the criteria you have specified. The Layout Wizard can later modify the form if you want to change its fundamental design or contents. You can also modify the layout manually, if you wish, to better suit your application's needs.

Creating a Layout Using the Layout Wizard

It is very simple to create a basic entry form using the Layout Wizard within Form Builder. Start by right-clicking the data block you would like to use as the basis for a form. (If you do not yet have a data block with the desired data, create one using the steps in the previous section.) For the purposes of this exercise, select the DEPARTMENT data block from the test data provided with this book.

Start the exercise by choosing Layout Wizard from the context menu that appeared when you right-clicked on your data block. You may or may not see the Layout Wizard Welcome screen, depending on how your system is configured. If you do see it, deselect the option labeled Display This Page Next Time and click the button labeled Next. You will see the dialog box shown in Figure 2-7.

The Canvas page starts by asking you which canvas you wish to use to display the form you are about to create. Remember, the canvas is the background that underlies all forms. If this is the first form you have created for this project, you will not have any existing canvases to select, so the proper choice for canvas is (New Canvas). For the canvas Type, leave the selection at the default choice of Content and click the Next button.

You should now be on Layout Wizard's Data Block page, shown in Figure 2-8. On this page, you select the data block that the Wizard will use as the basis for this layout. By default, the data block you started with is displayed. You will use this page to select which items (that is, data columns) from the data block you wish to have displayed in the layout. Most developers are familiar with selection interfaces like the one used on the Data Block page. The left area, labeled Available Items,

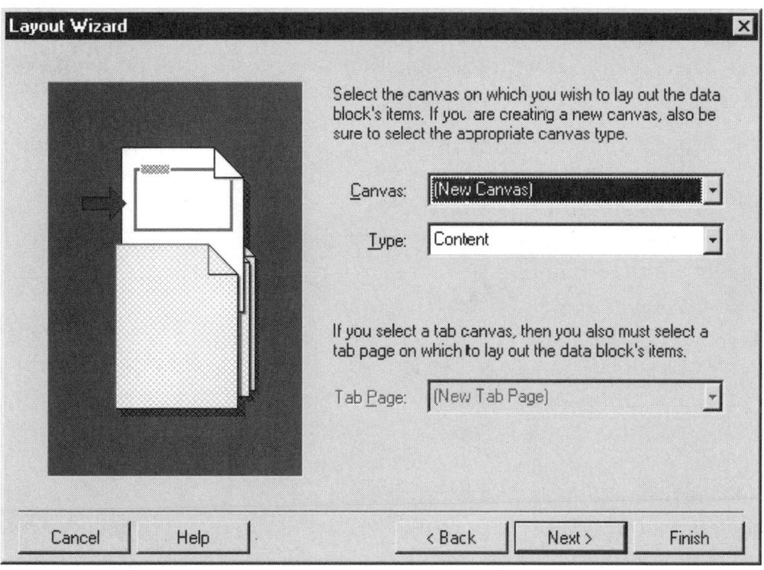

FIGURE 2-7. *Layout Wizard Canvas page*

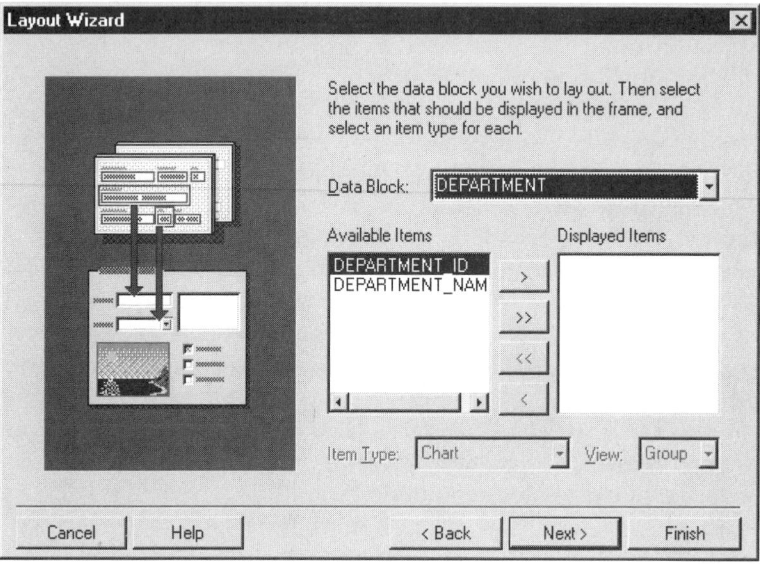

FIGURE 2-8. *Layout Wizard Data Block page*

contains all the items in the data block you have selected. The right area, labeled Displayed Items, shows the items you have selected for inclusion in the layout. Move the DEPARTMENT_ID and DEPARTMENT_NAME items into the Displayed Items column and click the Next button.

You should now be on the Layout Wizard's Items page, as shown in Figure 2-9. Here you can change the onscreen label that will be displayed next to each data item. To the right of the Prompt column are two columns showing the field width and height that the Layout Wizard is planning to give each item. By default, these measurements are shown in points. There is no reason to change the measurements at this time, so you can just click the Next button.

You will next see the Layout Wizard's Frame Style page, shown in Figure 2-10. This is where you specify whether the data you selected should be depicted in a form layout or in a table layout, which looks like a spreadsheet. For the purposes of this exercise, select the Tabular choice and click the Next button.

You should now be on the Layout Wizard's Rows page, shown in Figure 2-11. In this Layout Wizard page, you start by entering a title for the frame the Layout Wizard is going to place around your data items. This frame serves as a container for all of the items. For the purposes of this exercise, enter **DEPARTMENT Frame Title** as the frame title. The next field, Records Displayed, allows you to specify how many records are shown at a time in this layout. Since you chose a tabular layout, it makes

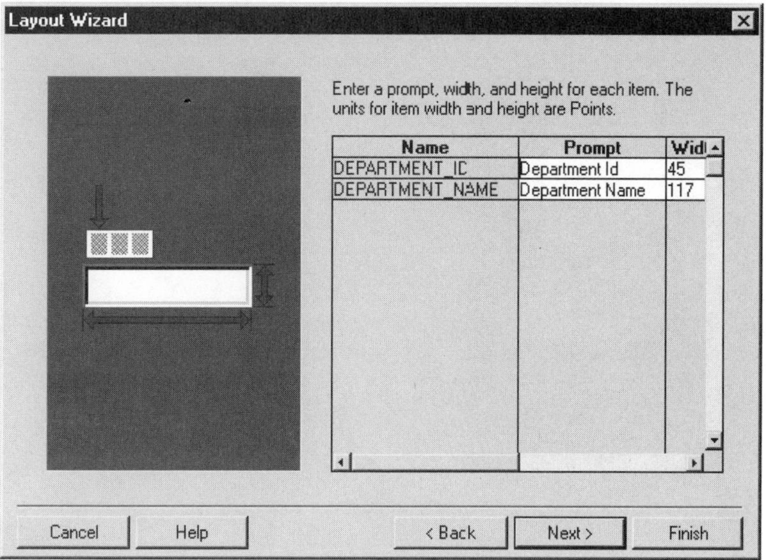

FIGURE 2-9. *Layout Wizard Items page*

sense to design the layout so that more than one record shows at a time. Specify that five records should be shown at a time.

The next field, Distance Between Records, specifies how much vertical space is placed between each row. This parameter only applies to layouts in which the Records Displayed option is set to more than one. Even then, it is generally better to leave the parameter at its default setting of zero. If for some reason the records prove to be too close together, you can increase the space between them easily in the Layout Editor, which provides versatile features for spreading items evenly and displays the results instantly so you can quickly determine the optimal amount of vertical space.

The final field on this page specifies whether the frame will include a scrollbar to move through records. This can be a good idea if your layout will be displaying more than one record at a time. Since your DEPARTMENT layout will show more than one record at a time, click on the Display Scrollbar checkbox so that it is enabled and click the Next button.

The Layout Wizard now displays its Finish page. Read the text on this page and then click the Finish button. Form Builder will generate your form and display it in the Layout Editor. Later sections of this book go into great detail about the editing changes you can make to your form in the Layout Editor. For now, the discussion will be limited to modifications you can make using the Layout Wizard you just employed.

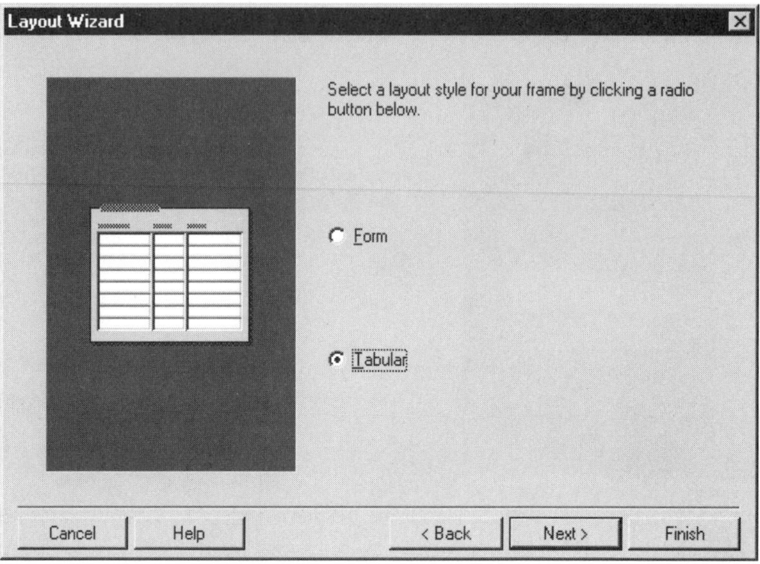

FIGURE 2-10. *Layout Wizard Frame Style page*

Modifying a Layout Using the Layout Wizard

By running the Layout Wizard again on an existing layout, you can make fundamental changes to the layout quickly. You can invoke the Layout Wizard from within the Layout Editor by clicking the Layout Wizard toolbar button, which looks like this:

This is called running the Layout Wizard in *reentrant mode*. The most useful reason to rerun the Layout Wizard on an existing form is to add or remove data items from the displayed canvas. For instance, if you have an Employee form that includes sensitive information such as Social Security Number, you may be asked at some point to remove that information from a canvas so it is not displayed to all employees. It may seem natural to just open the canvas in the Layout Editor, select the item you no longer want to display, and press the Delete key. Doing this will certainly remove the item from your layout, but *it will also remove the item from the underlying data block*. If the form needs that item for some other purpose, but you

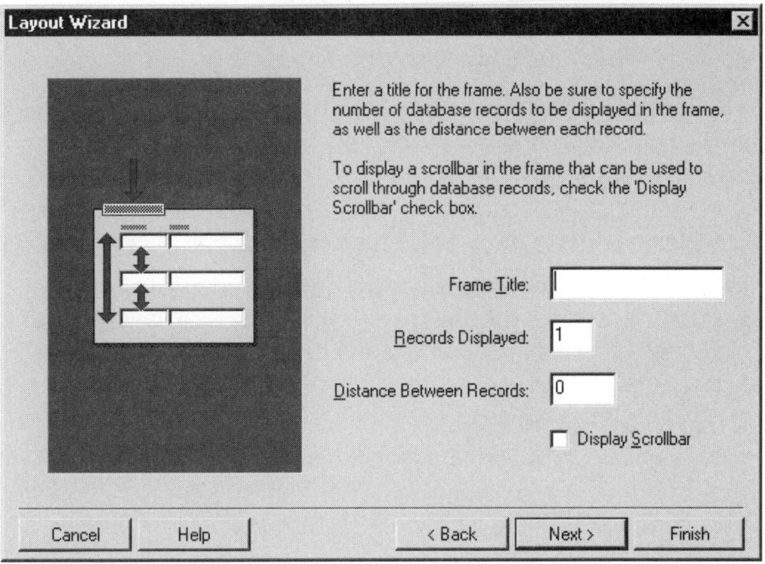

FIGURE 2-11. *Layout Wizard Rows page*

do not want to display the item, that's the time to use the Layout Wizard. You can restart the Layout Wizard on that block in your layout and move the appropriate items from the Displayed Items column back to the Available Items column. Once you have finished, your form will display only the items you want, while your data block continues to contain all the items it had originally.

You can also use the Layout Wizard to change the size of your data items. While you can do this in the Layout Editor just by clicking on an item's field and dragging its edges to make it shorter or longer, the Layout Wizard incorporates more intelligence about the block's physical layout on the canvas. If you use the Layout Wizard, rather than the Layout Editor, to increase the length of a field beyond what the data block's frame can contain, the Layout Wizard automatically increases the size of the frame and even rearranges the fields within the frame if necessary. Because of this ability, the Layout Wizard is your best tool for increasing a field's size when the increase is enough to make the field extend outside the data block's current frame. To finish this section, close the Layout Editor and return to the Object Navigator. Then rename your new canvas by clicking the canvas's icon, clicking again the canvas name, and then typing **DEPARTMENT** as the canvas name. Be sure to save your work afterward.

Exercises

1. **What is the best way to remove an item from a form layout without removing it from the underlying data block?**
2. **What is the best way to increase the display width of a field when there is plenty of space around the field? What is the best way when there is no extra space around the field?**

Saving, Compiling, and Running a Form Module

As you know, you can create form modules in Form Builder, but you cannot run them there. For that, you must invoke the Forms Runtime program. Before you do, however, you need to save the form and compile it.

Saving a Form in Form Builder

You will find saving a form in Form Builder extremely easy. To do so, perform either of these actions. Either execute the File | Save command from Form Builder's menu, or click the familiar Save button, whose icon is shown here:

TIP

You can configure Form Builder to save your work automatically each time you compile it. Go to Tools | Preferences, and, under the General tab, select the Save Before Building option. The rest of this chapter assumes that the Save Before Building option is enabled, so enable it on your system now.

Compiling a Form in Form Builder

The form modules you create in Form Builder cannot be run directly. There is an interim step in which the form module file is converted into a separate, executable file in a format that the Forms Runtime program can read. This process is called *compiling*. You can compile your form modules at any time by executing the File | Administration | Compile File menu command. Take this step now, and you will see that Form Builder creates a new file on your hard disk with the same name as your Form Builder .fmb file, but its extension will be .fmx.

You can configure Form Builder to compile your module automatically before you run it. Go to Tools | Preferences, and, under the General tab, select the Build

Before Running option. The rest of this chapter assumes that the Build Before Running option is enabled, so you should enable it on your system now. Note that this option does not cause the module to be saved, so you will need to either save the module manually or enable the Save Before Building preference option discussed previously. In addition, the Build Before Running option does not cause Library or Menu modules attached to a form to be compiled when the form is compiled, so when you have an application that includes custom Library or Menu modules, you need to compile them manually before running the form.

Running a Form Module

To run your form module, perform either of these actions. Either execute the Program | Run Form command, or click the Run Form button, as shown in this illustration:

Form Builder will start the Forms Runtime program, which will load the executable version of your form. Figure 2-12 shows how the form will look.

The first thing you're likely to notice is that the form does not display any data. The Forms Runtime program is making an assumption that when you first open a form, you want to enter new data. If you want to see existing data, you must query the database. To do that, take either of these actions. Either run the Query | Execute menu command, or click the Execute Query button shown here:

Later in this book, you will learn how to customize the form so it displays data as soon as it opens. For the time being, complete this exercise by exiting out of the Forms Runtime program.

Exercises

1. **What is a compiled file?**
2. **What Forms Developer 6*i* program runs the form modules you create in Form Builder?**
3. **When you initially run a form, why doesn't it show any data?**

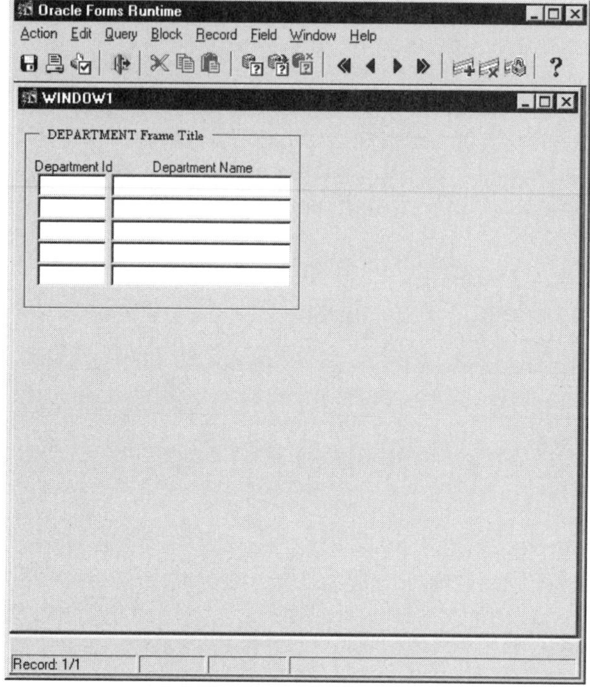

FIGURE 2-12. *Form in Forms Runtime program*

Form Builder File Formats and Their Characteristics

Now that you have gone through a complete cycle of creating, compiling, and running a form module, it is time to step back for a moment and discuss a bit more theory: the different types of Form Builder files. Each of the main Form Builder nodes generates a different set of files, and each file has a different purpose.

The Form node generates three file types. The design file you work with directly is given an extension of **.fmb** (Form Module Binary). The executable file generated when you compile a form module is given an extension of **.fmx** (Form Module Executable). The form module's parameters can be exported to an ASCII text file using the File | Administration | Convert menu command, and that file's extension is **.fmt** (Form Module Text).

The Menu node also generates three file types. The design file you work with (coming up later in this book) has an extension of **.mmb** (Menu Module Binary). The executable file generated when you compile has an extension of **.mmx** (Menu Module Executable). The menu module can be exported to an ASCII text file whose extension is **.mmt** (Menu Module Text).

The PL/SQL Library node generates three file types, but their file extensions follow a different pattern than those presented so far. The design file is given an extension of **.pll** (Programming Language Library), and unlike any other node, the design version contains both source and executable code, and thus can be used at runtime. The executable file, whose file extension is **.plx** (PL/SQL eXecutable), contains only the executable code-no source code. The PL/SQL Library can be exported to an ASCII text file, and that file's extension is **.pld** (PL/SQL Documentation).

The Object Library node generates only two file types. The design file has the extension **.olb** (Object Library Binary). The Object Library can be exported to an ASCII text file, and that file's extension would be **.olt** (Object Library Text).

Table 2-2 summarizes each of the Form Builder file types and characteristics.

Module	**Extension**	**Characteristic**
Form	**.fmb**	Form design file
.fmx	Form executable runfile	
.fmt	Form text export file	
Menu	**.mmb**	Menu design file
.mmx	Menu executable runfile	
.mmt	Menu text export file	
PL/SQL Library	**.pll**	PL/SQL Library design file (can also be executed—contains both source and executable code)
	.plx	PL/SQL Library executable runfile (contains no source code)
	.pld	PL/SQL Library text export file
Object Library	**.olb**	Object Library design file
	.olt	Object Library text export file

TABLE 2-2. *Form Builder File Types*

Exercises

1. **What is the difference between an .fmb file and an .fmx file?**
2. **What Form Builder file type contains compiled menu data?**
3. **What Form Builder file type contains both source code and executable code?**

Creating Data Blocks with Relationships

The sample tables used in this chapter include the DEPARTMENT and EMPLOYEE tables. The contents of these tables have inferred relationships; for instance, a department has one or more employees. This particular type of relationship is often called a *master/detail* relationship (also called a *parent/child* relationship). In order for this type of relationship to exist, the master or parent table must have a *primary key*. A primary key consists of one or more columns that cannot be empty and that must contain unique values for every record. These unique primary key values are what the detail or child table stores and uses to refer to master table records. The detail table column(s) that store values from the master table's primary key are called the *foreign key* to the master table's primary key. So in a master/detail relationship, the master table's primary key is referred to by the detail table's foreign key.

It is common for database applications to use a single form to display data that is in a master/detail relationship. Form Builder makes it easy to define master/detail relationships between data blocks. Once this is done, any canvas containing both the master and the detail data block will also have automatic query synchronization between the two, so the detail data block will only show those records that are related to the selected record in the master data block.

Data Blocks and Relationships in Action

In order to experiment with this, you will modify the DEPARTMENT canvas so it displays two data frames: the current one for department data and a new one that will show employees assigned to the selected department. To do this, you will create a new data block to get data from the EMPLOYEE table, and assign a master/detail relationship between the new Employee data block and the DEPARTMENT data block.

Within your Form Builder file, start the Data Block Wizard by either executing the Tools | Data Block Wizard command, or right-clicking on the Data Blocks item in the Forms node and selecting Data Block Wizard from the context menu that appears. On the Type page, specify that the data block should be based on a Table or View. On the Table page, specify that the data block should be based on the EMPLOYEE table. Move all six EMPLOYEE table columns from the Available Columns area to the Database Items area. Notice that the EMPLOYEE table includes a column called DEPARTMENT_ID. This will be the foreign key to the DEPARTMENT table's primary key. The next page you will see is new: the Master/Detail page. Click the Create Relationship button. From the list of tables that appears, select DEPARTMENT and click OK. Your screen should now look like the one shown in Figure 2-13.

Note that the field labeled Detail Item currently shows EMPLOYEE_ID. This is the primary key for the EMPLOYEE table, but it is not the correct item to serve as the foreign key back to the DEPARTMENT table. Open the drop-down list for the Detail Item field, and you will see the DEPARTMENT_ID item in the list. Select the DEPARTMENT_ID item from the list. You will see that not only did the Detail Item change to the DEPARTMENT_ID item you selected, but the Data Block Wizard also automatically placed DEPARTMENT_ID in the Master Item field. You can see the SQL join condition that this relationship creates in the following code:

L 2-2

```
EMPLOYEE.DEPARTMENT_ID = DEPARTMENT.DEPARTMENT_ID
```

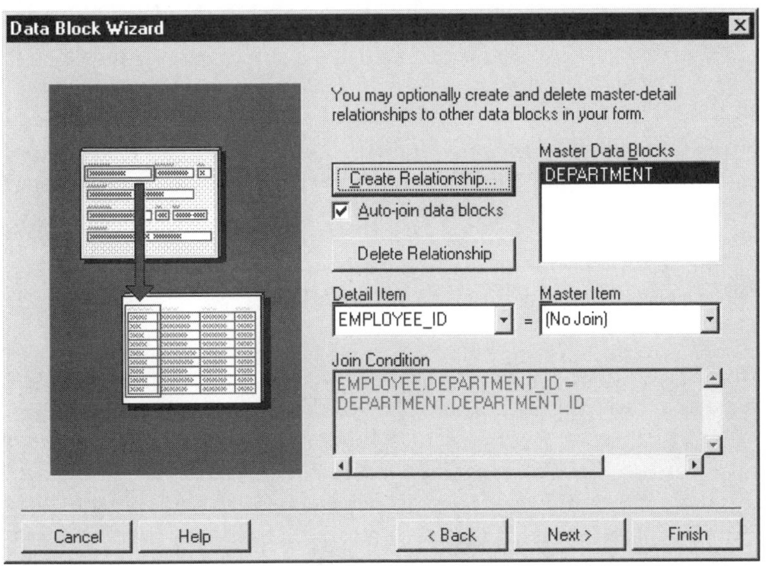

FIGURE 2-13. *Creating a master/detail relationship*

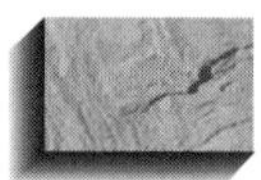

NOTE
The syntax for the SQL join condition is as follows:

```
master_data_block_name.item_name = detail_data_block_name.item_name
```

Those of you familiar with SQL are familiar with creating join conditions similar to this, using table names instead of data block names. In Oracle Forms, remember to use data block names instead of table names.

Now click the Next button. This takes you to the Finish page. Select the option titled "Create The Data Block, Then Call The Layout Wizard," and click the Finish button. When the Layout Wizard starts, ensure that the Canvas field shows your DEPARTMENT canvas, not New Canvas. Click the Next button. On the Data Block page, note that the Data Block field is grayed out. That is because you have already selected the data block indirectly by calling the Layout Wizard from the Data Block Wizard. In the Available Items column, select every item *except* DEPARTMENT_ID. (There is no reason to show the department ID in both the list of departments and the list of employees, when the purpose of this exercise is to show only the employees in the department selected elsewhere on the form.) Click the Next button.

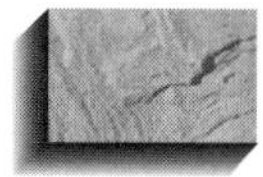

TIP
There is no need to display the DEPARTMENT_ID item in the Employee data frame, since the current department will be displayed elsewhere on the canvas. It was essential to have DEPARTMENT_ID in the Employee data block, however, because that item is the foreign key to the DEPARTMENT data block.

You're close to the end. On the Items page, simply click the Next button to accept all default values for item prompt, width, and height. On the Style page, select Tabular. On the Rows page, enter a frame title of **Employees in this department:** Increase the Records Displayed value to **5**, and enable the Display Scrollbar option. Click the Finish button to close the Layout Wizard. You will now see your form in the Layout Editor, with data frames for both Department and Employees. Close your form to return to the Object Navigator. Notice that the Object Navigator now shows two frames beneath your DEPARTMENT canvas: the first frame holds the DEPARTMENT data block, and the second frame holds the Employee data block.

Exercises

1. **What must be true about a pair of tables in order to create a master/detail relationship between them?**
2. **What is a foreign key?**
3. **Does the detail frame of a master/detail form need to display the foreign key used to join the tables?**

Running a Master/Detail Form Module

Running a master/detail form module is even easier than creating one. From within Form Builder, follow this process. First, select the Form module you want to run by clicking on the module name. (If you have been following the exercises in this chapter, you will have only one form module available.) Then, run the module using the Run button or the Program | Run Form menu command. When the form opens in the Forms Runtime program, populate it with data using the Execute Query button or the Query | Execute command. After that, select different Department records by clicking on either the records directly or the Next Record and Previous Record buttons. Note that each time you select a different department record, the Employees frame changes to show only those employees in that department. When you are done experimenting with your form, use the Action | Exit menu command to close the Forms Runtime program and return to Form Builder.

Exercise

1. **What steps do you have to take in a master/detail form to change the records included in the detail frame?**

Running a Form Builder Application

In this section, you will cover the following points related to running a Form Builder application:

- Understanding the runtime environment
- Navigating a Form Builder application
- Understanding the two modes of Forms Runtime operation
- Retrieving data into a Form Builder application
- Inserting, updating, and deleting records
- Displaying database errors using the Help facility

Now that you have used the Developer 6*i* Forms Runtime program to run your first form a couple of times, this is a good time to go into detail about the Forms Runtime program's purpose, requirements, and operational techniques. This section will help you understand the runtime environment and navigate Form Builder applications when they are running. You will also learn the two modes of Forms Runtime operation, and you will gain experience retrieving data into a Form Builder application. In addition, you will practice **insert**, **update**, and **delete** operations, as well as learn how to display database errors using the Help facility.

Understanding the Runtime Environment

Each of the Builder programs provides an environment for creating application modules. However, the Builder programs do not run those modules, but rather call the runtime program. For that, you use runtime programs supplied with the Forms Developer 6*i* package. There are two runtime programs: one each for the Form and Graphics Builders. The runtime programs must be present on the client machine when the application is distributed, but the development programs do not need to be and generally are not. Keeping the development environment separate from the runtime environment allows the development tool to be rich with convenience-enhancing features, while the runtime program can be lean and efficient. It also allows companies to distribute applications to many users while only having to purchase development-tool licenses for the actual developers.

To run an application built in Forms Developer 6*i*, you call the appropriate runtime program. When you are developing an application and testing it, you usually call the Forms Runtime program directly from within the Builder you are using. This is done by either clicking the Run button—which was introduced earlier—or using the Program | Run Form command.

If you want to run the Forms Runtime program independently of any Builder, you can do so by opening the Start menu in Windows environments and navigating to Programs | Oracle Forms 6i | Forms Runtime. When you do, you see a dialog similar to the one depicted in Figure 2-14.

Using this dialog, you can enter all the information necessary to open and run a form module: the filename (remember that it will be looking for an **.fmx** file), the user ID and password for logging into the database, and the alias for the database itself. There are also a number of other options, which are beyond the scope of discussion at this point.

To have the Forms Runtime program run the form you created earlier in this book, fill in the filename, userid, password, and database alias. When filled in, the Forms Runtime Options screen looks similar to the one shown in Figure 2-15. Once you have filled in the necessary information, click the OK button to run your form.

When you distribute an application, the client computers need to have the runtime programs installed, as well as all the compiled files for your application. To enable you to start your application from a user-friendly icon and still specify

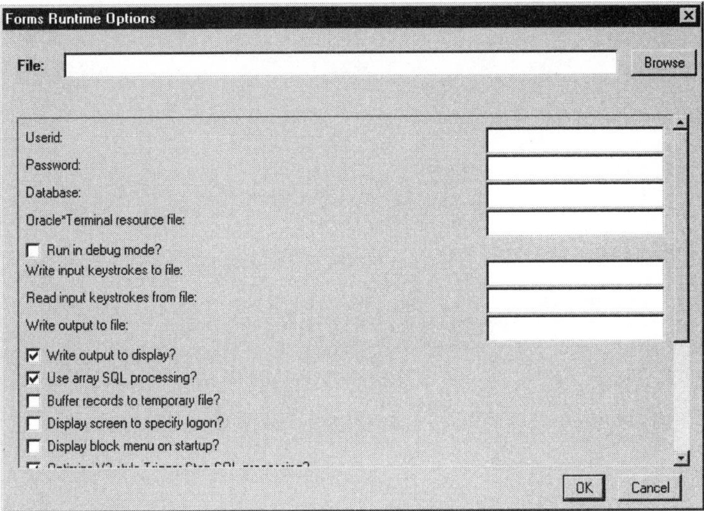

FIGURE 2-14. *Forms Runtime Options dialog*

Forms Runtime Options

File: W:\OCP_Forms6i_Form_1.fmx

Browse

Userid: forms6i

Password: xxxxxxx

Database: orcl8i

Oracle*Terminal resource file:

Run in debug mode?

Write input keystrokes to file:

Read input keystrokes from file:

Write output to file:

Write output to display?

Use array SQL processing?

Buffer records to temporary file?

Display screen to specify logon?

Display block menu on startup?

OK

Cancel

FIGURE 2-15. *Forms Runtime Options dialog with essential data*

runtime arguments, Forms Developer 6*i* provides a way for you to include the desired application's name and other parameters as command-line arguments. For instance, this is an example of a command line that could call the department/employee form you have created:

L 2-3

```
"D:\Dev6i\BIN\ifrun60.EXE" W:\Form_1.fmx user/password@db_name
```

Exercises

1. **What is meant by the term "runtime environment" in Forms Developer 6*i*?**
2. **What are the advantages of separating development and runtime tools?**

Navigating a Form Builder Application

Navigating a Form Builder application in the Forms Runtime program is relatively straightforward. This section will discuss the four parts of a standard Forms Runtime display: the Menu, Toolbar, Form Area, and Console.

Looking at the Menus

The default menu used in the Forms Runtime program is shown here:

Action Edit Query Block Record Field Window Help

If you do not create a custom menu for your application, this is the menu that Forms Runtime provides. It is somewhat unusual in that its first menu category is not File. This is because a Runtime instance is specific to the **.fmx** file opened within it; if you close the **.fmx** file, the Forms Runtime program closes as well. Thus, there is no need for commands like File | Open.

Within the menu bar, the Action menu provides choices to commit data inserts, updates, and deletes; to clear all displayed records from the form (which does not remove them from the underlying tables—it simply blanks the form); to print the form; and to exit the Runtime program. The Edit menu provides the standard cut, copy, and paste commands, which operate at field-level granularity. Further down this menu, the Edit | Edit command opens a dialog box containing the contents of the currently selected field, with a convenient search-and-replace function for making repetitive changes within a large text field. The final choice on this menu, Edit | Display List, opens a List of Values (LOV) if the currently selected field has one.

Two other menus include the Query and Block menus. The Query menu provides functions to enter and utilize data-filtering criteria, including a handy Counts Hits function to determine how many records will match your current criteria without having to actually retrieve the records. The Block menu provides navigational control, enabling the user to move between data blocks on a multiple-block canvas. The menu also includes a command to clear, or blank out, the records in the currently selected block. As with the Action | Clear All command, the Block | Clear command does not actually remove any data from the database; its function is purely cosmetic.

The Record menu provides standard navigation functions: previous and next record, along with scroll up and down (which act similar to a page down and page up within the data block's frame). It also provides commands to insert, lock, and remove records; Remove will actually delete the record from the underlying table when the action is committed, unlike the clear command farther down the menu. A convenient duplicate function copies the values from whichever existing record was more recently current when invoked within a new blank row. Many of these functions are also available from the Runtime toolbar, which will be addressed shortly.

Other menus abound. The Field menu provides a subset of the functions described on the Record menu: move to previous or next, clear, and duplicate. In this case, each function operates at the field level instead of the record level. For instance, when invoked from a new blank record, the Field | Duplicate command copies the contents of that field from the record just above the new one and places the contents into the new record. This can be useful when entering repetitive data. The Window menu offers standard windows-management commands for applications that employ more than one window. The Help menu provides a limited amount of help: details about the field you are currently in, a reminder of the keyboard shortcut keys available, and information about errors, if any have occurred.

Looking at the Toolbar

The next area for study is the toolbar. The default toolbar used in the Forms Runtime program looks like this:

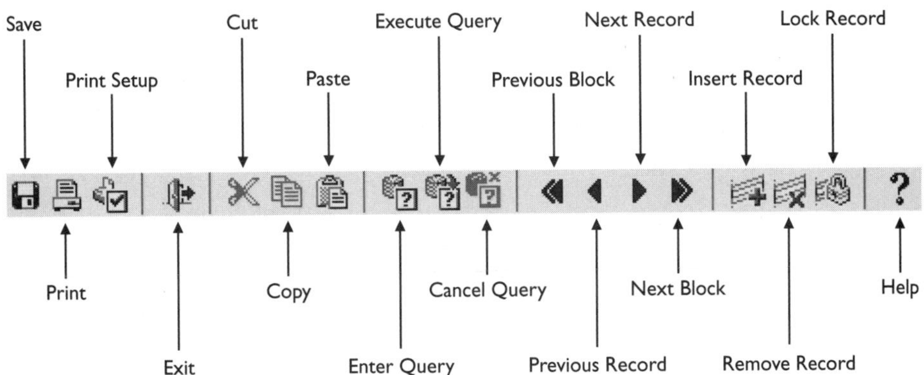

If you do not create a custom toolbar canvas for your application, this is the toolbar Forms Runtime provides. Several of its buttons are undoubtedly familiar to you, while others are specific to the Forms Developer 6*i* environment. The Save button performs a SQL **commit** command, saving any inserts, updates, or deletions the user has performed. Its menu equivalent is Action | Save. The Print button prints the current form and its contents. Its menu equivalent is Action | Print. The Print Setup button provides standard options for page size, source, orientation, and margins. Its menu equivalent is Action | Print Setup. The Exit button closes the application and the Forms Runtime program. Its menu equivalent is Action | Exit. The Cut, Copy, and Paste buttons provide exactly the functions you would expect in any Windows program. Their menu equivalents are Edit | Cut, Edit | Copy, and Edit | Paste. Like their menu equivalents, the buttons operate at field-level granularity.

The Enter Query button places users in a mode where they can enter query-by-example (QBE) data into the form. (This function will be covered later in more detail.) The button's menu equivalent is Query | Enter. The Execute Query button performs a **select** statement against the database, using whatever criteria are present from the Enter Query mode. If no criteria have been entered, all records are returned. The button's menu equivalent is Query | Execute. The Cancel Query button clears any criteria that were entered in Enter Query mode. It does not cause an additional **select** statement to be run, however, so the contents of the form will not change until the Execute Query function is performed again. The button's menu equivalent is Query | Cancel.

The Previous Block button moves the user's cursor to a prior data block on the current canvas. If the canvas has no prior data block but the form module contained additional canvases, the button causes the prior canvas to be displayed, with the cursor in the last data block on that canvas. The button's menu equivalent is Block | Previous. The Next Block button moves the user's cursor to the next data block on the current canvas. If the canvas has no succeeding data block but the form module contained additional canvases, the button causes the next canvas to display, with the cursor in the first data block on that canvas. The button's menu equivalent is Block | Next.

The Prior Record button causes the user's cursor to move up one record in the current data block. If the user is already on the block's first record, the button does nothing. Its menu equivalent is Record | Previous. The Next Record button causes the user's cursor to move down one record in the current data block. If the user is already on the block's last record, the button moves the cursor to a blank row and allows the user to enter a new record. Its menu equivalent is Record | Next. The Insert Record button creates a blank row below the user's current cursor location (or a blank form if the form is designed to show one record at a time) and allows the user to enter new data. The insertion will occur in the database when the user's next **commit** occurs. The button's menu equivalent is Record | Insert. The Remove Record button deletes the current record from the table. The deletion will occur in the database when the user's next **commit** occurs. The button's menu equivalent is Record | Remove. The Lock Record button attempts to lock the database row corresponding to the record at which the user's cursor is currently located. Its menu equivalent is Record | Lock.

Finally, the Help button shows detailed information about the field in which the user's cursor currently resides. This can be handy during development, but it is of little interest to most users, and so you may want to reprogram its function in a custom menu.

Looking at the Form Area

Beneath the default Forms Runtime toolbar is the form area. This is the area where your users will focus most of their attention—as will you as a developer. Because this area simply displays the canvases you create, it will be covered in greater detail later in the book, in the portions dealing with customizing the canvas contents.

Looking at the Console

At the bottom of the Forms Runtime display is the console area. This area consists of two lines. The bottom line displays the record number your cursor is on, along with status information, such as Enter-Query when you are in Enter Query mode. Above that is a line that displays tips for each toolbar item, as well as Oracle messages, such as "FRM-40400: Transaction complete: 10 records applied and saved." when data is saved.

Exercises

1. **What can you do if you decide that most of the buttons in the Forms Runtime toolbar are not of value to your users?**
2. **List all the ways you can cause a commit to occur from an application in the Forms Runtime program.**
3. **Explain the purpose of the console. Describe how it is laid out.**

Understanding the Two Modes of Forms Runtime Operation

The phrase "Enter Query mode" has been used a few times already in this section, and it is time to explain this mode in more detail. A form running in the Forms Runtime program is always in either of two states: the normal insert/update/delete mode, or Enter Query mode. When the user invokes Enter Query mode, the form blanks its contents and waits for the user to enter data into the form that will serve as filtering criteria for a **where** clause when the user invokes the Execute Query command. The user can enter only one record's worth of criteria, although he or she can enter criteria into multiple fields on that record. This means that there is no record-to-record movement while in the Enter Query mode.

To test this operation, follow these steps. First, open your sample application in the Forms Runtime program. Then, invoke Enter Query mode by either clicking the Enter Query button, performing the Query | Enter command, or pressing the F7 function key. Next, move to the Department Name field and type **Maintenance** (remember that queries are case sensitive). Finally, execute the query by either clicking the Execute Query button, performing the Query | Execute menu command, or pressing function key F8. You will see that the Maintenance department record appears, along with the employee record related to that department. You are now back in the normal mode—the only difference is that you are viewing a filtered subset of the available records. Since you are no longer in Enter Query mode, executing another query will produce a result set containing all records.

Exercises

1. **Describe the difference between Enter Query mode and the Forms Runtime normal mode for a form.**
2. **How is the user's movement among records restricted while in Enter Query mode?**

Retrieving Data into a Form Builder Application

By doing the chapter exercises up to this point, you have already retrieved data into a Form Builder application by opening the application with the Forms Runtime program and doing the Execute Query command. When you retrieve records without using selection criteria to limit the number of records returned, you are performing an *unrestricted query*. It's the same as using a **select** statement with no **where** clause. Unrestricted queries win points for simplicity, but they can hurt overall application performance by clogging the available network bandwidth with records the user does not really need.

The solution to this can be a *restricted query*, which uses selection criteria to limit the number of records returned. In the last section, you used Enter Query mode to limit the department records retrieved to just those matching the name Maintenance. That was a restricted query. You can perform more sophisticated restricted queries as well, using Oracle wildcard characters and SQL statements.

Restricting Queries with Field-Level Criteria

There are a number of characters you can use as wildcards and comparison operators when entering field criteria for Enter Query mode. These characters are shown in Table 2-3.

Character	Function
_	Wildcard replacing any single character
%	Wildcard replacing any number of characters, including none
> and <	Greater than and less than (usable for numbers, strings, and dates)
<> or !=	Not equal to (usable for numbers and strings)
>= and <=	Less than or equal to, and greater than or equal to

TABLE 2-3. *Criteria-Field Characters for Enter Query Mode*

All of these would be valid criteria to enter into a field in Enter Query mode:

- Sm_th%
- Pine Ave%
- >50000
- <50000
- >G
- <01-JUL-2003
- <>Backup
- <>5
- !=5
- >=5
- <=5

If you enter search criteria into more than one field while entering a query, all of your search criteria will be combined with **and** clauses in the query's **where** clause.

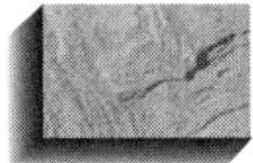

TIP
While you are experimenting with different combinations of criteria, this is an excellent time to practice using the F7 function key to invoke Enter Query mode, and the F8 key to execute a query. Small timesavers like these can add up to a sizable overall timesavings.

Restricting Queries with SQL Statements

You can also employ full SQL statements to restrict the records returned in a query, and even to control their sort order. To try this, open your sample application in the Forms Runtime program, if it is not open already. If necessary, execute a query to populate the Department frame with all four departments. Then, place your cursor on the department record Information Technology. Place your cursor on any record in the Employees data frame. Next, invoke Enter Query mode by either clicking the Enter Query button, performing the Query | Enter menu command, or pressing function key F7. After that, move to the Hire Date field and type **:HIRE_DATE**. (The variable name does not have to be the same as the column name, but you might find it provides more clarity to make it so.) The colon at the beginning of the name indicates that the name is to be treated as a variable. Then move to the Salary field and type **:SALARY**. Your screen should now look like Figure 2-16.

Continuing the process, execute the query by either clicking the Execute Query button, performing the Query | Execute menu command, or pressing function key F8. You will see a dialog box titled Query/Where. Enter the text from L 2-4 as your query's **where** clause. After doing so, click OK. You will see that the number of Information Technology employees displayed has dropped from two to one, and that the one shown is the one who fulfills the criteria you specified.

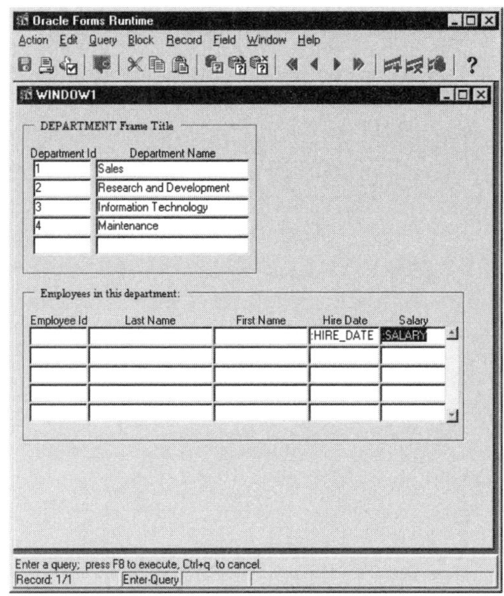

FIGURE 2-16. *Using variables in a Forms Runtime query*

L 2-4

```
HIRE_DATE between '01-JAN-1972' and '31-DEC-2001'
     and SALARY < 90000
```

Exercises

1. **Which of the following is *not* a valid criterion to place in a field while in Enter Query mode: SEL_CT, WILDC*RD, >JKL or <6-DEC-1999?**
2. **What must you place in front of a field name in Enter Query mode to cause the Forms Runtime program to treat the name as a variable?**

Inserting, Updating, and Deleting Records

So far in this chapter, you have only queried existing records. Now it is time to add records of your own, change their contents, and delete them. Before you do, it is important to note that each of these Data Manipulation Language (DML) functions occurs with the records you are looking at locally; changes you make are not made in the underlying database until you **commit** the changes with a Save command. Each of the three topics that follows requires that you have your sample application open in the Forms Runtime program.

Inserting Records

To learn how to **insert** records, start by clicking anywhere in the Department record frame. Proceed in any of the following ways: choose the Record | Insert menu option, click the Insert Record button in the toolbar, or navigate to the last record in the table, and then use the DOWN ARROW cursor key to move to a blank record. To add a new record to the DEPARTMENT table, enter a Department ID of **5** and a Department Name of **Quality Assurance**. Now add two employees to this department with information shown in Table 2-4. **Commit** the records to the database using the Save command or the Save button.

Employee ID	Last Name	First Name	Hire Date	Salary
1009	Unca	Bob	25-NOV-2002	68000
1010	Paterson	Lois	01-MAR-2003	72000

TABLE 2-4. *Sample Employee Records to Add*

Updating Records

Updating records is straightforward. You simply navigate to the desired record, move your cursor to the field you want to change, make the change, and then **commit** the change with a Save command. Experiment with this process by changing the hire date for Lois Paterson to **March 2**. Be sure to **commit** the change.

Deleting Records

Deleting records is even easier than updating them. To begin, create and execute a query that produces the record you want to delete (or just move through the record set already displayed until you find the record you want). Put your cursor in any field in the record, and then **delete** the record by either performing the Record | Remove menu command, clicking the Remove Record button in the toolbar, or pressing SHIFT-F6 keys on your keyboard. Finally, **commit** the change with a Save command. Experiment with this process by deleting the record for Bob Unca. Be sure to **commit** the deletion.

Exercise

1. **You have just performed a Record | Remove command on the wrong record. What steps do you need to take to get the record back?**

Displaying Database Errors Using the Help Facility

As a foundation for this topic, add the record shown in Table 2-5 to your sample application. If you have been following the exercises, this **insert** should fail when you try to **commit** it. As you probably noticed, the new record has the same Employee ID as a record that already exists. The Employee ID is the primary-key column for the EMPLOYEE table, so all records must have unique Employee ID values.

Look down at the console area at the bottom of your Forms Runtime program, and you will see a message like the one shown in the code block in L 2-5.

Department ID	Employee ID	Last Name	First Name	Hire Date	Salary
1	1010	Trumble	Laren	10-JAN-2003	60000

TABLE 2-5. *Record with Duplicate Employee ID*

L 2-5

```
FRM-40508: ORACLE error: unable to INSERT record.
```

Unfortunately, the error message doesn't say *why* the **insert** failed. To get more information, you can use the Forms Runtime program's Help facility. Here is the process. First, choose the Help | Display Error menu option. You should see a dialog box similar to the one shown in Figure 2-17. The top half of the dialog box shows a segment of the code the application was attempting to execute. The bottom half has more useful information: the Oracle database error message. Here, you learn that the table has a unique constraint that your new record would violate. When you are finished reading the error information, click the OK button to close the Database Error dialog box and exit the Forms Runtime program without saving the new record.

Exercise

1. **What information is available from the Forms Runtime program's Help | Display Error command that is not available in the console area?**

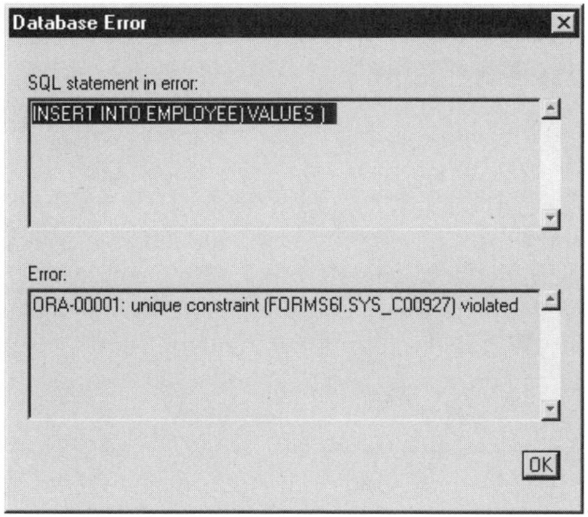

FIGURE 2-17 *Forms Runtime Database Error dialog box*

Chapter Summary

In this chapter, you have covered a substantial amount of information on Form Builder. You started by learning about the Form Builder environment: the main Form Builder executables (Form Builder, Form Compiler, and Forms Runtime), and the main Form Builder components (form modules, menu modules, PL/SQL Libraries, and Object Libraries). You then learned the main objects in a form module: window, canvas, block, and item.

In the next section, you covered the basics of creating form modules. You learned the four steps involved in creating and using a Forms Developer 6*i* form: creating a new form module in Form Builder; creating a data block to supply the new form module with data; creating a form layout depicting the data block's items on one or more canvases; and saving, compiling, and running the module using the Forms Runtime program. You then took the steps to actually create a new form module, and then used the Data Block Wizard to create data blocks to use within the module to access database data. Once you had access to data, you employed the Layout Wizard to create a basic form layout on a canvas, which you then viewed in the Layout Editor. Next, you modified the layout by rerunning the Layout Wizard in reentrant mode and changing specific parameters in the already-existing layout. You then learned about compiling form modules, and once your sample application was compiled, you ran it using the Forms Runtime program.

Next you learned to identify Form Builder file formats and their characteristics. The Form module file types are **.fmb** (Form Module Binary), **.fmx** (Form Module Executable), and **.fmt** (Form Module Text). The Menu module file types are **.mmb** (Menu Module Binary), **.mmx** (Menu Module eXecutable), and **.mmt** (Menu Module Text). The PL/SQL Library file types are **.pll** (PL/SQL Library), **.plx** (PL/SQL eXecutable), and **.pld** (PL/SQL Documentation). The Object Library file types are **.olb** (Object Library Binary) and **.olt** (Object Library Text). To finish up the section, you learned how to use the Data Block Wizard to create data blocks with relationships, generating a master/detail relationship between two data blocks. You then used the Layout Wizard to modify your single-table form layout so that it displayed both tables involved in the master/detail relationship. When you ran the resultant form in the Forms Runtime program, you saw how Forms Developer 6i automatically synchronizes the two tables so the contents of the details table changes each time a different master record is selected.

In the final section, you learned about running a Form Builder application. You started by getting an overview of the runtime environment, which included information about how to specify information about your compiled forms on the Forms Runtime command line. You then learned more about navigating a Form Builder application, learning details about the four sections of the runtime display: the menu, the toolbar, the form area, and the console. Next, you discovered the difference between the two modes of Forms Runtime operation: normal insert/update/delete mode and Enter Query mode. Then, you learned how to control what data a Form Builder application retrieves, either by employing field-level criteria utilizing the _, %, <, >, =, and **!=** operators, or by implementing form variables allowing you to use statements similar to SQL **where** clauses. You learned the fine points of inserting, updating, and deleting records, including how to save time by using record-level and field-level duplicate commands to speed the entry of repetitive data. Finally, you learned how to display detailed database error information using the Help facility in the Forms Runtime program. All in all, the material in this chapter comprises about 12 percent of material tested on *OCP Exam 3*.

Two-Minute Drill

- The main Form Builder executables are Form Builder, Form Compiler, and Forms Runtime.
- The main Form Builder components are form modules, menu modules, PL/SQL Libraries, and Object Libraries.
- The four steps involved in creating and using a Forms Developer 6*i* form are (1) creating a new form module in Form Builder, (2) creating a data block to supply the new form module with data, (3) creating a form layout depicting the data block's items on one or more canvases, and (4) saving, compiling, and running the module using the Forms Runtime program.
- The main objects in a form module are, from largest to smallest: window, canvas, block, and item. When a data block is placed on a canvas, it is automatically surrounded by a frame that assists in selecting the data block for moving and editing.
- Form Builder provides a Data Block Wizard to simplify creating and modifying data blocks.
- Form Builder also provides a Layout Wizard to simplify creating and modifying form layouts.
- Form Builder generates different file types for each of its four main components. All of the components generate binary source files and text documentation files. All but the Object Library component create compiled executable files.
- The Form module file types are **.fmb** (Form Module Binary), **.fmx** (Form Module eXecutable), and **.fmt** (Form Module Text).
- The Menu module file types are **.mmb** (Menu Module Binary), **.mmx** (Menu Module eXecutable), and **.mmt** (Menu Module Text).

- The PL/SQL Library file types are **.pll** (PL/SQL Library), **.plx** (PL/SQL eXecutable), and **.pld** (PL/SQL Documentation).
- The Object Library file types are **.olb** (Object Library Binary) and **.olt** (Object Library Text).
- A master/detail relationship—also known as a parent/child relationship—is the most common relationship between two data blocks. In it, the master table's primary key is referenced by a foreign key in the detail table.
- Form Builder automatically synchronizes master/detail relationships so the detail table only shows records related to the currently selected record in the master table.
- Before a form can be run, it must be compiled. This can be done manually within Form Builder, or you can set Form Builder to do it automatically when you run a form.
- There are three ways to cause a form to run in the Forms Runtime program: (1) use the Run command in Form Builder, (2) start the Forms Runtime program and fill in the necessary filename/userid/password/database information when it presents its starting dialog box, or (3) invoke the Forms Runtime program from a command line or shortcut and append all the necessary data to the end of the command line.
- There are four sections in a standard Forms Runtime display: the menu, the toolbar, the form area, and the console.
- A form running in the Forms Runtime program is always in one of two states: normal insert/update/delete mode, or Enter Query mode.
- Enter Query mode allows you to control what data are retrieved into a Form Builder application.
- While in Enter Query mode, you can specify data filters using either field-level criteria with the _, %, <, >, =, and **!=** operators, or form variables that enable you to use statements similar to SQL **where** clauses. Each form variable name must begin with a colon in the form, but not in the SQL clause.
- The Record | Duplicate menu command copies the values from the most recently selected record into a new record. The Field | Duplicate menu command does the same thing, but only for the field currently selected.
- When you encounter an error in the Forms Runtime program, you can often get more detailed information by invoking the Help | Display Error command.

Chapter Questions

1. **What are the main Form Builder executables?**

   A. Forms, menus, PL/SQL Libraries, Object Libraries

   B. Form module, data block, layout, runtime file

   C. .fmb, .fmx, .fmt

   D. Form Builder, Form Compiler, Forms Runtime

2. **What are the main Form Builder components?**

   A. Form module, data block, layout, runtime file

   B. Form modules, Menu modules, PL/SQL Libraries, Object Libraries

   C. Form Builder, Form Compiler, Forms Runtime

   D. .fmb, .fmx, .fmt

3. **You want to create a basic form module. What main steps will you take, and in what order? (Choose four.)**

   A. Create a data block.

   B. Create a master/detail relationship.

   C. Create a form module.

   D. Save, compile, and run the form module.

   E. Create a layout.

4. **You have created a DEPARTMENT data block and layout, both of which contain the items Department ID and Department Name. Now your requirements have changed: while you still need the Department ID in the data block for relational integrity reasons, you no longer want the layout to display it to the user. What is the best way to remove Department ID from the layout without removing it from the underlying data block?**

   A. It is not possible to remove a data item from a layout when it is still in the underlying data block. Thus, to remove it from the layout, you must remove it from the data block first.

   B. Open the Data Block Wizard and move the Department ID item from the Displayed Items column back to the Available Items column.

C. Open the layout in the Layout Editor. Locate the Department ID item, select it, and press Delete.

D. Open the canvas in the Layout Editor. Select the frame around the DEPARTMENT data block, and start the Layout Wizard. Move the Department ID item from the Displayed Items column back to the Available Items column.

5. Which of the following file types is *not* ready to be run in the Forms Runtime program? (Choose one.)

A. .fmx

B. .pll

C. .mmt

6. What is the purpose of the Data Block Wizard?

A. Simplify saving data blocks to disk

B. Simplify creating data blocks in a database

C. Simplify creating and modifying data blocks in forms

D. Simplify creating and modifying form layouts

7. When a new form module is created, what object does it automatically include?

A. Window

B. Toolbar

C. Tab canvas view

D. Stacked canvas view

8. What are the main objects in a form module, and what is their size precedence, from largest to smallest? (Choose four.)

A. Frame

B. Layout

C. Block

D. Window

E. Item

F. Canvas

9. What is the purpose of the Layout Wizard?

A. Simplify creating and modifying form layouts

B. Simplify saving data blocks to disk

C. Simplify creating form layouts in a database

D. Simplify creating and modifying data blocks in forms

10. You would like to create a master/detail relationship in Form Builder between two database tables. What must be true about the tables in order to accomplish this? (Choose three.)

A. The detail table must have a primary key.

B. The master table must have a primary key.

C. The form module must contain data blocks for at least one of the database tables.

D. The form module must contain data blocks for both of the database tables.

E. The master table must have a foreign-key column referencing the primary key of the detail table.

F. The detail table must have a foreign-key column referencing the primary key of the master table.

11. Which of the following represent the two states a form can be in while running in the Forms Runtime program?

A. Builder

B. Toolbar

C. Insert/update/delete

D. Sorted

E. Enter Query

12. Which of the following are *not* defining characteristics of Enter Query mode in the Forms Runtime program? (Choose as many as necessary.)

A. Allows entering SQL statements for record filtering

B. Is the default mode

C. Allows updating records

D. Allows wildcard criteria such as the "*" character

E. Allows movement from record to record

13. **You are creating a form for the DEPARTMENT table using the Data Block Wizard and the Layout Wizard. You know that the table's DEPARTMENT NAME column is wider than any of the actual department names, so you decide to change the width of that item on your display. Unfortunately, you underestimated the amount of screen space the department names would require, and as a result some of them are being cut off when displayed. On the canvas, the Department Name is tightly clustered with other data items, and there is no additional space within its data block's frame. What is the best way to increase the width of the Department Name item?**

    A. Open the canvas in the Layout Editor, click the Department Name item, and drag its right side to increase its display length.

    B. Open the Property Palette of the DEPARTMENT data block and change the Department Name's Maximum Length property to a larger number. The layout will update automatically to the new length the next time the module is compiled.

    C. Use the Data Block Wizard in reentrant mode to change the field's display size.

    D. Use the Layout Wizard in reentrant mode to change the field's display size.

    E. Both C and D.

14. **Which of the following are *not* ways to cause a form to run in the Forms Runtime program? (Choose as many as necessary.)**

    A. Use the Run command in Form Builder.

    B. Start the Forms Runtime program and fill in the necessary filename/userid/password/database information when it presents its starting dialog.

    C. Include all the necessary data in the command line that calls the Forms Runtime program.

    D. None of the above.

15. You create a form module that does not have a custom menu or toolbar defined. Which of the following items will be present when the form is run in the Forms Runtime program, and in what order, from the top of the display to the bottom? (Choose as many as necessary.)

A. Toolbar

B. Layout

C. Form area

D. Console

E. Menu

16. You have created a new application and would like to customize it. Which of the following is a Form component that you can customize or replace altogether?

A. Message line

B. Console

C. Graph

D. MDI window

E. Default menu

Answers to Chapter Questions

1. D. Form Builder, Form Compiler, Forms Runtime

Explanation The *executables* are the programs that make up this portion of the Forms Developer 6*i* package.

2. B. Form modules, Menu modules, PL/SQL Libraries, Object Libraries

Explanation The *components* are the nodes you see in the Form Builder object tree. They are the pieces that make up a Form Builder application.

3. C, A, E, D. Create a form module; create a data block; create a layout; and save, compile, and run the form module

Explanation A master/detail relationship is not an essential part of a basic form module. Of the remaining steps, you must create a form module first, because it contains the other components. The next essential step is creating a data block—without a data block, you have nothing to lay out. Once the data block is created and laid out, you have an application you can save, compile, and run in the Forms Runtime program.

4. D. Open the canvas in the Layout Editor. Select the frame around the DEPARTMENT data block, and start the Layout Wizard. Move the Department ID item from the Displayed Items column back to the Available Items column.

Explanation It is possible to keep an item in a data block while not displaying it in a layout. The Layout Wizard's Data Block page provides two areas for items: Available Items and Displayed Items. You select which items are displayed on a layout by moving them into or out of the Displayed Items area.

5. C. **.mmt**

Explanation **.pll** files contain both source code and executable code. The **.mmt** file, however, is a simple ASCII text file and, as such, cannot be executed.

6. C. Simplify creation and modification of data blocks in forms

Explanation For a refresher on this topic, review the section "Using the Data Block Wizard to Create and Modify Data Blocks."

7. A. Window

Explanation Form Builder automatically creates a default window in each new form module it creates. No other items are created automatically.

8. D, F, C, E. Window, Canvas, Block, Item

Explanation A layout is the combination of all of these items; it is not an item itself. A window contains one or more canvases, each of which can contain one or more blocks. Each block is comprised of one or more items. A frame is not considered an item itself, but rather a boundary around a block. Review Figure 2-1 for a visual refresher.

9. A. Simplify creating and modifying form layouts

Explanation For a refresher on this topic, review the section "Creating and Modifying Layouts Using the Layout Wizard."

10. B, D, F. The master table must have a primary key, the form module must contain data blocks for both of the database tables, and the detail table must have a foreign-key column referencing the primary key of the master table.

Explanation In order for database tables to be visible in a Form Builder application at all, there must be a Form Builder data block for each table. Once that is done, a master/detail relationship is possible as long as the master table has a unique primary key, which the detail table stores in one or more columns called a foreign key. Forms Developer 6*i* uses a detail record's foreign-key value to determine whether to display the record when a new master record is displayed.

11. C, E. Insert/update/delete, Enter Query

Explanation These two modes relate to the main purposes of a form: inserting new records, updating and deleting existing records, and filtering records to view.

12. B, C, D, E. Is the default mode, Allows updating records, Allows wildcard criteria such as the "*" character, Allows movement from record to record

Explanation The default mode for the Forms Runtime program is the normal insert/update/query mode. In Enter Query mode, any data you enter is treated as selection criteria, thus it is not possible to **update** records while in it. And while the Enter Query mode does allow for wildcards, the multiple-character wildcard is "%", not "*". Finally, because Enter Query mode is inherently a one-record query-by-example form, it does not accommodate any movement from record to record.

13. D. Use the Layout Wizard in reentrant mode to change the field's display size.

Explanation While you can increase the display size of an item by clicking and dragging its borders in the Layout Editor, the question stated that the data block in question has no additional space. The Layout Wizard's Items page contains parameters controlling display width, and the Layout Wizard will redo the layout of a data block if size changes to the items within the block cause them to no longer fit within the old data block layout. The Maximum Length property controls the length of data that can be displayed in an item, but does not affect the size of the field used to display that data. In addition, the Data Block Wizard has nothing to do with display size.

14. D. None of the above.

Explanation All of these are valid ways to cause a form to run in the Forms Runtime program.

15. E, A, C, D. Menu, Toolbar, Form area, Console

Explanation Review the section "Navigating a Form Builder Application" for a refresher.

16. E. Default menu

Explanation While you can place messages into the message line, you cannot replace it entirely. Since the message line is part of the console, the same holds true for the console. A graph is not inherently part of a form module, so you cannot modify it. The MDI window cannot be replaced. That leaves the default menu, which you can in fact modify or replace.

CHAPTER 3

Forms Design I

In this chapter, you will learn about the following facets of building forms:

- Working with data blocks and frames
- Working with text items
- Creating Lists of Values (LOVs) and editors

To create Form Builder applications in Oracle Forms 6*i*, you must understand the components that work together on a finished form. Most forms are based on data blocks that provide the link between the form and the source of the data being displayed. In this chapter, you will learn quite a bit about data blocks, as well as the nondata version of form blocks: control blocks. You will also be introduced to the components of the Property Palette, where you specify how every object on a form will look and function. Once you are familiar with navigating the Property Palette, you will learn about specific groups of properties important for form development: properties that control the appearance and behavior of data blocks, the frames surrounding data blocks, and control blocks, among others. Next you will learn about text items—the objects on a form that enable the user to see and edit text, numbers, dates, or long data. You will learn about text item properties, including those you can use to enforce data-quality standards at the point of input. You will see how to create tooltips and hints for your users. Finally, you will practice creating LOVs and editors on your forms to enhance productivity.

Overall, the contents of this chapter comprise about 13 percent of *OCP Exam 3* test content.

Working with Data Blocks and Frames

In this section, you will cover the following points related to working with data blocks and frames:

- Property Palette components
- Manipulating properties
- Controlling the behavior of data blocks
- Controlling frame properties
- Creating blocks that do not correspond to a database object
- Deleting data blocks and their components

In the previous chapter you used wizards to effect changes on a variety of objects and properties—the items included in data blocks, the relationships between blocks, the items displayed on a canvas, and so forth. Whereas the wizards are helpful for certain tasks, they give you access to only a small portion of the properties you can change. This section will introduce the Property Palette, which gives you much greater control over the objects you create. You will learn how the Property Palette works, how to use it to control the behavior of data blocks, and how to control frame properties with it. Building on this knowledge, you will learn about blocks that do not correspond directly to a database, and you will create a block of this type. Rounding out this section, you will learn how to delete data blocks and their components in two different ways, observing the characteristics of each approach as you experiment.

Property Palette Components

The Property Palette provides complete control over many facets of your objects. Using it efficiently requires understanding its components so you can select the best approach to setting the parameters you need.

To start learning about the Property Palette, start Form Builder and open the file containing your sample application from Chapter 2. Then open the Data Blocks node and double-click on the DEPARTMENT data block to open its Property Palette. You will see a window that looks similar to Figure 3-1.

Toolbar

The toolbar contains buttons giving convenient access to functions relevant to setting properties, such as property copy and paste, property add and delete, and property-class create and inherit. You will also see a button shaped like an upside-down "U" that determines what properties are shown when you use a single Property Palette to show properties for multiple objects. When the "U" is upside down (the default setting), the Property Palette is in *Intersection mode* and shows only the properties that are common among all the objects you have selected. Clicking the button switches the Property Palette to *Union mode,* in which every property related to the selected items is displayed, even if a property relates to only a single item. In either mode, a shared property that has the same value for all selected objects shows that value, but if the value is not the same for every selected object, the property displays ***** instead of a value.

The next toolbar button, labeled Freeze/Unfreeze, helps work around a feature of the Property Palette that can be annoying in certain circumstances. Usually the Palette changes its contents each time you select a different object, so that the current object's properties are displayed. This is generally a convenience. However, when you have more than one Property Palette open, *all* of the Palettes change their contents each time you select a new object. The Freeze/Unfreeze button solves this by forcing a Property Palette to continue showing properties for its current object, regardless of what objects you select from that point on.

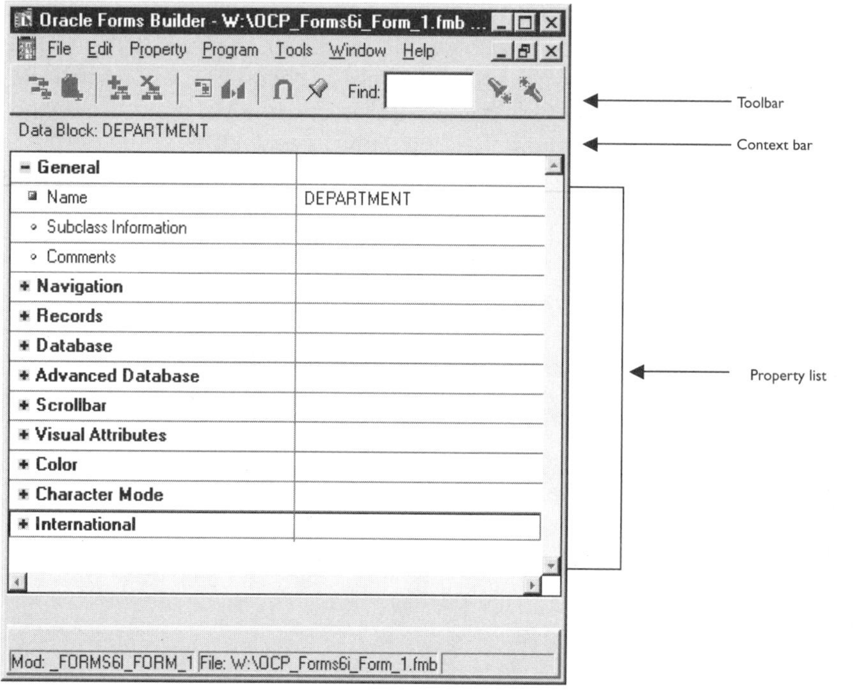

FIGURE 3-1. *Property Palette for DEPARTMENT data block*

To see this in action, open your sample application. Open the Data Blocks node so you can see the DEPARTMENT and EMPLOYEE data blocks. Then open a Property Palette for the DEPARTMENT data block by double-clicking its icon, or by right-clicking it and selecting Property Palette from the Layout Wizard. Open a second Property Palette by holding down the SHIFT key and double-clicking the icon for the EMPLOYEE data block. The second Property Palette will open in exactly the same position as the first one, so you need to move or resize the second Property Palette in order to see both. Click once again on the DEPARTMENT data block. You will see that *both* Property Palettes shift their display to show properties for that data block. Click on the EMPLOYEE data block, or any other object, and you will see that both Property Palettes continue to follow your selection in lockstep. To solve this, click on the DEPARTMENT data block, and then in the first Property Palette you opened, click on the Freeze/Unfreeze button. This forces the Palette to keep its focus on the DEPARTMENT data block. Click on other objects in the Object Navigator, and you will see that the second Property Palette changes its contents to follow your selections, while the first Palette continues displaying properties for the DEPARTMENT data block. Click on the EMPLOYEE data block, and then in the second Property Palette you opened, click on the Freeze/Unfreeze button. This will force the second Property Palette to keep its focus on the EMPLOYEE data block. Click on other objects in the Object Navigator. You will see that no matter what item you select, both Property Palettes remain on their "frozen" objects.

To the right of the toolbar is a field labeled Find. This search field is handy, because it makes the Property Palette quickly jump to specific properties. Even if the group containing the matching property is closed, the Find field opens it up for you. For instance, if you want to change the sort order of the data returned by a data block, you can jump to that property by just typing the letter **O** in the data block's Property Palette's Find field. The focus immediately moves to the **order by** clause property.

Context Bar

Located beneath the toolbar, the context bar identifies which object is currently having its properties displayed by the Property Palette. The first text on the context bar line identifies the type of object: form module, trigger, data block, item, relation, and so forth. (When you test this on your own system, remember to unfreeze the Property Palette first.) The object type is followed by a colon and then the name of the selected object.

Property List

The main portion of the Property Palette, of course, is the property list. This two-column display shows the property names in the left column with their current values in the right column. The properties are grouped by category, and a + in front of a category name indicates that the category is collapsed and not displaying its properties, while a – in front of a category name means that the category is expanded and that the properties within that category are all visible. You can toggle between these two states on a category-by-category basis by clicking on the + or – in front of each category name. Each object type in your application has different properties, and the Property Palette is smart enough to remember which property categories you like to have open and closed for each type of object.

Exercises

1. **What is the difference between the Intersection and Union display modes of the Property Palette?**
2. **How can you find a specific property quickly in the Property Palette?**
3. **What does freezing the Property Palette do?**

Manipulating Properties

The Property Palette contains several different types of value fields. As you move from property to property, you will encounter the following field types in the Property Palette's value column:

- Alphanumeric fields for typing values
- Fields containing a button labeled More, which opens a dialog box for setting values
- Fields with a button showing an ellipsis (. . .), which opens a window for entering and editing lengthy text, such as comments or **where** clauses
- Drop-down lists of fixed, predefined values (such as Yes/No fields, or a data block's fixed Navigation Style options of Same Record, Change Record, and Change Data Block)
- LOVs containing lists whose contents can change (such as a canvas frame's *Layout Data Block* property, whose list will show whatever data blocks your application has)

You can change properties simply by clicking on the value field for the desired property and either typing in the correct value, selecting it from a list, or specifying it in a dialog box. For properties that have lists, you can iterate through the choices in the list by double-clicking on the property name. This can be particularly handy for Yes/No properties.

You can compare the properties of two or more objects by selecting all of the items you want to compare, and then looking at the Property Palette. As long as you are in the Property Palette's default Intersection display mode, the Palette only shows properties that are common among all of the selected objects. Properties having the same value in all selected objects show the shared value, while properties that do not have the same value display ***** for that property instead of a value. When you are showing the properties for multiple objects in a single Palette, any property you change will be changed in all of the selected objects, overwriting whatever prior settings the objects had for that property.

TIP
You can select multiple objects in the Object Navigator by employing the same techniques that work in Windows Explorer. After selecting an initial object, SHIFT*-clicking on another object will select a contiguous range containing all the objects between*

the first selection and the second one. For noncontiguous sets of objects, use CTRL-clicking after the initial object is selected.

If you want to contrast the properties for more than one object, you can open multiple Palettes by SHIFT-double-clicking on the second and subsequent object icons.

The Property Palette's copy and paste functions operate just as you would expect for individual properties: you select the property that contains the value you want to copy, click the Copy Properties button, move to the property to which you would like to copy the value, click the Paste Properties button, and the value from the source property is written into the destination property. Now for the interesting information about copying and pasting:

- You can select multiple properties to copy all at once, using the SHIFT and CTRL keys along with the mouse.
- If any of the properties you selected are displaying *****—meaning your Property Palette is reflecting multiple objects, and some of those objects' shared properties do not have the same value—the Copy command ignores those properties. The Copy command only copies values from properties whose values are the same among all the source objects.
- The destination object does not need to be the same type as the source object. For instance, you can copy the *Visual Attribute Group* properties from a data block to a canvas. The Paste command is flexible enough to only paste the properties that are appropriate for the destination object.

Exercises

1. **What types of value fields are in a Property Palette?**
2. **What happens when you double-click on the name of a property that has a LOV?**
3. **What problem could arise from pasting a group of properties into another object?**

Controlling the Behavior of Data Blocks

The properties for a data block are divided into nine categories: General, Navigation, Records, Database, Advanced Database, Scrollbar, Font & Color,

Character Mode, and International. From a developer's perspective, you can divide these categories into three main groups:

- **General properties** This is where you can change the data block's name, subclass the data block beneath another object or property class, and enter comments about the data block. The General category offers similar properties for all Form Builder objects.
- **Behavior properties** This includes the Navigation group, Records group, Database group, and Advanced Database group.
- **Appearance properties** This includes the Scrollbar group, Font & Color group, Character Mode group, and International group.

The behavior properties are particularly important to developers. Several deserve special attention.

The Query Array Size property controls how many records are fetched from the database at a time.

The Number of Records Buffered property specifies how many records the Forms Runtime program keeps in the client computer's memory when the form is run (records beyond this quantity are stored in a temporary disk file on the client). Increasing the number improves client performance but requires more RAM; decreasing it saves client RAM. The default value for Number of Records Buffered is the Number of Records Displayed + 3.

The Query Allowed property determines whether the user (or application code) can execute a query in this data block. The **where** clause allows you to enter filtering criteria to limit the types of records returned. The **order by** clause lets you select how the returned data should be sorted.

The Insert/Update/Delete Allowed property relates to the Create/Read/Update/ Delete control of your block (known unofficially as C.R.U.D).

The Update Changed Columns Only property specifies that when the user changes an existing record, the **update** command sent to the server only includes the fields that were changed. While that may seem like a good idea in general, it forces Oracle Forms 6*i* to reparse the **update** statement for every record being updated, which can degrade performance. It is useful when the record contains LONG values that are not likely to be updated, or if the user is likely to be updating the same one or two columns, or if you have column-specific triggers in your database that you do not want firing unnecessarily.

The DML Array Size property controls the number of records sent to the server in a batch. Increasing the number reduces network traffic and therefore improves system-wide performance, but requires more memory on the client computer. Since this command creates batch processing, it forces the Update Changed Columns Only property to No, regardless of the property's set value. This property is ignored if the block includes a LONG RAW item.

Exercises

1. **Which data block properties manipulate the balance between client computer memory and network traffic?**
2. **Which data block property gives you control over whether the block allows records to be inserted? Updated? Deleted? Which property determines whether the block accepts query criteria?**
3. **Which data block property would you consider changing if your records include LONG items that are not likely to be edited?**

Controlling Frame Properties

A number of properties will be of particular interest to you as you work with frames on your application's canvases.

- **Frame Title Alignment** Lets you select the horizontal position of your frame title within the top border of the frame.
- **Number of Records Displayed property** A value that you initially specify while running the Layout Wizard. If you want to change it later, this is the property to use. You can also change this value by rerunning the Layout Wizard on a frame.
- **Distance Between Records property** Also specified while running the Layout Wizard. If you decide you want a little more space between rows, you can make that modification using this property. You can also change this value by rerunning the Layout Wizard on a frame.
- **Bevel property** Lets you select from six different types of frame borders. The choices are Raised, Lowered, None, Inset (the default), Outset, and Plain. Figure 3-2 shows how each bevel type looks.
- **Frame Title Font & Color Group property** Gives you control over the frame title's appearance—its font, size, spacing, and color, among other things. In order to standardize these frame appearance properties across your application, you may want to specify them as a Visual Attribute (one of the nodes under Forms in the Object Navigator) and then assign that visual attribute to the appropriate frames.

Exercises

1. **What bevel types are available for your frames?**
2. **What is the purpose of a Visual Attributes object?**

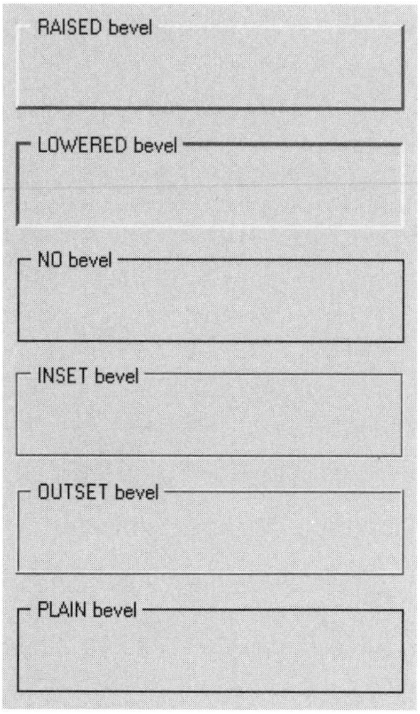

FIGURE 3-2 *Frame bevel types*

Creating Blocks That Do Not Correspond to a Database Object

So far, all the blocks you have created have been data blocks that serve to provide a data link between a form and a database. Another type of block is not associated with a database object and is called a *control block*. The items in a control block are not related to database columns. Instead, a control block contains either controls (such as buttons), or a group of items with single values (such as calculated subtotals).

Unlike data blocks, control blocks have a two-part creation process: create the control block, and then manually create the items that go in the block. To get a taste of how this is done, open Form Builder. Within the Object Navigator form module where you wish to create the control block, click on the Data Blocks node. Start the process of creating a new block by clicking on the Create button, or executing the Navigator | Create command. From the New Data Block dialog box that appears, select the *Build a new data block manually* option, and then click on the OK button. You will see a new block appear under your Data Blocks node. Double-click on the icon for the new block to open its Property Palette. Under the Database node in the Property Palette, change the property named Database Data Block to No. Change the block's name (under the General node) to **DEPARTMENT_EXIT**.

You now have an empty control block. You will place within it a single item: a button that the user may click to exit a form. In the Object Navigator, click on the Items subnode beneath the DEPARTMENT_EXIT block. Click the Create button, or execute the Navigator | Create command. In the new item's Property Palette, change the item's Name property to **EXIT_BUTTON**. While in the General property node, change the Item Type to Push Button. Under the Functional node, change the Label value to Exit Form. Under the Physical node, change the Canvas property to the canvas containing your DEPARTMENT data block.

You now have a control item on your DEPARTMENT canvas. But the item doesn't do anything yet; it has no code beneath it. To add code, open the canvas containing your DEPARTMENT data block in the Layout Editor. Drag the control button from the top-left corner of the canvas to a position centered beneath the DEPARTMENT data block. Right-click the button and select SmartTriggers from the context menu that appears. In the list of SmartTriggers, select WHEN-BUTTON-PRESSED. Form Builder will open the PL/SQL Editor. Enter this code to give the button its functionality:

L 3-1

```
BEGIN
  EXIT_FORM (ASK_COMMIT, NO_ROLLBACK);
END;
```

Run the form. When it opens in the Forms Runtime program, click your new Exit Form button to see it perform.

Exercises

1. **What is the definitive difference between a data block and a control block?**
2. **When a control block is created, what items does it contain?**

Deleting Data Blocks and Their Components

Two ways you can delete data blocks and data block components are from the Object Navigator and from the Layout Editor. Each has as slightly different impact. The important thing to know is how closely linked Object Navigator objects are with those in the Layout Editor. It probably won't surprise you to find out that deleting an object in the Object Navigator causes that object to be removed from any canvas in which it was used. Not so obvious, however, is that the reverse is also true: deleting an object from a canvas in the Layout Editor removes that object from the Object Navigator as well.

To see this demonstrated, open the Form Builder and your sample project from this chapter, if it is not already open. If it is already open, save it now. This is important, because in this exercise you will be deleting items that cannot be undeleted. Then open the Data Blocks node so you can see the data blocks displayed. Open the Canvases node and double-click on the canvas that displays your DEPARTMENT data block. Arrange the Object Navigator window and Layout Editor window so you can see the contents of both simultaneously. In the Object Navigator, click on the DEPARTMENT data block and press the Delete key to delete it. Answer Yes to the confirmation prompt. Notice what happens on the canvas in the Layout Editor. The frame that contained your DEPARTMENT data block is now empty. The data block and its items are gone, while the frame and the frame title are still there.

TIP
Any text in a Oracle Forms 6i application that you type is called boilerplate text. This is in contrast to text that is derived from the database, such as item names. The frame title is an example of boilerplate text, as is the label you placed on your Exit Form button earlier.

Open the Edit menu. Notice that the Undo command is not available. When you delete a data block or data block component from the Object Navigator, it cannot be undone with the Undo command. Now use the File | Revert command to revert your sample project to the state it was in before you deleted the data block. Your sample application is now exactly as it was before you deleted any objects.

Now it is time to see what happens when you delete data block items from the Layout Editor. Once again open the Data Blocks node. Then click on the + next to the DEPARTMENT data block so you can view its components, and click on the + next to the Items subnode so you can see the DEPARTMENT_ID and DEPARTMENT_NAME items. Open the Canvases node, then open the canvas containing your DEPARTMENT data block and position the windows again, if necessary, so you can see the contents of both the Object Navigator and the Layout Editor. In the Layout Editor, select the entire DEPARTMENT data block by clicking outside one of the block's corners and dragging the mouse to the opposite corner. You should see the entire block display selection marks, including the items, titles, and scroll bar within it. Notice that in the Object Navigator, several items are selected: the DEPARTMENT_ID and DEPARTMENT_NAME items in the data block, as well as the frame in your canvas that holds those items. Now delete the selected items in the Layout Editor by pressing the Delete key. Notice the difference in the result this time. In the Layout Editor, everything has been deleted except the scroll bar: the frame and its boilerplate text are gone, as well as the items the frame contained. In the Object Navigator, you can see that the items are also gone from the DEPARTMENT data block's Items subnode. The data block itself is still there as an empty data structure, but its triggers and relations remain intact. Now open the Edit menu. Notice that the Undo command is available this time. When you delete a data block or data block component from the Layout Editor, you can get it back if you immediately issue an Edit | Undo command. Use the File | Revert command now to revert your sample project to the state it was in before you deleted the data block.

Exercises

1. **Which approach to deleting data block items gives you the opportunity to undo the deletion?**
2. **Which approach to deleting a data block removes the data block's data structure but leaves its triggers and relations?**
3. **What is the only way to delete an entire data block, structure and all?**

Working with Text Items

In this section, you will cover the following points about working with text items:

- Introduction to text items
- Modifying a text item's appearance
- Controlling the data in a text item
- Modifying the navigational behavior of a text item
- Enhancing the relationship between a text item and a database
- Modifying the functionality of a text item
- Including help messages in your applications

This section covers the most ubiquitous part of any form: text items. You will learn what text items are, and how they differ from display items. You will learn which properties are available to control the appearance of data within text items, and you will learn more about Visual Attribute Groups, which enable you to specify and store named sets of appearance properties that can be referred to by objects in your forms. This helps ensure that similar items look identical throughout your application, and it can save you an immense amount of time if you need to make application-wide changes to appearance later, because you simply change the appropriate Visual Attribute Groups. Next you will learn about the properties that give you control over what the users can, or must, enter. After that, you will be introduced to the properties that affect how users can move around your application, and then you will see which properties control how your Form Builder application interacts with a database. Next, you will learn about properties that affect the scope of queries, along with properties determining what items the user can insert or update. Following this, you will discover properties that control how text items get their value, whether they hide data entered by the user, and whether they are available for user interaction. Finally, you will learn about properties you can use to add user hints and tooltips to your application.

Introduction to Text Items

Form Builder uses the term *text item* to describe any control on your form that displays text, numbers, dates, or long data, and allows the data to be edited by the user. For instance, the fields that display your database items are text items. A text item differs from a *display item* in that the latter does not allow the user to change the data shown. A text item can be either single-line—the type used to display most database data—or multiple-line, which responds to the ENTER key by creating another line of text, instead of moving to the next item.

Exercises

1. **What is the difference between a text item and a display item?**
2. **Describe how a multiple-line text item differs from a single-line text item.**

Modifying a Text Item's Appearance

Since a text item is all about displaying data, it's important to understand how to control the appearance of the data it displays. You can access the appearance-oriented properties by opening your canvas in the Layout Editor, selecting the text item whose appearance you would like to change, and opening that item's Property Palette. Table 3-1 contains a number of the more relevant properties.

You undoubtedly noticed that Table 3-1 shows two Visual Attribute Group properties. These handy features allow you to create named groups of visual properties—font, colors, and fill, among other things—and then apply those properties to your forms. This feature is similar to the style sheets used in many word processors. If you change any of the default item appearance properties in your forms, it makes sense to use a Visual Attribute Group to do it. That way you can later modify the display properties in a single, centralized location, and have those modifications automatically propagate throughout your forms.

Property Node	Property Name	Function
Functional	Justification	Horizontal alignment of the item's contents in relation to the item's width
Data	Format Mask	Allows you to tailor how text, numbers, dates, and times are displayed
Records	Distance Between Records	Vertical distance between each row in a data block
Physical	Visible	Determines whether item is displayed to user
Visual Attributes	Visual Attribute Group	Allows you to reference an object in which you have already specified appearance properties
Visual Attributes	Prompt Visual Attribute Group	Allows you to reference an object in which you have already specified appearance properties
Prompt	Prompt	Text label to be displayed for the item
Prompt	Prompt Justification	Horizontal justification of the prompt text in relation to the item's width

TABLE 3-1. *Text Item Appearance Properties*

Exercises

1. **Why would someone want to change the appearance of a text item?**
2. **What are the benefits of using a Visual Attribute Group to control the appearance of text items?**

Controlling the Data in a Text Item

While controlling the appearance of a text item is important, the content of the data is even more important. Table 3-2 shows properties that give you control over what the users can, or must, enter.

Property Node	Property Name	Function
Functional	Multi-Line	Determines whether the item allows for multiple lines of text data
Functional	Case Restriction	Converts value entered by user to uppercase or lowercase
Data	Data Type	Specifies what type of data the item accepts: number, date, and so on
Data	Maximum Length	Longest entry the item accepts
Data	Fixed Length	Only accepts entries containing exactly the number of characters specified by the Fixed Length property
Data	Initial Value	Default value for the item
Data	Required	When set to Yes, will not allow user to save the record unless the item contains a value
Data	Format Mask	Allows you to restrict the content of each character typed, and to control the length of each portion in a multiportion entry such as a date
Data	Lowest Allowed Value	Minimum valid value
Data	Highest Allowed Value	Maximum valid value
Calculation	Calculation Mode	Specifies that a formula or summary should populate the item

TABLE 3-2. *Text Item Data Control Properties*

To use the current date as a value in a text item property, set the Initial Value property to $$DATE$$. To use the current date and time, set it to $$DATETIME$$.

Exercises

1. **Which properties would you use to set valid range of values for a number field?**

2. **How can you ensure that a date is entered with a four-digit year?**
3. **Which property would enable you to specify that an item must contain three letters, a two-digit number, and another letter?**
4. **How could you configure a Date/Time field to have the current date and time automatically inserted each time a new record is created?**

Modifying the Navigational Behavior of a Text Item

Once you have taken care of the quality of data users enters, you can focus on the ease with which they can move around the application. Table 3-3 shows the properties you can employ that help in this endeavor.

Property Node	Property Name	Function
Functional	Automatic Skip	Specifies that cursor automatically jumps to next item when the last character in the field has been added or changed.
Navigation	Keyboard Navigable	When set to No, the item never receives the input focus via "default navigation" (tabs, ARROW keys, ENTER key)—item can only receive input focus if the user clicks on it.
Navigation	Previous Navigation Item	Identifies which item the default navigation should move to if the user moves backward.
Navigation	Next Navigation Item	Identifies which item the default navigation should move to if the user moves forward.
Physical	Show Vertical Scroll Bar	Specifies that the block should display a scroll bar.

TABLE 3-3. *Text Item Navigational Behavior Properties*

Exercises

1. **Which text item navigation property would help you minimize the number of keystrokes your users need to type?**
2. **If you wanted to change the default navigation in a table so users move down a column before they move across a row, which text item navigation properties would you change?**

Enhancing the Relationship Between the Text Item and a Database

This section identifies properties that allow you to exert greater control over how your Form Builder application interacts with a database. There are properties that limit or expand the scope of queries users can perform, as well as properties to specify what items the user can **insert** or **update**, and under what conditions. Table 3-4 lists each of these properties in order and describes their purpose.

Exercises

1. **Which text item database properties can restrict whether a user can** insert **new data?**
2. **Which text item data properties can expand the scope of a query beyond what the user explicitly entered?**
3. **What text item data property allows you to specify that an item cannot be changed once it is populated?**

Modifying the Functionality of a Text Item

Quite a few properties are available that enable you to modify a text item's functionality. These properties control how a text item gets its value, whether it displays data as the user enters it, and whether the item is active in the first place. Table 3-5 lists these properties and describes each one.

Exercises

1. **What text item properties would you use to specify that a text item's value should be derived from the sum of an item in a different block?**
2. **If you want a Date field in your form to automatically be populated with today's date for every new record, what text item property would you use to make that happen?**
3. **What text item property can increase a field's security?**

Property Node	Property Name	Function
Database	Primary Key	Item corresponds to a database data block's primary-key column
Database	Query Only	Specifies that item can be queried but cannot be part of an **insert** or **update** command
Database	Query Allowed	Determines whether users or applications can perform a query using this block
Database	Query Length	Maximum length for a restricted query operation; a value of 0 means no limit
Database	Case Insensitive Query	When set to Yes, any text queries constructed by Form Builder will be case-insensitive; these rely on the queried column being indexed
Database	Insert Allowed	Determines whether user can manipulate the content of the item when inserting a new record
Database	Update Allowed	Determines whether user can change the contents of the item
Database	Update Only if NULL	Handy feature stating that the item can be changed only if it does not already have contents

TABLE 3-4. *Text Item Database Relationship Properties*

Including Help Messages in Your Applications

Form Builder provides properties that make it easy to add helpful information for your users to see as they move from item to item. The helpful information can take two different forms: *hints* and *tooltips*. When the user enters a particular text item, a hint displays in the message line (the first line of the two-line area called the console, at the bottom of the form display). A tooltip displays adjacent to the mouse pointer when the pointer is hovering over a text item. Table 3-6 lists the properties that provide you with these capabilities.

Property Node	Property Name	Function
Functional	Enabled	Specifies whether the user can navigate to an item using the mouse or keyboard (Keyboard Navigable must also be Yes for keyboard access)
Functional	Conceal Data	Instructs Form Builder to hide characters typed into this item (often used for password fields)
Functional	Popup Menu	Allows you to attach a pop-up menu of your own design to an item
Data	Initial Value	Specifies a default value to populate the item each time a new record is created; value can be a hard-coded value, a form item, a global variable, a form parameter, or a sequence
Data	Copy Value from Item	Used primarily in master/detail relationships, specifies the item in the master block that should be used to filter records in the detail block, or should be automatically copied into this item in the detail block when a new detail record is created
Calculation	Calculation Mode	Allows you to specify that an item should derive its value from a formula or summary, rather than from a database column
Calculation	Formula	Stores a PL/SQL expression used to create the item's value if Calculation Mode property is set to Formula
Calculation	Summary Function	Works in conjunction with the Summarized Block and Summarized Item properties to define a calculation used to populate this item; choices are Average, Count, Max, Min, Standard Deviation, Sum, and Variance

TABLE 3-5. *Text Item Functionality Properties*

Property Node	Property Name	Function
Calculation	Summarized Block	Works in conjunction with the Summary Function and Summarized Item properties to define a calculation used to populate this item
Calculation	Summarized Item	Works in conjunction with the Summary Function and Summarized Block properties to define a calculation used to populate this item
LOV	LOV	Defines the LOV that should be attached to the text item
LOV	Validate from List	Used in a field that has an attached LOV, specifies whether data typed by the user should be validated against the LOV

TABLE 3-5. *Text Item Functionality Properties* (continued)

Exercise

1. **What is the difference between a hint and a tooltip in Form Builder?**

Creating LOVs and Editors

In this section, you will cover the following points about creating LOVs and editors:

- Introduction to LOVs and editors
- Creating LOVs
- Creating editors

This section covers two features that can make the forms you create much easier for users to work with: *LOVs* and *editors.* A LOV is a pop-up window that displays a series of choices from which the user selects. LOVs incorporate a feature called *autoreduction* that makes it possible for users to select the list item they want with an absolute minimum of keystrokes, which can save a substantial amount of time in

Property Node	Property Name	Function
Help	Hint	Stores the hint text you would like to display to the users when they enter this text item
Help	Display Hint Automatically	Yes causes the hint to display in the message line instantly when the user enters the field; No keeps the hint from displaying until the user presses the HELP function key or executes the menu Help command
Help	Tooltip	Stores the tooltip text you would like to display to the user when the mouse pointer hovers over this text item
Help	Tooltip Visual Attribute Group	Allows you to specify a Visual Attribute Group for the tooltip text (the default <Null> setting results in the familiar black-on-yellow tooltip text)

TABLE 3-6. *Text Item Help Properties*

high-volume production environments. In this section, you will create a new form and incorporate your own LOV into the form. After learning about LOVs, you will move on to editors. An editor is a dialog box that appears when the user is in a text item. You will see how to create custom editors that incorporate your own titles, visual attributes, and even a different editing program, if you wish.

Introduction to LOVs and Editors

An LOV is a specific type of pick list used in Oracle Forms 6*i*. It consists of a pop-up window that displays a series of choices relevant to the operation or text item from which it was called. The LOV window is modal, so the user has to either make a selection or dismiss the list. A sample LOV window is depicted in Figure 3-3, which shows the LOV of available triggers you would see if you created a new trigger from the Object Navigator.

One useful feature in the LOV window is autoreduction, which filters the list's entries in real time as the user enters characters to identify the desired item.

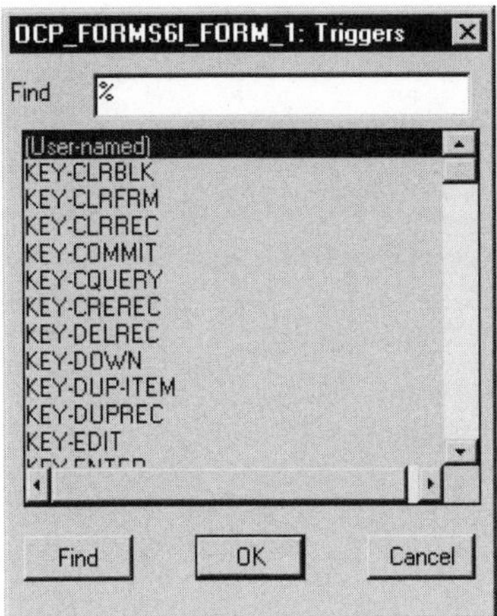

FIGURE 3-3. *LOV window*

Whereas many word processors offer a similar-sounding feature for operations like font selection, this feature in Oracle Forms 6*i* is smarter: if the list includes items whose names have many identical characters, the user only needs to type the characters that differentiate one item from the next.

For example, consider a situation where you want to create a trigger for a KEY-DOWN event. (This book covers triggers later, so just read along for now—don't try to follow this as an exercise.) To do this you would click on the Triggers node in your module and then invoke the Create procedure. You would immediately be presented with a list of the triggers available in Form Builder, as you saw in Figure 3-3. Since you want a KEY-DOWN trigger, you could type a **k** to reduce the list to only the items that start with "K." The result of this action is depicted in Figure 3-4. The only items showing are those that start with the same letter: "K." In fact, they all start with the same word: "KEY," followed by a hyphen. All you need to do next is identify *which* key you want; you do not need to type the "EY-" that would be required in, for instance, a font list. So you could type a letter **d**, and the list would diminish to only those values whose second word started with "D." This is depicted in Figure 3-5. To select from that list, you would only need to type a letter **o**, and the list shortens to a single entry: the KEY-DOWN trigger, as shown in Figure 3-6. With only three keystrokes, you could select the desired trigger from a list of over 100 potential triggers.

You can also search an LOV for strings that occur anywhere within the values, not just at their start. For instance, if you wanted to create a trigger that fires when an item is changed but cannot remember the exact name of the trigger, you can type

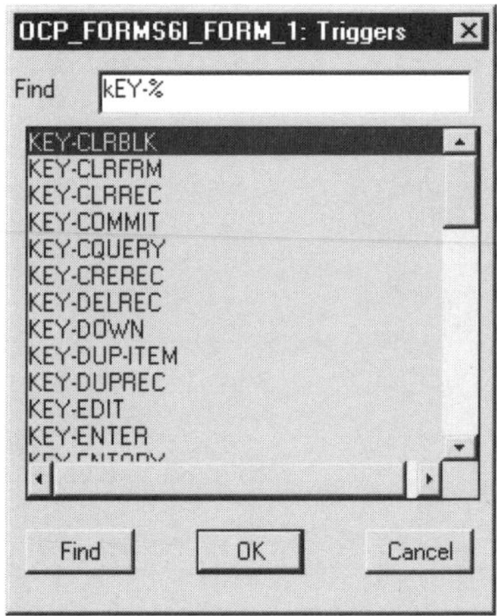

FIGURE 3-4. *LOV filtered with using letter "k"*

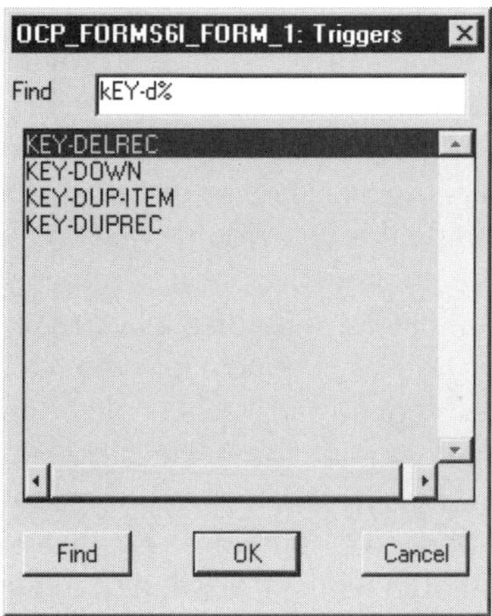

FIGURE 3-5. *LOV filtered with using letters "k d"*

the word **update** after the "%" in the Find field and click the Find button. The list of triggers will be filtered to show only the values that have "update" somewhere within their names, as shown in Figure 3-7. This same versatile functionality is

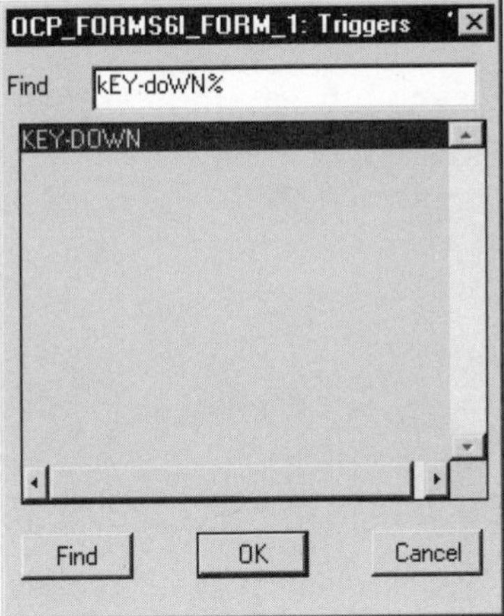

FIGURE 3-6. *LOV filtered with using letters "k d o"*

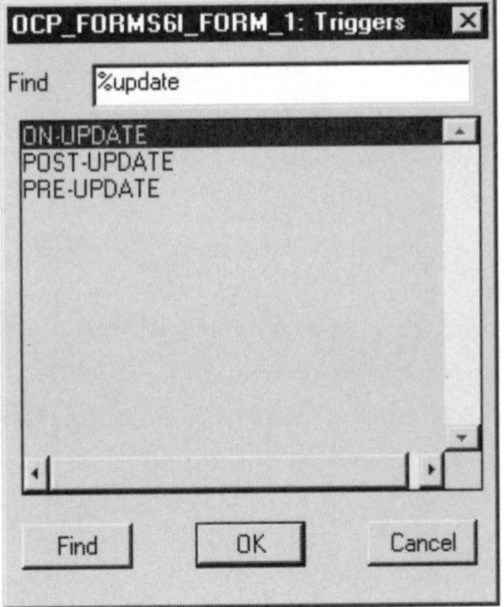

FIGURE 3-7. *LOV filtered to show UPDATE triggers*

available in LOVs you create for your users, enabling them to find people, products, or anything else quickly and easily.

Exercises

1. **What is a LOV?**
2. **How many ways does an LOV give the user to find items in the list? What are the differences between them?**

Creating LOVs

It is quite easy to create an LOV and use it in your forms. In this section, you will go through the steps of creating an LOV, configuring its properties, and assigning it to an item on a form. You will create an Employee form and design the Department ID field so it can be filled in from an LOV.

Start by creating a new data block to get data from the EMPLOYEE table. (If you use the existing EMPLOYEE data block in a new canvas, it will be removed from the DEPARTMENT canvas where it already resides.) You then create an LOV for DEPARTMENT data. Next, you create a new canvas to display records from the EMPLOYEE data block. After testing your new canvas by running it in the Forms Runtime program, return to the Layout Editor and attach the DEPARTMENT LOV to the EMPLOYEE canvas. You then run the Employee form again and see how it allows users to select a department by name and have the appropriate department number appear in the employee's record.

Using the Data Block Wizard, create a new data block. Base it on the EMPLOYEE table, and include all of that table's columns. Do not establish any relationships for the data block, and when the Data Block Wizard asks if you would like it to proceed to the Layout Wizard, tell it to just create the data block. Once the new data block has been created, change its name to **EMPLOYEE_2**. In the Object Navigator, select the LOVs node and then click the Create button. In the New List-Of-Values dialog box, ensure that the choice Use The LOV Wizard is selected, and click the OK button. Go past the LOV Wizard's welcome screen if it appears, and select the LOV Wizard option labeled New Record Group Based On A Query. Then enter the following code as the source query for the LOV:

L 3-2

```
SELECT DEPARTMENT_ID, DEPARTMENT_NAME
FROM DEPARTMENT
ORDER BY DEPARTMENT_NAME
```

Click on the Next button, and in the following wizard dialog indicate that both columns from the EMPLOYEE table should be included in the LOV. Click on the Next button, and in the following dialog change the Department_ID column's display width to **0**. (This ensures that when a user opens the LOV in a form, he or she will see only the Department_Name values, not the IDs linked to those values.) Then click the FINISH button to complete the procedure.

Next open the Property Palette for the new LOV, and change its name to **DEPARTMENT_LOV**. Navigate to the LOV's Functional properties group, and open the dialog box for Column Mapping properties. The dialog box should look like Figure 3-8. For the DEPARTMENT_ID column name, enter a Return Item property of **EMPLOYEE_2.DEPARTMENT_ID**. This specifies the *destination* into which the LOV will place the DEPARTMENT_ID value of whatever department record the user selects. Then enter a display width of **0**, which will cause DEPARTMENT_ID to become a *hidden* column. Click on the OK button to close the dialog box. In the Object Navigator, you will see that a record group has automatically been created under the Record Groups node to supply data to your new LOV. Change the record group's name to **DEPARTMENT_LOV**.

Now you have an LOV, but it isn't yet attached to a form. To do that, navigate to the Object Navigator's Canvases node and change the name of your existing canvas to **DEPARTMENT** (if it isn't named that already). Then start the Layout Wizard to create a new canvas. Select (New Canvas) as the canvas name, click on the Next button, and move the Available Items into the Displayed Items area in the following order: LAST_NAME, FIRST_NAME, EMPLOYEE_ID, HIRE_DATE, SALARY, DEPARTMENT_ID. Click the Next button twice, and select a layout style of Form. Click the Next button again, and enter a frame title of **Employee**. Click the Finish button, and when the finished canvas is displayed in the Layout Editor, click on the

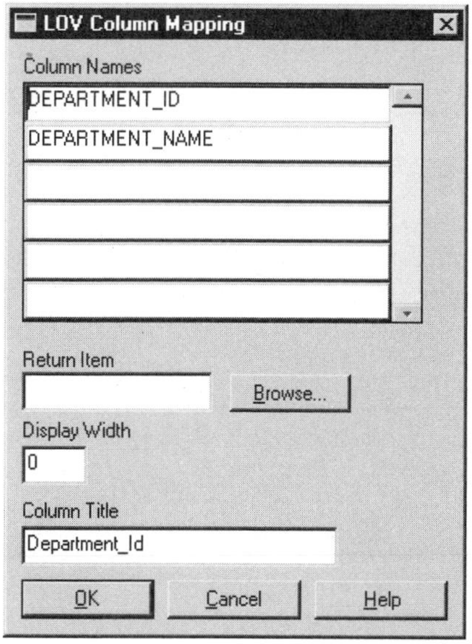

FIGURE 3-8. *Column Mapping properties dialog box for LOV*

background of the form to select the entire canvas. Open the Property Palette for the canvas (function key F4 is a shortcut to do this), and change the new canvas's name to **EMPLOYEE**.

Next, click on the Department_ID field on the form canvas. Back in the Property Palette—which is now showing properties for the selected field—go to the LOV group and set the item's LOV property to DEPARTMENT_LOV. Move farther down the Property Palette to the property named Validate from List, and set that property to Yes. Then run your form. Click on the Next Block button on the toolbar twice to change the form from the original department/employee combination to the new EMPLOYEE form. Enter the following values in a new record: Last Name **Carilla**, First Name **Bianca,** Employee ID **1011**, Hire Date **10-MAY-2002**, Salary **65000**.

When you move into the Department ID item, notice that the bottom line in the console displays the indicator "List of Values." This is your clue that you can enter data into this item using a list, as well as by typing directly. To see the LOV, press function key F9 or use the menu command Edit | Display List. You should see an LOV appear that looks like the one shown in Figure 3-9. Select the Quality Assurance department either by typing **Q** and clicking on the OK button, or by double-clicking on the Quality Assurance value in the list. When you do, you will see the Quality Assurance department's ID automatically appear in the item. Save the record by clicking on the Save button, and then exit out of the Forms Runtime program.

Once you have returned to Form Builder, close the Layout Editor and then open the Property Palette for the LOV named DEPARTMENT_LOV. Table 3-7 shows a number of properties you can use to tailor the look and feel of the LOV.

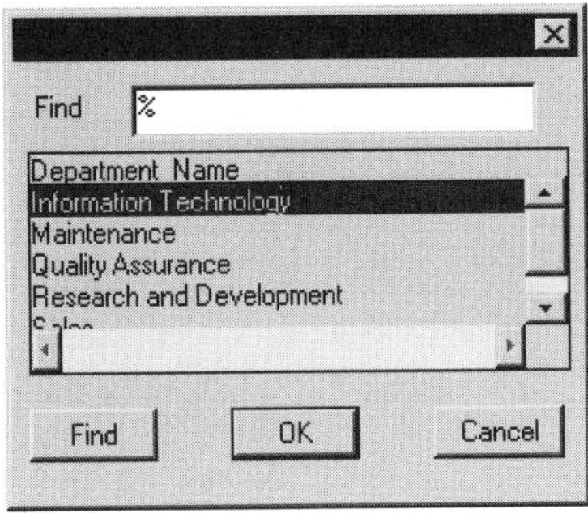

FIGURE 3-9. *DEPARTMENT LOV*

Property Node	Property Name	Function
Functional	Automatic Display	Causes the LOV to display automatically any time the user navigates into the relevant item
Functional	Automatic Refresh	A setting of Yes causes the LOV's underlying query to reexecute each time the LOV is displayed or the item's contents are validated, which takes additional time but ensures that the LOV contents are up-to-date; a setting of No means the query runs only the first time the LOV is used, a bandwidth-saving approach useful when the list's contents are not likely to change during the session
Functional	Automatic Select	When set to Yes, the LOV automatically acts on a list entry as soon as the user types enough characters to uniquely identify a single row in the list; eliminates need for user to click OK to return to the form
Functional	Automatic Skip	A setting of Yes causes focus to move immediately to next field on form after user makes an LOV selection
Functional	Automatic Position	Enables Oracle Forms 6*i* to automatically position an LOV near the item that invoked it
Functional	Automatic Column Width	Lets Oracle Forms 6*i* automatically set the widths of the LOV columns wide enough to accommodate their titles if the Display Width isn't wide enough to do so
Physical	X Position Y Position	Enables you to position an LOV precisely where you want it on the screen

TABLE 3-7. *LOV Functional Properties* (continued)

Property Node	Property Name	Function
Physical	Width Height	Enables you to tailor the size and shape of the LOV
Visual Attributes	Visual Attribute Group	Convenient way to control the appearance of all LOVs in your application from a single Visual Attribute Group

TABLE 3-7. *LOV Functional Properties* (continued)

Exercises

1. **What are the two purposes of a LOV?**
2. **Which LOV properties give you control over the LOV's appearance?**
3. **What LOV property would you set to cause the LOV to appear automatically when the user enters a field?**
4. **What LOV property ensures that the values in the LOV are always up-to-date, as of the moment the LOV is opened?**

Creating Editors

In Oracle Forms 6*i*, an *editor* is a dialog box that can appear when the user is in a text item. In addition to giving the user more space in which to type text, an editor provides Find and Replace functions that can be useful when modifying large blocks of text. You can open an editor any time your cursor is in a character, number, or date/time field by pressing CTRL-E (remember that in Oracle Forms 6*i* the CTRL-key commands are case sensitive, so this command will work only if your CAPS LOCK key is off). This keystroke command produces an editor window similar to the one shown here:

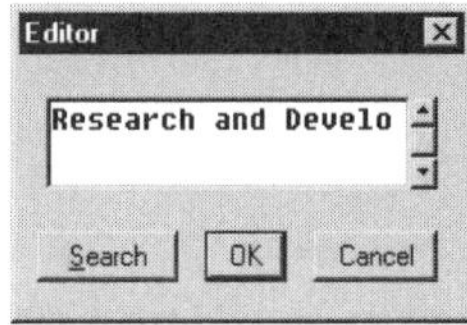

Clicking the Search button takes you to the Search/Replace dialog box shown in the following illustration:

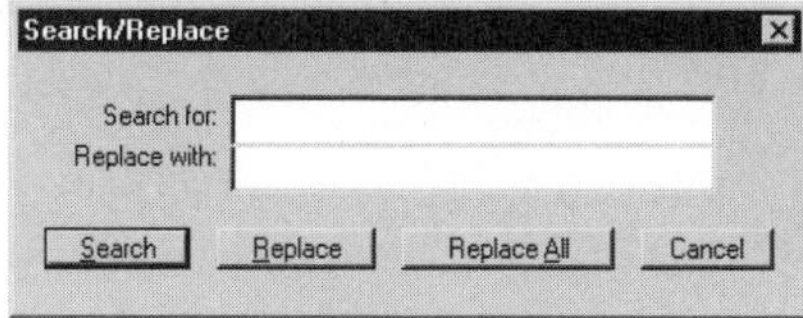

Since you can call up an editor any time already, why create your own? Customization. Designing your own editor allows you to specify what editing program is opened for the user, as well as customize the editor window's size, shape, title, and appearance.

Editor windows are most useful for character fields that will hold large amounts of text. The sample application you have created for this unit does not have any fields of this type, so to learn how to make a custom editor you will create one for the DEPARTMENT_NAME item. In Object Navigator, select the Editors node and then click the Create button. Open the Property Palette for the new editor. Change the editor's Name property to **DEPARTMENT_NAME_EDITOR**. Enter a Title property of **Department Name Editor**, and then a Bottom Title property of **Sample Bottom Title**. Change the X Position property to **100**, the Y Position property to **25**, the Width to **400,** and the Height to **300**. Change the Show Vertical Scroll Bar property to **Yes**.

Next, open your DEPARTMENT canvas. Display the Property Palette for the item called DEPARTMENT_NAME. Change the item's Editor property to the name of the editor you just created: **DEPARTMENT_NAME_EDITOR**. Then run your application. When the DEPARTMENT form opens in the Forms Runtime program, populate the form using the Execute Query button. Then move to a Department Name item, and press CTRL-E to invoke the editor you created. The editor window that appears should look very similar to Figure 3-10. When you are finished, close the editor window, exit from the Forms Runtime program, and return to Form Builder.

If you just want your user to have a more flexible editing window and do not care about custom titles or visual attributes, you can tell Oracle Forms 6*i* to use the default system editor (Notepad in Windows systems) instead of Developer's internal editor. You can do this by opening the canvas in Layout Editor, selecting the relevant text item, and changing its Editor property to **SYSTEM_EDITOR**.

Exercises

1. **What benefits does the user derive from using an editor window while working with large text blocks?**
2. **What are the advantages of creating a custom editor?**

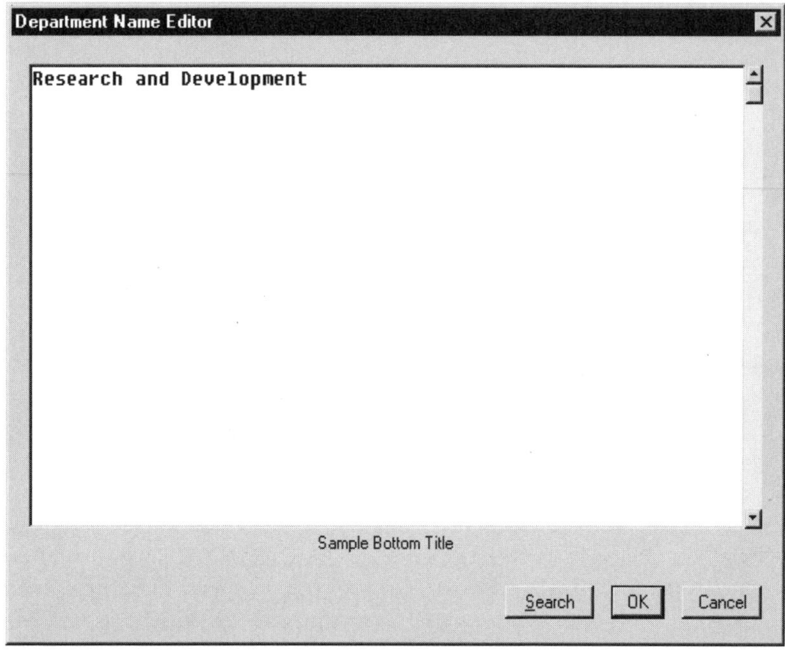

FIGURE 3-10. *Custom editor window*

Chapter Summary

In this chapter, you have covered quite a bit of information about Forms design. You began by learning about the components of the Property Palette, which consist of the toolbar, context bar, and property list. The toolbar contains buttons giving convenient access to functions relevant to setting properties: property copy and paste, property add and delete, and property—class create and inherit. It also provides buttons that control whether a Property Palette invoked for multiple objects shows only the properties those objects have in common (Intersection mode), or shows all of the properties for all objects (Union mode). The next Property Palette toolbar button, labeled Freeze/Unfreeze, forces the Palette to continue showing properties for its current object, regardless of what objects you select from that point on. To the right of that button is a field labeled Find that lets you quickly jump to specific properties in the Property Palette.

Beneath the toolbar is the context bar, which identifies the object whose properties are currently being displayed by the Property Palette. Below that is the property list, the main portion of the Property Palette. The property list arranges properties into groups and provides the familiar + or – in front of each group name to open or close the group's properties. Each object type in your application has different properties, and the Property Palette remembers which property categories you like to have open and closed for each type of object.

Next you learned how to manipulate properties using the Property Palette. The Property Palette contains several different types of value fields: alphanumeric fields for typing values, fields containing a button labeled More . . . that opens a dialog box for setting values, fields with a button showing an ellipsis (. . .) that opens a window for entering and editing lengthy text such as comments or **where** clauses, pop-up lists of predefined values, and Lists of Values (LOVs) containing lists whose contents can change. You can compare the properties of two or more objects by selecting all of the items you want to compare: SHIFT-clicking allows you to quickly select contiguous groups of objects, and CTRL-clicking lets you select noncontiguous objects. When a Property Palette is displaying properties for multiple objects, it displays ***** for properties that do not have the same value for all the objects selected. You can change the properties for multiple objects simultaneously by selecting all the objects and then changing the desired property in the Property Palette. The Property Palette offers copy and paste functions for individual and multiple properties. When copying more than one property at a time, the Palette pastes only the properties for which an actual value is shown (as opposed to *****), and only the properties that are relevant in the object receiving the pasted properties.

You then learned about properties that control the behavior of data blocks. The General group of properties allows you to change the data block's name, subclass the data block beneath another object or property class, and enter comments about the data block. The data block behavior properties include the Navigation group, Records group, Database group, and Advanced Database group. The data block appearance properties include the Scrollbar group, Font & Color group, Character Mode group, and International group. Behavior properties that are especially useful to developers are Query Array Size, which controls how many records will be fetched from the database at a time; Number of Records Buffered, which specifies how many records the Forms Runtime program keeps in the client computer's memory when the form is run; and Query Allowed, which determines whether the user (or application code) can execute a query in a data block. The property named **where** clause enables you to enter filtering criteria to limit the types of records returned; **order by** clause allows you specify how the returned data should be sorted; Insert/Update/Delete Allowed lets you enable or disable the respective DML functions; Update Changed Columns Only specifies that when the user changes an existing record, the **update** command sent to the server only includes the fields that were changed; and DML Array Size controls the number of records that will be sent to the server in a batch. The properties relevant to the frame surrounding a data block include Frame Title Alignment, Number of Records Displayed, Distance

Between Records, Bevel, and the Frame Title Font & Color group.

Next you learned how to create control blocks-blocks that do not directly correspond to a database. A control block contains either controls such as buttons, or a group of items with single values, such as calculated subtotals. Unlike data blocks, control blocks have a two-part creation process: create the control block, and then manually create the items that go into the block. When you delete data blocks and their components from the Object Navigator, the frame that contained the data block remains on the canvas, as well as the frame's title, which is an example of boilerplate text. The frame no longer contains the data block or data block items, and the deletion cannot be undone. In contrast, when you delete a data block's items and frame from the canvas in the Layout Editor, everything related to those items is deleted from the Layout Editor except the scroll bar: the frame and its boilerplate text are gone, as well as the items the frame contained. In the Object Navigator, the data block is still present but as an empty data structure. This action can be undone.

You then moved on to a new section discussing text items. A text item is any control on your form that displays text, numbers, dates, or long data, and allows the data to be edited by the user. This is in contrast to display items, which do not allow the user to change the data shown. You can modify a text item's appearance by manipulating properties such as Justification, Format Mask, Distance Between Records, Visible, Visual Attribute Group, Prompt, Prompt Justification, and Prompt Visual Attribute Group. For controlling the data within a text item, Oracle Forms 6*i* offers properties such as Case Restriction, Data Type, Maximum Length, Initial Value, Required, Lowest and Highest Value, and Calculation Mode. You can change the navigational behavior of a text item with properties like Automatic Skip, Keyboard Navigable, Previous and Next Navigation Item, and Show Vertical Scroll Bar. To enhance the relationship between a text item and a database, you can utilize such properties as ******** Primary Key, Query Only, Query, Insert, Update Allowed, Query Length, Case Insensitive Query, and Update Only if NULL. The properties designed to modify the functionality of a text item include Enabled, Conceal Data, Popup Menu, Initial Value, Copy Value from Item, Calculation Mode, Formula, Summary Function, Summarized Block, Summarized Item, LOV, and Validate from List.

After digesting the capabilities of those properties, you proceeded to learn about others enabling you to provide item-level assistance for your user by creating hints and tooltips. These invaluable text item properties include Hint, Display Hint Automatically, Tooltip, and Tooltip Visual Attribute Group. Further enhancing individual text items are LOVs and editors. An LOV is a window that displays a series of choices users can use to populate a text item. The LOV window is modal, so users has to either make a selection from the list or dismiss it. When presented with an LOV, users can employ a feature called autoreduction to select the list item they want with a minimum of keystrokes. Users can also search an LOV for strings that occur anywhere within the list's values, not just at their start. An LOV can be customized using properties such as Automatic Display, Automatic Refresh, Automatic Select, Automatic Skip, Automatic Position, Automatic Column Width, X and Y Position, Width, and Height to tailor the look and feel of the LOV.

An editor is a dialog box that gives the user a larger space in which to type text. An editor provides Find and Replace functions, and you can customize its look and feel. You can also tell Oracle Forms 6*i* to employ the operating system's default editor instead of Developer's internal editor by setting the Editor property to SYSTEM_EDITOR for the relevant text item.

All in all, this chapter comprises about 13 percent of material tested on OCP Exam 3.

Two-Minute Drill

- The components of the Property Palette are the toolbar, context bar, and property list.
- The toolbar on the Property Palette contains buttons giving convenient access to functions relevant to setting properties: property copy and paste, property add and delete, and property-class create and inherit.
- The Intersection/Union button on the Property Palette toolbar controls whether a Property Palette invoked for multiple objects shows only the properties those objects have in common (Intersection mode), or all of the properties for all objects (Union mode).
- The Property Palette toolbar button labeled Freeze/Unfreeze forces the Palette to continue showing properties for its current object, regardless of what objects you select from that point on.
- The Property Palette toolbar field labeled Find causes the Property Palette to place its focus on the first property matching the characters you type.
- The Property Palette context bar identifies the object whose properties are currently being displayed by the Property Palette.
- The Bevel property lets you select from six different types of frame borders. The choices are Raised, Lowered, None, Inset (the default), Outset, and Plain.
- The Property Palette can contain alphanumeric fields for typing values, fields containing a button labeled More . . . that opens a dialog box for setting values, fields with a button showing an ellipsis (. . .) that opens a window for manipulating lengthy text, pop-up lists of predefined values, and LOVs containing lists whose contents can change.

- You can compare the properties of two or more objects using just one Property Palette by selecting all of the items you want to compare. The Property Palette displays ***** for properties that do not have the same value for all the objects selected.
- You can change the properties for multiple objects simultaneously by selecting all the objects and then changing the desired property in the Property Palette. In doing so, you overwrite whatever settings the selected objects had for those properties.
- The Property Palette can copy and paste individual or multiple properties. When copying multiple properties, the Palette pastes only the properties for which an actual value is shown, and only the properties that are relevant to the object receiving the pasted properties.
- The behavior of data blocks can be controlled using properties such as Query Array Size, Number of Records Buffered, Query Allowed, **where** clause, **order by** clause, Insert/Update/Delete Allowed, Update Changed Columns Only, and DML Array Size.
- The properties relevant to the frame surrounding a data block include Frame Title Alignment, Number of Records Displayed, Distance Between Records, Bevel, and the Frame Title Font & Color group.
- A control block does not directly correspond to a database, tables, or columns.
- Control blocks have a two-part creation process: create the control block, and then manually create the items that go in the block.
- When you delete data blocks and their components from the Object Navigator, the data blocks and components are irreversibly deleted, but the frame that contained them remains on the canvas, along with the boilerplate text you entered for the frame's title.
- When you delete a data block's items from the canvas in the Layout Editor, everything related to that block is deleted from the Layout Editor except the scroll bar, and the data block remains in the Object Navigator but as an empty data structure. This action can be reverted.
- A text item is any control on your form that enables the user to view and edit text, numbers, dates, or long data.
- A display item shows data but does not allow the user to change it.
- You can modify a text item's appearance by manipulating properties such as Justification, Format Mask, Distance Between Records, Visible, Visual

Attribute Group, Prompt, Prompt Justification, and Prompt Visual Attribute Group.

- For controlling the data within a text item, Oracle Forms 6*i* offers properties such as Case Restriction, Data Type, Maximum Length, Initial Value, Required, Lowest and Highest Value, and Calculation Mode.
- You can change the navigational behavior of a text item with properties like Automatic Skip, Keyboard Navigable, Previous and Next Navigation Item, and Show Vertical Scroll Bar.
- To enhance the relationship between a text item and a database, you can use such properties as Primary Key, Query Only, Query,Insert, Update Allowed, Query Length, Case Insensitive Query, and Update Only if NULL.
- The properties that can modify the functionality of a text item include Enabled, Conceal Data, Popup Menu, Initial Value, Copy Value from Item, Calculation Mode, Formula, Summary Function, Summarized Block, Summarized Item, LOV, and Validate from List.
- The item properties enabling you to provide item-level assistance for your user are Hint, Display Hint Automatically, Tooltip, and Tooltip Visual Attribute Group.
- A LOV is a modal window that populates a text item based on a selection made by the user from the list.
- LOVs utilize autoreduction to filter the list in real time as the user types differentiating characters, making it possible to select the desired list item with an absolute minimum of keystrokes.
- The user can also search an LOV for strings that occur anywhere within the values, not just at their start. Only the first column in the LOV will be searched.
- A LOV can be customized using properties such as Automatic Display, Automatic Refresh, Automatic Select, Automatic Skip, Automatic Position, Automatic Column Width, X and Y Position, Width, and Height.
- An editor is a dialog box that can give the user a larger space in which to type text, as well as providing Find and Replace functions.
- You can customize the look and feel of the editor, and you can tell Oracle Forms 6*i* to bring up the operating system's default editor instead of Developer's internal editor by setting the Editor property to SYSTEM_EDITOR for the relevant text item.

Chapter Questions

1. **Which of the following are components of the Property Palette? (Choose three.)**

   A. Context bar

   B. Next Block button

   C. Property list

   D. Save icon

   E. Toolbar

2. **You open a single property sheet to display properties for your DEPARTMENT data block and DEPARTMENT canvas simultaneously. Which Property Palette display mode is likely to show more properties?**

   A. Intersection

   B. Union

3. **Which of the following activities are available from buttons on the Property Palette toolbar? (Choose six.)**

   A. Add property

   B. Combine property

   C. Copy property

   D. Create property class

   E. Delete property

   F. Inherit property class

   G. Paste property

   H. Print property

   I. Retrieve property

   J. Save property

4. **Which of the following are valid frame bevel types? (Choose six.)**

   A. Bump

   B. Flat

C. Inset

D. Lowered

E. None

F. Outset

G. Plain

H. Raised

I. Rigid

5. What types of fields are in the Property Palette?

A. Alphanumeric fields for typing values

B. Fields containing a button labeled More . . . that opens a dialog box for setting values

C. Fields with a button showing an ellipsis (. . .) that opens a window for manipulating lengthy text

D. Pop-up lists of predefined values

E. LOVs containing lists whose contents can change

F. All of the above

G. None of the above

6. What does it mean when the Property Palette displays *** as a property's value?**

A. The property is not applicable for the object you have selected.

B. The value "*****" will be inserted into the field automatically.

C. Two or more objects are selected, and their values for that property are not the same.

D. You cannot update that property for the object you have selected.

7. What happens if you select multiple objects, open the Property Palette, and change a property's value?

A. The changed value displays as *****.

B. The change is applied to all selected objects.

C. The Property Palette shows each object's old and new values for that property.

D. You cannot change a property for multiple objects at one time.

8. **Which data block property would you consider changing if your records include LONG items that are not likely to be edited?**

A. Query Allowed

B. Update Allowed

C. Update Changed Columns Only

D. DML Array Size

9. **What does the Property Palette toolbar field labeled Find do?**

A. Locates other objects containing the same property as the one you currently have selected

B. Forces the Palette to place its focus on the first property matching the characters you type

C. Locates Form Builder files on your hard disk

D. Allows you to search-and-replace a given property value with a different value

10. **What would be the result of completely deleting a data block from the Object Navigator?**

A. The data blocks and components are deleted but can be retrieved using the Edit | Undo command.

B. The data blocks and components are irreversibly deleted, and all components from the data block stay on the canvas and must be deleted manually.

C. The data blocks and components are irreversibly deleted, and all components from the data block are removed from any canvas that contained them, including the data block's frame and boilerplate title text.

D. The data blocks and components are irreversibly deleted, and all components from the data block are removed from any canvas that contained them, but the data block's frame and boilerplate title text will stay on the canvas.

11. Which of the following describe a LOV?

- **A.** Best when used with fields with few possible values
- **B.** Context-sensitive
- **C.** List
- **D.** Modal
- **E.** Populates an item based on a selection made by the user
- **F.** Window
- **G.** All of the above
- **H.** None of the above

12. What of the following are properties you can use to customize a LOV?

- **A.** Automatic Column Width
- **B.** Automatic Display
- **C.** Automatic Position
- **D.** Automatic Refresh
- **E.** Automatic Select
- **F.** Automatic Skip
- **G.** Height
- **H.** Width
- **I.** X Position
- **J.** Y Position
- **K.** All of the above
- **L.** None of the above

13. What does the Property Palette context bar do?

- **A.** Identifies which object's properties are currently being displayed by the Property Palette
- **B.** Identifies which program you are in when you open the Property Palette
- **C.** Provides help instructions based on your location in the Property Palette
- **D.** Nothing

14. Which of the following occur if you copy multiple properties from one object and paste them into another?

- **A.** It is not possible to copy multiple properties at one time.
- **B.** Properties with blank properties will be pasted.
- **C.** Properties not relevant to the destination object will be added to that object.
- **D.** If the destination is a different type of object than the source, the destination object will be changed to the same type of object as the source.
- **E.** All of the above.
- **F.** None of the above.

15. You created a LOV for stock items and included a Quantity Currently In Stock column in the LOV. How can you ensure that the user sees accurate "in stock" numbers each time the LOV is invoked?

- **A.** Enable the LOV's Automatic Select property.
- **B.** Programmatically requery all tables in the application when the user opens that canvas.
- **C.** Enable the LOV's Automatic Refresh property.
- **D.** There is no way to ensure this.

16. You have created a SALES_TICKET form for a point-of-sale application. You now want to modify the Transaction_Date_Time item in the form so it is automatically populated with the current date and time each time a new record is created. How can you accomplish this?

- **A.** Set the Default Value property to $$DATETIME$$.
- **B.** Set the Initial Value property to SYSDATE.
- **C.** Set the Default Value property to SYSDATE.
- **D.** Set the Initial Value property to $$DATETIME$$.

17. What does freezing the Property Palette do?

- **A.** Enables you to change a property in multiple objects at one time
- **B.** Forces the Palette to continue displaying properties for the currently selected object(s), regardless of what object(s) you select from that point on

C. Opens a second Palette for comparing multiple objects' properties

D. When multiple objects are selected, shows only those properties that all selected objects share in common

18. What is the best way to ensure that an item cannot accept query criteria?

A. Set the item's Query Allowed property to No.

B. Set the item's Disable Query property to Yes.

C. Set the item's Queryable property to No.

D. Set the item's Query Length property to 0.

19. How many characters would you need to type in a LOV to select the WHEN-KEY-UP item from a list containing WHEN-BUTTON-PRESSED, WHEN-KEY-DOWN, and WHEN-KEY-UP, assuming they are the only items in the list and the LOV's properties are set to automatically display the LOV and automatically enter the value once a row is selected?

A. 1

B. 2

C. 3

D. 10

20. Which of the following data block properties affect the balance between client computer memory and network traffic? (Choose all that apply.)

A. DML Data Target Type

B. DML Array Size

C. DML Data Target Name

D. Number of Records Buffered

E. Number of Records Displayed

F. Record Orientation

21. What is the definition of the term "text item?"

A. The label preceding a field on a form

B. Any control on your form that allows the user to view and edit text

C. Any control on your form that allows the user to view and edit text or numbers

D. Any control on your form that allows the user to view and edit text, numbers, or dates

E. Any control on your form that allows the user to view and edit text, numbers, dates, or long data

22. You have created a LOV for a text item on your canvas, and you would like the LOV to appear automatically each time the user enters that text item. What is required to make that happen?

A. Set the Automatic Refresh property in the LOV Property Palette to Yes.

B. Set the Automatic Refresh property in the text item Property Palette to Yes.

C. Set the Automatic Display property in the LOV Property Palette to Yes.

D. Set the Automatic Display property in the text item Property Palette to Yes.

E. Set the Automatic Select property in the LOV Property Palette to Yes.

F. Set the Automatic Select property in the text item Property Palette to Yes.

G. You must code a trigger to make this happen.

23. Which of the following properties enable you to provide item-level assistance for your user?

A. Display Hint Automatically

B. Hint

C. Justification

D. Prompt

E. Prompt Justification

F. Summary Function

G. Tooltip

24. Which of the following actions can a user do with a display item?

A. View existing database values.

B. Insert new database values.

C. Update existing database values.

D. Delete existing database values.

E. All of the above.

F. None of the above.

25. To which of the following items does a control block directly correspond?

A. Database

B. Table

C. Column

D. All of the above

E. None of the above

26. When a control block is created, what items does it contain?

A. Text items for all columns in the related database table.

B. None. You must manually create any items that will go into a control block.

C. None, because, you cannot put items in a control block.

27. Which text item data properties can restrict whether a user can insert new data? (Choose all that apply.)

A. Primary Key

B. Query Only

C. Query Allowed

D. Insert Allowed

E. Lock Record

28. What are the benefits of incorporating a LOV in your application? (Choose as many as apply.)

A. Faster record retrieval

B. Enables user to make selections with minimum keystrokes

C. Efficient use of client computer memory

D. Can ensure that detail values are valid in master table

E. Makes application much cooler

29. Which of the following are benefits of creating a custom editor for an application? (Choose as many as apply.)

A. Allows you to control the position of the editing box

B. Enables user to include bold, italics, and underlining in text

C. Gives the user a larger area for editing text

D. Provides Find and Replace functions

E. Allows you to title the editing window

F. Enables you to specify an editing program other than the system default

G. All of the above

H. None of the above

30. Which of the following properties change the navigational behavior of a text item? (Choose as many as apply.)

A. Automatic Skip

B. Calculation Mode

C. Case Restriction

D. Display Hint Automatically

E. Keyboard Navigable

F. Maximum Length

G. Next Navigation Item

H. Previous Navigation Item

I. Query Only

J. Show Vertical Scroll Bar

Answers to Chapter Questions

1. A, C, E. Context bar, Property list, Toolbar

Explanation For a refresher on this topic, review the section "Property Palette Components."

2. B. Union

Explanation The Intersection display mode shows only the properties that multiple selected objects have in common, whereas the Union display mode shows all properties for all selected objects, whether the objects share the properties in common or not.

3. A, C, D, E, F, G. Add property, Copy property, Create property class, Delete property, Inherit property class, Paste property

Explanation For a refresher on this topic, review the section "Property Palette Components."

4. C, D, E, F, G, H. Inset, Lowered, None, Outset, Plain, Raised

Explanation For a refresher on this topic, review the section "Controlling Frame Properties."

5. F. All of the above

Explanation For a refresher on this topic, refer to the section "Manipulating Properties."

6. C. Two or more objects are selected, and their values for that property are not the same

Explanation Because the Property Palette cannot display more than one value per property, the only way it can deal with multiple objects is to display something special when those objects' values are different. The special display is *****.

7. B. The change is applied to all selected objects

Explanation For a refresher on this topic, review the section "Manipulating Properties."

8. C. Update Changed Columns Only

Explanation If your records include LONG items that are not likely to be edited, this data block property can improve application performance by keeping the application from sending the voluminous LONG data back to the server during an **update** command.

9. B. Forces the Palette to place its focus on the first property matching the characters you type

Explanation The Property Palette toolbar field labeled Find makes the Property Palette quickly jump to specific properties. If the group containing the matching property is closed, the Find field will even open it up for you.

10. D. The data blocks and components are irreversibly deleted, all components from the data block are removed from any canvas that contained them, but the data block's frame and boilerplate title text will stay on the canvas.

Explanation Review the section "Deleting Data Blocks and Their Components" if you need a reminder on this topic.

11. B, C, D, E, F. Context-sensitive, List, Modal, Populates an item based on a selection made by the user, Window

Explanation A LOV is a modal window that populates an item based on a selection made by the user from the list. Since a LOV uses autoreduction to navigate through its list with the fewest possible keystrokes, its benefits are most noticeable when used with long lists.

12. K. All of the above

Explanation For a refresher on this topic, refer to the section titled "Creating LOVs."

13. A. Identifies which object's properties are currently being displayed by the Property Palette.

Explanation For a refresher on this topic, review the section titled "Property Palette Components."

14. F. None of the above

Explanation The Property Palette can copy and paste individual or multiple properties. When copying multiple properties, the Palette pastes only the properties for which an actual value is shown, and only the properties that are relevant to the object receiving the pasted properties.

15. C. Enable the LOV's Automatic Refresh property

Explanation The Automatic Refresh property determines whether the LOV's underlying query executes every time the LOV is invoked, or only the first time it is invoked. Setting the property to Yes configures it to requery every time.

16. D. Set the Initial Value property to $$DATETIME$$.

Explanation The is no Item property called Default Value, and whereas SYSDATE is a valid parameter in a SQL query, it will not work in the Initial Value property; you must use $$DATETIME$$.

17. B. Forces the Palette to continue displaying properties for the currently selected object(s), regardless of what object(s) you select from that point on

Explanation Review the section "Understanding the Components of the Property Palette" for a refresher on this topic.

18. A. Set the item's Query Allowed property to No

Explanation There are no properties named Disable Query or Queryable. Setting the Query Length property to 0 simply tells Oracle Forms 6*i* to use the item's length as the maximum query length.

19. B. 2

Explanation Because all three choices begin with "WHEN-," the LOV only cares about the first differentiating character, which is the "K" that identifies the KEY group. The next character needed is the "D" to select DOWN, after which the row's key value will automatically be entered into the text item.

20. B, D. DML Array Size, Number of Records Buffered

Explanation Review the section "Controlling the Behavior of Data Blocks" if you need a reminder on this topic.

21. E. Any control on your form that allows the user to view and edit text, numbers, dates, or long data

Explanation For a refresher on this topic, review the section "Working with Text Items."

22. C. Set the Automatic Display property in the LOV Property Palette to Yes

Explanation No text item property would effect this change. Of the LOV properties listed, Automatic Refresh determines whether the LOV's contents are requeried each time it is opened, and Automatic Select specifies whether the selected LOV row is placed into the specified text item without the user having to double-click on the row or click the OK button.

23. A, B, G. Display Hint Automatically, Hint, Tooltip

Explanation For a refresher on this topic, refer to the section "Including Help Messages in Your Applications."

24. A. View existing database values

Explanation A display item shows data but does not allow the user to change it. In essence, it is a read-only field.

25. E. None of the above

Explanation A control block is not associated with a database object. Instead, it contains either controls (such as buttons), or a group of items with single values (such as calculated subtotals).

26. B. None. You must manually create any items that will go into a control block.

Explanation By definition, a control block is not related to a database table. And you can put items into a control block—that is what it's for. But you must do it manually after the block is created.

27. B, D. Query Only, Insert Allowed

Explanation When the Query Only property is set to Yes, records cannot be inserted. The same is true if the Insert Allowed property is set to No.

28. B, D. Enables user to make selections with minimum keystrokes, Can ensure that detail values are valid in master table

Explanation The autoreduction feature of LOVs allows them to select records with minimum keystrokes, and the fact that the LOV can be populated from a detail item's master table ensures that the selected values are valid as long as the item is set to validate entries against the LOV. Answer E was not intended as a serious answer, but don't reduce your score if you selected it.

29. A, C, D, E, F. Allows you to control the position of the editing box, Gives the user a larger area for editing text, Provides Find and Replace functions, Allows you to title the editing window, Enables you to specify an editing program other than the system default

Explanation When you create a custom editor, you can control its size and position, the titles it displays, and even what program will be started to perform the editing. The custom editor also provides Find and Replace functions. It does not, however, allow saving text attributes such as bold, italics, or underlining.

30. A, E, G, H, I. Automatic Skip, Keyboard Navigable, Next Navigation Item, Previous Navigation Item, and Query Only

Explanation For a refresher on this topic, review the section "Modifying the Navigational Behavior of a Text Item."

CHAPTER 4

Forms Design II

In this chapter, you will cover the following aspects of building forms:

- Creating additional input items
- Creating noninput items
- Creating windows and content canvases
- Working with other canvases

This chapter covers a wealth of information you can use to make your applications much more sophisticated. You will learn about all the input item types available in Form Builder, and then practice creating check boxes, lists, and radio button groups. Next you will cover noninput item types, with practice at creating buttons, read-only fields, calculated fields, and items to display pictures and play sounds. Then, you will learn how to create applications with multiple windows, and you will create forms that incorporate toolbars, tabbed interfaces, and stacked canvases.

The *OCP Exam 3* will consist of test questions in this subject area worth 18 percent of the final score.

Creating Additional Input Items

In this section, you will cover the following points related to creating additional input items:

- Introduction to item types that allow input
- Creating a check box
- Creating a list item
- Creating a radio group

The most obvious task when creating forms is placing items on the form for the user to interact with. Several of the items you can place on a form are designed to let the reader enter or modify data. This section introduces those *input items* and takes you through exercises creating several different types of them.

Introduction to Item Types that Allow Input

Input items are form objects enabling the user to enter and change data. Table 4-1 shows the input items available in Form Builder, along with usage recommendations for each item type.

Item Type	Usage
Text Item	Allows user to enter and view data. Best for nonrepeating data that does not lend itself to being in a list of often-used choices.
Check Box	Used singly or in groups. Each check box represents a data item that can have only one of two values. They are used for yes/no status fields such as "transaction completed," "currently active," "include in report," and "flagged for review."
Radio Button	Used in groups of two or more. Represents data that has a fixed number of choices that are mutually exclusive. Examples include gender, ratings, and day of week.
Poplist	Familiar drop-down list that allows user to select one value. Autofills entry with matching list item as user types. Will not accept nonlist entries. Designed to be used with lists containing 15 or fewer choices.
T-List	Shows multiple rows of list options and highlights the one currently selected. Designed to be used when the user selects one row from a list containing 15 to 30 choices. The default display size shows at least five rows from the list, so it is best suited for a form that has plenty of screen space available.
Combo Box	Drop-down list that allows user to select one value. Does not autofill entry with matching list item as user types. Can accept nonlist entries if the developer has written appropriate code.
List of Values (LOV)	Can display an unlimited number of choices, and can display multiple columns of information for each choice.

TABLE 4-1. *Item Types that Allow Input*

Exercises

1. **What item type would you use to allow users to select rows from a multicolumn list?**
2. **What is the main functional difference between a group of check boxes and a group of radio buttons?**

Creating a Check Box

In order to add a check box to a form layout, the form's data block needs to include an item that can contain only one of two possible values. Currently, the sample application being used in this unit does not have a column that matches this criterion, so you will add one. Using SQL*Plus, add a profit-sharing column to the EMPLOYEE table by entering the following code:

L 4-1

```
ALTER TABLE employee
  ADD (profit_sharing_indicator NUMBER(1,0) NULL
       CONSTRAINT between_0_and_1 CHECK (
            profit_sharing_indicator BETWEEN 0 AND 1
            )
      )
;
```

Now that the database can store a true/false value for profit sharing for each employee, you need to add the profit-sharing column to the data block underlying your Employee form. Open your sample application in Form Builder, open the Data Blocks node, right-click on the EMPLOYEE_2 data block, and select Data Block Wizard from the context menu that appears. In the wizard, click the Table tab and then click the Refresh button. (The Form Builder program will prompt you to log into Oracle at this point if you haven't yet logged into the database.) After you see the PROFIT_SHARING_INDICATOR column appear in the Available Columns area, click once on the SALARY item in the Database Items area (to tell the wizard where it should add the new column), and then click the > button to move PROFIT_SHARING_INDICATOR into the Database Items area. Complete the change by clicking the Finish button.

Next, open your EMPLOYEE canvas in the Layout Editor. Right-click on the frame surrounding the Employee data block, and select Layout Wizard from the context menu that appears. In the Layout Wizard's Data Block tab, click on DEPARTMENT_ID in the Displayed Items area and then click the > button to move PROFIT_SHARING_INDICATOR from the Available Items area to the bottom of the Displayed Items area. While PROFIT_SHARING_INDICATOR is still selected, open the Item Type drop-down list and choose Check Box from its choices. Then click the Finish button. Your form should look very similar to the one shown in Figure 4-1.

Before you can run your modified form, you must set properties identifying the check box's on and off values. Click the check box to select it, open the Property Palette, set the Value When Checked property to **1**, and the Value When Unchecked property to **0**. In the property named Check Box Mapping of Other Values, change the property to Unchecked. Finally, change the Prompt property from Profit Sharing Indicator to simply **Profit Sharing**.

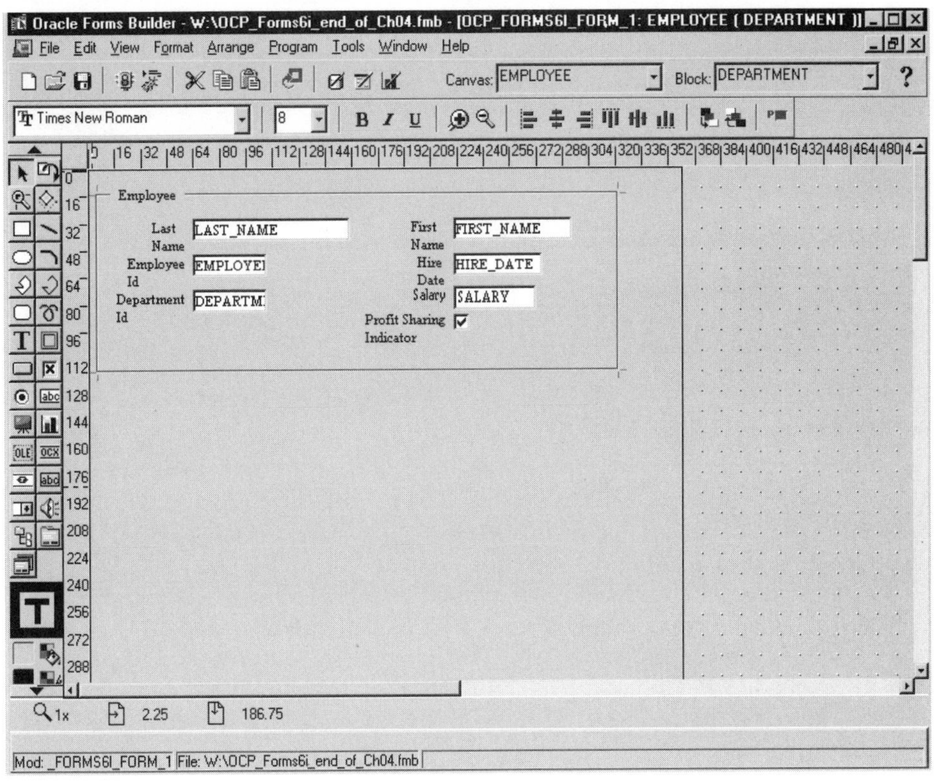

FIGURE 4-1. *Check box added to employee layout*

Your form is ready to run now, but none of the EMPLOYEE records currently have a true value for profit sharing, so it won't be immediately apparent if your check box is working. Using SQL*Plus, enter the following code to set the first record's profit sharing to true:

L 4-2

```
UPDATE employee
  SET profit_sharing_indicator = 1
  WHERE employee_id = 1001;

COMMIT;
```

Now run your form. In the Forms Runtime program, use the Next Block button, if necessary, to make the EMPLOYEE canvas display. Then, click the Execute Query button to retrieve records from the database. You will see that the Profit Sharing Indicator is checked for the first record—the one you set from SQL*Plus—but not for the other records.

Exercises

1. **What limitation does a check box place on values within a database column?**
2. **What check box property controls the text that displays on the form next to the check box?**

Creating a List Item

Lists are a common way to improve the usability of your form. In order to gain experience with creating list items, modify your EMPLOYEE canvas so it displays a drop-down list for Department. Start by opening the EMPLOYEE canvas in the Layout Editor. Select the **DEPARTMENT_ID** item and open its Property Palette. Change its Item Type property to List Item, and set its List Style property to Poplist. Locate the Elements In List property, click on the empty field to the right of it, and then click the More button that appears. Amazingly, you must manually type the elements of the list the user will see, and Forms Developer 6*i* offers no way to automatically read the contents of a table to initially create the list elements. There is also no automatic sorting of the list, so the list elements you type must be in the order in which you want them displayed. Type the following values for the list elements and their corresponding list item values:

List Element	List Item Value
Information Technology	3
Maintenance	4
Quality Assurance	5
Research and Development	2
Sales	1

When you are done, click the OK button to continue. Change the Prompt property to **Department**. Return to the Layout Editor, and drag the right side of the DEPARTMENT_ID item so it is long enough to display "Research and Development" along with the Drop-Down List button (you will need to expand the data block's frame to the right to make the field large enough). Save your form and then run it.

When the form compiles, the Form Compiler displays the following error message, which may be quickly covered up by the Forms Runtime program:

L 4-3

```
FRM-30188: No initial value given, and other values are not allowed
(item EMPLOYEE_2.DEPARTMENT_ID).

List DEPARTMENT_ID

Block: EMPLOYEE_2
```

Forms Developer 6*i* prefers that list boxes have a default value. Since that is not appropriate for a Department field, none was specified in the item's Property Palette. The form runs perfectly, however.

In the Forms Runtime program, navigate to the Employee form and then click the Execute Query button to populate it. You will see that the Department field now displays department names, instead of their numbers. When you are done, exit the Forms Runtime program and dismiss the Compilation Errors dialog box presented by the Form Compiler. To keep the Compilation Errors dialog box from appearing dozens of times as you work with this form module, open the Property Palette for the DEPARTMENT_ID item in your EMPLOYEE_2 data block and change the item's Initial Value property to **1**.

Exercise

1. **What are the differences between the various types of lists available in Form Builder?**

Creating a Radio Group

Radio buttons are a popular way to depict data when an item has two or more possible values, and only one of the values can be true at a given time. Neither the DEPARTMENT nor EMPLOYEE tables contain columns that satisfy this criterion, but another table you created does: EMPLOYEE_SKILL. This table is designed to link the EMPLOYEE and SKILL tables, and it includes a column named SKILL_LEVEL that rates an employee's ability in a given skill, using a ranking of 1, 2, 3, 4, or 5. This column is a good candidate for a group of radio buttons. To use the column, you must first create a data block for the EMPLOYEE_SKILL table and add that data block to the EMPLOYEE canvas. Then modify the EMPLOYEE_SKILL data block so the SKILL_LEVEL item displays as a radio group.

Start by right-clicking on the Data Blocks node in the Object Navigator. From the context menu that appears, select Data Block Wizard. Identify that the data block is to be based on a Table or View, and specify the EMPLOYEE_SKILL table as the source. Move all available columns into the Database Items area.

Click the Next button to proceed to the Master/Detail dialog page, and then click the Create Relationship button. In the list of data blocks that appears, select EMPLOYEE_2 as the master data block. Ensure that both the Detail Item and the Master Item are set to EMPLOYEE_ID. Click the Next button, select *Just create the data block*, and click the Finish button.

In the Object Navigator, move to the new EMPLOYEE_SKILL data block and open the Items node beneath it. Select the SKILL_LEVEL item and open its Property Palette. Change the Item Type property to Radio Group. Back in the Object Navigator, click the + to the left of the SKILL_LEVEL item to open the subnodes beneath it. Note that while there is an entry for Radio Buttons, there are no buttons beneath it. The Data Block Wizard does not generate radio buttons automatically—in order to do so, it would have to read the database and determine the unique values for the assigned column, and while this would be a handy feature, it doesn't exist, so you will add radio buttons to the radio group manually.

There are two ways to add radio buttons to a radio group: in the Object Navigator, and in the Layout Editor. In order to give you experience with both approaches, the following exercise will have you create some radio buttons in the Object Navigator and others in the Layout Editor. Normally, you would choose one location or the other to perform this task.

Start by opening the Property Palette for the SKILL_LEVEL item and changing its Initial Value property to **1** (this avoids an error message similar to the one seen for the poplist on the DEPARTMENT_ID field). Back in the Object Navigator, click once on the Radio Buttons subnode beneath SKILL_LEVEL, and then click the Create button. A radio button will appear. Open its Property Palette and change its Name property to **SKILL_RADIO_1**. Change its Label property to **1** so the button has a "1" next to it when it is laid out, and change its Radio Button Value property to **1** so the button relates to a value of "1" in the SKILL_LEVEL data block column. Set the button's Width property to **36** so the button and its label have plenty of space. Then, return to the Object Navigator and click the SKILL_RADIO_1 radio button object. Copy it by pressing CTRL-C and then paste four copies of it by pressing CTRL-V four times. Change the properties of each copy so that the Name, Label, and Radio Button Value for each button increment by one. When you are done, your Object Navigator should show radio buttons like those depicted in Figure 4-2.

TIP
You can also use the Label property to place text next to a radio button. The prompt text goes to the left of the button; the label text goes to the right of it. Remember both of these for the exam!

You now have a data block for the EMPLOYEE_SKILL table, and a set of radio buttons to depict the values for the SKILL_LEVEL column in that table. The next step

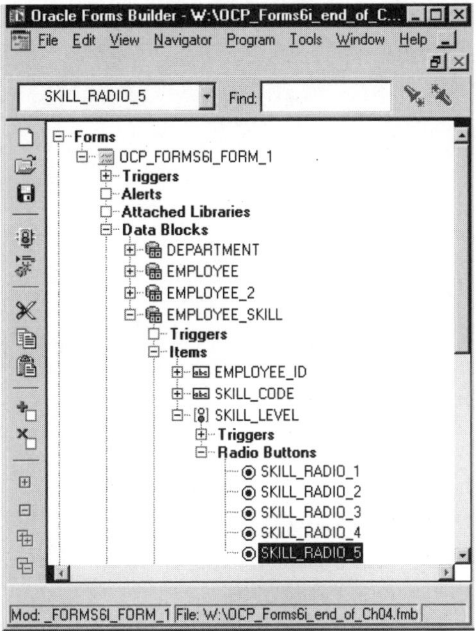

FIGURE 4-2. *Radio buttons in the Object Navigator*

is to lay the data block out on the EMPLOYEE canvas. To do this, right-click on the EMPLOYEE_SKILL data block and select Layout Wizard from the context menu that appears. In the Layout Wizard, select the EMPLOYEE canvas as the destination for your new data block. On the next Wizard dialog page move SKILL_CODE and SKILL_LEVEL into the Displayed Items area. Continuing forward through the Wizard dialog pages, accept the default sizes for each item, and then specify that the layout style for the frame be Tabular. In the next dialog page, enter a Frame Title of **Skills for this employee:** and specify that the frame display **5** records at a time. Click on the Finish button to complete the process. Your EMPLOYEE canvas should now look similar to Figure 4-3.

Now run your form. In the Forms Runtime program, navigate to the Employee form, and then click the Execute Query button to populate the form. Move forward through the employee records using the Next Record button and you will see that the SKILL_LEVEL radio buttons change to reflect each employee shown. When you are done viewing records, exit the Forms Runtime program and return to Form Builder.

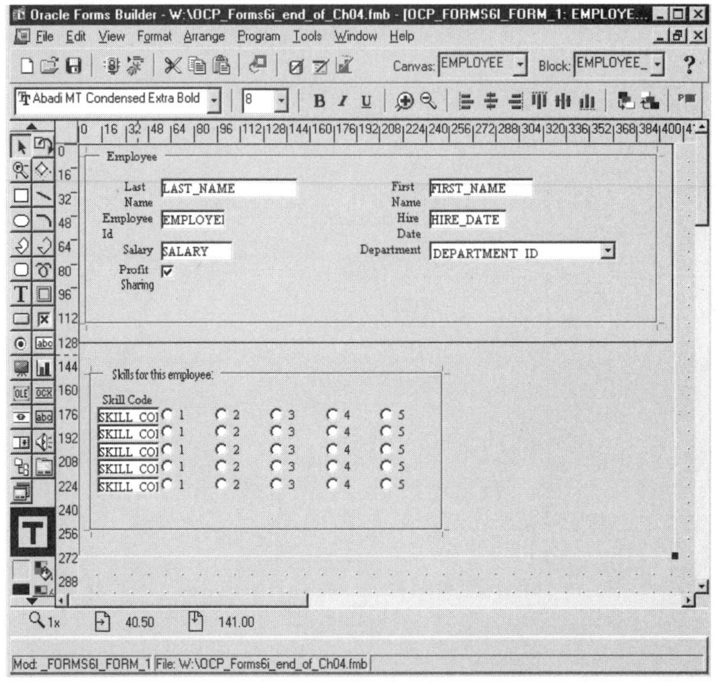

FIGURE 4-3. *EMPLOYEE canvas with radio button group*

To see what happens when you add a radio button using the Layout Editor, view your layout for the EMPLOYEE canvas, click the Radio Button button, shown here:

Then click anywhere within the EMPLOYEE_SKILL block. A modal window appears asking whether you want to place the new radio button in an existing radio group—and if so which one—or if you would rather create a new radio group for this button. This window is shown in Figure 4-4. Click the OK button to select the SKILL_LEVEL radio group. You will see that five closely positioned copies of the new radio button appear within the data block. There are five copies of the radio button because this data block's properties specify that it displays five records at a time. The spacing of the new radio button's instances does not match the record spacing already in place in the data block, however. If you were going to keep this radio button, you would

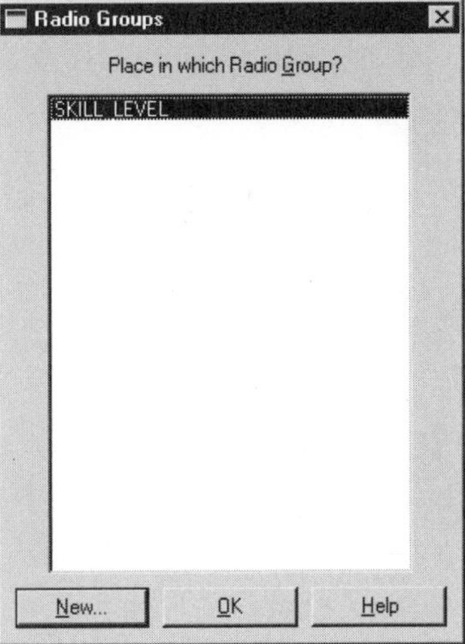

FIGURE 4-4. *Radio Groups selection window in Form Builder*

alter its properties to make it fit with the existing data block. Since this new radio button is not going to be used, however, press the DELETE key to delete it now.

Exercises

1. **You create a data block and specify that one of its items be represented as a radio group. How many radio buttons will be generated?**
2. **What does the Layout Editor do when you add a radio button to a block that contains a radio group?**

Creating Noninput Items

In this section, you will cover the following points about creating noninput items:

- Introduction to item types that do not allow input
- Creating a display item
- Creating an image item
- Creating a sound item

- Creating a button
- Creating a calculated field

In addition to items through which users can enter and change data, a form usually needs items that display read-only data or initiate actions. This section covers such *noninput* items. You will start by learning about the different types of noninput items. After that, you will experiment with creating noninput items of your own, including a display item, an image item, a sound item, a group of buttons, and a calculated field.

Introduction to Item Types that Do Not Allow Input

In contrast to input items, noninput items do not enable the user to enter or change data. Instead, they present nonchangeable data to the user and/or generate actions. Table 4-2 shows the noninput items available in Form Builder, along with a description for each item type.

Item Type	Description
Boilerplate Text	Any form text that was typed in manually rather than derived from the database by Form Builder.
Display Item	Form field that displays data but does not allow input. Useful for calculated data such as subtotals or totals, as well as read-only data such as a city based on ZIP code.
Image	Provides access to graphics files.
Sound	Provides access to audio files.
Push Button	Ubiquitous object for initiating actions; displays text or picture indicating what it does.
Icon	Button on a toolbar, best suited for frequently used operations. Displays text or picture indicating what it does.

TABLE 4-2. *Item Types that Do Not Allow Input*

Exercises

1. **What is the difference between input items and noninput items?**
2. **Which noninput items present nonchangeable data to the user? Which provide informative text? Which generate actions?**

Creating a Display Item

As its name suggests, a *display item* is a form object that shows data to the user but does not allow that data to be changed. The data can be calculated, or it can come directly from a database column.

Open your sample application, if it is not already open. In the Object Navigator, open your EMPLOYEE canvas in the Layout Editor, click on the Salary item, and in the Property Palette, change its Item Type property to Display Item. Now run the form. Once the form is open in the Forms Runtime program, populate it using the Execute Query button, and then move among the records using the Next Record and Previous Record buttons. The data in the display item changes with the current record, but it cannot be changed, or even selected.

When you are done, close the Forms Runtime program and return to Form Builder. Execute the File | Revert command to return the Employee form to its fully changeable state.

You can also create a read-only field by changing a text item's Insert Allowed, Update Allowed, and Keyboard Navigable properties to No, and—to make it obvious that the field is read only—changing its Background Color property to gray. However, even an unchangeable text item consumes more memory than a display item, so it is to your advantage to use display items whenever you want to display read-only data.

Exercises

1. **What is the difference between a text item and a display item?**
2. **What are the benefits of using a display item instead of a text item for read-only data?**

Creating an Image Item

Using Forms Developer 6*i* to load and store images is really quite easy. In order to experiment with this feature, create a table capable of holding image files. In SQL*Plus, enter the code that follows:

L 4-4

```
CREATE TABLE av_data (
     blob_id        NUMBER(10,0) NOT NULL,
```

```
     blob_type      VARCHAR2(10) NOT NULL,
     description    VARCHAR2(25) NOT NULL,
     blob_data      BLOB
     )
;

ALTER TABLE av_data
     ADD CONSTRAINT av_primary_key PRIMARY KEY (
          blob_id
          )
;
```

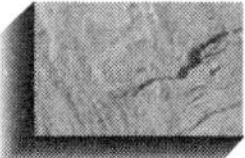

NOTE
If your Oracle database version is prior to version 8, replace the BLOB data type in the above CREATE TABLE command with LONG RAW.

Next, you need to create a new data block to forge a link between your new table and the sample application you have been working with. To do this, open the application, click on the Forms node (at the top of the Object Navigator), and then click the Create button. Navigate to the new module that is created and change its name to **IMAGE_MODULE**. Click the + to the left of the module's name in order to see the nodes it contains, and then click on its Data Blocks node, followed by the Create button. Elect to use the Data Block Wizard and specify that the block be based on a Table or View. Select the AV_DATA table as the source, and move all columns into the Database Items area. Click the Next button to proceed to the final Data Block Wizard page, select the *Just create the data block* option, and then click the Finish button. When you see your new data block appear in the Object Navigator, change its name to **AV_DATA_IMAGE**. Open the Property Palette for the data block and change its **WHERE** Clause property to **blob_type = 'IMAGE'**. (Because the AV_DATA table is going to store both image and sound files, this **WHERE** Clause property ensures that the AV_DATA_IMAGE data block only retrieves image records from the table.)

In order to ensure that all records entered through this data block are identified as image records you need to write some code. Return to the Object Navigator and click on the Triggers subnode beneath the AV_DATA_IMAGE data block. Click the Create button and select the PRE-INSERT trigger, which fires before a record is inserted. Type the following code into the PL/SQL Editor for the trigger:

L 4-5

```
av_data_image.blob_type := 'IMAGE';
```

Click the Compile button and look for the message "Successfully Compiled" in the bottom right corner of the PL/SQL Editor. (If you do not see that message, correct the syntax of the code and recompile it.) When the trigger code is successfully compiled, click the Close button to close the PL/SQL Editor. The code you just entered causes the value of 'IMAGE' to be placed into the BLOB_TYPE item of any new record you create using this data block.

Now it is time to create a form for the data block. Right-click on the AV_DATA_IMAGE data block and select Layout Wizard from the context menu that appears. Specify that you want to lay the data out on a New Canvas. In the next dialog page, move the BLOB_ID, DESCRIPTION, and BLOB_DATA items into the Displayed Items area. Click the Next button, accept the default sizes for each item, proceed to the next dialog page, and select Form as the layout style. Click the Next button, enter **Picture Test** as the Frame Title and then click the Finish button. You should see a form that looks like Figure 4-5.

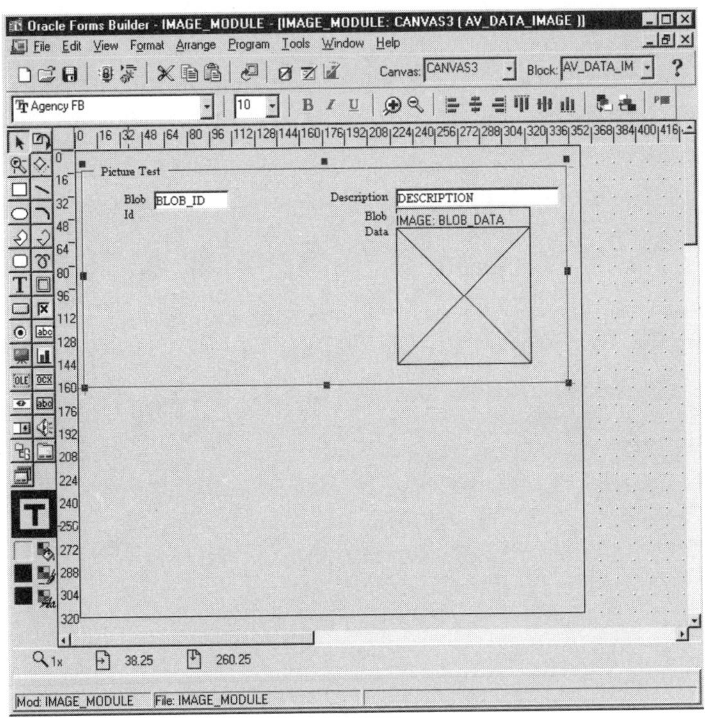

FIGURE 4-5. *Form Builder form with image item*

Click on the BLOB_DATA item and change its Sizing Style property to Adjust so that images show in their entirety on your form, regardless of their size. (At least, that is the theory; in reality, large images are still cropped.) Then, close the Layout Editor and return to the Object Navigator. Change the name of your new canvas to **AV_DATA_IMAGE**.

In order to make this form useful, you need to give it the ability to read image files from disk and load them into your database. To do this, open the AV_DATA_IMAGE canvas in the Layout Editor. Locate the Button Tool button in the Tool Palette (shown next) and click it.

Then click on an open area in your form, and a button will appear. Open the button's Property Palette and change its Name property to **LOAD_DISK_IMAGE**, its Label property to **Load Disk Image**, its Keyboard Navigable property to No, its Mouse Navigate property to No, and its Tooltip property to **Load image stored on disk**.

Now you need to add code to the button. Return to the Object Navigator and beneath your AV_DATA_IMAGE data block locate the new item named LOAD_DISK_IMAGE. Click on the + to the left of this item, and then click on the Triggers subnode. Click the Create button and select the WHEN-BUTTON-PRESSED trigger. In the PL/SQL Editor, enter the following code:

L 4-6

```
DECLARE
     v_dirname    VARCHAR2(255);
     v_filename   VARCHAR2(255);
BEGIN
     v_dirname := 'C:\';  --C: drive is assumed, change if appropriate

     v_filename := GET_FILE_NAME(
          v_dirname,
          NULL,
          'Bitmap files (*.bmp)|*.bmp|'   ||
          'JPEG files (*.jpg)|*.jpg|'
          )
     ;

     IF v_filename IS NOT NULL THEN
          READ_IMAGE_FILE(
               v_filename,
               'ANY',
```

```
                'av_data_image.blob_data'
                )
            ;
    END IF;
END;
```

Click the Compile button, and, when the trigger code is successfully compiled, click on the Close button. You are done! Save your work, and then run your form. When the Forms Runtime program opens, navigate to the AV_DATA_IMAGE canvas and click your Load Disk Image button. Navigate to any disk directory you know contains graphics files; your Windows directory is a safe bet, because it usually contains **.bmp** files used for wallpaper. Wherever you choose to search, select a graphics file and then click the OK button. Your image will appear inside the BLOB_DATA item, similar to the form shown in Figure 4-6. Enter values for the BLOB_ID and DESCRIPTION items, and then click the Save button to store the image and description into your AV_DATA table. If you would like to store more image records, click the Next Record button and repeat the process just described. When you are finished, exit the Forms Runtime program and return to Form Builder.

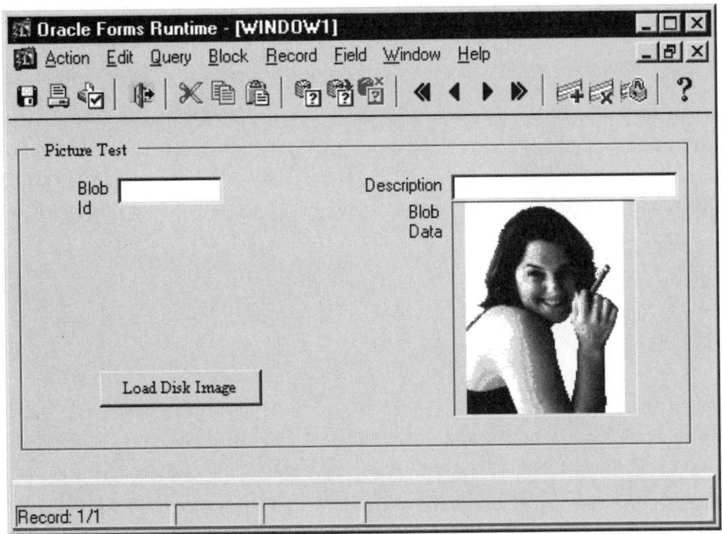

FIGURE 4-6. *Form Builder form with image item populated*

Exercises

1. **What are the major steps necessary to create an image item and load images into it?**
2. **What database column types are used to store image data?**

Creating a Sound Item

The process for adding a sound item is similar to the process for adding an image item. Like images, sounds are stored in Oracle in a binary "blob" column: either a LONG RAW data type for Oracle versions 7 and earlier, or a BLOB data type for Oracle versions 8 and later. You already have a database table suitable for storing sounds, so all you need to do is create a new data block to access that table, and then a form for reading sound files from disk and storing them in the table.

Starting in the Object Navigator, click on the Forms node, and then click the Create button. Navigate to the new module that is created, and change its name to **SOUND_MODULE**. Back in the Object Navigator, click on the new module's Data Blocks node, followed by the Create button. Elect to use the Data Block Wizard, and specify that the block be based on a Table or View. Select the AV_DATA table as the source, and move all columns into the Database Items area. Click the Next button to proceed to the final Data Block Wizard page, select the *Just create the data block* option, and then click the Finish button. When you see your new data block appear in the Object Navigator, change its name to **AV_DATA_SOUND**. Open the Property Palette for the data block and change its **WHERE** Clause property to **blob_type = 'SOUND'**. In order to ensure that all records entered through this data block are identified as sound records, return to the Object Navigator and click on the Triggers subnode beneath your AV_DATA_SOUND data block. Click the Create button and select the PRE-INSERT trigger. Type the following code into the PL/SQL Editor for the trigger:

L 4-7

```
av_data_sound.blob_type := 'SOUND';
```

Click the Compile button. When the trigger code is successfully compiled, click the Close button to close the PL/SQL Editor. To create the form, right-click on the AV_DATA_SOUND data block and select Layout Wizard from the context menu that appears. Specify that you want to lay the data out on a New Canvas. Move the BLOB_ID, DESCRIPTION, and BLOB_DATA items into the Displayed Items area, and while in that Layout Wizard page, change the Item Type for BLOB_DATA to Sound. Accept the default sizes for each item, and select Form as the layout style. Enter **Sound Test** as the Frame Title and then click the Finish button. You should see a form that looks like Figure 4-7.

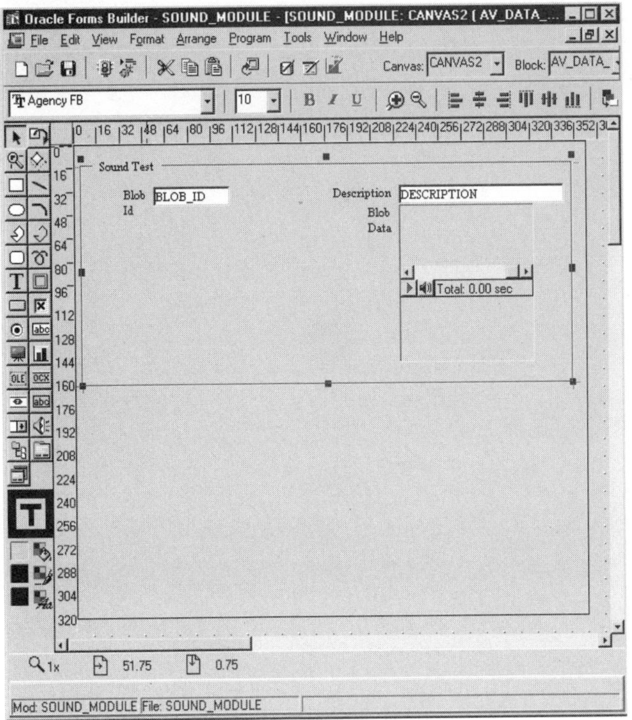

FIGURE 4-7. *Form Builder form with sound item*

Click on the BLOB_DATA item and open its Property Palette. Change its Distance Between Records property to **0** and its Number Of Items Displayed property to **1**. Change its Width property to **140** and its Height property to **24**. Set Yes values for the properties Show Record Button, Show Rewind Button, and Show Fast Forward Button. If the changes to the BLOB_DATA item size have caused it to extend outside the data block frame, use your mouse to reposition the item to a more suitable location. Then, close the Layout Editor and return to the Object Navigator. Change the name of your new canvas to **AV_DATA_SOUND**.

In order to give this form the ability to read sound files from disk and load them into your database, open the AV_DATA_SOUND canvas once again in the Layout Editor. Click the Button Tool button in the Tool Palette and then click on an open area in your form. Open the newly created button's Property Palette and change its Name property to **LOAD_DISK_SOUND**, its Label property to **Load Disk Sound**, its Keyboard Navigable property to No, its Mouse Navigate property to No, and its Tooltip property to **Load sound stored on disk**.

Now you need to add code to the button. Return to the Object Navigator and locate the new item named LOAD_DISK_SOUND. Click the + to the left of the item to see the subnodes beneath it, and then click on the Triggers subnode. Click on the Create button and select the WHEN-BUTTON-PRESSED trigger. In the PL/SQL Editor, enter the following code:

L 4-8

```
DECLARE
     v_dirname    VARCHAR2(255);
     v_filename   VARCHAR2(255);
BEGIN
     v_dirname := 'C:\'; -- C: drive is assumed, change if appropriate

     v_filename := GET_FILE_NAME(
          v_dirname,
          NULL,
          'Wave files (*.wav)|*.wav|'
          )
     ;

     IF v_filename IS NOT NULL THEN
          READ_SOUND_FILE(
               v_filename,
               'ANY',
               'av_data_sound.blob_data'
               )
          ;
     END IF;
END;
```

Click the Compile button, and when the trigger code is successfully compiled, close the PL/SQL Editor. Save your work, and then run your form. When the Forms Runtime program opens, navigate to the AV_DATA_SOUND canvas, click the Insert Record button, and then click the Load Disk Sound button. Navigate to any directory you know contains sound files, such as your Windows **\media** subdirectory, which usually contains **.wav** files. Wherever you choose to search, select a sound file and then click the OK button. Your sound will appear inside the BLOB_DATA item. Enter values for the BLOB_ID and DESCRIPTION items, such as the ones shown in Figure 4-8, and then click the Save button to store the sound and description into your AV_DATA table. (Remember that your BLOB_ID cannot duplicate a BLOB_ID for an image file, since a single table is storing both types of data. In a production system, you would probably create an Oracle sequence to generate the BLOB_ID numbers, but that is not germane to this example.) If you would like to store more sounds, click the Insert Record button and repeat the

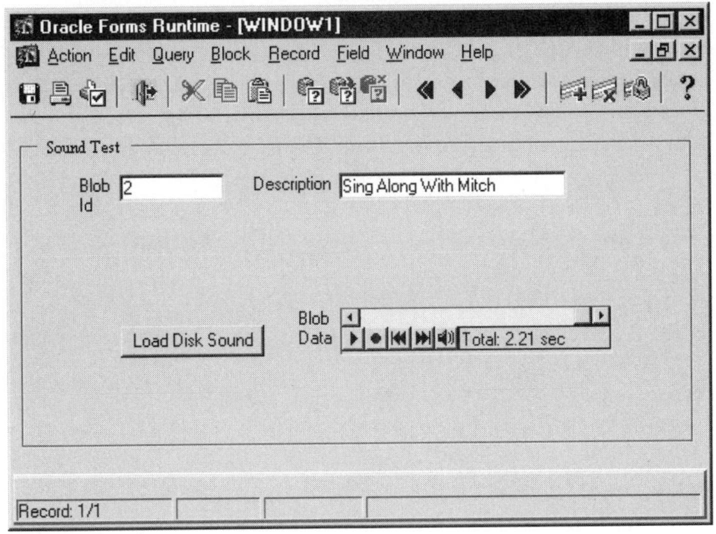

FIGURE 4-8. *Form Builder form with sound item populated*

process just described. Since the sound item's Show Record Button property was set to Yes, you can also record new sounds from a microphone, your computer's CD-ROM drive (playing audio CDs), or any other audio input source your computer accommodates. When you are finished, exit the Forms Runtime program and return to Form Builder.

Exercises

1. **What properties must you change on a sound item to enable it to record sound?**
2. **What properties must you change on a sound item to shuttle back and forth within a recording?**

Creating a Button

Since you have already learned the basics of creating individual buttons in Form Builder, it is time to extend that knowledge by creating a group of buttons. You will add buttons to your AV_DATA_SOUND canvas to navigate between records, as well as to create a new record, delete an existing record, save your work, and exit the application.

Start by opening the AV_DATA_SOUND canvas in the Layout Editor. Create six buttons in close proximity to each other. Select all six buttons, and in the property sheet set their Iconic property to No. Set their Background Color property to gray. Change their Keyboard Navigable and Mouse Navigate properties to No. Next set their Width properties to **36** and their Height properties to **18**. To set button-specific properties, click individual buttons and change their properties to match those shown here:

Button Number	Name	Label	Tooltip
1	PREV_REC	Previous	Move to previous record
2	NEXT_REC	Next	Move to next record
3	SAVE	Save	Save work
4	NEW_REC	Add	Add new record
5	DEL_REC	Delete	Delete current record
6	EXIT	Exit	Exit this application

After you have set the button-specific properties, select all of the buttons and use the Arrange | Align Objects menu command to line them up the way you wish. While they are all still selected, execute the Arrange | Group menu command to group the buttons. You will see that when this is done, the selection marks around the buttons change to indicate that a single group is selected, instead of six individual objects. In fact, it is impossible to select an individual object in the Layout Editor once that object has been made part of a group. To see this for yourself, click on any other object on the canvas, and then click any of the six buttons you just created. You will see that clicking a single button now results in the entire group of buttons being selected.

Close the Layout Editor now and return to the Object Navigator. Beneath the AV_DATA_SOUND data block, open the Items node and you will see items representing each of the six buttons you just created, in addition to the original items for database columns. Click the + to the left of the PREV_REC item, and then click on the Triggers subnode beneath it. Click the Create button and select the WHEN-BUTTON-PRESSED trigger. Once the PL/SQL Editor opens, type **previous_record;** as the trigger code. Compile the trigger and close it. Perform the same task with the other five buttons, using the following table as your guide:

Button Name	WHEN-BUTTON-PRESSED Trigger Code to Add
PREV_REC	previous_record;
NEXT_REC	next_record;

SAVE	commit work;
NEW_REC	create_record;
DEL_REC	delete_record;
EXIT	exit_form(ask_commit, no_rollback);

Save your form, and then run it to test the buttons you have created. When you are done, close the Forms Runtime program and return to Form Builder.

Exercises

1. **When you create a new button, what function is it automatically programmed to perform?**
2. **If you have combined numerous objects into a group, and you click on a single object within that group, what is selected?**

Creating a Calculated Field

Calculated fields are an excellent way to keep the user updated on important status information without giving them the opportunity to change that information directly. Form Builder gives you functions to easily select a data block item and perform sum, average, count, min, max, variance, and standard deviation calculations on it. You can also specify your own formulas to fulfill more complicated mathematical requirements.

To see how to create a calculated field, open your AV_DATA_SOUND canvas in the Layout Editor. Click the Display Item button in the Tool Palette. Then click on the canvas at the location where you would like to display the number of records in the underlying data table. Open the new display item's Property Palette and change its Name property to **TOTAL_RECORDS**. Change its Data Type property to Number, and its Calculation Mode property to Summary. Change its Summary Function property to Count, its Summarized Block property to **AV_DATA_SOUND**, and its Summarized Item property to **BLOB_ID**. Change its Width property to **25**. Then move back to the Tool Palette and click the Text button, which is shown here:

Click on your canvas just to the right of the display item you just created. Type **Sound records in database** inside the text box, and line it up with the display item so they can be read as a single phrase. Close the Layout Editor and return to the Object Navigator. Under the Data Blocks node, click on the AV_DATA_SOUND data block and change its Precompute Summaries property to Yes so the calculated field shows the correct number as soon as you retrieve records. Then save the form, run it, retrieve records using the Forms Runtime program's Execute Query button, and watch your new TOTAL_RECORDS item display the calculated total as you add and delete sound records. When you are done, exit from the Forms Runtime program and return to Form Builder.

Exercises

1. **What mathematical functions are automatically available for calculated fields in the Layout Editor?**
2. **What property must be changed in a canvas's underlying data block in order for a calculated field to work?**

Creating Windows and Content Canvases

In this section, you will cover the following points about creating windows and content canvases:

- Introduction to windows and content canvases
- Window and content canvases properties
- Displaying a form module in multiple windows

Windows and content canvases are relatively simple objects, but not knowing how to work with them can cost you time, productivity, and quality in the final application. In this section, you will learn about key properties of windows and content canvases. You will then put your knowledge to use by creating a multiple-window application.

Introduction to Windows and Content Canvases

You may recall from Chapter 2 that whenever you create a new form module, Form Builder generates a multiple document interface (MDI) window for the module (assuming you are working in a Windows environment). The MDI window serves as a parent window containing all the other document windows, and it usually holds the application's main menu and toolbar. All other document windows—in other words, the ones you create—must fit within the confines of the MDI window. A window is the outermost boundary for a form—an empty frame to hold objects. All of the visual objects in a Form Builder application are contained within windows.

There are two types of windows: *document* and *dialog*. A document window is used for standard data entry forms. When users are in a document window, they can generally enter and query data, move to other windows within the application, and use the application's menu and toolbars. In contrast, a dialog window usually serves as a modal dialog box, requiring users to acknowledge the dialog box in one way or another before proceeding to any other action.

Canvases are displayed within windows, and a single window can be used by one or more canvases. If a window contains more than one canvas, you can use the Next Block and Previous Block buttons to move from one canvas to another. There are four types of canvases: content, stacked, tab, and toolbar. All four types can coexist within a single window. The default canvas type, and the most common, is the content canvas. The content canvas completely occupies the content pane of its window, and every window must have at least one content canvas. All of the canvases you created in this unit so far have been content canvases.

Exercises

1. **What are the four types of canvases?**
2. **Is it possible to have a window without a canvas? A canvas without a window?**
3. **Which is the outermost object, a window or a canvas?**

Window and Content Canvases Properties

In order to thoroughly understand how to use windows and content canvases, you must be well versed in their properties. This section presents the most important properties for you to know.

Window Properties

Table 4-3 shows key properties for use with windows.

Content Canvas Properties

Table 4-4 shows key properties for use with content canvases.

Exercises

1. **Which window property controls what title appears in the window's title bar?**
2. **Which canvas property controls what title appears in the window's title bar?**
3. **What canvas property controls which window the canvas displays in?**

Property Node	Property Name	Function
General	Name	Name of the window as it appears in the Object Navigator.
General	Subclass Information	Allows you to subclass this window's properties under another window's in order to simplify changing window properties globally.
Functional	Title	Allows you to specify text to display in the window's title bar at run time. If NULL, the window's name appears in the title bar by default.
Functional	Primary Canvas	Name of canvas that will be this window's primary content view.
Functional	Window Style	Selection between document and dialog window styles.
Functional	Hide on Exit	Applicable only to nonmodal windows, and specifies whether the window becomes hidden if the user navigates to another window.
Functional	Close Allowed	Specifies whether user can close the window.
Functional	Move Allowed	Specifies whether user can move the window.
Functional	Resize Allowed	Specifies whether user can resize the window.
Functional	Maximize Allowed	Specifies whether user can maximize the window.
Functional	Minimize Allowed	Specifies whether user can minimize the window.
Functional	Minimized Title	Specifies the title that appears with a window's icon if it is minimized.

TABLE 4-3. *Windows Properties*

Property Node	Property Name	Function
Physical	X Position	Horizontal location of window's top-left corner.
Physical	Y Position	Vertical location of window's top-left corner.
Physical	Width	Width of window.
Physical	Height	Height of window.

TABLE 4-3. *Windows Properties* (continued)

Property Node	Property Name	Function
General	Name	Name of the canvas as it appears in the Object Navigator.
General	Canvas Type	Select between content, stacked, tab, or vertical or horizontal toolbar.
General	Subclass Information	Allows you to subclass this canvas under another in order to simplify changing global properties.
Functional	Raise on Entry	If the user navigates to an item that is covered by another canvas, should this canvas be raised to make the item visible?
Physical	Window	If the form module has more than one window, this property specifies which window should be used to display this canvas.
Physical	Width	Width of canvas.
Physical	Height	Height of canvas.

TABLE 4-4. *Content Canvas Properties*

Displaying a Form Module in Multiple Windows

To practice controlling the relationship between windows and content canvases, you will create a second window in your sample application. You will then assign the DEPARTMENT canvas to one window, and the EMPLOYEE canvas to the other.

Open your original sample form module in Form Builder and navigate to the Windows node. Click on it and then click the Create button. Once the new window object appears, change its Name property to **DEPARTMENT_WINDOW**. Then, select your original window in the Object Navigator and change its Name property to **EMPLOYEE_WINDOW**. Move to the Canvases node in the Object Navigator, and select the DEPARTMENT canvas. Change its Window property to DEPARTMENT_WINDOW. Then, select the EMPLOYEE canvas and ensure that its Window property is set to EMPLOYEE_WINDOW. Run your application. Once it opens in the Forms Runtime program, click the Next Block button until the second window opens. It may open directly on top of the first window if both windows have default settings for size and location. You can drag the windows to different locations on the screen, resize them, and position them so both windows are open at once. Thus, you can cause two or more canvases to appear in your application simultaneously simply by assigning each canvas to its own window. You can also use the window size and position properties to ensure that the windows do not overlap, if you wish.

Exercises

1. **What must you do in Form Builder to enable two or more canvases to display simultaneously at run time?**
2. **What canvas property allows you to specify the window in which a canvas will be viewed?**

Working with Other Canvases

In this section, you will cover the following points about working with other canvases:

- Introduction to canvas types
- Creating an overlay effect using stacked canvases
- Creating a toolbar
- Creating a tabbed interface

You have created numerous canvases in your sample application, but they have all been the same type: content. Now it is time to learn about the other canvas types Forms Developer 6*i* offers for forms.

Introduction to Canvas Types

In addition to the content canvas type, Form Builder enables you to create stacked, tab, and toolbar canvases. Each of these types is ideal for fulfilling certain requirements. In this section, you will practice creating all three types.

Stacked Canvas

As its name implies, a stacked canvas lies on top of, or "stacks" onto, a content canvas. In doing so, it hides whatever is beneath it; the user can see what is part of a stacked canvas, but not what it covers. Because of this, stacked canvases are useful for controlling the visibility of entire groups of objects. You can use a stacked canvas to display information that only needs to be viewed in certain situations—information such as sensitive data, highly detailed data, or help text. A stacked canvas is also handy if you want to make a portion of the screen static, displaying a predictable group of data, while the user moves among other content canvases in the rest of the screen. Finally, because a stacked canvas can have its own set of scroll bars separate from those on the underlying content canvas, you can use a stacked canvas to show data in a tabular format that the user can scroll around in, while keeping important data (like record IDs) visible in a fixed location on the underlying content canvas.

Tab Canvas

Familiar to most computer users, the tab canvas is a useful tool when you need to display a lot of information about a single subject but want to break the information into logical groups for reasons of simplicity or limited screen space. The tabs on a tab canvas essentially represent a group of stacked canvases, with each canvas page obscuring the rest when its tab is selected by the user.

Toolbar Canvas

Unlike the stacked or tab canvases, the toolbar canvas is not designed to display data from a data source. Instead, it contains the components that make toolbars for individual windows. You can make a toolbar either horizontal or vertical, and you can even have multiple toolbars in a single window.

Exercises

1. **What type of canvas would most help you create an application that doesn't need a menu (assuming that the application already has a content canvas)?**
2. **How would you describe the difference between a tab canvas and a stacked canvas?**

Creating an Overlay Effect Using Stacked Canvases

To see how stacked canvases work, modify your EMPLOYEE canvas so that it only shows the employee work skills when a button is activated. Start by opening your sample application. Click on the application's form module node—the one that displays the module's name—and open the Property Palette. Change the First Navigation Data Block property to **EMPLOYEE_2** so your EMPLOYEE canvas will show immediately each time the module is run. Next, move to the Object Navigator's Canvases node and double-click on the EMPLOYEE canvas to open it in the Layout Editor. Click the Button tool button, and then click anywhere on your canvas. Open the new button's Property Palette, and change the Number Of Items Displayed property to **1**. Then move the button to the location shown in Figure 4-9. This button ends up being covered by the stacked canvas, and will therefore become visible to the user only when the stacked canvas is hidden. The button's job will be to make the stacked canvas visible again, thereby covering the button and the Employee Skills area at the same time.

Returning to the button's Property Palette, change its Name property to **HIDE_SKILLS**. Change its Label property to **Hide Skills**. Set its Keyboard Navigable property to No and its Mouse Navigate property to No. Then, right-click the button and select PL/SQL Editor from the context menu that appears. Select the WHEN-BUTTON-PRESSED trigger and enter the following code in the PL/SQL Editor:

L 4-9

```
GO_BLOCK('employee_2');
SHOW_VIEW('employee_skill_cover');
```

This command names a canvas that does not yet exist: EMPLOYEE_SKILL_COVER. You will create that canvas after setting the properties of this button, which will be hidden beneath it. To continue, compile your code and then close the PL/SQL Editor.

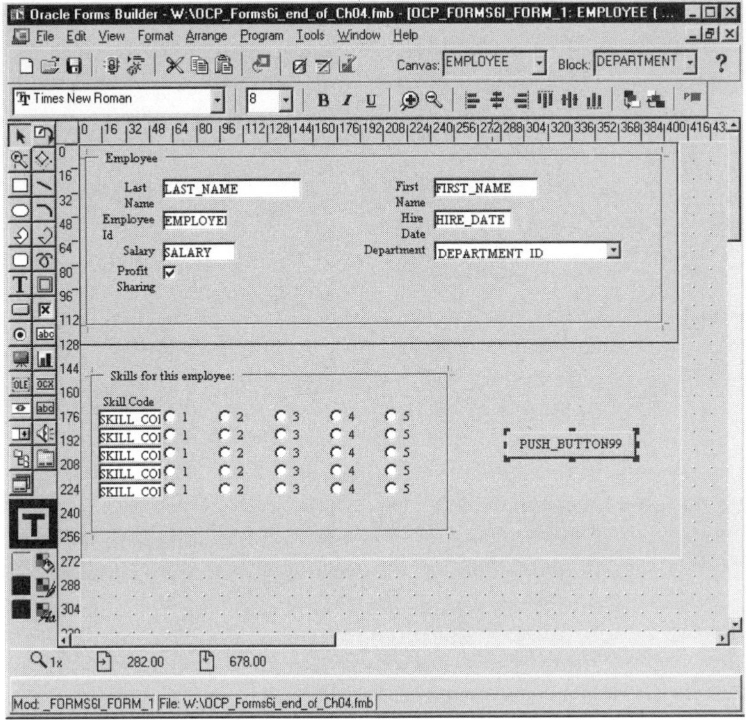

FIGURE 4-9. *Location of button to redisplay stacked canvas*

Now it is time to create the stacked canvas that will cover the employee skills area. Locate the Stacked Canvas button in the Tool Palette. The Stacked Canvas button looks like this:

Position your mouse over the top left corner of the EMPLOYEE_SKILL frame in the bottom half of the canvas, hold down the mouse button, drag the mouse to the bottom right corner of the EMPLOYEE_SKILL frame, and let the mouse button go. The EMPLOYEE_SKILL frame will disappear from view, because it is covered by the stacked canvas. While the stacked canvas is still selected, open its Property Palette and change its Name property to **EMPLOYEE_SKILL_COVER**. Change the stacked canvas's Bevel property to None, and change its Background Color to gray.

All that is left to do now is give the user the ability to make the skill information visible, which requires hiding the stacked canvas. To do this, click the Button tool button, and then click on the stacked canvas in approximately the same location where you placed the first button. Change the second button's Name property to **SHOW_SKILLS**. Change its Label property to **Show Skills**. Set its Keyboard Navigable property to No, its Mouse Navigate property to No, and its Number Of Items Displayed property to **1**. Then, right-click the new button and select PL/SQL Editor from the context menu that appears. Select the WHEN-BUTTON-PRESSED trigger and enter the following code in the PL/SQL Editor window:

L 4-10

```
HIDE_VIEW('employee_skill_cover');
```

Compile the code and then close the PL/SQL Editor. Save your form module and then run it. In the Forms Runtime program, click on the Next Block button until the EMPLOYEE_WINDOW window appears. Then populate the Employee form in the Forms Runtime program by clicking on the Execute Query button. Then, click your Hide Skills button. The skills for each employee will disappear, and they will stay invisible until you click the Show Skills button. When you are finished experimenting with the form, close it and return to Form Builder.

Exercises

1. **For what types of uses are stacked canvases best suited?**
2. **When you add a stacked canvas to a layout, what is the default visibility status of items beneath the stacked canvas?**

Creating a Toolbar

You can create a toolbar containing exactly the functions your application's users need. To see how to do this, open your original sample form module, if it is not already open. In the Object Navigator, click on the module's Data Blocks node and then the Create button. From the dialog box that appears, select Build A New Data Block Manually, and click the OK button. Change the new data block's Name property to **TOOLBAR_ITEMS** and set its Database Data Block property to No.

Back in the Object Navigator, click on the Canvases node and then the Create button. Set the new canvas's Name property to **TOOLBAR_HORIZONTAL**, and set its Canvas Type property to Horizontal Toolbar. In the Object Navigator, double-click the new canvas's icon to open it in the Layout Editor. Create four buttons, and set their properties to those shown in Table 4-5.

Property	Button 1	Button 2	Button 3	Button 4
Name	SAVE	DEPT	EMP	EXIT
Label	Save	Department form	Employee form	Exit
Keyboard Navigable	No	No	No	No
X Position	0	36	112	188
Y Position	3	3	3	3
Width	30	70	70	30
Height	18	18	18	18
Tooltip	Save work	Open Department form	Open Employee form	Exit this application

TABLE 4-5. *Properties for Sample Toolbar Buttons*

Click on the background canvas that all the buttons are located on. Change the canvas's Height property to **24**. Then, use the PL/SQL Editor to place the code shown in Table 4-6 into WHEN-BUTTON-PRESSED triggers behind each button.

Close the Layout Editor. At the top of the Object Navigator, click on the sample module's name, and then change its Form Horizontal Toolbar Canvas property to **TOOLBAR_HORIZONTAL**. Then, save your work and run the form to see the toolbar in action. When you are done, close the Forms Runtime program and return to Form Builder.

Exercise

1. **What type of block stores the contents of a custom toolbar?**

Creating a Tabbed Interface

A tabbed interface is an excellent way to squeeze large amounts of related information into a limited display space. It can also be useful for separating information into logical groups for purposes of clarity. To see how to produce one, create a new form module and name it **EMPLOYEE_TAB**. Using the Data Block Wizard, create new data blocks for the EMPLOYEE and EMPLOYEE_SKILL tables. Establish an appropriate relationship between the two tables. Then select the

Button	WHEN-BUTTON-PRESSED Trigger Code
SAVE	commit work;
DEPT	go_block('DEPARTMENT');
EMP	go_block('EMPLOYEE_2');
EXIT	exit_form(ask_commit, no_rollback);

TABLE 4-6. *Trigger Code for Sample Toolbar Buttons*

EMPLOYEE_SKILL data block and change its Number Of Records Displayed property to **5** so the user will be able to see up to five skills for each employee.

Form Builder doesn't like it when a single data block's items are split between a main canvas and a tab page residing on the same canvas; the program responds by hiding the main canvas items at run time. To avoid this, create a second data block for the EMPLOYEE table. In the Data Block Wizard page for relationships, deselect the Auto-Join Data Blocks option, and then click the Create Relationship button. When the Relation Type dialog appears, select the option labeled Based On A Join Condition and click the OK button. Select the EMPLOYEE data block next, and then specify EMPLOYEE_ID for both the Detail Item and the Master Item. This causes Form Builder to keep the two employee data blocks synchronized on any form that uses them both, such as the form you are about to create. Keep the new data block's default name of EMPLOYEE1.

Right-click on the EMPLOYEE data block and start the Layout Wizard. Create a new canvas containing the LAST_NAME and FIRST_NAME items from the EMPLOYEE data block. Select a form layout style, and enter a frame title of **Employee Data Sheet**. Once you are in the Layout Editor, click on the background to select the canvas, and change the canvas's Name property to **EMPLOYEE**. Then click the Tab Canvas button, shown next:

Move your mouse to a location just below the Employee Data Sheet's bottom left corner, hold down the left mouse button, and drag the mouse down and to the right so it creates a rectangle approximately the same width as the Employee Data Sheet area and twice as deep. Your screen should look similar to Figure 4-10 at this point. Change the tab canvas's Name property to **EMPLOYEE_TAB**, and change its Background Color property to gray.

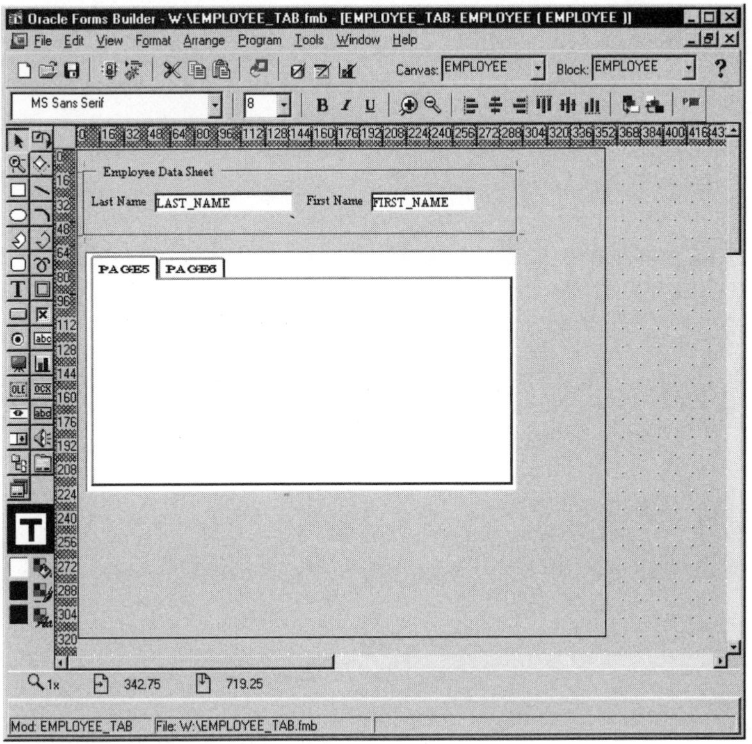

FIGURE 4-10. *Empty tab canvas*

Return to the Object Navigator. Locate the EMPLOYEE_TAB canvas and click the + to the left of its name in order to see its objects. Click the + to the left of the Tab Pages node, and then select the first tab page beneath it. Change the first tab page's Name property to **GENERAL_INFO**, and change its Label property to **General Info**. Change the second tab page's Name property to **SKILLS**, and change its Label property to **Skills**. Then, locate the EMPLOYEE1 data block (the "extra" employee data block) in the Object Navigator, and select its EMPLOYEE_ID, HIRE_DATE, DEPARTMENT_ID, SALARY, and PROFIT_SHARING_INDICATOR items. Set the Canvas property for all five items to EMPLOYEE_TAB, and the Tab Page property to GENERAL_INFO. Next, move to the EMPLOYEE_SKILL data block and select its SKILL_CODE and SKILL_LEVEL items. Set the Canvas property for both items to EMPLOYEE_TAB, and set the Tab Page property to SKILLS. Return to the Layout Editor, and you will see that the items you selected now appear on the tabbed pages. Arrange the items into an effective layout—one possible layout is shown in

Figure 4-11. When you are done, return to the Object Navigator. In the Windows node, select the WINDOW1 window and change its Primary Canvas property to EMPLOYEE.

Now run your form, populate it using the Execute Query button, and move between the two tab pages you created to see the results of your efforts.

Exercise

1. **What uses are tabbed interfaces well suited for?**

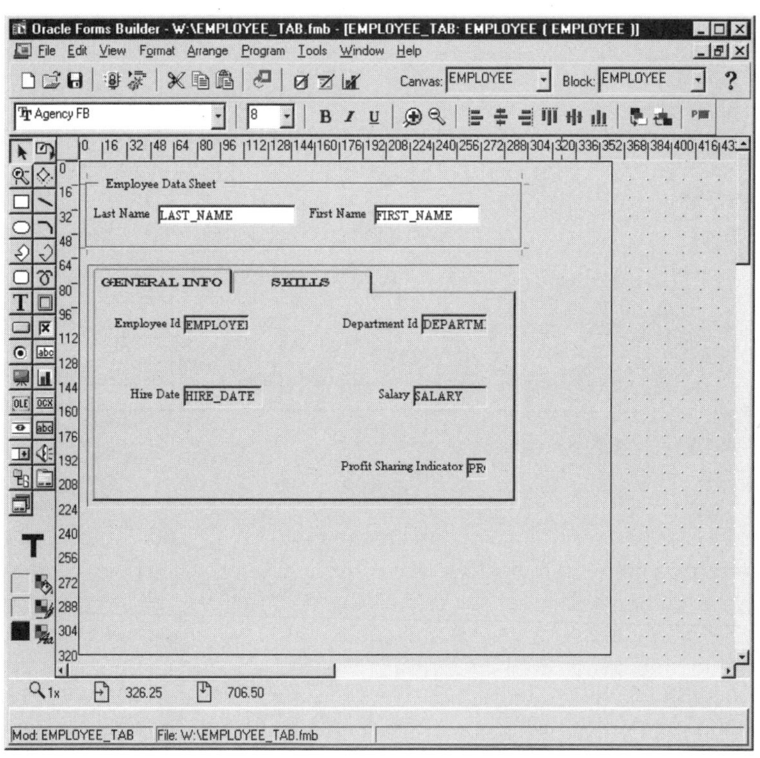

FIGURE 4-11. *Employee information on a tabbed canvas*

Chapter Summary

In this chapter, you have covered a substantial amount of information on forms design. Topics included creating additional input items, as well as creating noninput items. You also learned to create windows and several kinds of canvases, including content canvases, toolbar canvases, stacked canvases, and tab canvases.

The first area you covered was creating additional input items. During the introduction you learned that an input item is a form object that enables the user to enter and change data. The input-item category includes text items, check boxes, drop-down lists, radio button groups, poplists, T-lists, combo boxes, and Lists Of Values (LOVs). A text item is most commonly used for entering and changing data, and it is best suited to data that is not repetitive and therefore does not belong in a list. A check box can be used singly or in groups, with each check box representing a data item that can have only one of two values. A radio button group is comprised of two or more radio buttons, and it represents data comprised of a limited number of mutually exclusive choices. A poplist provides a familiar drop-down list that allows users to select one value. It can autofill an entry by matching the user's typing with a list item as the user types, and it does not accept nonlist entries. A T-List is designed for applications where the user selects one row from a list containing 15 to 30 choices. By default, a T-list shows at least five rows from the list, so it is best suited for layouts that have plenty of screen space available. A combo box provides a drop-down list that allows the user to select one value. It does not autofill an entry as the user types, and it can accept nonlist entries as long as the developer has written appropriate code. A List of Values (LOV) can display an unlimited number of choices, and it can display multiple columns of information for each choice.

Next, you learned the steps necessary to create a check box. After adding a column to a database table to hold the yes/no data for which a check box is suited, you added the check box and set the properties necessary to make it work. You established the check box's on and off values by setting the Value When Checked property and the Value When Unchecked property. The property named Check Box Mapping Of Other Values tells the check box what to display if it encounters other values in the data source. Next, you learned to create a list item. You created a poplist, which required you to manually type the list elements in the exact order in which they should be displayed to the user. One benefit of attaching a poplist to a field containing codes or ID numbers is that it allows that field to display as user-friendly text instead of codes or numbers—as long as the codes or numbers are in the list.

You then proceeded to create a group of radio buttons. This allowed the SKILL_LEVEL values stored in the EMPLOYEE_SKILL table to display in a more graphical fashion by having one radio button assigned to each possible value. You can produce a radio group from the Layout Wizard by specifying that a column in the Displayed Items area should be represented as a radio group; you can also create a radio group in the Object Navigator or the Layout Editor. Once a group is created, radio buttons can be added to it from the Object Navigator, as well as from the Layout Editor. Each radio button within a radio group must be assigned a unique number that it will represent for existing records and generate in new records. When you add a radio button to an existing radio group in the Layout Editor, a modal window appears asking whether you want to place the new radio button in an existing radio group—and, if so, which one—or if you would rather create a new radio group for this button.

You then moved on to a new section covering noninput items. This section provided an introduction explaining what noninput items are available in Forms Developer 6*i*, and then gave detailed instructions for creating display items, image items, sound items, buttons, and calculated fields. Noninput items do not enable the user to enter or change data. Instead, they provide the user with information to view but not change, and they generate actions. The types of noninput items include boilerplate text, which is any form text that was typed in manually rather than derived from the database by Form Builder; display items, which are read-only form fields that are useful for calculated data such as subtotals or totals, as well as read-only data such as ZIP-based cities; image items, which provide access to graphics files; sound items, which provide access to audio files; and push buttons, which initiate actions. You then created a table capable of holding image files, followed by a canvas that could load and save them. Here, you got your first taste of a form PRE-INSERT trigger, which fires before a record is inserted; the trigger ensured that any record entered through the image canvas was given a blob type of "IMAGE". You added a variety of buttons to the canvas, and since new buttons contain no code by default, you utilized WHEN-BUTTON-PRESSED triggers to store the code each button would execute when activated. After the buttons were combined into a group, you learned that selecting any object in a group causes the entire group to be selected. Then, you applied your knowledge to creating a canvas for loading and storing sound files. Sound items allow you to customize how many controls are given to the user by setting properties such as Show Play Button, Show Record Button, Show Rewind Button, Show Fast Forward Button, Show Volume Control, Show Time indicator, and Show Slider.

The next subject you covered was creating calculated fields, which let you easily create display items showing sum, average, count, min, max, variance, and standard deviation values. In order for calculated fields to work automatically, the summarized data block's Precompute Summaries property must be enabled. Form Builder also lets you specify your own formulas to fulfill more complicated mathematical requirements.

Next you worked through a thorough discussion on creating windows and content canvases. Whenever you create a new form module, Form Builder generates a multiple document interface (MDI) window that serves as a parent window containing all the other document windows. There are two types of windows: document and dialog. A document window is used for standard data entry forms, allowing a user to enter and query data, move to other windows within the application, and interact with the application's menu and toolbars, while a dialog window usually presents a modal dialog box requiring the user to acknowledge the dialog box before proceeding to any other action. Both types of windows display canvases. The four types of canvases are content, stacked, tab, and toolbar. All four types can coexist within a single window, meaning that a single window can contain numerous canvases. Every window must have a content canvas, which completely occupies the content pane of its window. You can create multiple-window applications simply by creating additional windows and assigning canvases to them by setting each canvas's Window property to the appropriate window.

The final area covered in this chapter is working with stacked, toolbar, and tab canvases. A stacked canvas lies on top of, or "stacks" onto, a content canvas, hiding anything beneath it. Stacked canvases are useful for controlling the visibility of entire groups of objects, and because they can have their own scroll bars separate from those on the underlying content canvas, they can provide a scrollable window separate from the main content canvas. A tab canvas is essentially multiple stacked canvases with handy tabs at the top to simplify moving from one canvas to another. Tab canvases are ideal for displaying a lot of information about a single subject in a small amount of screen space. Content, stacked, and tab canvases are all designed to display data. In contrast, a toolbar canvas contains buttons giving users quick access to whatever functions you choose. You can have multiple horizontal and vertical toolbars in a single window.

The content covered in this chapter represents about 18 percent of the material tested on *OCP Exam 3*.

Two-Minute Drill

- An input item is a form object that enables the user to enter and change data.
- Input items include text items, check boxes, drop-down lists, radio button groups, poplists, T-lists, combo boxes, and Lists of Values (LOVs).
- A text item is most commonly used for entering and changing data, and it is best suited to nonrepeating data that could not be in a list of often-used choices.

- A check box can be used individually or in groups, with each check box representing a data item that can have only one of two values.
- A radio button group is comprised of two or more radio buttons, and it represents data containing a limited number of mutually exclusive choices.
- A poplist provides a familiar drop-down list that allows a user to select one value, and it can autofill an entry by matching the user's typing with matching list items as the user types. It will not accept nonlist entries.
- A T-list is designed for applications where the user selects one row from a list containing 15 to 30 choices. By default, a T-list shows at least five items from the list, so it is best suited for layouts that have plenty of screen space available.
- A combo box provides a drop-down list that allows a user to select one value. It does not autofill an entry as the user types. It can accept nonlist entries as long as the developer has written appropriate trigger code.
- A List of Values (LOV) can display an unlimited number of choices, and it can display multiple columns of data for each choice.
- A check box item must have mutually exclusive on and off values defined by setting the Value When Checked property and the Value When Unchecked property.
- A poplist allows a text field to display as user-friendly text instead of codes or numbers.
- A radio button group allows values stored in a data source column to display in a more graphical fashion, by having one radio button assigned to each possible value.
- You can create a radio button group in the Object Navigator, Layout Wizard, or Layout Editor.
- Once a radio group is created, each radio button within it must be assigned a unique value that it represents for existing records or generates in new records.
- When you add a radio button to an existing radio group in the Layout Editor, a modal window appears asking whether you want to place the new radio button in an existing radio group—and if so, which one—or if you would rather create a new radio group for that button.
- Noninput items do not enable the user to enter or change data. Instead, they provide the user with information to view but not change, and they can generate actions.

- The types of noninput items include boilerplate text, display items, image items, sound items, and push buttons.
- Boilerplate text is any form text that was typed in manually rather than derived from the database by Form Builder.
- Display items are read-only form fields that are useful for calculated data such as subtotals or totals, as well as unchangeable data such as ZIP-based cities.
- Image items provide access to graphics files, and sound items provide access to audio files.
- Push buttons initiate actions stored in their trigger code.
- A form PRE-INSERT trigger fires before a record is inserted. It allows you to tailor the environment for the form by establishing the contents of memory variables or other parameters important to your application.
- A button's functionality is specified in its WHEN-BUTTON-PRESSED trigger.
- Once items are combined into a group, selecting any object in the group causes the entire group to be selected.
- Calculated fields display read-only information that is computed based on database or other data, rather than retrieved directly from the database.
- Form Builder gives you functions to easily perform sum, average, count, min, max, variance, and standard deviation calculations on any data block item. Form Builder also lets you specify your own formulas for more complicated mathematical requirements.
- Whenever you create a new form module, Form Builder generates a multiple document interface (MDI) window that serves as a parent window containing all the other document windows.
- The two types of windows are document and dialog. A document window is used for standard data entry forms, while a dialog window usually presents a modal dialog box that the user must acknowledge before proceeding to any other action.
- The four types of canvases are content, stacked, tab, and toolbar. All four types can coexist within a single window. A single window can display many canvases.
- A content canvas is the basic background for all windows. Every window, regardless of type, must have at least one content canvas.
- A stacked canvas lies on top of, or "stacks" onto, a content canvas, hiding anything it covers.

- A tab canvas is essentially multiple stacked canvases with handy tabs at the top to simplify moving from one canvas to another. Tab canvases are ideal for displaying a lot of information about a single subject in a small amount of screen space.
- A toolbar canvas contains buttons giving users quick access to whatever functions you choose.
- You can have multiple horizontal and vertical toolbars in a single window.
- You can create multiple-window applications by creating additional windows and assigning canvases to them by setting each canvas's Window property to the appropriate window.

Chapter Questions

1. What is the definition of an input item?

A. A dialog box

B. A form object through which the program can enter and change data

C. A form object through which the user can enter and change data

D. A form object through which the user can view data

E. A graphics element affecting how a chart will look

2. What mathematical functions are automatically available for calculated fields in the Layout Editor, without having to write any formulas? (Choose as many as apply.)

A. Average

B. Mean

C. Count

D. Max

E. Min

F. Standard deviation

G. Sum

H. Variance

3. **Users of your application have requested that they be able to see STOCK and CUSTOMER canvases on the screen simultaneously. You add a second window to the application. How can you make the CUSTOMER canvas use the second window?**

   A. Change the canvas's Visual Attributes group.

   B. Change the canvas's Window property.

   C. Change the window's Primary Canvas property.

   D. It is not possible to change a canvas's display window.

4. **Which check box property controls the text that displays next to the check box?**

   A. Text

   B. Name

   C. Label

   D. A check box's text is fixed and cannot be changed.

5. **Which type of canvas is best suited for displaying tutorial text on the same canvas as the form about which the user is being taught?**

   A. Toolbar

   B. Tab

   C. Viewport

   D. Stacked

   E. Content

6. **What visual controls can you add or remove from a sound item? (Choose all that apply.)**

   A. Sound format

   B. Play button

   C. Compression

   D. Record button

   E. Mono/stereo

   F. Rewind button

G. Fast Forward button

H. Sound quality

I. Volume control

J. Time indicator

K. Progress slider

7. **You are working with an existing radio group in the Layout Editor and try to add a radio button to the group. The Layout Editor responds by:**

   A. Offering to create a check box instead, since a radio button group already exists

   B. Displaying a warning message, and then returning you to the Layout Editor

   C. Presenting a dialog box giving you the chance to select a radio group for the new radio button, or create a new radio group for it

8. **Your Employee form includes a SALARY text item. You want to ensure that standard users cannot input or change a salary value, but you want the value to look exactly like a regular field. What is the best way to do this?**

   A. Set the item's Insert Allowed property to No, and its Update Allowed property to No.

   B. Set the item's Enabled property to No.

   C. Set the item's Enabled property to No, and its Update Allowed property to No.

   D. It is not possible for an unchangeable item to look like a changeable item.

9. **Which of the following are input items? (Choose all that apply.)**

   A. Push button

   B. Check box

   C. Radio button

   D. Sound item

10. What type of canvas can easily eliminate the need for a menu in your application?

A. Content

B. Stacked

C. Toolbar

D. Tab

11. The DEPARTMENT table in your database has been augmented with a BUDGET column. You want to add BUDGET as an item on your Department form, but the item should be a read-only text box so users cannot change it. The best way to do this is:

A. In the Layout Editor, create a display item and set its Insert Allowed property to No, its Update Allowed property to No, and its Database Item property to No.

B. In the Data Block Wizard, move the BUDGET column into the Available Items area. Change the new data block item's Insert Allowed and Update Allowed properties to No. Proceed to the Layout Editor and add BUDGET as a text item.

C. In the Layout Editor, create a display item and set its Column Name property to BUDGET.

D. In the Data Block Wizard, move the BUDGET column into the Available Items area. Proceed to the Layout Editor and add BUDGET as a text item, and change the item's Insert Allowed and Update Allowed properties to No.

12. You have created a form that contains two canvases, ten database items, and four buttons. The items have all been placed into a group, and the buttons have been placed into a separate group. What happens when you click one of the buttons in the Layout Editor?

A. Nothing is selected.

B. The button is selected.

C. The group of buttons is selected.

D. All groups are selected.

E. All items on the button's canvas are selected.

F. All items on all canvases are selected.

13. Which canvas type is most dissimilar to the others?

A. Content

B. Stacked

C. Toolbar

D. Tab

14. What is the primary difference between tab and stacked canvases?

A. A stacked canvas can contain push buttons.

B. A tab canvas can contain multiple pages.

C. A stacked canvas obscures what is beneath it.

D. A tab canvas looks much cooler.

Answers to Chapter Questions

1. C. A form object through which the user can enter and change data

Explanation Input items are the basis of forms; they enable a user to add or edit data. A dialog box may contain input items, but the dialog itself is a window, not an input item.

2. A, C, D, E, F, G, H. Average, Count, Max, Min, Standard Deviation, Sum, Variance

Explanation Review the section "Creating a Calculated Field" if you need a refresher on this topic.

3. B. Change the canvas's Window property.

Explanation A canvas's Window property determines which window the canvas is visible in. The Visual Attributes Group has no window selection properties, and a window's Primary Canvas property specifies the primary canvas for a window that displays multiple canvases.

4. C. Label

Explanation Remember that both Prompt and Label can place text next to a radio button.

5. D. Stacked

Explanation The requirement that the tutorial text be visible on the same form limits the choices to either stacked or tab. A tab canvas might be useful for a multipage tutorial, but the requirements did not state the need for multiple pages, so a simple stacked canvas will fulfill the requirement.

6. B, D, F, G, I, J, K. Play button, Record button, Rewind button, Fast Forward button, Volume control, Time indicator, Progress slider

Explanation Review the section "Creating a Sound Item" if you need a refresher on this topic.

7. C. Presenting a dialog box giving you the chance to select a radio group for the new radio button, or create a new radio group for it

Explanation The Layout Editor is willing to add buttons to an existing radio group. It just needs to know which group will get the new button, or if a completely new group is what you desire.

8. A. Set the item's Insert Allowed property to No, and its Update Allowed property to No.

Explanation Changing an item's Enabled property to No causes its contents to display with light gray characters instead of black. Therefore, the only valid choice is A.

9. B, C. Check box, Radio button

Explanation The definition of an input item is an item that allows the user to enter data. You cannot enter data through a push button; you can only run trigger code. A check box can enter data, as can a radio button. A sound item can only play back existing items; you must code a trigger to populate a sound item.

10. C. Toolbar

Explanation A toolbar canvas's sole purpose is holding buttons that initiate actions. The buttons can replace every menu action your users would need to take.

11. C. In the Layout Editor, create a display item and set its Column Name property to BUDGET.

Explanation Setting an item's Database Item property to No keeps it from retrieving database data, so answer A cannot be correct. Answer B does work, but it creates a normal-looking text box that actually allows the user to type in data; it isn't until the user tries to save their work that the data block's Insert Allowed and Update Allowed properties halt the action. This is not optimal design. Answer D creates an application in which the field's data cannot be changed, but the user can still place focus on the field, which is also not optimal. Therefore, the best choice is answer C.

12. C. The group of buttons is selected.

Explanation The primary reason for groups is to ensure that when any item in the group is selected, all items are selected with it.

13. C. Toolbar

Explanation Content, stacked, and tab canvases are all intended to display database data. The toolbar canvas type is not; it is intended to display buttons that work in concert with the items on the other three canvas types.

14. B. A tab canvas can contain multiple pages.

Explanation The essence of a tab canvas is the fact that it consists of multiple pages of data, each page overlaying the others when it is selected by the user or developer. It is not possible to get this functionality from a single stacked canvas.

CHAPTER 5

Working with Triggers

In this chapter, you will understand and demonstrate knowledge in the following areas:

- Introduction to form triggers
- How to produce triggers
- Adding functionality to form items
- Using query triggers
- Debugging triggers

Triggers are the bread and butter of your work creating a Form Builder application. You have already worked briefly with triggers in prior chapters of this book. Now it is time for a more complete introduction. You will start by learning about trigger categories, types, scope, and properties. Next, you will learn how to attach triggers to a variety of different objects, using trigger-specific components and subprograms. You will practice adding functionality to form items by attaching triggers to them, and see how to exert greater control over query results by employing query triggers. Then, you will learn how to use the form Debugger, which can provide major assistance when you need to track down misbehaving code.

The content of this chapter represents about 22 percent of *OCP Exam 3* test content.

Introduction to Form Triggers

In this section, you will cover the following points related to form triggers:

- Definition of a trigger
- Form trigger categories
- Form trigger types and scope
- Form trigger properties

You will learn about the numerous categories of triggers that Form Builder offers; be introduced to the two form trigger types; learn how to control a trigger's scope; and see all of a form trigger's properties.

Definition of a Trigger

A *trigger* is a block of PL/SQL code that is attached to objects in your application to add functionality. When a trigger is activated, or *fired*, it executes the code it contains. Each trigger's name defines what event will fire it; for instance, a WHEN-

BUTTON-PRESSED trigger executes its code each time the user clicks the button to which the trigger is attached.

Form Trigger Categories

The triggers most commonly used in Form Builder fall into several functional categories. There are *block-processing* triggers such as ON-DELETE, *interface event* triggers like WHEN-BUTTON-PRESSED, *master/detail* triggers such as ON-POPULATE-DETAILS, *message-handling* triggers like ON-MESSAGE, *navigational* triggers such as WHEN-NEW-FORM-INSTANCE, *query-time* triggers like POST-QUERY, *transactional* triggers such as PRE-INSERT, and *validation* triggers like WHEN-VALIDATE-ITEM. Most of the triggers you deal with will fall into the category of interface event triggers. These fire as the user interacts with your application's GUI. Each time the user clicks on a button, chooses from a list, or changes a radio group or check box, a series of triggers is available to control the application's response.

Interface event triggers generally have names fitting the format WHEN-*object-action*. For instance, list-item triggers include WHEN-LIST-ACTIVATED and WHEN-LIST-CHANGED. For triggers that fire when a new instance of an object is created, the format WHEN-NEW-*object*-INSTANCE prevails. For instance, if you wanted to establish certain settings when a particular form opens, but did not want the application to bother reestablishing those settings just because the user navigated out of the form and then came back into it, the trigger WHEN-NEW-FORM-INSTANCE would do the trick. There are also quite a few triggers for mouse events, such as WHEN-MOUSE-CLICK, WHEN-MOUSE-DOUBLE-CLICK, WHEN-MOUSE-DOWN, WHEN-MOUSE-UP, WHEN-MOUSE-ENTER, and WHEN-MOUSE-LEAVE. In addition, there are over 40 triggers to respond to keystrokes; these use the naming format KEY-*keytype*. Examples include KEY-DOWN, KEY-UP, KEY-F1, KEY-ENTER, and a very useful addition, KEY-OTHERS. The KEY-OTHERS trigger fires whenever the user presses a key that could have a trigger *but does not.* It is an excellent way to disable unwanted function keys, or to perform one or more actions each time the user presses any key.

Exercises

1. **What are the most common trigger categories in Form Builder?**
2. **If you see a trigger named WHEN-CHECKBOX-CHANGED, what category does the trigger fall into?**
3. **What trigger would fire each time a new record is created?**
4. **What is the purpose of the KEY-OTHERS trigger?**

Form Trigger Types and Scope

Triggers can also be divided according to their *trigger type* and *trigger scope*. There are two types of triggers: *built-in* and *user-named*. Built-in triggers correspond to specific runtime events and are supplied with Form Builder. User-named triggers are not provided with Form Builder; they are written by developers like you, and their names can be whatever you, the developer, desire. User-named triggers are required only in special situations, and they can only be run using the EXECUTE_TRIGGER built-in procedure from within a user-named subprogram, built-in trigger, or menu item command.

A trigger's scope defines what event must occur in order for the trigger to fire as a result. The trigger scope is usually determined by the object to which it is attached: its scope encompasses the object itself, and any smaller objects contained therein. For instance, if you defined a WHEN-NEW-ITEM-INSTANCE trigger for a single item on a canvas, the trigger would fire whenever the user navigated to that item. If you moved the trigger to a block, it would fire each time the user navigated to any item in the block. Move the same trigger farther up to the form level, and it would fire when the user navigated to any item in any of the form's blocks.

Exercises

1. **What is the difference between a built-in trigger and a user-named trigger?**
2. **What is meant by a trigger's "scope?" What determines a trigger's scope?**

Form Trigger Properties

Triggers have relatively few properties. This makes sense for an object whose very name defines when it operates, and whose code content defines what it does. Table 5-1 shows the trigger properties and what they do.

Exercises

1. **Which property controls how a trigger interacts with other triggers?**
2. **Which property controls what actions a trigger will perform? (Hint: This is a trick question.)**

How to Produce Triggers

In this section, you will cover the following points about producing triggers:

- Writing trigger code
- Understanding the use of built-in subprograms
- Introduction to the WHEN-WINDOW-CLOSED trigger

Property Node	Property Name	Function
General	Name	Name of this trigger as it appears in the Object Navigator.
General	Subclass Information	Allows you to subclass this trigger under another in order to simplify changing global properties.
General	Comments	Developer comments about trigger.
Functional	Trigger Style	Allows you to select between a PL/SQL trigger and a V2-style trigger. The latter is available only for compatibility with previous versions, and it is not recommended.
Functional	Trigger Text	Contains a More . . . button that opens the PL/SQL Editor for entering and editing the trigger's code.
Functional	Fire in Enter-Query Mode	Specifies whether trigger should fire if the form is in Enter-Query mode. Only applicable for triggers related to actions that are valid in Enter-Query mode.
Functional	Execution Hierarchy	If a higher-level object contains a trigger with the same name, this property defines whether this trigger should override the higher-level one (the default), execute before it, or execute after it.
Help	Display in 'Keyboard Help'	Useful only for KEY-triggers, specifies whether a description of the trigger will appear in the list produced by the Forms Runtime program's Help | Keys menu command.
Help	'Keyboard Help' Text	Text to display for a key trigger in the runtime Keys help screen.

TABLE 5-1. *Trigger Properties*

This section covers the basics of writing trigger code. It starts with an overview of the components you can use in a trigger code block. It then introduces the built-in subprograms that are supplied with Form Builder. It wraps up with an exercise in which you use a built-in subprogram within a form trigger.

Writing Trigger Code

Triggers consist of PL/SQL code blocks. The structure of these blocks will be familiar if you have completed the first two units of this book. (If you have not yet worked through those units, be sure to do so; the information they contain is essential to your success as a Oracle Forms 6*i* developer.) Trigger code can contain a declaration section, a code section, and an error-trapping section. In addition, there are many new system variables enabling you to ascertain and control facets of the environment provided by Form Builder; these are as follows:

SYSTEM.BLOCK_STATUS
SYSTEM.COORDINATION_OPERATION
SYSTEM.CURRENT_BLOCK
SYSTEM.CURRENT_DATETIME
SYSTEM.CURRENT_FORM
SYSTEM.CURRENT_ITEM
SYSTEM.CURRENT_VALUE
SYSTEM.CURSOR_BLOCK
SYSTEM.CURSOR_ITEM
SYSTEM.CURSOR_RECORD
SYSTEM.CURSOR_VALUE
SYSTEM.DATE_THRESHOLD
SYSTEM.EFFECTIVE_DATE
SYSTEM.EVENT_WINDOW
SYSTEM.FORM_STATUS
SYSTEM.LAST_QUERY
SYSTEM.LAST_RECORD
SYSTEM.MASTER_BLOCK
SYSTEM.MESSAGE_LEVEL
SYSTEM.MODE
SYSTEM.MOUSE_BUTTON_PRESSED
SYSTEM.MOUSE_BUTTON_SHIFT_STATE
SYSTEM.MOUSE_ITEM
SYSTEM.MOUSE_CANVAS
SYSTEM.MOUSE_X_POS
SYSTEM.MOUSE_Y_POS
SYSTEM.MOUSE_RECORD
SYSTEM.MOUSE_RECORD_OFFSET
SYSTEM.RECORD_STATUS
SYSTEM.SUPPRESS_WORKING
SYSTEM.TAB_NEW_PAGE
SYSTEM.TAB_PREVIOUS_PAGE
SYSTEM.TRIGGER_BLOCK
SYSTEM.TRIGGER_ITEM
SYSTEM.TRIGGER_RECORD

There are also many, many object properties that you can read and set using PL/SQL code. For instance, you could change the background color of an item in response to an event by placing code like this in the event's trigger:

L 5-1

```
DECLARE
  item_id ITEM;
BEGIN
  item_id := FIND_ITEM('net_earnings');
  SET_ITEM_PROPERTY(item_id, VISUAL_ATTRIBUTE, 'green_text_group');
END;
```

In addition, there are many built-in packages containing PL/SQL constructs you can reference in your own code. Examples include CLEAR_ITEM, which clears a text item's current value, and GET_FILE_NAME, which causes a file-open dialog box to display and returns information about the file selected to the routine that called it. The next section covers built-ins in greater detail. As you work through this chapter and the chapters that follow, you will have many opportunities to expand your trigger-writing skills.

Exercises

1. **What features can you utilize as you write trigger code in Form Builder?**
2. **What are system variables?**

Understanding the Use of Built-In Subprograms

In addition to system variables and object properties, many built-in subprograms, also known as *built-ins,* contain PL/SQL constructs you can use in your own trigger and subprogram code. Form Builder comes with hundreds of built-ins, and they are always available for use within your code. Examples include navigational functions such as NEXT_ITEM, NEXT_RECORD, or NEXT_BLOCK, as well as programming conveniences like GET_FILE_NAME, which generates a file-open dialog box and returns information about the selected file to its calling routine. The built-ins provided with Form Builder are grouped by function into *packages.* You can view the built-in packages in the Object Navigator by opening the Built-In Packages node. Table 5-2 shows the packages and their functional areas.

You have already used built-ins while doing this book's exercises. For instance, when you created a form to display images you included a button employing the GET_FILE_NAME built-in to let the user specify a graphics file to be loaded. For reminder's sake, the code used is shown in L 5-2.

Built-In Package Name	Functional Area
DDE	Dynamic Data Exchange support for Developer/2000 components
Debug	Procedures, functions, and exceptions for debugging PL/SQL program units
List	Procedures, functions, and exceptions for creating and maintaining lists of character strings
OLE2	PL/SQL API for creating and manipulating attributes of OLE2 automation objects
Ora_FFI	Public interface to call foreign (C) functions from PL/SQL
Ora_NLS	Extracts high-level information about your current language environment
Ora_Prof	Procedures, functions, and exceptions for tuning PL/SQL program units
PECS	Tools to utilize Form Builder's Performance Event Collection Services measuring resource usage
Standard Extensions	Core Form Builder built-ins such as CALL_FORM and CREATE_RECORD
Standard Package Spec	Comparison, number, text, date, record, and logical operators such as >=, BETWEEN, DECODE, LTRIM, ADD_MONTHS, CHARTOROWID, and XOR
Text_IO	Support for reading and writing information from and to files
Tool_Env	Tools to interact with Oracle environment variables
Tool_Err	Allows you to manipulate error stack created by other built-in packages
Tool_Res	Extracts string resources from a resource file in order to make PL/SQL code more portable
VBX	Utilize VBX components in forms
Web	Utility for Web applications

TABLE 5-2. *Built-In Packages*

L 5-2

```
DECLARE
     v_dirname   VARCHAR2(255);
     v_filename  VARCHAR2(255);
BEGIN
     v_dirname := 'C:\';

     v_filename := GET_FILE_NAME(
          v_dirname,
          NULL,
          'Bitmap files (*.bmp)|*.bmp|'    ||
          'JPEG files (*.jpg)|*.jpg|'
          )
     ;

     IF v_filename IS NOT NULL THEN
          READ_IMAGE_FILE(
               v_filename,
               'ANY',
               'av_data_image.blob_data'
               )
          ;
     END IF;
END;
```

This code also used the READ_IMAGE_FILE built-in to load the selected image file into the application's current record memory. Both of these built-ins are part of the Standard Extensions package. When you use a built-in from a package other than the standard packages, you must precede its name with the name of the package, for example, WEB.SHOW_DOCUMENT.

Restricted and Unrestricted Built-Ins

Because some of the built-ins provided in the Standard Extensions package are designed to cause navigation, a potential problem exists: what if a developer writes a trigger in response to a navigation event, and the trigger contains a built-in generating another navigation event causing the original trigger to fire again? This sort of circular-reference mistake would cause the application to hang, and it can happen with database transactions as well as navigation events. To keep this from happening, Form Builder prohibits navigation triggers from containing built-ins that move input focus or involve database transactions. These *restricted* built-ins cannot be called from PRE- and POST- triggers, because these triggers fire while the user navigates from one item to another. Examples of restricted built-ins include CLEAR_FORM, COMMIT_FORM, DELETE_RECORD, DOWN, ENTER, GO_ITEM, and NEXT_ITEM, among others.

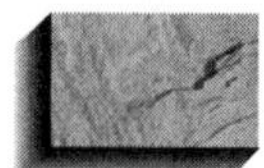

TIP

Trigger names have hyphens between the words, and built-in subprogram names have underscores between the words. This is a handy thing to remember while taking the certification exam, because some questions ask about triggers and offer some answers containing underscores, or ask about built-in subprograms and offer some answers containing hyphens. Keeping their respective naming conventions straight will help you eliminate answers that are in the wrong category altogether.

Exercises

1. **What is a built-in subprogram? A built-in package?**
2. **What naming convention must be observed when calling built-ins from packages other than the Standard packages?**
3. **Why are some built-ins classified as restricted? What is the restriction that is enforced?**

Introduction to the When-Window-Closed Trigger

The WHEN-WINDOW-CLOSED trigger fires whenever the user employs the window-manager Close command to close a window. To create one, open your SOUND_MODULE application. In the Object Navigator, open the Windows node and change the name of the application's only window to **SOUND_WINDOW**. Then, go back up to the top of the Object Navigator and select the Triggers node directly beneath the module name. Click the Create button, select the WHEN-WINDOW-CLOSED trigger, and click the OK button. Enter the following code in the PL/SQL Editor for the trigger:

L 5-3

```
MESSAGE(
  'Executing WHEN-WINDOW-CLOSED trigger. Preparing to exit form...',
  ACKNOWLEDGE
  )
;
EXIT_FORM;
```

Compile the code, close the PL/SQL Editor, and run your application. When the application opens in the Forms Runtime program, click the Windows Close button in the top-right corner of your form window. (The trigger does not fire if you use the Close button in the outer MDI window, or the Action | Exit menu command.) You should see a dialog box appear that looks similar to the one shown here:

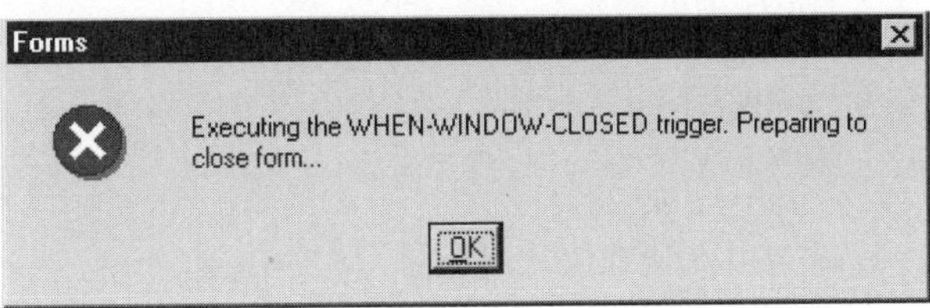

Click the dialog box's OK button to return to Form Builder.

A key fact to remember about the WHEN-WINDOW-CLOSED trigger is that it is not attached to a window. Why? Look in the Object Navigator within the Windows node for your module. See any trigger subnodes? No.Windows do not have triggers, so you have to go up a level, attaching the WHEN-WINDOW-CLOSED trigger at the form level, where it will fire when *any* window in the module is closed. Because of this, it is common to have the WHEN-WINDOW-CLOSED trigger contain an **if** statement that selects the trigger's actions based on which window's closing fired the trigger. An example of this, from the **d2khelp.fmb** demo file provided with an earlier version of Oracle Forms, follows. This sample assumes the application has two windows: one named WIN_REL_TOPICS, and the other named WIN_EXAMPLE.

L 5-4

```
IF      :SYSTEM.EVENT_WINDOW = 'WIN_REL_TOPICS' THEN
         TRT_HLP.HIDE_TOPICS;
ELSEIF :SYSTEM.EVENT_WINDOW = 'WIN_EXAMPLE' THEN
         TRT_HLP.HIDE_EXAMPLE;
ELSE
         DO_KEY('EXIT_FORM');
END IF;
```

Exercises

1. **When does the WHEN-WINDOW-CLOSED trigger fire?**
2. **At what level should a WHEN-WINDOW-CLOSED trigger be placed? Why?**

Adding Functionality to Form Items

In this section, you will cover the following points about adding functionality to items on your forms:

- Supplementing the functionality of input items
- Supplementing the functionality of noninput items

The study of the triggers and built-in subprograms Form Builder offers for its input and noninput items is likely to be an ongoing process in your life as a developer. Here is an overview to help you understand the forest as you learn about the trees.

Supplementing the Functionality of Input Items

All input items can have triggers attached to them. Because of the nature of their function—accepting data—input items commonly have triggers that fire when the user arrives on the item, leaves the item, or changes the item's data. Any input item can have a WHEN-NEW-ITEM-INSTANCE trigger that executes each time the user lands on the item, as well as a WHEN-VALIDATE-ITEM trigger containing code to determine whether the content entered by the user satisfies your integrity constraints. Input items that function by having the user change their state rather than enter a value—meaning all input items except text items—can have triggers that fire when their contents change; the format used in those triggers' names is WHEN-*itemtype*-CHANGED. Table 5-3 shows the common triggers for each type of input item.

Input item triggers can include built-ins to enhance their functionality. There are built-ins to manipulate data, such as CLEAR_ITEM, CLEAR_RECORD, ADD_LIST_ELEMENT, DELETE_LIST_ELEMENT, INSERT_RECORD, DELETE_RECORD, ENTER_QUERY, and EXECUTE_QUERY. There are also built-ins to move the input focus, such as GO_ITEM, GO_RECORD, GO_BLOCK; NEXT_ITEM, NEXT_RECORD, NEXT_BLOCK; and PREVIOUS_ITEM, PREVIOUS_RECORD, and PREVIOUS_BLOCK. In addition, there are built-ins to open specific items, such as SHOW_EDITOR and SHOW_LOV, as well as built-ins to control an item's availability, like DISABLE_ITEM and ENABLE_ITEM. These built-ins operate like a PL/SQL function, expecting specific input parameters when they are called.

Exercises

1. **Describe the difference between a trigger and a built-in.**
2. **What trigger would you use to store code that should fire when the user modifies a radio group's value?**
3. **Which built-in will cause an editor to display?**

Item Type	Common Triggers
Text Item	WHEN-VALIDATE-ITEM WHEN-NEW-ITEM-INSTANCE PRE-TEXT-ITEM POST-TEXT-ITEM
Check Box	WHEN-VALIDATE-ITEM WHEN-NEW-ITEM-INSTANCE WHEN-CHECKBOX-CHANGED
Radio Button	WHEN-VALIDATE-ITEM WHEN-NEW-ITEM-INSTANCE WHEN-RADIO-CHANGED
Poplist	WHEN-VALIDATE-ITEM WHEN-NEW-ITEM-INSTANCE WHEN-LIST-CHANGED
T-List	WHEN-VALIDATE-ITEM WHEN-NEW-ITEM-INSTANCE WHEN-LIST-CHANGED
Combo Box	WHEN-VALIDATE-ITEM WHEN-NEW-ITEM-INSTANCE WHEN-LIST-CHANGED
List of Values (LOV)	WHEN-VALIDATE-ITEM WHEN-NEW-ITEM-INSTANCE WHEN-LIST-CHANGED

TABLE 5-3. *Common Triggers for Input Items*

Supplementing the Functionality of Noninput Items

Like input items, noninput items can be augmented with triggers. Table 5-4 shows the common triggers for each type of noninput item.

Noninput item triggers can also employ built-ins to enhance their functionality. A noninput item trigger can employ any built-in used for an input item, as well as many other built-ins that control interface elements. Examples of such built-ins include CALL_FORM and CLOSE_FORM, ENTER_QUERY and EXECUTE_QUERY,

Item Type	Common Triggers
Boilerplate text	Not applicable
Display Item	Not applicable
Image	WHEN-NEW-ITEM-INSTANCE WHEN-IMAGE-PRESSED WHEN-IMAGE-ACTIVATED
Sound	Available, but no triggers are specifically designed for sound items
Push Button	WHEN-NEW-ITEM-INSTANCE WHEN-BUTTON-PRESSED
Icon	WHEN-NEW-ITEM-INSTANCE WHEN-BUTTON-PRESSED

TABLE 5-4. *Common Triggers for Noninput Items*

OPEN_FORM and EXIT_FORM, and GET_TAB_PAGE_ PROPERTY and SET_TAB_PAGE_PROPERTY. You may also find the following built-ins useful:

GET_BLOCK_PROPERTY, GET_CANVAS_PROPERTY, and GET_FORM_PROPERTY
SET_BLOCK_PROPERTY, SET_CANVAS_ PROPERTY, and SET_FORM_PROPERTY
SHOW_PAGE, SHOW_VIEW, SHOW_WINDOW; HIDE_PAGE, HIDE_VIEW, and HIDE_WINDOW
SHOW_MENU, HIDE_MENU, and EXIT_MENU

Exercises

1. **Which noninput items can you assign triggers to?**
2. **What built-in would you use to change a tab page's name?**

Using Query Triggers

In this section, you will cover the following points about query triggers:

- Data block query process and triggers
- Writing triggers that screen query conditions
- Writing triggers to supplement query results

Believe it or not, a single query can fire over half a dozen triggers. There is a reason that Oracle Corporation expended the effort to offer this many points at which you can insert trigger code: *control.* Query triggers allow you to exert an enormous amount of control over the queries your application generates—both before they are created and after their data results have been returned. In this section you will learn how to use query triggers.

Data Block Query Process and Triggers

A query seems like a simple process: you identify what must be true about the records you want to see, and Oracle fetches them for you. When this is done via an Oracle Forms 6*i* application, additional layers of actions are added relating to the presence of a user interface. The first group of actions falls under the category *entering the query*. When the user initiates a query in the Forms Runtime program, the program starts by checking whether the data block the user is in has its Query Allowed property set to Yes. If so, it checks to see if the block contains any items whose Query Allowed property is also Yes. If so, the Forms Runtime program allows the user to use Enter-Query mode to enter query conditions. The Forms Runtime program then takes the query conditions entered by the user in Enter-Query mode and adds whatever conditions were programmatically placed in the data block's **where** clause property (this property can be changed by a trigger at runtime, as you will soon see). The Forms Runtime program also appends any ordering specifications you have placed in the data block's **order by** clause property (which can also be changed programmatically at runtime).

The next stage is *executing the query*. Here, the Forms Runtime program once again checks whether the data block's Query Allowed property is set to Yes (it does this again because this point can be reached by other means). Once that succeeds, it navigates to the relevant data block, validates any records that aren't validated, and prompts the user to save any unsaved changes. Finally, it opens the query. If there are resulting records, it fetches the records, limiting their quantity to the number specified in the block's Query Array Size property if the property is set to a value other than zero.

In addition to performing the actions just described, Oracle Forms 6*i* has the ability to fire a variety of triggers during the process of fulfilling a query. For instance, there are PRE-QUERY and POST-QUERY triggers that you can attach to blocks or forms. These usually are attached to a block, where they can exert such control as specifying additional **where** column conditions (via a PRE-QUERY trigger) and setting values in fetched records before showing the records to the user (via a POST-QUERY trigger). To give you a more complete picture of when query triggers fire, Table 5-5 shows the order in which query triggers and actions execute. *Whenever a trigger is on the same line as an action,* the Forms Runtime program checks for the presence of the trigger first, and if the trigger exists, it is fired and the corresponding action does not occur.

Stage	Triggers	Actions
Enter Query		Check whether query is allowed on data block.
		Check whether data block contains any queryable items.
		Accept user's query conditions via Enter-Query mode.
Execute Query		Check whether query is allowed on data block.
		Navigate to block.
		Validate unvalidated records.
		Prompt to **commit** unsaved changes.
	Fire PRE-QUERY trigger	
		Check whether the block has a base table.
		Build **select** statement.
	Fire PRE-SELECT trigger	
	Fire ON-SELECT trigger	Execute **select** statement.
	Fire POST-SELECT trigger	
	Fire WHEN-CLEAR-BLOCK trigger	
		Flush example query record from block.

TABLE 5-5. *Chronology of Query Actions and Triggers*

Stage	Triggers	Actions
Fetch Records		Check whether buffer already contains fetched rows not yet placed in data block; if so, use those rows and skip to POST-CHANGE trigger.
	Fire ON-FETCH trigger	Fetch one record, or quantity specified in Query Array Size property.
		Place cursor at first record in buffer.
	Fire POST-CHANGE trigger	
		Mark record and items as valid.
	Fire POST-QUERY trigger once for each record	
		Loop to fetch next record.

TABLE 5-5. *Chronology of Query Actions and Triggers* (continued)

Exercises

1. **What are the three major steps in the process of querying a data block?**
2. **At what object level are PRE-QUERY and POST-QUERY triggers most often attached?**
3. **Does the PRE-QUERY trigger fire before or after the user enters criteria? Does the POST-QUERY trigger fire before or after records are shown to the user?**
4. **In what trigger would you place code to check whether the user specified criteria for an indexed item before running the query?**

Writing Triggers That Screen Query Conditions

The PRE-QUERY trigger gives you the ability to check a query entered by the user before that query is executed, and modify or stop the query if you wish. For instance, you can use a PRE-QUERY trigger to ensure that the user's query includes at least one column that has an index in order to maximize query turnaround speed and minimize server workload. You can also use a PRE-QUERY trigger to control how returned records are sorted, as well as to apply additional **where** clause criteria before the query is processed.

To practice this, modify your DEPARTMENT canvas so it lets users choose whether to sort departments by DEPARTMENT_ID or DEPARTMENT_NAME. Open your original sample application, click on the Data Blocks node, and click the Create button. Select the option labeled *Build A New Data Block Manually* and click the OK button. Change the new block's Name property to **DEPARTMENT_SORT_CONTROL**, and change its Database Data Block property to No to make it a control block. In the Object Navigator, click on the block's Items node, followed by the Create button. Change the item's name to **SORT_SELECT**, its Item Type property to Radio Group, its Initial Value to **DEPARTMENT_ID**, and its Canvas property to DEPARTMENT. Back in the Object Navigator, click on the SORT_SELECT item's Triggers node, click the Create button, select the WHEN-RADIO-CHANGED trigger, and enter the following code in the PL/SQL Editor:

L 5-5

```
GO_BLOCK('DEPARTMENT');
EXECUTE_QUERY;
```

Compile the trigger code and close the PL/SQL Editor. Now click on the SORT_SELECT item's Radio Buttons node, and then double-click the Create button. Change the first radio button's Name and Label properties to **ID**, and its Radio Button Value property to **DEPARTMENT_ID**. Change the second radio button's Name and Label properties to **NAME**, and its Radio Button Value property to **DEPARTMENT_NAME**. Next, in the Object Navigator, right-click on the DEPARTMENT_SORT_CONTROL block's name and select *Layout Wizard* from the context menu that appears. Specify that you want to lay the control block out on the DEPARTMENT canvas, specify a form type of Form, enter a frame title of **Department Sort Order**, and then click the Finish button. In the Layout Editor, change the control block's Frame Title property to **Department Sort Order**. Then move the control block so it is next to the DEPARTMENT block. Close the Layout Editor and return to the Object Navigator. Open the DEPARTMENT data block's node, click on its Triggers node, and click the Create button. Select the Pre-Query trigger and enter the following code in the PL/SQL Editor:

L 5-6

```
SET_BLOCK_PROPERTY(
     'DEPARTMENT',
     ORDER_BY,
     :DEPARTMENT_SORT_CONTROL.SORT_SELECT
     )
;
```

Compile the trigger code and close the PL/SQL Editor. Save your application and then run it. In the Forms Runtime program, navigate to the Department window, and then click the NAME radio button. That will initiate a query whose results look

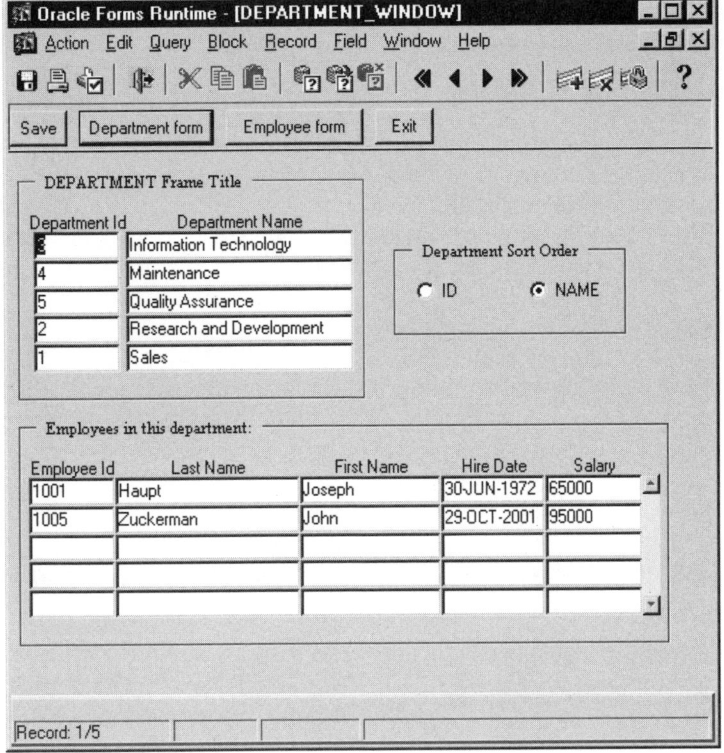

FIGURE 5-2. *Department form sorted by PRE-QUERY trigger*

similar to those in Figure 5-2. When you are through, close the Forms Runtime program and return to Form Builder.

If you wanted to create a PRE-QUERY trigger to ensure that a user's query includes criteria on the indexed column DEPARTMENT_ID, you could do so with code similar to this:

L 5-7

```
IF :DEPARTMENT.DEPARTMENT_ID IS NULL THEN
  MESSAGE('A Department ID is required. Please provide '||
          'a Department ID and re-run your query.');
  RAISE FORM_TRIGGER_FAILURE;
END IF;
```

You can also specify additional **where** clause filtering by using code like the following (which assumes, for the sake of demonstration, that a check box exists identifying whether the user wants the employee form to show only employees in the profit-sharing plan):

L 5-8

```
IF CHECKBOX_CHECKED('EMPLOYEE_FILTER_CONTROL.PROFIT_SHARE_ONLY') THEN
     SET_BLOCK_PROPERTY('EMPLOYEE',
                        DEFAULT_WHERE,
                        'PROFIT_SHARING_INDICATOR = 1'
                        );
END IF;
```

You can use all of these techniques together in a single PRE-QUERY trigger, giving you the assurance of index utilization while giving your users the ability to easily tailor the data returned without having to go through Enter-Query mode.

Exercises

1. **What type of trigger gives you the ability to modify query criteria before records are selected?**
2. **What types of items can you add to your user interface to give the user a simple method of changing query criteria and rerunning a query?**

Writing Triggers to Supplement Query Results

Because the POST-QUERY trigger fires after records are retrieved but before they are displayed to the user, you can use it to augment a query's records in a number of ways. The POST-QUERY trigger can contain code to calculate running totals, generate statistics about the records retrieved, or populate control items, as well as items in other blocks.

The following example builds on the techniques you practiced in the section you just completed. The example code, designed to be run from an Employee form, uses the employee's DEPARTMENT_ID to retrieve that department's mission statement from the DEPARTMENT table and display it on the EMPLOYEE canvas. The example code assumes that the DEPARTMENT table has a column named MISSION to store mission statements, and that the EMPLOYEE canvas has a display item named DEPT_MISSION_DISPLAY to show a mission statement.

L 5-9

```
DECLARE
  CURSOR mem_dept_mission IS
```

```
    SELECT mission
    FROM   department
    WHERE  department_id=:employee.department_id;
BEGIN
  OPEN mem_dept_mission;
  FETCH mem_dept_mission INTO :employee.dept_mission_display;
  CLOSE mem_dept_mission;
END;
```

Exercises

1. **When does the POST-QUERY trigger fire?**
2. **What are the potential benefits of using a POST-QUERY trigger?**

Debugging Triggers

In this section, you will cover the following points about debugging triggers in your forms:

- Running a form module in debug mode
- Understanding the components of the Debugger
- Debugging PL/SQL code

Nothing is more fun than debugging trigger code. Okay, that may not be true. But using decent debugging tools can make the process a lot more pleasant. This section covers the fundamentals of using the Forms Runtime program's Debugger. You will start with an overview of the debugging process used for Oracle Forms 6*i* forms. Then, you will learn specifics about debugging options and initiating the debugging process. Next, you will get a thorough explanation of the Debugger's screen components, followed by a walk-through on setting debugging breakpoints, altering memory values while the application is paused, and seeing the impact of altered values when the application resumes.

Running a Form Module in Debug Mode

When you run your form module in debug mode, the Forms Runtime program starts, but instead of going immediately into your application, it first displays the Debugger. While in the Debugger, you can create breakpoints and even write coded debug triggers that fire at specific times. After you have established breakpoints and debug triggers—or if you don't yet know where you will need them—you close the Debugger, and your application starts. From that point on, the evidence that you are in debug mode varies depending on how you configured your debug settings before running your form. You may see evidence that you are running in debug mode every time a trigger fires, or whenever the program's execution is interrupted with a **break** command in your code, or when you choose Help | Debug from the Forms Runtime menu.

One of the important debugging options you set from Form Builder controls how much information the Forms Runtime program shows you while it is running in debug mode. To change this option, execute the Tools | Preferences menu command and then select the Runtime tab. The resulting dialog box contains a check box labeled Debug Messages. When you run your form in debug mode with this option enabled, the Forms Runtime program displays an alert every time a trigger is about to fire. In addition, it displays in the form console the name of the trigger, along with the item that the trigger is attached to. This option can be valuable because it lets you pinpoint precisely the spot in an application where a problem is occurring. On the other hand, simple actions can generate a lot of trigger events, and if you already have a good idea where a problem is occurring, your debugging may be slowed down substantially by enabling the Debug Messages option. For the sake of learning, enable it now and close the dialog box.

You can start the Debugger from Form Builder by clicking the Run Form Debug button in the Object Navigator's top toolbar. The button is shown here:

When you click this button, the Debugger starts. Behind the scenes, enabling this button causes Form Builder to include source code in the **.fmx** and **.mmx** files it generates before calling the Forms Runtime program. Since part of the Debugger's job is letting you view and modify source code at runtime, it is necessary to have that source code in the executable file.

Click the Run Form Debug button now. Before your application starts, you will see the Debugger screen, which is discussed in detail in the next section.

Exercises

1. **Assuming you already have a form module application, what are the steps for running it in debug mode?**
2. **What does Form Builder do differently to the .fmx and .mmx files it creates when it knows you will be running the application in debug mode?**

Understanding the Components of the Debugger

In order to use the Debugger effectively you must be thoroughly acquainted with its components. Figure 5-3 shows the Debugger window and identifies its main components.

The Debugger toolbar provides quick access to functions commonly used while debugging. The toolbar is shown in detail in Figure 5-4. The Step Into button instructs the Debugger to step into subprogram calls. In contrast, the Step Over button disables stepping into called subprogram bodies. The Step Out button resumes execution, and stays in effect until the current subprogram has returned. The Go button also resumes program execution, remaining in effect until the thread currently executing terminates or is interrupted by a debug action. The Reset button stops program execution in the current debug level and returns program control to an outer level. The Close button closes the Debugger window so you can proceed to run your form. The Expand, Collapse, Expand All, and Collapse All buttons cause Object Navigator nodes to open and close, either individually or as a group.

Beneath the toolbar is the **Source Pane**, which displays the source code of whatever program unit you have selected in the Debugger's Object Navigator. The source code is read-only when viewed through the Source Pane; the pane is not designed for editing. The Source Pane also displays the program unit's line numbers along its left margin. In addition to line numbers, the left margin of the Source Pane sometimes shows other symbols. The pipe symbol (|) marks the current source location. The current scope location is marked with the symbol =>. If the current execution location is different from the current scope location, it is marked with the symbol à. Breakpoints are indicated with the letter *B* followed by a number representing the corresponding debug action ID. Debug triggers are marked with the letter *T* along with a number indicating the corresponding debug action ID.

Below the Source Pane is the Debugger's Object Navigator. This area lists all the modules that the Debugger is going to watch. You can see your module by clicking on the + to the left of the Modules node. When you do, you see your sample application module. Open it, open its Blocks node, open the DEPARTMENT node, open the Triggers subnode, and click on the PRE-QUERY trigger. You will see the trigger's code appear in the Source Pane above.

Underneath the Object Navigator is the Interpreter. This is an interactive prompt at which you can enter commands that control the actions of the Debugger, such as creating breakpoints. Much of what you can do at the Interpreter prompt can also be done by selecting items in the Source Pane or the Debugger Object Navigator, or by executing commands from the new menu command groups that appear in your Forms Runtime menu when the Debugger is active: View, Navigator, Program, and Debug.

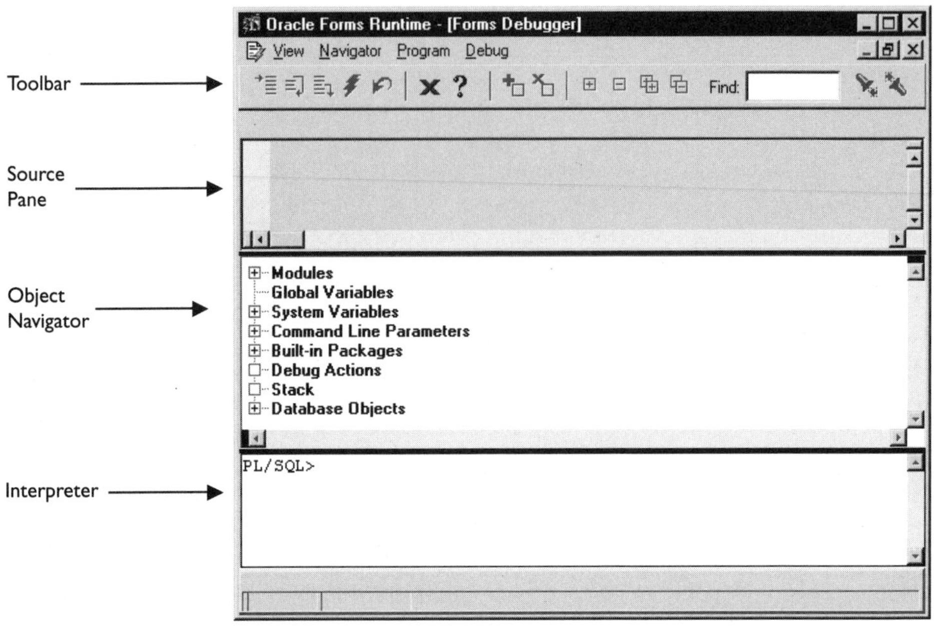

FIGURE 5-3. *Debugger components*

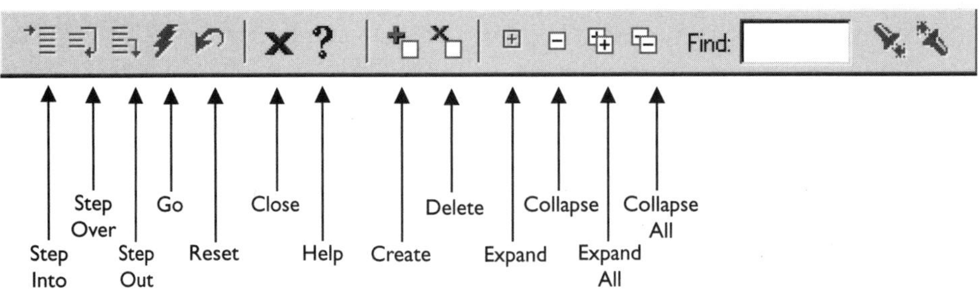

FIGURE 5-4. *Debugger toolbar*

Exercise

1. **Which Debugger menu buttons cause program execution to resume? What are the differences between them?**

Debugging PL/SQL Code

When you run a form module in debug mode and the Debugger presents its screen, it is likely you will want to simply dismiss the Debugger and run your application until you observe the problem you are trying to solve. Dismiss the Debugger now by clicking the Close button in its toolbar. Then navigate to your Department form. If you enabled the Debug Messages option in Form Builder, you are immediately presented with an alert dialog stating simply *"Please acknowledge message."* The message being referred to is down in the console: it reports that a trigger is about to fire; names the trigger, and specifies which object owns the trigger. Click the alert dialog's OK button to proceed, and then populate the Department form by clicking the NAME radio button in the Department Sort Order control block. This causes several alert messages to display—one for each trigger that fires while the program fulfills your request.

As you can see, the Debug Messages option gives you a very fine razor . . . and can get annoying after a while. To turn it off, exit from the Forms Runtime program, execute the Form Builder's Tools | Preferences command, and in the Runtime tab, uncheck the Debug Messages option. Then click the OK, followed by the Run Form Debug button to rerun your form in debug mode. This time, don't dismiss the Debugger right away. Within its Object Navigator, navigate to the PRE-QUERY trigger you created earlier for the DEPARTMENT data block. When you click on the trigger, its code will be displayed up in the Debugger's Source Pane. Double-click now on the **set_block_property** line in the trigger code. You will see that its line number changes to 'B(01)'. You have just set a breakpoint that will cause the Debugger to be invoked just before your application executes that line of trigger code. You can remove the breakpoint by double-clicking on the line again. You also could have established a breakpoint here when you created the trigger in Form Builder by including a line containing the following code:

L 5-10

```
BREAK;
```

The **break** command can be especially handy as part of an **if** statement that checks for valid conditions and executes the **break** command if it encounters unexpected conditions.

Ensure now that the **set_block_property** line in your trigger is marked as a breakpoint, and then click the window's Close button (in the top-right corner) to proceed to run your application. Navigate to the Department form and click the NAME radio button. When the Forms Runtime program encounters the breakpoint in your PRE-QUERY trigger, it will stop and open the Debugger. At this point your screen should look similar to Figure 5-5. If you were tracking down a real problem, you would now use the Debugger's Object Navigator to investigate the values stored in your module, global variables, or system variables. For example, open the Object Navigator's Modules node and navigate down to your DEPARTMENT_SORT_CONTROL block. Open its Items node and you see that the only item it has, SORT_SELECT, has a current value of DEPARTMENT_NAME. It has that value because the most recent action was initiated by the NAME radio button, and you assigned that radio button a value of DEPARTMENT_NAME when you created it. To see how you can use the Debugger to alter values during execution, click on the DEPARTMENT_NAME value to the right of the SORT_SELECT item, and replace the

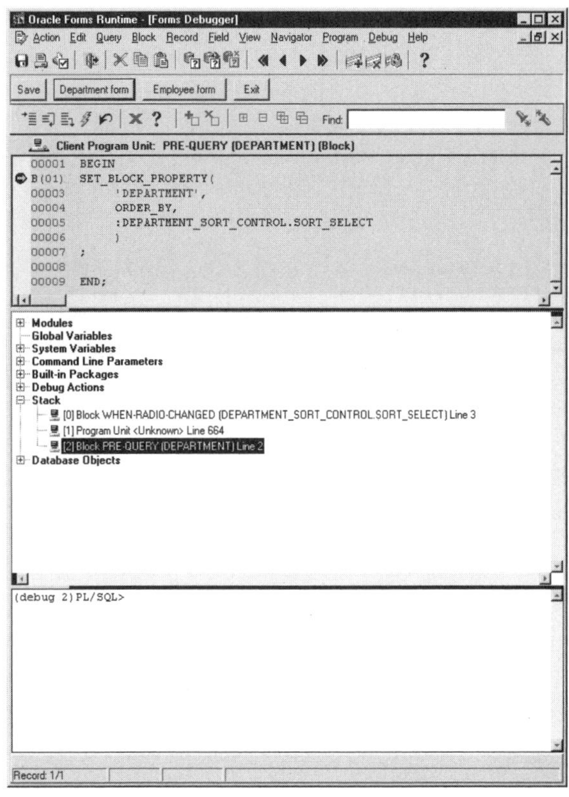

FIGURE 5-5. *Debugger open in response to breakpoint*

value with **DEPARTMENT_ID**. Press the ENTER key to make the new value "stick," and then click the Go button to continue. You will see that the department data has been sorted by ID, and the radio group has its ID button marked, even though it was the NAME button that initiated the action. The results were different because you altered the value midstream using the breakpoint and the Debugger.

Exercises

1. **What is the difference between the Step Into, Step Over, and Step Out menu commands?**
2. **When you run a form in debug mode, how many different actions can cause the Debugger to appear?**

Chapter Summary

In this chapter, you have covered a substantial amount of information on working with triggers. You started with an explanation of what triggers are and how they work. You then learned how to produce triggers, and you employed this knowledge while writing triggers that add functionality to items and queries. Next, you learned how to debug triggers using the Debugger.

The first area you covered was an introduction to form triggers. A trigger is a block of PL/SQL code that adds functionality to your application. Triggers are attached to objects in your application. When a trigger is fired, it executes the code it contains. Each trigger's name defines what event fires it; for example, a WHEN-BUTTON-PRESSED trigger executes its code each time the user clicks the button to which the trigger is attached. The triggers most commonly used in Form Builder fall into several functional categories: Block Processing, Interface Event, Master/Detail, Message Handling, Navigational, Query, Transactional, and Validation. Most of the triggers you deal with will be interface event triggers, which fire as the user interacts with your application's GUI objects.

Interface event triggers generally have names fitting the format of WHEN-*object-action*. Triggers that fire when a new instance of an object is created follow a naming format of WHEN-NEW-*object*-INSTANCE. Mouse event triggers use the naming format WHEN-MOUSE-*mouse action*, and triggers that respond to keystrokes use the format KEY-*keytype*. The KEY-OTHERS trigger fires whenever the user presses a key that can have a trigger but does not, and it is an excellent way to disable unwanted function keys. One trigger whose name does not represent the object it is attached to is WHEN-WINDOW-CLOSED. Because windows do not have triggers, the WHEN-WINDOW-CLOSED trigger is usually attached at the form level.

Triggers can also be grouped by their type and scope. The two types of triggers are "built-in" and "user-named." Built-in triggers are supplied with Form Builder, and they each correspond to a predefined runtime event. User-named triggers, on the other hand, are not provided with Form Builder; they are written by developers like you, and their names can be whatever the developer desires. A trigger's scope defines what event must occur in order for the trigger to fire, and is determined by the object to which the trigger is attached. Triggers have few properties, the most important of which are Execution Hierarchy, which determines how the Forms Runtime program handles triggers with identical names and overlapping scopes; and Display In Keyboard Help, which gives you the ability to add a description of a KEY-trigger to the key help in the Forms Runtime program.

After establishing the basic premises of trigger functions, categories, types, scopes, and properties, your attention turned to the techniques involved in producing triggers. Triggers consist of code blocks filled with PL/SQL instructions. Trigger code can also contain a variety of system variables, commands to read and set object properties, and built-in packages containing premade PL/SQL constructs for specific purposes. The built-ins provided with Form Builder are grouped by function into packages. When you use a built-in from a package other than the Standard packages, you must precede its name with the name of the package, for example, WEB.SHOW_DOCUMENT. Built-ins that move input focus or involve database transactions cannot be used in navigation triggers, so as to avoid circular references that generate endless command loops. These built-ins are called restricted built-ins.

When addressing how to use triggers to add functionality to form items, you learned that all input items can have triggers attached to them. Input items commonly have triggers that fire when the user arrives on the item, leaves the item, or changes the item's data. Any input item can have a WHEN-NEW-ITEM-INSTANCE trigger that executes each time the user lands on the item, as well as a WHEN-VALIDATE-ITEM trigger to check the item's contents for integrity. Input items that function by having the user change the items' state rather than enter a value—meaning all input items except text items—can have triggers that fire when their contents change; the format used in those triggers' names is WHEN-*itemtype*-CHANGED. Input item triggers can make use of built-ins that manipulate data, move the input focus, open editors and LOVs, and control an item's availability. Like input items, noninput items can be augmented with triggers, generally including a WHEN-NEW-ITEM-INSTANCE trigger and a trigger that fires when the item is clicked with the mouse. Noninput item triggers can also employ built-ins to enhance their functionality. A noninput item trigger can make use of any built-in used for an input item, as well as many other built-ins that control interface elements.

You then proceeded to learn about query triggers. You started by learning the process involved in executing a data-block query, which consists of three steps: entering the query, executing the query, and fetching the records. A data query can have several triggers attached to it, the most useful of which are the PRE-QUERY trigger (which fires before the **select** statement is finalized) and the POST-QUERY trigger (which fires before selected records are presented to the user).

The final area covered in this chapter is debugging. The Debugger can be invoked by enabling the Debug Mode option in Form Builder and then running your form. When the Debug Mode button is active, the Debugger starts each time you run your form from Form Builder. Enabling this button causes Form Builder to include source code in the **.fmx** and **.mmx** files it generates before calling the Forms Runtime program. You can also choose to enable Debug Messages, which cause the Forms Runtime program to display an alert every time a trigger is about to fire, along with a message in the console identifying the trigger and object that owns it. The Form Debugger has four visual components: the toolbar, which contains buttons for often-used actions; the Source Pane, which shows the PL/SQL instructions in whatever code object you select; the Object Navigator, which displays Debugger objects in a hierarchical layout; and the Interpreter, which is an interactive prompt at which you can type Debugger commands. While in the Debugger, you can create temporary breakpoints and write coded debug triggers that fire in response to specific actions. You can also create breakpoints in Form Builder by adding the command **break** to your PL/SQL code. Whenever the Forms Runtime program encounters either type of breakpoint, it pauses execution of your application and starts the Debugger, which allows you to examine and change memory variables and program code.

All in all, this chapter comprises about 22 percent of material tested on *OCP Exam 3*.

Two-Minute Drill

- A trigger is a block of PL/SQL code that adds functionality to your application.
- Triggers are attached to objects in your application.
- When a trigger is fired, it executes the code it contains.
- Each trigger's name defines what event will fire it.
- The triggers most commonly used in Form Builder fall into several functional categories: Block Processing, Interface Event, Master/Detail, Message Handling, Navigational, Query, Transactional, and Validation.
- Most of the triggers you deal with will be interface event triggers, which fire as the user interacts with your application's GUI objects.
- Interface event triggers generally have names fitting the format of WHEN-*object-action*.

- Triggers that fire when a new instance of an object is created use a naming format of WHEN-NEW-*object*-INSTANCE.
- Mouse event triggers use the naming format WHEN-MOUSE-*mouse action*.
- Triggers that respond to keystrokes use the naming format KEY-*keytype*.
- The KEY-OTHERS trigger fires whenever the user presses a key that can have a trigger but does not.
- Because windows do not have triggers, the WHEN-WINDOW-CLOSED trigger is usually attached at the form level.
- The two types of triggers are *built-in* and *user-named*. Built-in triggers are supplied with Form Builder, while user-named triggers are written by developers.
- A trigger's scope defines what event must occur in order for the trigger to fire, and is determined by the object to which the trigger is attached.
- Triggers consist of code blocks filled with PL/SQL instructions.
- Trigger code can also contain a variety of system variables, commands to read and set object properties, and built-in packages containing premade PL/SQL constructs for specific purposes.
- The built-ins provided with Form Builder are grouped by function into *packages*.
- When you use a built-in from a package other than the Standard packages, you must precede its name with the name of the package, for instance, WEB.SHOW_DOCUMENT.
- Built-ins that move input focus or involve database transactions cannot be used in navigation triggers, so as to avoid circular references that generate endless command loops. These built-ins are called restricted built-ins.
- Input items commonly have triggers that fire when the user arrives on the item, leaves the item, or changes the item's data.
- Any input item will accept a WHEN-NEW-ITEM-INSTANCE trigger that executes each time the user moves focus to the item, as well as a WHEN-VALIDATE-ITEM trigger to identify how the item's contents should be checked for integrity.
- All input items except text items can also have triggers that fire when their contents change; the format used in those triggers' names is WHEN-*itemtype*-CHANGED.

- Noninput items can also be augmented with triggers, generally including a WHEN-NEW-ITEM-INSTANCE trigger and a trigger that fires when the item is clicked with the mouse.
- A noninput item trigger can employ any built-in used for an input item, as well as many other built-ins that control interface elements.
- The query process involves three steps: entering the query, executing the query, and fetching the records.
- A data query can have several triggers attached to it, the most useful of which are the PRE-QUERY trigger (which fires before the **select** statement is finalized) and the POST-QUERY trigger (which fires before selected records are presented to the user).
- The Debugger can be invoked by enabling the Debug Mode option in Form Builder and then running your form.
- When the Debug Mode option is active, the Debugger will start each time you run your form from Form Builder.
- Enabling this button causes Form Builder to include source code in the **.fmx** and **.mmx** files it generates before calling the Forms Runtime program.
- If you enable Debug Messages, the Forms Runtime program will display an alert every time a trigger is about to fire, along with a message in the console identifying the item and trigger.
- The Form Debugger has four visual components: toolbar, Source Pane, Object Navigator, Interpreter.
- While in the Debugger, you can create temporary breakpoints and write coded debug triggers that fire in response to specific actions. You can also create breakpoints in Form Builder by adding the command **break** to your PL/SQL code.
- Whenever the Forms Runtime program encounters a breakpoint, it pauses execution of your application and starts the Debugger, which allows you to examine and change memory variables.

Chapter Questions

1. **What trigger would you use to execute code each time a user modifies the value of a check box?**

   A. WHEN-CHECKBOX-CLICKED

   B. WHEN-CHECKBOX-CHECKED

   C. WHEN-CHECKBOX-UNCHECKED

   D. WHEN-CHECKBOX-CHANGED

   E. ON-NEW-CHECKBOX-INSTANCE

2. **You would like to create a trigger that fires each time a window is closed by the user. You will most likely place the trigger at which of the following levels:**

   A. Item level

   B. Data block level

   C. Canvas level

   D. Window level

   E. Form level

3. **What trigger would fire each time a new record is created?**

   A. ON-NEW-RECORD

   B. WHEN-NEW-RECORD-INSTANCE

   C. WHEN-VALIDATE-RECORD

   D. WHEN-DATABASE-RECORD

4. **What do you need to do within Form Builder to run a form module in debug mode?**

   A. Enable the Debug Mode button, run the form, and the Debugger displays automatically.

   B. Run the form, and in the Forms Runtime program execute the Help | Debug menu command.

   C. Enable Debug Messages and then run your form. The Debugger will appear automatically.

D. Enable the Debug Mode button, run your form, and in the Forms Runtime program execute the Help | Debug menu command.

5. When does the PRE-QUERY trigger fire?

A. Before the form enters Enter-Query mode

B. After the form enters Enter-Query mode, but before the user enters query criteria

C. After the user enters query criteria, but before the query executes

D. After the query executes, but before records are shown to the user

6. Which built-in causes an editor to display for a text item?

A. SHOW-EDITOR

B. WHEN-NEW-ITEM-INSTANCE

C. SHOW_EDITOR

7. You want to write a trigger that screens a query condition. At what level will you place the trigger?

A. Item

B. Record

C. Block

D. Form

8. You wish to have certain values in a form initialized when the form is first opened. What trigger will you use?

A. WHEN-NEW-FORM

B. WHEN-NEW-CANVAS

C. WHEN-FORM-OPENED

D. WHEN-NEW-FORM-INSTANCE

E. WHEN-NEW-CANVAS-INSTANCE

9. What part of a trigger specifies the trigger's actions?

A. Name

B. Type

C. Code

D. Scope

10. **Which built-in causes an LOV to display for a text item that has one defined?**

A. WHEN-NEW-ITEM-INSTANCE

B. WHEN-NEW-LOV

C. GO_ITEM

D. SHOW_LOV

11. **What trigger can you use to ensure that a query entered by the user includes at least one item that is indexed, and keep the query from occurring if not? (Choose all that apply.)**

A. PRE-QUERY

B. ON-SELECT

C. POST-SELECT

D. WHEN-CLEAR-BLOCK

E. ON-FETCH

F. POST-CHANGE

G. POST-QUERY

12. **What is the purpose of the KEY-OTHERS trigger?**

A. Provides code to execute if a key's own trigger fails

B. Provides code to execute if user presses wrong key

C. Provides code to execute if user presses a key that has no trigger attached, but could

D. Provides code that accesses another key's trigger and executes the code it contains

13. Your data analysis application is slowing the network to a crawl. You analyze the queries users are performing and discover that the majority of their queries are too broad, returning many more records than necessary. You decide to require that any query have at least three fields containing criteria. What type of trigger can you use to enforce that requirement?

A. ON-NEW-QUERY-INSTANCE

B. PRE-QUERY

C. PRE-UPDATE

D. POST-QUERY

E. POST-UPDATE

Answers to Chapter Questions

1. D. WHEN-CHECKBOX-CHANGED

Explanation See the section "Supplementing the Functionality of Input Items" for a refresher on this topic.

2. E. Form level

Explanation Windows do not have triggers. Placing the WHEN-WINDOW-CLOSED trigger at the Form level allows it to fire when any window in the module is closed.

3. B. WHEN-NEW-RECORD-INSTANCE

Explanation Choice A is not a valid trigger name, and choices C and D fire at other times. Review the section "Supplementing the Functionality of Input Items" if you need a reminder on this topic.

4. A. Enable the Debug Mode button, run the form, and the Debugger displays automatically.

Explanation See the section "Running a Form Module in Debug Mode" for a refresher on this topic.

5. C. After the user enters query criteria, but before the query executes

Explanation The PRE-QUERY trigger fires after Enter-Query mode but before a query's **select** statement has been finalized, and therefore before the query is executed.

6. C. SHOW_EDITOR

Explanation Choice A is formatted as a trigger, not a built-in, and doesn't exist. Choice B exists but is also a trigger, not a built-in.

7. D. Form

Explanation See the section "Writing Triggers that Screen Query Conditions" for a refresher on this topic.

8. D. WHEN-NEW-FORM-INSTANCE

Explanation None of the other choices are valid triggers.

9. C. Code

Explanation A trigger's actions are defined entirely by its code.

10. D. SHOW_LOV

Explanation The first two choices are triggers, not built-ins. GO_ITEM navigates to an item but does not open an LOV.

11. A. PRE-QUERY

Explanation While the other triggers listed are query triggers, only the PRE-QUERY trigger fires before the **select** statement is executed.

12. C. Provides code to execute if user presses a key that has no trigger attached, but could

Explanation See the section "Form Trigger Categories" for a refresher on this topic.

13. B. PRE-QUERY

Explanation The PRE-QUERY trigger fires before a query's **select** statement has been finalized, and is therefore ideal for screening query criteria before the query is executed.

CHAPTER 6

Forms Processing

In this chapter, you will understand and demonstrate knowledge in the following areas:

- Forms Runtime messages and alerts
- Data validation
- Navigation
- Transaction processing

This chapter builds on the knowledge you gained in the preceding chapter about triggers and shows you how to apply it in several new areas. The chapter starts with an introduction to the messages produced by the Forms Runtime program. With that basis established, it goes on to show how you can create and present your own messages to the user. You will also learn about numerous triggers and techniques that can ensure the integrity of the data entered through your applications. Next, you will see how to move the focus from form object to form object programmatically. The chapter wraps up by thoroughly covering the processes and triggers used in transaction processing, including information on how to use Oracle sequences and array DML in your applications.

The *OCP Exam 3* will consist of test questions in this subject area worth 23 percent of the final score.

Forms Runtime Messages and Alerts

In this section, you will cover the following points related to Forms Runtime messages and alerts:

- Introduction to the default messaging
- Handling errors using built-in subprograms
- Controlling system messages
- Creating and controlling alerts

At some point in your application's operation you will need to communicate with users in a way they cannot ignore. The message may simply be informative; it may require them to make a decision; or it could be a warning about a problem. In this section, you will learn how to create these messages and redirect your code's execution path based on user response. You will also learn the basics of trapping error conditions. This is an essential part of creating robust, reliable, bulletproof applications.

Introduction to the Default Messaging

The Forms Runtime program has the ability to generate a wide variety of error messages in response to anomalous conditions. It displays these messages in either of two places: the message line within the console at the bottom of the Forms Runtime display, or in pop-up windows called *alerts*. Each message has an internally assigned severity level that defines how strongly it tries to be seen. The severity levels can be grouped into the categories shown in Table 6-1.

As the last row in this table indicates, by setting a system variable named SYSTEM.MESSAGE_LEVEL in your code, you can instruct the Forms Runtime program to suppress messages whose severity level is below a certain value. The technique to do this is covered in detail later in this chapter.

Forms Runtime messages are divided into four types. The first type is the *Working* message, also known as a *Hint*. These Hints tell the user that the Forms Runtime program is processing data or instructions. They appear in the console message line. They are useful for messages that the user can ignore without interfering with processing. The second type of Forms Runtime message is the *Informative* message, which appears when the user needs to acknowledge the message but will not be required to make a choice in order to proceed. Informative messages consist of the message text, an OK button, and the Information icon. They are useful for messages such as "No records matching your criteria were found." The

Message Severity Level	Message Severity Category
5	Describes a condition that is already apparent
10	Identifies a procedural mistake made by the user
15	User is trying to execute a function the form is not designed for
20	Outstanding condition or trigger problem that will keep user from continuing the action they intended
25	Condition that could cause the form to perform incorrectly
>25	Extreme severity; messages in this category cannot be suppressed by using the SYSTEM.MESSAGE_LEVEL system variable

TABLE 6-1 *Message Severity Levels*

third type of Forms Runtime message is the *Warning* message, which appears when the user needs to make a choice before processing can continue. Warning messages consist of the message text, up to three buttons, and the Warning icon. They are useful when you want the user to answer a question or verify an action before processing proceeds. The last type of Forms Runtime message is the *Error* message, which appears when a condition has occurred that prevents the user from continuing whatever action they were taking. Error messages consist of the message text, the OK and Help buttons, and the Error icon.

Exercises

1. **Which message type does not display a pop-up message window?**
2. **What is the function of the severity level assigned to each message?**

Handling Errors Using Built-In Subprograms

Errors are bound to happen, and it is important that your application be ready to handle them gracefully. When a Forms application encounters an error, it *raises an exception*, halts execution of the PL/SQL code that was active when the error occurred, and looks in the current PL/SQL block for an EXCEPTION section to tell it what to do about the error. Forms 6*i* divides errors into two types: *internal exceptions*, which include all the situations for which either Oracle Server or Oracle Forms already has preprogrammed error messages; and *user-specified exceptions*, which are exceptions defined by the developer. Form Builder provides a variety of built-ins for error handling. Table 6-2 shows the relevant built-ins along with explanations of each one.

All of the built-ins shown in Table 6-2 can be used in any PL/SQL code in your application. The ON-MESSAGE and ON-ERROR triggers can be defined at the form, block, or item level; form level is recommended, because it can be difficult for the Forms Runtime program to trap block- and item-level errors while it is performing internal navigation functions like committing records. The following code demonstrates a simple error-trapping routine that works when installed as an ON-ERROR trigger at the form level. This routine traps record-insertion problems and displays a message in the console's message line.

L 6-1

```
DECLARE
  dberr_num NUMBER        := DBMS_ERROR_CODE;
  err_num   NUMBER        := ERROR_CODE;
  err_txt   VARCHAR2(80)  := ERROR_TEXT;
  err_typ   VARCHAR2(3)   := ERROR_TYPE;
BEGIN
  IF err_num = 40508 THEN
```

Built-In Name	Data Returned
DBMS_ERROR_CODE	Error number of the most recent Oracle database error
DBMS_ERROR_TEXT	Message number and text of the most recent Oracle database error
ERROR_CODE	Error number of the most recent Forms Runtime error
ERROR_TEXT	Error-message text from the most recent Forms Runtime error
ERROR_TYPE	Three-character code indicating the message type of the most recent Forms Runtime error: FRM = Form Builder error, ORA = Oracle error
MESSAGE_CODE	Message number of the most recent Forms Runtime message
MESSAGE_TEXT	Message text from the most recent Forms Runtime message
MESSAGE_TYPE	Three-character code indicating the message type of the most recent Forms Runtime message: FRM = Form Builder message, ORA = Oracle message

TABLE 6-2. *Form Builder Error-Handling Built-Ins*

```
      IF dberr_num = -1 THEN
        MESSAGE(
          'Primary key for new record duplicates key in existing record.'
          );
      ELSE
        MESSAGE(
          'Cannot insert this record...reason undetermined.'
          );
      END IF;
    ELSE
      MESSAGE(
        ERR_TYP||'-'||to_char(ERR_NUM)||': '||ERR_TXT
        );
    END IF;
  END;
```

Exercises

1. **At what level are error-trapping triggers best defined? Why?**
2. **Which built-ins are designed for handling error conditions? Which are designed to handle messages?**
3. **What is the difference between the DBMS_ERROR_CODE built-in and the ERROR_CODE built-in?**

Controlling System Messages

There are two ways you can control system messages in Form Builder. The first approach is similar to the technique you just learned for handling errors: You simply place the trapping code in an ON-MESSAGE trigger instead of an ON-ERROR trigger, and the trapping code contains MESSAGE_CODE, MESSAGE_TEXT, and MESSAGE_TYPE built-ins instead of ERROR_CODE, ERROR_TEXT, and ERROR_TYPE built-ins. An example of this type of code follows, using the DISPLAY_ERROR built-in to show the error screen:

L 6-2

```
DECLARE
  msg_num NUMBER        := MESSAGE_CODE;
  msg_txt VARCHAR2(80)  := MESSAGE_TEXT;
  msg_typ VARCHAR2(3)   := MESSAGE_TYPE;
BEGIN
  IF msg_num = 40301 THEN
    MESSAGE('No records matching your criteria were found.');
    DISPLAY_ERROR;
  ELSE
    MESSAGE(msg_typ||'-'||TO_CHAR(msg_num)||': '||msg_txt);
  END IF;
END;
```

If your goal is to suppress low-priority messages entirely, you can do so using the SYSTEM.MESSAGE_LEVEL system variable. For instance, when the Forms Runtime program is at the first record of a table and the user clicks the Previous Record button, the console's message line displays a rather terse "FRM-40100: At first record" in the console's message line. You could use the ON-MESSAGE trigger to change the message, using code similar to that shown in the previous listing. Or, you can set the SYSTEM.MESSAGE_LEVEL system variable so that the Forms Runtime program doesn't display the message at all. The severity level of the FRM-40100 message is 5, so the following instruction in a Form module's WHEN-NEW-FORM-INSTANCE trigger will keep the message from displaying the following:

L 6-3

```
:SYSTEM.MESSAGE_LEVEL := 5;
```

One other type of system message that is sometimes useful to suppress is the "Working . . . " message that appears in the console's message line while records are being retrieved. The message itself isn't the problem, but rather the fact that it usually causes the screen to update, which can generate unwanted delays. Because the message is generally useful, you may find it makes sense to suppress it only when you need to, rather than globally. The following code will do it:

L 6-4

```
:SYSTEM.SUPPRESS_WORKING := 'TRUE';
GO_BLOCK('EMPLOYEE');
  EXECUTE_QUERY;
GO_BLOCK('EMPLOYEE_SKILL');
  EXECUTE_QUERY;
GO_BLOCK('EMPLOYEE');
:SYSTEM.SUPPRESS_WORKING := 'FALSE';
```

Exercises

1. **What are the different types of control you can exercise over system messages?**
2. **What is the purpose of the SYSTEM.MESSAGE_LEVEL system variable?**

Creating and Controlling Alerts

Form Builder offers a premade dialog box called an *alert* that shows the user a message of your choosing and provides one, two, or three buttons for their response. Your PL/SQL code then reads the user's response and selects subsequent actions based on it. There are three types of alerts: Note, Caution, and Stop. To experiment with alerts in your own application, take the following steps.

Start by opening your SOUND_MODULE application. In the Object Navigator, click on the Alerts node, followed by the Create button. An alert object will appear in the Object Navigator (as opposed to all the other objects, which are probably snoozing). Open the alert's Property Palette, and change the following properties:

- Change Name to **TEST_ALERT_NOTE**.
- Change Title to **Test Alert Note**.
- Change Message to **This is your sample message for the Test Alert Note**.

- Change Alert Style to **Note**.
- Change Button 1 Label to **OK**.

If the Button 2 Label or Button 3 Label properties have contents, delete those contents; this causes your alert to only display one button. Your alert is now complete. To make it display, you must create a trigger or subprogram that calls for it. To do that, open the AV_DATA_SOUND canvas and create a new push button on it named **TEST_ALERT_NOTE**. Set the button's Label property to **Test Alert Note**. Right-click the button and select SmartTriggers from the context menu that appears. Select the WHEN-BUTTON-PRESSED trigger, and enter the following code in the PL/SQL Editor:

L 6-5

```
DECLARE
  v_alert_user_response NUMBER;
begin
  v_alert_user_response := SHOW_ALERT('TEST_ALERT_NOTE');
END;
```

Compile your code and then close the PL/SQL Editor. Run your application, click the Execute Query button to populate the form with records, and click your Test Alert Note button. You should see a dialog box that looks like the following:

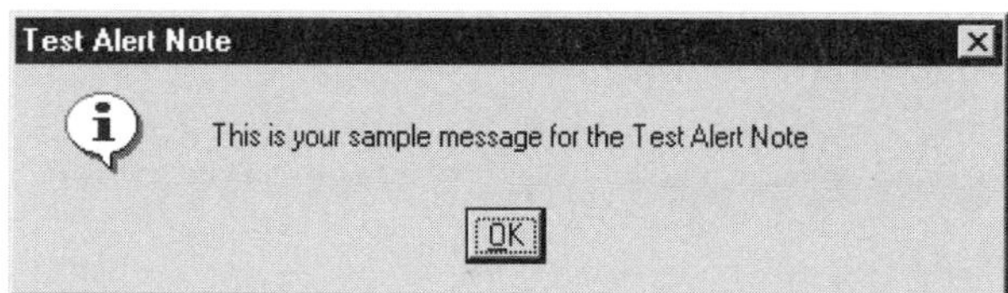

Click the OK button to dismiss the alert and then exit the Forms Runtime program to return to Form Builder.

Informative alerts like this are useful, but there will be times when you want the alert to ask the user to make a choice. The SHOW_ALERT built-in returns specific numeric constant values depending on which of its three buttons the user selects. If the user clicks the first button, the SHOW_ALERT built-in returns the value **alert_button1**, regardless of the label the button displays. If the user clicks the second button, the SHOW_ALERT built-in returns the value **alert_button2**. Clicking the third button, or exiting the alert without choosing a button, generates a return value of **alert_button3**. To see this in action, create another alert in the Object Navigator and name it **TEST_ALERT_STOP**. Change the alert's Title property to **Test Alert Stop**, and its Message property to **You are about to do something destructive.**

Continue? Set its Alert Style property to **Stop**, and change its three button labels to **Yes**, **Help**, and **No**. Then open your AV_DATA_SOUND canvas once again and add another push button. Set the button's Name property to **TEST_ALERT_STOP** and its Label property to **Test Alert Stop**. Right-click on the button and select SmartTriggers from the context menu that appears. Select the WHEN-BUTTON-PRESSED trigger, and enter the following code in the PL/SQL Editor:

L 6-6

```
DECLARE
  v_alert_user_response NUMBER;
BEGIN
  v_alert_user_response := SHOW_ALERT('TEST_ALERT_STOP');
  IF v_alert_user_response = ALERT_BUTTON1 THEN
    MESSAGE('User selected button 1.');
  ELSIF v_alert_user_response = ALERT_BUTTON2 THEN
    MESSAGE('User selected button 2.');
  ELSE MESSAGE(
    'User selected button 3 or cancelled alert without making a selection.'
    );
  END IF;
END;
```

Notice how this code compares the variable V_ALERT_USER_RESPONSE, which stores the user's response, with numeric constants NAMED **ALERT_BUTTON1**, **ALERT_BUTTON2**, and **ALERT_BUTTON3**. This is how it determines which button the user clicked.

Compile your code and then close the PL/SQL Editor. Run your application, click the Execute Query button to populate the form with records, and click your Test Alert Stop button. You should see a dialog box that looks like the following:

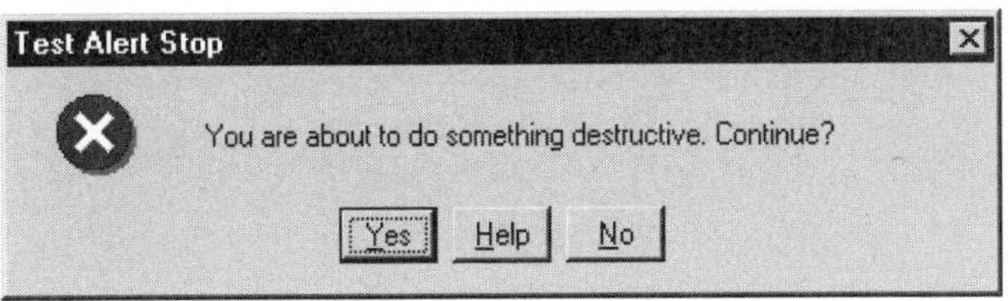

Each time you select a button, your message will appear in the console's message line. (In your own applications, you would have the buttons perform other actions. This example is just to show you how the alert code should be written.) Experiment now by clicking each of the three available buttons. Find out what happens when you bypass the buttons by closing the alert with the ESC key. When you are done, exit the Forms Runtime program and return to Form Builder.

Exercises

1. **What type of window does an alert produce?**
2. **When the SHOW_ALERT built-in is used, what value will it return for the first button in the alert? What value for the second button? The third button?**

Data Validation

In this section, you will cover the following points about data validation:

- Effects of the validation unit on a form
- Introduction to Form Builder validation properties
- Controlling validation using triggers

As anyone who has studied popular psychology can tell you, validation is an important part of any interaction. In this section, you will learn everything you need to know to ensure that your data is properly validated. You will see how a validation unit affects a form, learn about the validation properties available in Form Builder, and practice controlling data validation by employing triggers.

Effects of the Validation Unit on a Form

The term *validation* refers to the process of ensuring that data satisfies whatever requirements you have specified. For example, it makes sense to use validation to guarantee that a State field contains one of the 50 recognized two-character abbreviations; that a gender field contains only M or F; and that a salary figure is greater than zero. Validation can occur in the Oracle database, as well as in the client application.

On the client side, validation can occur each time the user enters an item, completes a record, leaves a data block, or leaves a form. This is known as the *validation unit:* the largest chunk of information a user can enter before the form starts the validation process. You specify this at the form module level, using a property named Validation Unit. *By default, the validation unit is at the Item level,* which causes the Forms Runtime program to perform validation when the user navigates out of an item, presses the ENTER key, or attempts to commit their changes to the database. If you change the validation unit to Record, data will not be evaluated until the user navigates out of the current record, or attempts to changes; when this occurs, all items within the current record will be validated. If the validation unit is set to Data Block or Form, the Forms Runtime program waits until the user tries to navigate out of the block or form, respectively, or until they attempt to commit changes to the database. At that time, *all* records in the block are validated.

The validation unit is rarely set at the block or form level.

Exercises

1. **What does the phrase "validation unit" mean?**
2. **What are the different units, or levels, at which validation can occur?**
3. **What is the default Form Builder validation unit?**
4. **At what level do you normally specify the Validation Unit property?**

Introduction to Form Builder Validation Properties

Client-side validation properties are usually defined at the item level. Text items have a number of properties that affect how they are validated. These properties are listed in Table 6-3. If the text item has an attached List of Values (LOV), setting the item's Validate From List property to Yes causes the Forms Runtime program to check what the user has typed against the values in the LOV's first column. If no LOV entry exactly matches what the user entered, the Forms Runtime program opens the LOV and autoreduces its contents so that only those rows that match what the user typed will be displayed. For instance, if the user enters just **A** in a State field with an attached LOV, when the field is validated the LOV will open and only those states that start with "A" will be shown.

Exercises

1. **At what level are validation properties usually defined?**
2. **How does the behavior of a text item with an attached LOV change when you set the text item's Validate From List property to Yes?**

Controlling Validation Using Triggers

You can augment the default validation of items or records by employing triggers. All you have to do is put PL/SQL code within the appropriate trigger to check the value you are concerned about. You can use the WHEN-VALIDATE-ITEM trigger to perform item-level validity checking. It is the last trigger to fire during item validation for new or changed items and can be assigned to the item, block, or form level. For record-level validity checking, the WHEN-VALIDATE-RECORD trigger comes into play. It is the last trigger to fire during record validation for new or changed records and can be assigned to the block or form level.

Property Node	Property Name	Function
Data	Data Type	Ensures that, for instance, a number field does not contain alphabetic characters.
Data	Maximum Length	Defines the maximum number of characters the field will accept.
Data	Fixed Length	If this property is set, requires input value to be exactly the maximum length.
Data	Required	Value must be entered.
Data	Lowest Allowed Value	Minimum value acceptable for the item.
Data	Highest Allowed Value	Maximum value acceptable for the item.
Data	Format Mask	Checks that user input matches the visual format defined by the developer.
Database	Insert Allowed	Does field allow input at all?
Database	Update Allowed	Can the field's contents be changed?
Database	Update Only If NULL	When set to Yes, item can only be altered if it was NULL before.
List of Values	Validate From List	Determines whether value entered by user should be validated against an attached List of Values.

TABLE 6-3. *Form Builder Item Validation Properties*

As an example, you could place the following PL/SQL code in a WHEN-VALIDATE-ITEM trigger connected to the EMPLOYEE_SKILL.SKILL_LEVEL item. Doing so would ensure that the skill values stay between 1 and 5. Combined with the fact that the SKILL_LEVEL item has a NUMBER(1,0) datatype that excludes decimal places, this trigger ensures that the user can only enter the values 1, 2, 3, 4, or 5.

L 6-7

```
IF NOT(:EMPLOYEE_SKILL.SKILL_LEVEL BETWEEN 1 AND 5) THEN
  MESSAGE(
    'WHEN-VALIDATE-ITEM trigger failed on field '
    || :SYSTEM.TRIGGER_FIELD ||' - Specified value not allowed.'
    );
  RAISE FORM_TRIGGER_FAILURE;
END IF;
```

Exercise

1. **Which triggers can help you expand on the Forms Runtime program's default validation functions?**

Navigation

In this section, you will cover the following points about navigation:

- Internal versus external navigation
- Using navigation triggers
- Introduction to built-ins that cause navigation

Controlling where the focus is in your application and what happens at each point when movement occurs, is essential to creating a smooth, stable experience for the user. This section provides a thorough introduction to navigation in Form Builder applications. It starts by explaining the difference between internal and external navigation. You will learn how to employ navigation triggers to achieve an extremely high degree of control over movement-related actions, and you will be presented with step-by-step tables showing the order in which these triggers fire. After that, you will discover all the built-ins Form Builder provides for controlling movement and focus from within your PL/SQL code.

Internal versus External Navigation

As a programmer, you undoubtedly already understand the difference between a movement the user makes from one object to another, and **goto**-like functions in code that occur behind the scenes. A similar dynamic exists in the realm of form navigation in Form Builder, and understanding it will help you determine where to place triggers to achieve the desired scope.

From the perspective of the Forms Runtime program, clicking on any input or noninput item that fires a trigger, or pressing a keyboard key to move from one object to another, creates an *external navigation* event. For instance, consider a user who is working with a form displaying two blocks. The user sees an object he or she wishes to change, clicks on it, and the focus naturally moves to that object. That is external navigation. However, what the Forms Runtime program actually does to move from one object to another is substantially more involved. In the example just offered, the Forms Runtime program would respond to the user's click by going up the tree of object hierarchy: validating the item the user was on at the time, leaving the item, moving up to the next-larger object in the item's hierarchy (a record, in this case) and validating it, leaving the record, and leaving the block that contained the record. It would then go down the desired branch by entering the destination block, entering the destination record, entering the destination item, preparing the block for input, preparing the record for input, and preparing the item for input. This is *internal navigation*, and in this case it consisted of 11 discrete events, each of which could fire its own trigger.

Exercises

1. **Describe the difference between internal and external navigation.**
2. **Which type of navigation does the user see?**
3. **Which type of navigation is more complicated? Why?**

Using Navigation Triggers

Navigational triggers fire when internal navigation is occurring. There are triggers for each level in the object hierarchy: form, block, record, and item. Table 6-4 lists the navigation triggers, describes each one, and identifies the level(s) at which each can be used. To help you visualize the order of trigger firing and how it relates to actions perceivable by the user, Tables 6-5, 6-6, and 6-7 provide a chronology of user actions, triggers fired in response, and perceivable results when the user starts a Forms Runtime application, moves among records, and exits the Forms Runtime program.

Exercises

1. **Which triggers can help you add auditing functions to your application?**
2. **If you set a data block's validation unit to Form, and then place a PRE-TEXT-ITEM trigger at the block level, will the trigger fire? Why or why not?**

Trigger Name	Description	Level
PRE-FORM	First trigger that fires when a form is run; fires before the form is visible. Useful for setting access to form items, initializing global variables, and assigning unique primary key from an Oracle sequence.	Form
PRE-BLOCK	Second trigger that fires when a form is run; fires before the form is visible. Useful for setting access to block items, and setting values of variables.	Block or form
POST-TEXT-ITEM	Fires when user leaves a text item. Useful for calculating or changing item values.	Item, block, or form
PRE-TEXT-ITEM	Fires when user navigates to a text item, before they are given the opportunity to change the item. Useful for storing the item's current value for later use.	Item, block, or form
WHEN-NEW-FORM-INSTANCE	Fires when form is entered.	Form
WHEN-NEW-BLOCK-INSTANCE	Fires when block is entered.	Block or form
WHEN-NEW-RECORD-INSTANCE	Fires when record is entered.	Block or form
WHEN-NEW-ITEM-INSTANCE	Fires when item is entered.	Item, block, or form
POST-BLOCK	Fires once when the user attempts to leave a block. Useful for validating the current record in the block.	Block or form
POST-FORM	Last trigger to fire before Forms Runtime program closes. Useful for erasing global variables and other cleanup tasks, as well as displaying an exit message to the user.	Form

TABLE 6-4. *Form Builder Navigation Triggers*

User Action	Trigger Fired	Visual Result on Form
Starting application in Forms Runtime program	PRE-FORM	
	PRE-BLOCK	
		Form appears without any data
	WHEN-NEW-FORM-INSTANCE	
	WHEN-NEW-BLOCK-INSTANCE	
	WHEN-NEW-RECORD-INSTANCE	
	WHEN-NEW-ITEM-INSTANCE	
		User is given access to form

TABLE 6-5. *Triggers That Fire When Starting Forms Runtime Application*

User Action	Trigger Fired	Visual Result on Form
TAB	WHEN-NEW-ITEM-INSTANCE	
		Focus moves to next field
NEXT RECORD	WHEN-NEW-RECORD-INSTANCE	
	WHEN-NEW-ITEM-INSTANCE	
		Next record appears

TABLE 6-6. *Triggers That Fire While Moving Among Records*

User Action	Trigger Fired	Visual Result on Form
Action | Exit	POST-BLOCK	
	POST-FORM	
		Forms Runtime program closes

TABLE 6-7. *Triggers That Fire When Exiting Forms Runtime Application*

Introduction to Built-Ins That Cause Navigation

A key requirement of coding routines in a GUI environment is controlling the focus within the GUI. Form Builder provides several built-in subprograms you can use in your PL/SQL code to move the focus to different objects (shown in Table 6-8). These navigation built-ins are restricted, so they cannot be used in the PRE- or POST-navigational triggers. Instead, place them inside WHEN- triggers such as WHEN-BUTTON-PRESSED, WHEN-CHECKBOX-CHECKED, WHEN-NEW-FORM-INSTANCE, WHEN-NEW-BLOCK-INSTANCE, WHEN-NEW-RECORD-INSTANCE, and WHEN-NEW-ITEM-INSTANCE.

Exercises

1. **You place a GO_ITEM built-in in a PRE-BLOCK trigger, and an error message results. Why?**
2. **Which navigation built-in would move focus one record down and keep it on the same item it was on when invoked?**

Transaction Processing

In this section, you will cover the following points about transaction processing:

- Commit processing, transaction processing, and triggers
- Allocating automatic sequence numbers to records
- Implementing array DML

The information in this section will enable you to exert a high degree of control over the behind-the-scenes processing of your application's records. You will begin

Built-In Name	Description	Sample Code
GO_ITEM	Moves focus to named item	`Go_item('EMPLOYEE. EMPLOYEE_ID');`
GO_RECORD	Moves focus to record matching number given	`Go_record( :control. last_record_number);`
GO_BLOCK	Moves focus to named block	`Go_block ('EMPLOYEE_2');`
GO_FORM	Moves focus to named form	`Go_form ('AV_DATA_SOUND');`
FIRST_RECORD	Moves focus to first record in current block	`First_record;`
LAST_RECORD	Moves focus to last record in current block	`Last_record;`
NEXT_RECORD	Moves focus to next record in current block, first navigable and enabled item	`Next_record;`
PREVIOUS_ RECORD	Moves focus to prior record in current block, first navigable and enabled item	`Previous_record;`
UP	Moves focus to current item in previous record	`Up;`
DOWN	Moves focus to current item in next record	`Down;`

TABLE 6-8. *Built-Ins That Cause Navigation*

with a detailed account of the triggers available for your use during commit and transaction processing. Next, you will create an autonumbering sequence for one of your application's tables, and instruct the relevant data block in your application to use that sequence as its source for ID numbers. Finally, you will see how to cut transaction-processing time to a minimum using array DML.

Commit Processing, Transaction Processing, and Triggers

The phrase *commit processing* refers to posting data from a client application to the database, and then committing that data. *Posting* the data involves sending all of the client application's inserts, updates, and deletes to the database. *Committing* the data involves making the posted data permanent in the database, and therefore available to other users. A **commit** command causes both **post** and **commit** operations to take place, although you can use the **post** command to cause only the posting stage to occur. This is especially useful when you have entered new data in a master form and are going to open a detail form to augment it. Table 6-9 shows the most important commit and transaction triggers available in Form Builder applications.

The actual process of committing records and performing other transactions varies depending on the nature of the transaction. Table 6-10 shows the steps that occur when records are retrieved from a database into the client application. Tables 6-11 through 6-13 show the steps when records are added, changed, and deleted.

Trigger Name	Description	Level
ON-COMMIT	Replaces normal **commit** processing, and is therefore most useful for creating special conditions to accommodate committing to a non-Oracle database.	Form
ON-INSERT	Replaces normal **insert** processing.	Block or form
ON-UPDATE	Replaces normal **update** processing.	Block or form
POST-BLOCK	Fires once when the user attempts to leave a block. Useful for validating the current record in the block.	Block or Form
POST-CHANGE	Fires when an item contains changed data. (Included for backward compatibility with older Forms versions, and not recommended for current use.)	Item, block, or form
POST-DATABASE-COMMIT	Fires once following a database **commit**, just after the POST-FORMS-COMMIT trigger.	Form

TABLE 6-9. *Commit and Transactional Triggers* (continued)

Trigger Name	Description	Level
POST-FORM	Fires once when a form is exited. Useful for clearing global variables, or for displaying a message to user when form is closed.	Form
POST-FORMS-COMMIT	Fires once between the time when changes are written to the database and the time when the Forms Runtime program issues the **commit** to finalize those changes. Useful for audit trails and other operations requiring an action each time a database **commit** is imminent.	Form
POST-INSERT	Fires once for each record inserted in a **commit** process. Useful for auditing transactions.	Block or form
POST-QUERY	Fires once for each record fetched into a block's list of records.	Block or form
POST-RECORD	Fires once when focus moves out of a record.	Block or form
POST-SELECT	Fires once between a query's **select** phase and the actual retrieval of records. Useful for performing record counts or other actions reliant on the **select** phase.	Block or form
POST-TEXT-ITEM	Fires when user leaves a text item. Useful for calculating or changing item values.	Item, block, or form
POST-UPDATE	Fires once after each updated row is saved in a **post** or **commit** process.	Block or form
PRE-BLOCK	Fires once as user enters a block. Useful for controlling block access, or setting variable values.	Block or form
PRE-COMMIT	Useful for initiating an action before a database **commit** occurs. Fires before the Forms Runtime program processes records to change, and only fires if records have been inserted, updated, or deleted.	Form

TABLE 6-9. *Commit and Transactional Triggers* (continued)

Trigger Name	Description	Level
PRE-DELETE	Fires once for each record marked for deletion. Fires before the **post** or **commit** processes occur. Useful for master/detail referential integrity checks.	Block or form
PRE-FORM	Fires once during form startup. Useful for controlling access to form, initializing global variables, and assigning a primary key from a sequence.	Form
PRE-INSERT	Fires once before each new record is inserted in a **post** or **commit** process. Useful for modifying item values or populating auditing fields such as User ID or Date.	Block or form
PRE-QUERY	Fires once just before a query. Useful for modifying query criteria.	Block or form
PRE-RECORD	Fires when user navigates to a different record.	Block or form
PRE-SELECT	Fires during query operations, after the **select** statement is constructed but before the statement is issued. Useful for preparing a query string for use by a non-Oracle database.	Block or form
PRE-TEXT-ITEM	Fires when user navigates to a text item, before they are given the opportunity to change the item. Useful for storing the item's current value for later use.	Item, block, or form
PRE-UPDATE	Fires once before each updated record is saved in a **post** or **commit** process. Useful for modifying item values or populating auditing fields such as User ID or Date.	Block or form
WHEN-NEW-BLOCK-INSTANCE	Fires when focus changes from one block to another. Useful for executing restricted built-ins for navigation.	Block or form

TABLE 6-9. *Commit and Transactional Triggers* (continued)

Trigger Name	Description	Level
WHEN-NEW-FORM-INSTANCE	Fires at form startup after focus has been moved to first navigable item. Useful for executing restricted built-ins for navigation.	Form
WHEN-NEW-RECORD-INSTANCE	Fires when focus moves to an item in a different record. Useful for executing restricted built-ins for navigation.	Block or form
WHEN-NEW-ITEM-INSTANCE	Fires when focus moves to an item. Useful for executing restricted built-ins for navigation.	Item, block, or form

TABLE 6-9. *Commit and Transactional Triggers* (continued)

User Action	Trigger Fired	Visual Result on Form
Open form in Forms Runtime module	PRE-FORM	Form not yet visible
	PRE-BLOCK	Form appears without any data
	WHEN-NEW-FORM-INSTANCE	
	WHEN-NEW-BLOCK-INSTANCE	
	WHEN-NEW-RECORD-INSTANCE	
	WHEN-NEW-ITEM-INSTANCE	Form is available to user
Click Execute Query button	PRE-QUERY	
	PRE-SELECT	
	POST-SELECT	
	POST-CHANGE	
	POST-CHANGE	
	POST-CHANGE	
	POST-QUERY	
	WHEN-NEW-RECORD-INSTANCE	
	WHEN-NEW-ITEM-INSTANCE	Data appears in form

TABLE 6-10. *Triggers That Fire When Retrieving Data*

User Action	Trigger Fired	Visual Result on Form
Insert record	WHEN-NEW-RECORD-INSTANCE	
	WHEN-NEW-ITEM-INSTANCE	Form data clears
Enter first field's data, then TAB to next field	WHEN-NEW-ITEM-INSTANCE	Focus moves to next field
. . .	. . . (loop through as many fields) as necessary	. . .
Save	POST-CHANGE	
	POST-CHANGE	
	WHEN-VALIDATE-RECORD	
	POST-BLOCK	
	PRE-COMMIT	
	PRE-INSERT	
	POST-INSERT	
	POST-FORMS-COMMIT	
		Console message line says "FRM-40400: Transaction complete: 1 records applied and saved."
	POST-DATABASE-COMMIT	
	PRE-BLOCK	
	WHEN-NEW-ITEM-INSTANCE	Control returns to user

TABLE 6-11. *Triggers That Fire When Adding a Record*

When Oracle performs the **commit**, it processes record deletions before inserts or updates, because getting the deleted records out of the way could speed up subsequent **update** processes. Next it processes updates, again with the idea that waiting until after new records are inserted would only cause the **update** process to churn through additional records that presumably do not need updating. Finally, the

User Action	Trigger Fired	Visual Result on Form
Change the data and click on Save button	POST-CHANGE	
	WHEN-VALIDATE-RECORD	
	POST-BLOCK	
	PRE-COMMIT	
	PRE-UPDATE	
	POST-UPDATE	
	POST-FORMS-COMMIT	
		Console message line says "FRM-40400: Transaction complete: 1 records applied and saved."
	POST-DATABASE-COMMIT	
	PRE-BLOCK	
	WHEN-NEW-ITEM-INSTANCE	Control returns to user

TABLE 6-12. *Triggers That Fire When Changing a Record*

new records are inserted. The whole process is depicted in Table 6-14, which shows the triggers that fire if you commit after adding one record, changing one record, and deleting one record. Looking at the chronology of events points out just how many triggers are available to you for controlling transactions.

Exercises

1. **What is one common use for the WHEN-NEW-*object*-INSTANCE triggers?**
2. **What is the order in which** insert, update, **and** delete **functions are executed during a** commit **process?**

User Action	Trigger Fired	Visual Result on Form
Remove record	WHEN-NEW-RECORD-INSTANCE	
	WHEN-NEW-ITEM-INSTANCE	Record counter decrements; control is returned to user
Save	POST-BLOCK	
	PRE-COMMIT	
	PRE-DELETE	
	POST-DELETE	
	POST-FORMS-COMMIT	
		Console message line says "FRM-40400: Transaction complete: 1 records applied and saved."
	POST-DATABASE-COMMIT	
	PRE-BLOCK	
	WHEN-NEW-ITEM-INSTANCE	Control is returned to user

TABLE 6-13. *Triggers That Fire When Deleting a Record*

Allocating Automatic Sequence Numbers to Records

A *sequence* is an Oracle construct that produces unique numbers, usually in sequential order. You can easily instruct your Form Builder applications to use sequences to get unique ID values for new records. To experiment with this, create a sequence using the code in L 6-8.

User Action	Trigger Fired	Visual Result on Form
Change the data and click Save button	POST-CHANGE	
	WHEN-VALIDATE- RECORD	
	POST-CHANGE	
	POST-CHANGE	
	WHEN-VALIDATE- RECORD	
	POST-BLOCK	
	PRE-COMMIT	
	PRE-DELETE	
	POST-DELETE	
	PRE-UPDATE	
	POST-UPDATE	
	PRE-INSERT	
	POST-INSERT	
	POST-FORMS-COMMIT	
		FRM-40400: Transaction complete: 3 records applied and saved.
	POST-DATABASE- COMMIT	
	PRE-BLOCK	
	WHEN-NEW-ITEM- INSTANCE	
		Control returned to user

TABLE 6-14. *Triggers That Fire During a Combined DML Commit*

L 6-8

```
CREATE SEQUENCE seq_employee
  START WITH 1050
  NOMAXVALUE
  NOCYCLE
;
```

Now, open your sample application in Form Builder, open the EMPLOYEE_2 data block node, and then the Items node beneath it. Select the EMPLOYEE_ID item and set its Initial Value property to **:SEQUENCE.seq_employee.NEXTVAL** to tell the item to retrieve ID values from the sequence you just created. Save the form and run it. When it opens in the Forms Runtime program, you will immediately see that the Employee ID field is already populated with a new number. Go ahead and fill out the new record with last name **Faltiss**, first name **Jeremy**, hire date **31-DEC-1998**, salary **102500**, department **Information Technology**, and profit sharing **True**. Save your record and exit the Forms Runtime program.

Exercises

1. **When creating a sequence for an existing table, which sequence-creation parameter must take into account the table's existing contents?**
2. **What is the syntax for the parameter referred to in question 1?**
3. **Which property in Form Builder do you use to cause an item to use a sequence?**

Implementing Array DML

You can control how many record inserts, updates, and deletes the Forms Runtime program can send in a single commit transaction. Increasing this number can improve overall application performance because each commit transaction has a certain amount of inherent overhead; combining multiple records into a single commit reduces that overhead as compared to issuing a commit for every individual record. The trade-off is that those uncommitted records have to be stored somewhere, and of course that somewhere is the client computer's memory. The larger the batch of records the client computer stores between each commit, the more memory it requires.

The need for this ability, known as *array data manipulation language* (DML), varies depending on the content of each data block. Therefore, you can set the array DML quantity for each data block individually. The name of the property is DML Array Size.

Exercises

1. **What does the word "array" refer to in the phrase "array DML"?**
2. **At what object level do you establish array DML?**
3. **Which property do you use to establish array DML?**

Chapter Summary

In this chapter, you have covered quite a bit of information on forms processing. The topics covered include Forms Runtime messages and alerts, data validation, external and internal navigation, and transaction processing. All in all, this chapter comprises about 23 percent of material tested on *OCP Exam 3*.

The first area you covered was Forms Runtime messages and alerts. Topics included an introduction to Form Builder's default messaging, how to handle errors with built-in subprograms, controlling system messages, and creating and controlling alerts. Messages can be presented in the console's message line or in pop-up alert windows. Every message has an internally assigned severity level that defines how strongly it tries to be seen. Forms Runtime messages are divided into four types. The first Forms Runtime message type is the *Working* message, also known as a *Hint*. These hints tell the user that the Forms Runtime program is processing data or instructions. They appear in the console message line. The second type of Forms Runtime message is the *Informative* message, which appears when the user needs to acknowledge the message but will not be required to make a choice before the message goes away. Informative messages consist of the message text, an OK button, and the Information icon. The third Forms Runtime message type is the *Warning* message, which appears when the user needs to make a choice before processing can continue. Warning messages consist of the message text, up to three buttons, and the Warning icon. The last type of Forms Runtime message is the *Error* message, which appears when a condition has occurred that prevents the user's action from continuing. Error messages consist of the message text, the OK and Help buttons, and the Error icon.

When a Forms application encounters an error, it raises an exception, halts PL/SQL code execution, and looks in the current PL/SQL block for an EXCEPTION section to tell it what to do about the error. Forms 6*i* divides errors into two types: *internal exceptions*, which include all the situations for which Oracle Server or Oracle Forms already has preprogrammed error messages; and *user-specified exceptions*, which are defined by the developer. Form Builder provides a variety of built-ins for error handling, including DBMS_ERROR_CODE, DBMS_ERROR_TEXT, ERROR_CODE, ERROR_TEXT, ERROR_TYPE, MESSAGE_CODE, MESSAGE_TEXT, and MESSAGE_TYPE. All of these can be used in any PL/SQL code in your application. It is best to define the ON-MESSAGE and ON-ERROR triggers at the form level, because it can be difficult for the Forms Runtime program to trap block- and item-level errors while performing internal navigation functions like committing records. When you are trapping system messages with the ON-MESSAGE trigger, the useful built-ins are MESSAGE_CODE, MESSAGE_TEXT, and MESSAGE_TYPE, instead of ERROR_CODE, ERROR_TEXT, and ERROR_TYPE. You can use the SYSTEM.MESSAGE_LEVEL system variable to suppress low-level system messages entirely by placing a command like **system.message_level := 5**; in your form's

WHEN-NEW-FORM-INSTANCE trigger. You can also control the display of the "Working . . ." message in the console's message line by including **system.suppress_working := 'TRUE';** and **system.suppress_working := 'FALSE';** commands at appropriate points in your code.

Next you learned about alerts. An alert is a modal dialog box containing message text, an icon indicating the severity of the alert, and from one to three buttons. Alerts are displayed via the PL/SQL command **show_alert**, which is usually placed in a trigger. The PL/SQL code can respond to the user's button selection by executing different code segments for each button. There are three types of alerts: Note, Caution, and Stop. The only inherent difference between them is the icon they display with the text, although you will generally use them to convey the alert's importance to the user. The button the user selects is returned to the PL/SQL code in the form of numeric constants named **alert_button1**, **alert_button2**, and **alert_button3**.

The next subject you covered was data validation. Topics here included the effects of the validation unit on a form, an introduction to Form Builder's validation properties, and how to control validation using triggers. The term *validation* refers to the process of ensuring that data satisfies whatever requirements you have specified. Validation can occur in the Oracle database, as well as in the client application. On the client side, text items have several properties that assist with data validation, including Data Type, Maximum Length, Fixed Length, Required, Lowest Allowed Value, Highest Allowed Value, Format Mask, Insert Allowed, Update Allowed, Update Only If NULL, and Validate From List. If the text item has an attached List of Values (LOV), setting the item's Validate From List property to Yes causes the Forms Runtime program to check the user's entry against the LOV, and if no matching LOV value exists, the LOV is opened and autoreduced based on the user's entry. You can also use triggers to augment the default validation of items or records. The WHEN-VALIDATE-ITEM trigger performs item-level validity checking, while the WHEN-VALIDATE-RECORD trigger performs record-level validity checking. The form-level property Validation Unit determines the largest chunk of information a user can enter before the form fires validation triggers. The validation unit can be Item, Record, Block, or Form, with the default validation unit being the smallest one, Item.

Next, your attention turned to navigation. There are two types of navigation: external, which encompasses any change in focus on the GUI, and internal, which consists of the steps taken by the Forms Runtime program as it moves up and down object hierarchies to execute external navigation initiated by the user. Form Builder provides navigational triggers that fire at different stages of the navigation process. There are triggers for each level in the object hierarchy: form, block, record, and item. These triggers include PRE-FORM, PRE-BLOCK, PRE-TEXT-ITEM, POST-TEXT-ITEM, WHEN-NEW-FORM-INSTANCE, WHEN-NEW-BLOCK-INSTANCE, WHEN-NEW-RECORD-INSTANCE, WHEN-NEW-ITEM-INSTANCE, POST-BLOCK, and

POST-FORM. Form Builder also provides a variety of built-ins to cause navigation, including GO_ITEM, GO_RECORD, GO_BLOCK, GO_FORM, FIRST_RECORD, LAST_RECORD, NEXT_RECORD, PREVIOUS_RECORD, UP, and DOWN. Because these navigation built-ins create movement, they are restricted and cannot be used in PRE- or POST- navigational triggers, so as to avoid endless navigation loops. They can, however, be used in WHEN-triggers.

The final area you covered was transaction processing. Committing, or saving, data to the database actually includes two steps: posting the data to the database (available by itself via the **post** command) and then committing the data to make it permanent. Many triggers can fire during a **commit** transaction, including PRE-BLOCK, PRE-COMMIT, PRE-DELETE, PRE-FORM, PRE-INSERT, PRE-QUERY, PRE-RECORD, PRE-SELECT, PRE-TEXT-ITEM, and PRE-UPDATE; POST-BLOCK, POST-CHANGE, POST-DATABASE-COMMIT, POST-FORM, POST-FORMS-COMMIT, POST-INSERT, POST-QUERY, POST-RECORD, POST-SELECT, POST-TEXT-ITEM, and POST-UPDATE; and WHEN-NEW-BLOCK-INSTANCE, WHEN-NEW-FORM-INSTANCE, WHEN-NEW-RECORD-INSTANCE, and WHEN-NEW-ITEM-INSTANCE. When Oracle performs the **commit**, it processes record deletions first, then updates, and then inserts.

Implementing a sequence to provide unique numbers for a data block item is quite simple. After you create the database sequence with the **create sequence** command, you set the Initial Value property for the appropriate data block item to **:sequence.*sequence_name*.nextval**. Implementing array DML to gain the speed benefits of batch transactions is equally easy: you just set the relevant data block's DML Array Size property to the number of records that should be in each batch.

Two-Minute Drill

- The four types of messages are Working, Informative, Warning, and Error. Working messages display in the console's message line; the other three types display in modal pop-up windows.
- The three types of alerts are Note, Caution, and Stop.
- All messages have severity levels that work together with the SYSTEM.MESSAGE_LEVEL system variable to let you suppress low-level messages from being displayed.
- Error-trapping triggers are best defined at the form level, because it can be difficult for the Forms Runtime program to trap block- and item-level errors while it is performing internal navigation functions like committing records.
- Error messages can be trapped with the ON-ERROR trigger, and system messages can be trapped with the ON-MESSAGE trigger.

- The built-ins designed to handle error conditions are DBMS_ERROR_CODE, DBMS_ERROR_TEXT, ERROR_CODE, ERROR_TEXT, and ERROR_TYPE. The DBMS_ built-ins handle Oracle database messages, and the ERROR_ built-ins handle Forms messages.
- The built-ins designed to handle system messages are MESSAGE_CODE, MESSAGE_TEXT, and MESSAGE_TYPE.
- When the SHOW_ALERT built-in is used, its buttons return the values **alert_button1**, **alert_button2**, and **alert_button3**, regardless of the labels displayed by the buttons.
- The phrase *validation unit* defines the object size from which the user must navigate in order for validation triggers to fire. The choices are Item (the default), Record, Block, and Form.
- Client-side validation properties are usually defined at the item level. These properties include Data Type, Maximum Length, Fixed Length, Required, Lowest Allowed Value, Highest Allowed Value, Format Mask, Insert Allowed, Update Allowed, Update Only If NULL, and Validate From List.
- The item property Validate From List causes the Forms Runtime program to check the user's entry against the attached LOV, and if no matching LOV value exists, the LOV opens with an autoreduced list based on the user's entry.
- The WHEN-VALIDATE-ITEM and WHEN-VALIDATE-RECORD triggers can help you expand on the Forms Runtime program's default validation functions.
- External navigation consists of the GUI focus moving from one object to another. Internal navigation is the movement the Forms Runtime program goes through to move up the object hierarchy from the source object, and then down the object hierarchy to the destination object.
- The Navigation built-ins UP and DOWN move to the prior or next records, respectively, placing the focus on the same item it was on when invoked.
- You can work around the restriction prohibiting the use of navigational built-ins in navigational triggers by using WHEN-NEW-*object*-INSTANCE triggers.
- When records are committed to the database, **delete** operations are processed first, followed by **update** operations, and then **insert** operations.
- You can make an item refer to a sequence to get default values for new records by setting the item's Initial Value property to **:sequence.*sequence_name*.nextval**.

- You establish array DML at the data block level by setting the DML Array Size property.

Chapter Questions

1. **You have created an alert with three buttons. What value will be returned if the user selects the second button?**

   A. BUTTON2

   B. DIALOG_BUTTON2

   C. ALERT_BUTTON2

   D. It depends on the choice being offered by the button.

2. **What is the default level at which validation occurs in the Forms Runtime program?**

   A. Item

   B. Record

   C. Form

   D. Block

3. **How does the Forms Runtime program respond when a user enters text into a text item that has an LOV attached and the VALIDATE_FROM_LIST property set to Yes?**

   A. The Forms Runtime program ignores the LOV if the user types a value directly into the field.

   B. The Forms Runtime program populates the item automatically with the first value in the LOV that matches the user's entry.

   C. The Forms Runtime program opens the LOV and shows only items that match what the user has typed so far.

   D. Validate From List is a Data Block property, not an Item property.

4. **How can you cause a block to use a database sequence to get unique IDs?**

   A. Set the Validate From List property to :sequence.*sequence-name*.nextval.

   B. Set the DML Array Size property to :sequence.*sequence-name*.nextval.

C. Set the Initial Value property to :sequence.*sequence-name*.nextval.

D. This action is not possible.

5. You have written a contact-tracking application that includes a field for the last date a client was contacted. You want to use a trigger to guarantee that whenever the date in that field is changed, the date entered is later than the date that was there before. What is the best trigger to use?

A. ON-UPDATE

B. PRE-UPDATE

C. PRE-COMMIT

D. ON-COMMIT

E. POST-UPDATE

F. POST-COMMIT

6. Your form module's Validation Unit property is set to Form. The module includes a data block that has a PRE-TEXT-ITEM trigger. At what point will the trigger fire?

A. Never

B. When data is committed

C. Before the form is validated

D. After the form is validated

7. You want to add a delete-confirmation dialog to your application. You can do so by creating which type of object?

A. Editor

B. Message box

C. Message

D. Alert

8. You would like to keep the user from seeing the Forms Runtime program's "nn records applied and saved" messages. What would you put in the form's WHEN-NEW-FORM-INSTANCE trigger?

A. :system.suppress_working := 'TRUE';

B. :system.suppress_working := 'FALSE';

C. :system.message_level := 0;

D. :system.message_level := 5;

9. **Which of the following are alert styles? (Choose all that apply.)**

A. Working

B. Note

C. Informative

D. Caution

E. Warning

F. Error

G. Stop

10. **What is the last DML statement processed during a commit transaction?**

A. INSERT

B. UPDATE

C. DELETE

D. POST

11. **Which of these built-ins can you use in a PRE-UPDATE trigger? (Choose all that apply.)**

A. COMMIT_FORM

B. DOWN

C. GO_ITEM

D. All of the above

E. None of the above

12. **Which navigational built-in will move the focus to a subsequent record and place it on the same item it was on in the original record?**

A. DOWN

B. NEXT_ITEM

C. NEXT_BLOCK

D. The described action is not possible from a single built-in.

13. You would like to modify your form so it uses array processing to send DML statements to the server in batches of 50. How would you do this?

A. Set the data block's DML Array Size property to 50.

B. Set the canvas's DML Array Size property to 50.

C. Set the window's DML Array Size property to 50.

D. Array processing is limited to 25 records per batch.

Answers to Chapter Questions

1. C. ALERT_BUTTON2

Explanation See the section "Create and Control Alerts" for a refresher on this topic.

2. A. Item

Explanation By default, the Forms Runtime program validates an item immediately when the user tries to leave the item.

3. C. The Forms Runtime program opens the LOV and shows only items that match what the user has typed so far.

Explanation See the section "Introduction to Form Builder Validation Properties" for a refresher on this topic.

4. D. This action is not possible.

Explanation Data blocks cannot read sequences, and in fact cannot store values at all. Items, on the other hand, can. Give yourself half a point if you answered C, which would have been the right answer if the question had referred to an item instead of a block, and remember to pay closer attention to the wording of questions. In some Oracle exam questions, a single word defines why one choice is right and another choice wrong.

5. C. PRE-COMMIT

Explanation PRE-COMMIT is a form-level trigger that fires only once at the beginning of a transaction, so it cannot perform validation on a row-by-row basis. ON-UPDATE and ON-COMMIT only occur if you have replaced the default Forms Runtime transaction processing. POST-UPDATE occurs after the update has occurred, so it is too late for a validity check. POST-COMMIT does not exist. The remaining trigger, PRE-COMMIT, is perfect.

6. A. Never

Explanation The trigger will not fire because the object level defined in the trigger name item is smaller than the module's validation unit.

7. D. Alert

Explanation See the section "Creating and Controlling Alerts" for a refresher on this topic.

8. D. :system.message_level := 5;

Explanation See the section "Controlling System Messages" for a refresher on this topic.

9. B, D, G. Note, Caution, and Stop

Explanation Working, Informative, Warning, and Error are message types.

10. A. INSERT

Explanation The **post** command does not perform a **commit**. Of the three remaining choices, their processing order is **delete**, **update**, and then **insert**.

11. E. None of the above

Explanation Each built-in listed is a navigational built-in, which cannot be used within the navigational trigger PRE-UPDATE.

12. A. DOWN

Explanation See the section "Introduction to Built-Ins that Cause Navigation" for a refresher on this topic.

13. A. Set the data block's DML Array Size property to 50.

Explanation See the section "Implementing Array DML" for a refresher on this topic.

CHAPTER 7

Forms Programming

n this chapter, you will cover the following areas of forms programming:

- Writing flexible code
- Sharing code and objects
- Managing multiple-form applications

As your applications become more complex, you need to start employing more sophisticated techniques to produce robust, powerful applications in a minimum of time. This chapter is here to help. It shows you how to leverage your effort by writing code that is flexible and reusable, employing techniques such as indirect object referencing, property classes, object groups, object libraries, and PL/SQL code libraries. The chapter wraps up by showing you how to create and manage applications incorporating multiple form modules.

Overall, the contents of this chapter comprise about 12 percent of *OCP Exam 3* test content.

Writing Flexible Code

In this section, you will cover the following points related to writing flexible code:

- Flexible code and system variables
- Advantages of using system variables
- Built-in subprograms that assist flexible coding
- Writing code to reference objects by internal ID
- Writing code to reference objects indirectly

The more flexible your code is, the more easily it can be reused, maintained, and expanded. This results in an overall reduction in the time you take to complete a project, which makes *you* more valuable to your employer or clients. There are an infinite number of ways to use the techniques shown in this section, so instead of showing every possible use, one or two simple examples of each technique is provided. Once you understand how the techniques work, you can apply them in your own applications.

Flexible Code and System Variables

Flexible code is code that can be used by a variety of objects, in a variety of modules, without requiring changes to the code. While this type of code often takes longer to write initially, the investment of additional time pays major dividends later, with the benefits increasing each time the code is reused. Code flexibility comes from the way the code is written, as well as from its availability for use in applications other than the one for which it was originally written.

One technique that makes code substantially more flexible is giving it the ability to refer to objects and values with generic names that are evaluated at runtime. Form Builder comes with dozens of *system variables* to provide this ability; they are listed in Table 7-1.

System Variable Name	Returns . . .
$$DATE$$	Current operating system date
$$DATETIME$$	Current operating system date and time
$$DBDATE$$	Current database date from an Oracle database
$$DBDATETIME$$	Current database date and time from an Oracle database
$$DBTIME$$	Current database time from an Oracle database
$$TIME$$	Current operating system time
SYSTEM.BLOCK_STATUS	NEW if all records in current block are new, CHANGED if one or more records in block have been changed, QUERY if all records are unchanged since being retrieved
SYSTEM.COORDINATION_OPERATION	Type of event that is causing coordination between related master and detail blocks
SYSTEM.CURRENT_BLOCK	NULL if current navigation unit is a form; name of current block if current navigation unit is block, record, or item
SYSTEM.CURRENT_DATETIME	Current operating system date and time in DD-MON-YYYY HH24:MI:SS format
SYSTEM.CURRENT_FORM	Name of current form
SYSTEM.CURRENT_ITEM	NULL if current navigation unit is record, block, or form; name of current item (without block name) if current navigation unit is item

TABLE 7-1. *System Variables* (continued)

System Variable Name	Returns . . .
SYSTEM.CURRENT_VALUE	Value of the current item
SYSTEM.CURSOR_BLOCK	NULL if current navigation unit is form; name of block where cursor is located if current navigation unit is block, record, or item
SYSTEM.CURSOR_ITEM	Name of item that has input focus, in format *block_name.item_name*
SYSTEM.CURSOR_RECORD	Number representing current record's physical order in a block's records
SYSTEM.CURSOR_VALUE	Value of item where cursor is located
SYSTEM.DATE_THRESHOLD	Changeable variable; used with $$DBDATE$$, $$DBTIME$$, and $$DBDATETIME$$, specifies how many minutes must have passed since the last database date/time retrieval to make the Forms Runtime program retrieve the information from the database again, instead of just adding the amount of elapsed local time to the last retrieved date/time value
SYSTEM.EFFECTIVE_DATE	Changeable variable; enables you to set the effective database date
SYSTEM.EVENT_WINDOW	Name of last window that fired a window event trigger
SYSTEM.FORM_STATUS	NEW if all records in current form are new, CHANGED if one or more records in block have been changed, QUERY if all records are unchanged since being retrieved
SYSTEM.LAST_QUERY	Most recent **select** statement used to populate a block
SYSTEM.LAST_RECORD	TRUE if current record is last record in block; FALSE if not
SYSTEM.MASTER_BLOCK	Name of master data block involved in a firing of an ON-CLEAR-DETAILS trigger
SYSTEM.MESSAGE_LEVEL	Changeable variable; message severity level at or beneath which messages will not be displayed

TABLE 7-1. *System Variables* (continued)

System Variable Name	Returns . . .
SYSTEM.MODE	NORMAL during normal processing, QUERY when query is being processed, ENTER-QUERY when form is in Enter-Query mode
SYSTEM.MOUSE_BUTTON_PRESSED	1 if left mouse button was pressed, 2 if right button (on 2-button mouse) or middle button (on 3-button mouse) was pressed
SYSTEM.MOUSE_BUTTON_SHIFT_STATE	Shift+ if SHIFT key was held down when mouse button was clicked; Ctrl+ for CONTROL key; Alt+ for ALT key; Shift-Control+ for SHIFT-CONTROL keys
SYSTEM.MOUSE_CANVAS	NULL if mouse is not in a canvas; canvas name if it is
SYSTEM.MOUSE_FORM	Name of form mouse is in
SYSTEM.MOUSE_ITEM	NULL if mouse is not in an item; item name in *block_name.item_name* format if it is
SYSTEM.MOUSE_RECORD	0 if mouse is not in a record; number of record if it is
SYSTEM.MOUSE_RECORD_OFFSET	Used in multirecord blocks with more than one visible record, number representing offset from first visible record to record the mouse is in; 0 if mouse is not in a record
SYSTEM.MOUSE_X_POS	Horizontal position of mouse in relation to top-left corner of canvas, or top-left corner of item's bounding box if mouse is in an item
SYSTEM.MOUSE_Y_POS	Vertical position of mouse in relation to top-left corner of canvas, or top-left corner of item's bounding box if mouse is in an item
SYSTEM.RECORD_STATUS	NEW if current record is new, CHANGED if it has been changed since last validated, QUERY if its status is valid and it was retrieved from a database, or INSERT if it contains invalidated data and has not been saved to the database
SYSTEM.SUPPRESS_WORKING	Changeable variable; TRUE is "Working . . . " messages are suppressed, FALSE if not

TABLE 7-1. *System Variables* (continued)

System Variable Name	Returns . . .
SYSTEM.TAB_NEW_PAGE	Name of destination of tab-page navigation
SYSTEM.TAB_PREVIOUS_PAGE	Name of source of tab-page navigation
SYSTEM.TRIGGER_BLOCK	Name of block that was current when trigger fired
SYSTEM.TRIGGER_ITEM	Name of item that was current when trigger fired
SYSTEM.TRIGGER_RECORD	Number of record that was current when trigger fired

TABLE 7-1. *System Variables* (continued)

Exercises

1. **What is the difference between the $$DATE$$ and $$DBDATE$$ system variables?**
2. **What system variable will tell you the name of the current item? The number of the current record? The name of the current block?**

Built-In Subprograms that Assist Flexible Coding

Form Builder provides quite a few built-ins that are useful when you want to make your code more flexible. The bulk of these either read or set specific properties for a wide variety of objects. These property-manipulation built-ins have names that make clear what they do. The built-ins that read object properties include the following:

- GET_APPLICATION_PROPERTY
- GET_BLOCK_PROPERTY
- GET_CANVAS_PROPERTY
- GET_FORM_PROPERTY
- GET_ITEM_PROPERTY
- GET_LIST_ELEMENT_LABEL
- GET_LIST_ELEMENT_VALUE
- GET_LOV_PROPERTY

- GET_MENU_ITEM_PROPERTY
- GET_RADIO_BUTTON_PROPERTY
- GET_RECORD_PROPERTY
- GET_RELATION_PROPERTY
- GET_TAB_PAGE_PROPERTY
- GET_VIEW_PROPERTY
- GET_WINDOW_PROPERTY

The built-ins that set object properties are almost, but not quite, an exact mirror of the GET_ list; they include the following:

- SET_ALERT_BUTTON_PROPERTY
- SET_ALERT_PROPERTY
- SET_APPLICATION_PROPERTY
- SET_BLOCK_PROPERTY
- SET_CANVAS_PROPERTY
- SET_FORM_PROPERTY
- SET_ITEM_PROPERTY
- SET_LOV_COLUMN_PROPERTY
- SET_LOV_PROPERTY
- SET_MENU_ITEM_PROPERTY
- SET_RADIO_BUTTON_PROPERTY
- SET_RECORD_PROPERTY
- SET_RELATION_PROPERTY
- SET_TAB_PAGE_PROPERTY
- SET_VIEW_PROPERTY
- SET_WINDOW_PROPERTY

These built-ins require as parameters the name of the item you are interested in, the name of the property to read or set—use the property name from the Property Palette, with underscores to replace spaces between words—and the value to place into the property, if it is a SET_ built-in. For example, the code in L 7-1 would make your sample application's SALARY item unavailable for editing.

L 7-1

```
SET_ITEM_PROPERTY('EMPLOYEE_2.SALARY', ENABLED, PROPERTY_FALSE);
```

Some of the more useful properties you can control when working with text items include ITEM_NAME, ITEM_TYPE, DATATYPE, ENABLED, LABEL, PROMPT TEXT, and VISIBLE. There are also properties you can GET_ and SET_ that do not show up in the Property Palette. For the GET_ITEM_PROPERTY built-in, for example, additional properties include BLOCK_NAME and ITEM_IS_VALID.

In addition to the GET_ and SET_ built-ins, Form Builder offers a handful of other built-ins that are useful when you are writing flexible code. Table 7-2 lists these and describes what they do. Of the built-ins in the list, the most unusual is SHOW_LOV, because it has the combined task of displaying an object (an LOV) and also returning a Boolean value to the calling program indicating whether the user selected a value from the LOV.

Built-In Name	**Description**
ADD_GROUP_COLUMN	Adds a column to a record group
ADD_GROUP_ROW	Adds a row to a record group
ADD_LIST_ELEMENT	Adds an element to a list
ADD_PARAMETER	Adds a parameter to a parameter list
COPY	Copies a value from a literal, text item, or global variable into a text item or global variable; used to write values into items referenced via the NAME_IN built-in
DEFAULT_VALUE	Copies a value to a variable if the variable is currently NULL; creates the variable if it is an undefined global variable
DISPLAY_ITEM	Assigns a display attribute to an item
NAME_IN	Returns a value from a named variable or object
SHOW_LOV	Displays a list of values at specified coordinates, returns TRUE if user selects value from list and FALSE if user dismisses list with the Cancel button

TABLE 7-2. *Additional Built-Ins for Flexible Coding*

Exercises

1. **What built-in lets you determine whether a specific field can be seen by the user?**
2. **What built-in has the ability to create a global variable?**
3. **What pair of built-ins could you use to control the labels on radio buttons programmatically? To set the labels for tab pages? To change canvas background colors?**

Writing Code to Reference Objects by Internal ID

Each built-in example you have seen so far has used an object's name as a parameter. It is also possible to use an internal ID to reference objects in many built-ins. The internal object ID is created by Form Builder when the object is created, and it is not visible to the user. Referring to objects by their ID rather than by name benefits you in two ways. First, it speeds up program execution if an object is referred to more than once. Form Builder's native way of addressing objects is their object ID, and if you refer to an object by name, Form Builder has to go find that object's ID before processing can continue. Subsequent references to the object name cause Form Builder to look up the object ID each time. Each of these lookups after the first one can be avoided by declaring a variable in your code to store the object's ID the first time it is looked up. After that, the ID is immediately available each time the object needs to be referenced: you just use the variable name in the referencing code statement. The second benefit is that it improves your code's flexibility and maintainability by storing the object name just once in a section of code, at the beginning. If you wish to modify the object name in the code for maintenance reasons or so the routine can be used elsewhere; you need only change the object name once, because that is the only time the object is referred to by name.

You can obtain an object's ID by using the FIND_ built-in functions. Each object class has a matching FIND_ built-in; for instance, FIND_WINDOW, FIND_BLOCK, and FIND_LOV. Each of these built-ins returns its own unique VARCHAR2 value type; Table 7-3 shows each object type's FIND_ function and return data type.

For example, the following code would return the object ID of the AV_DATA_SOUND form and then move focus to that form:

L 7-2

```
DECLARE
  v_form_id  FORMMODULE;
BEGIN
  v_form_id := FIND_FORM('AV_DATA_SOUND');
  GO_FORM(v_form_id);
END;
```

Object Type	FIND_ Function	Return Data Type
Alert	FIND_ALERT	ALERT
Block	FIND_BLOCK	BLOCK
Canvas	FIND_CANVAS	CANVAS
Editor	FIND_EDITOR	EDITOR
Form	FIND_FORM	FORMMODULE
Item	FIND_ITEM	ITEM
List of Values	FIND_LOV	LOV
Menu Item	FIND_MENU_ITEM	MENUITEM
Parameter List	GET_PARAMETER_LIST	PARAMLIST
Record Group	FIND_GROUP	RECORDGROUP
Record Group Column	FIND_COLUMN	GROUPCOLUMN
Relation	FIND_RELATION	RELATION
Timer	FIND_TIMER	TIMER
View	FIND_VIEW	VIEWPORT

TABLE 7-3. *FIND_* Built-In Return Data Types*

Once you have included code such as that just shown in a PL/SQL code block, you can refer to the object using the variable name (in the prior example, "v_form_id") instead of the object name. You can also use the FIND_ function directly as a parameter in another built-in, with a statement like **go_form(find_form('AV_DATA_SOUND'));**. However, because the form's ID does not get stored in a reusable variable, this approach provides no benefit over simply saying **go_form('AV_DATA_SOUND');**.

Exercises

1. **What are the benefits of referencing objects by ID instead of by name?**
2. **How do you determine an object's ID?**

Writing Code to Reference Objects Indirectly

There are probably going to be times when you need to write code that refers to variables and objects in a way that is even more abstract than using object IDs. One reason to do this is to make your code even more flexible; a routine that receives a value, processes it, and places it somewhere else can achieve its maximum flexibility when it does not have the names of *any* source or destination objects hard-coded. Another reason is that you will soon be building applications that contain menu modules, library modules, and/or multiple form modules, and because each of these modules is compiled independently of the others, they cannot directly reference items or variables stored in a module other than their own. The solution in both of these situations is referencing objects indirectly.

The types of objects that cannot be referenced directly across modules are form items, system and global variables, and parameters. These are called *form bind variables*. There are two built-ins you can use to reference form bind variables: one to read values, and the other to write them. This technique is called *indirect referencing*. The built-in to read values is NAME_IN, and if you interpret its name somewhat loosely, it means "the name that is in" a named object. The built-in to write values is COPY. The structure of each built-in follows:

L 7-3

```
NAME_IN('block_name.item_name')
NAME_IN('GLOBAL.variable_name')
NAME_IN('SYSTEM.variable_name')
NAME_IN('PARAMETER.parameter_name')
COPY('value', 'block_name.item_name');
COPY('value', 'GLOBAL.variable_name');
COPY('value', 'SYSTEM.variable_name');
COPY('value', 'PARAMETER.parameter_name');
```

You can nest NAME_IN inside the COPY built-in to give COPY the ability to place values into indirectly referenced locations. An example of this follows:

L 7-4

```
DECLARE
  gv_user_type VARCHAR2(10);
BEGIN
  IF :radio.choice = 1 THEN
    GV_USER_TYPE := 'STANDARD';
  ELSE
    GV_USER_TYPE := 'ADMIN';
  END IF;

  COPY(NAME_IN('logon_screen.userid'), 'GLOBAL.' || GV_USER_TYPE || '_ID'
);
END;
```

The return value from a NAME_IN built-in is always a character string, even when it is retrieving data from an item with a datatype of NUMBER or DATE. Use the TO_NUMBER and TO_DATE conversion functions to convert the character string to the appropriate type, as shown in the following code:

L 7-5

```
numeric_variable := TO_NUMBER(NAME_IN('block.numeric_item'));
date_variable := TO_DATE(NAME_IN('block.date_item'));
```

Exercises

1. **What are the benefits of writing code that references objects indirectly?**
2. **What built-in enables you to derive the contents of a variable referenced indirectly?**
3. **What built-in enables you to place a value into a variable referenced indirectly?**

Sharing Objects and Code

In this section, you will cover the following points about sharing code and objects:

- Inheriting properties from property classes
- Grouping related objects for reuse
- Reusing objects from an object library
- Reusing PL/SQL code

The allure of being able to reuse objects and code is powerful. It saves time and money. It reduces errors by eliminating re-creation of existing procedures and functions. It helps ensure uniform appearance and functionality with little effort. Form Builder offers sophisticated features to help you reuse objects and code, such as property classes, object groups, object libraries, and PL/SQL libraries.

Inheriting Properties from Property Classes

Every form module contains a node called Property Classes. A *property class* is an object that holds a collection of properties and property values that can be *inherited* by other objects. This enables you to create objects that automatically incorporate the properties you have taken the trouble to define previously, thereby cutting development time. It also assists in creating applications with a uniform look and behavior. An added benefit is that if you need to change a property later, you can change it in the property class and the change is automatically propagated throughout your application, once again improving your productivity. A property class can hold any number of properties, including properties that apply to different object types. Once you have created a property class, you can use it as the basis for other objects that will inherit the properties appropriate for their object types. In the objects based on the property class, you decide which properties are inherited by the object and which are overridden. A property class can also be subclassed into other modules.

Consider, for example, text items that display dollar values; the Salary field in your EMPLOYEE canvas is one example. By default the salary figures appear flush left in the field, without any commas or dollar signs, whereas numeric values are traditionally aligned to the right. You might also wish to have salary values of zero display with a red background to attract the user's attention. These design features would also be useful in *any* item showing dollar values. You can create a property class containing the properties that produce these features and then have each dollar-oriented item refer to that property class, thereby producing the appearance and behavior you want in each item without having to set the properties manually every time.

To make this example more concrete, open your sample application in Form Builder. Open the EMPLOYEE canvas in the Layout Editor, and open the Property Palette for the HIRE_DATE item. Select the following properties (remember that you can hold down the CTRL key to select multiple properties):

- Item Type
- Justification
- Data Type
- Maximum Length
- Fixed Length
- Format Mask
- Width
- Height
- Hint

In the Property Palette toolbar, click the Property Class button, shown here:

A dialog box will appear informing you that a property class was created; click the OK button to dismiss it. Close the Layout Editor and open the Property Classes node in the Object Navigator. Double-click on your new property class to open its Property Palette, and then look at its contents. Change the new property class's name to **DATE_PROPERTIES**. Change its Justification property to Right, and its Format Mask property to MM-DD-YYYY.

If you want to add additional properties to the property class, you can do so by clicking the Add Property button in the Property Palette toolbar, shown here:

You can also delete unneeded properties by clicking the Delete Property button in the Property Palette toolbar, shown next:

You now have a usable property class. To cause form items to inherit its properties, open your EMPLOYEE canvas once again in the Layout Editor and select the HIRE_DATE item. Open its Property Palette and select the Subclass Information property. Click the More . . . button that appears in the property's value location, and you will see a dialog box similar to the Subclass Information dialog box:

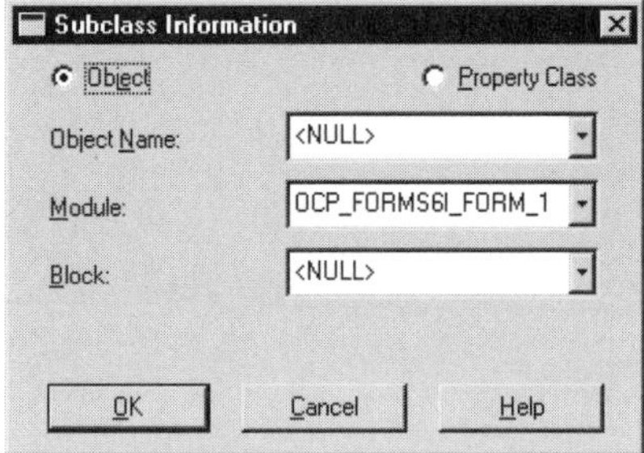

Click the Property Class radio button, open the Property Class Name list, and select your DATE_PROPERTIES property class from the list. Then click the OK button. When you do, you will see that some new symbols appear in the Property Palette to the left of the property names. The standard symbol is a small dot signifying that the property's value is unchanged from the default, as follows:

Properties whose values have been changed manually are marked with a slightly larger square that looks like this:

Properties whose values are inherited from a property class are marked with an arrow pointing to the right, as shown here:

Properties whose values were inherited from a property class *and then manually overridden* are marked with an inheritance arrow whose point is replaced with a red "X," like the following:

Exercises

1. **What are the benefits of using property classes?**
2. **How are inherited properties indicated in a Property Palette? Inherited properties that have been manually overridden?**

Grouping Related Objects for Reuse

An *object group* is a logical container you can create to hold pointers to other objects in a module. This enables you to group related objects—even objects of different types—so they can be easily copied to, or subclassed within, another module. Object groups are available within form and menu modules. They are easy to create: you simply click on the Object Groups node in the Object Navigator and then click the Create button. To add pointers to the object group, just select the items you want to group together and drag them onto the object group's name. To remove an item from an object group, select the item within the object group (*not* the original item!) and click the Delete button or press the DELETE key.

Exercise

1. **What is the purpose of object groups?**

Reusing Objects from an Object Library

While grouping objects into an object group is convenient, there are limitations inherent in this approach; for example, subclassing the object group into another form module does not always work. A more powerful approach is to copy the original items into an *object library* and subclass the object library items into each form module that needs them. Besides being a more robust approach to reusing objects, an object library lets you divide the objects visually onto tab pages of your own design so you can locate and select the ones you want more quickly.

To see this in action, create an object library to hold the objects necessary to save and load images to and from your AV_DATA table. Start by clicking on the Object Libraries node in Form Builder and then clicking the Create button. Change the object library's name to **IMAGE_LIBRARY**. Beneath its entry in the Object Navigator you will see a subnode named Library Tabs; double-click on the subnode to create your first tab, and then click the Create button to create a second tab. Change the first tab's Name property to **BLOCKS** and its Label property to **Blocks**. Change the second tab's Name property to **CANVASES** and its Label property to **Canvases**. Now, double-click the object library's icon in the Object Navigator to open it. You will see a window similar to Figure 7-1.

To place items into your new object library, open the IMAGE_MODULE form in Form Builder. Drag its AV_DATA_IMAGE data block into the object library. Click on the object library's Canvases tab, and then drag the IMAGE_MODULE's AV_DATA_IMAGE canvas into the object library. Click the object library's Save button to save the object library to disk under the name **IMAGE_LIBRARY.olb**. Then, close the IMAGE_MODULE form module so that it is no longer present in the Object Navigator.

Next, create a new form module in the Object Navigator. Then return to the object library, click on the Blocks tab, and drag the AV_DATA_IMAGE data block from the object library onto the new form module's name. Form Builder will display a dialog box asking if you want to subclass the object library object or copy it. Select the Subclass option. Then, click on the object library's Canvases tab and drag the AV_DATA_IMAGE canvas from the object library onto the new form module. When asked, select the Subclass option for this object as well. Save your new module with the name **IMAGE_MODULE_SUBCLASSED.fmb**. Then click the Object Navigator's Run button to run your new form. You will see that it runs exactly as the original IMAGE_MODULE form did. Bringing the functionality of the IMAGE_MODULE form into your new form module took only seconds—a good demonstration of the productivity benefits you can enjoy from using object libraries. When you are finished experimenting with your new form, close it and return to Form Builder.

Object libraries are a powerful way to enforce standards across an organization's applications. One common approach is to have two object libraries used in a project: an enterprise-wide object library containing objects applicable to

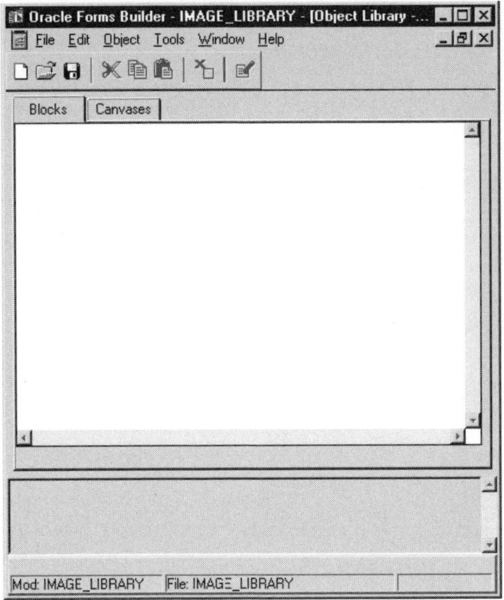

FIGURE 7-1. *Object Library window*

any application created for the company, and a second object library containing objects for a particular application or group, if necessary.

Exercises

1. **What are the benefits of using an object library?**
2. **How is using an object library different from using an object group?**

Reusing PL/SQL code

With all this talk about reusing objects, it is natural that the discussion turn to the subject of reusing code. You can copy and paste code just like any other object, of course, but Form Builder offers a far more elegant solution: *PL/SQL libraries.* A PL/SQL library allows you to store client-side program units and make them available to any form, menu, or library module. A PL/SQL library stores subprograms, including functions, procedures, and packages. Once attached to a module, a PL/SQL library's program units can be called from your own routines, triggers, and menu item commands. You can attach multiple PL/SQL libraries to a single module, and many modules can attach to the same PL/SQL library. A library can even be attached to another library. A PL/SQL library is intelligent enough to only load its program units as an application needs them, thereby minimizing the demand for client-computer memory. This is called *dynamic loading*. PL/SQL libraries can also be handy for applications that need to be distributed in multiple languages: you can store different language versions of the display text in separate language-specific PL/SQL libraries and then attach the appropriate library before the application is distributed to a specific region. PL/SQL libraries are created and modified under Form Builder's PL/SQL Libraries node. To use a PL/SQL library in a module, attach it under the Attached Libraries node within the appropriate module; the attached library is read-only. Forms 6*i* comes with several PL/SQL libraries to simplify common tasks; look in the directories <**forms_6i_home**>**\oca60\plsqllib** and <**forms_6i_home**>**\tools\open60\plsqllib**.

Exercises

1. **What features do PL/SQL libraries offer to reduce the amount of memory needed on the client computer?**
2. **How do you work with server code in a PL/SQL library? (This is a trick question.)**

Managing Multiple-Form Applications

In this section, you will cover the following points about multiple-form applications:

- Defining multiple-form functionality
- Calling one form from another

You have already seen how a single form module can contain different canvases. You can also integrate multiple form modules into a larger, coordinated application. Put on your seat belt!

Defining Multiple-Form Functionality

The Forms Runtime program can have more than one form module open simultaneously during a session. The application starts in the same familiar way—with a single form—but incorporates PL/SQL built-ins to invoke other forms. The additional forms can call other forms of their own, and so on. This propagation can assist development of complicated applications by dividing functional groups into different forms. It also helps maximize the usability of client-computer memory because forms only consume memory when they are called, and their memory is released when they are closed. As an added bonus, using separate form modules lets you exercise a higher degree of control over what records are committed when the user performs a save procedure.

Form Builder gives you plenty of options related to running multiple forms. A newly opened form can run simultaneously with the one that called it, or the new form can replace the old one, causing the calling form to close. Multiple instances of the same form can be run. A form can be opened but kept in the background. And multiple forms can either share the same database connection or they can have multiple independent database connections, as if they were running on separate client computers. The next section provides all the dirty details.

Exercises

1. **What are the benefits of creating multiple-form applications?**
2. **What kinds of multiple-form options are available to you as a developer? When might you use each?**

Calling One Form from Another

To experiment with calling one form from another, start creating a new form module in Form Builder. Give it the name **START_SCREEN**. Create a new data block within the module; change its name to **BUTTON_BLOCK**, and change its Database Data Block property to No. Create a new canvas manually by double-clicking on the Canvases node; name the new canvas **BUTTON_CANVAS**. Open the canvas in the Layout Editor and add four push buttons to it. Set the properties of the buttons as shown in Table 7-4.

Your canvas should look similar to the one shown in Figure 7-2.

Button Name	Button Label	Width
RUN_SAMPLE_APP	Run Sample Application	100
RUN_SOUND_APP	Run Sound Application	100
RUN_IMAGE_APP	Run Image Application	100
EXIT_FORM	Exit	50

TABLE 7-4. *Button Properties for Exercise*

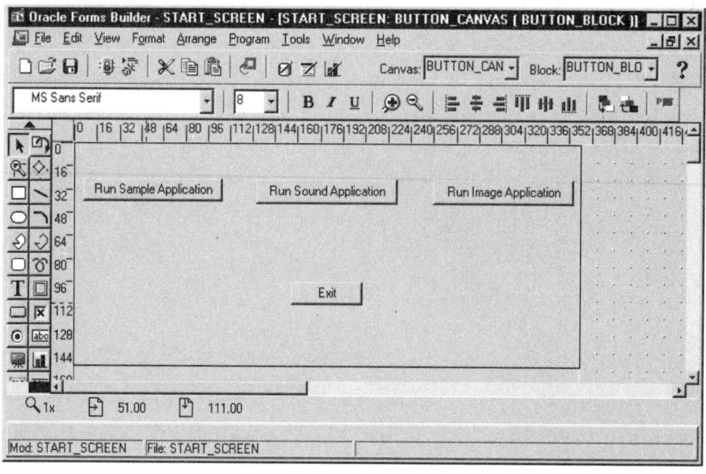

FIGURE 7-2. *Canvas with buttons to open other forms*

Now create a WHEN-BUTTON-PRESSED trigger for the RUN_SAMPLE_APP button, and place inside it code similar to this:

L 7-6

```
OPEN_FORM('sample_application_name');
```

Replace the *sample_application_name* with the name of your sample application as it appears on disk, not as it appears in the Object Navigator. You do not need to include a file extension of **.fmb** or **.fmx**. *You must have a compiled version of the application with an extension of* ***.fmx*** *on the disk, however.* If you have been storing the sample application somewhere other than Form Builder's default path, you need to specify that path in the OPEN_FORM built-in command (this is an excellent place to use a global variable in an application you are going to distribute). If your file specification includes spaces, you may need to use the old 8.3 filename format from DOS, which limits file and directory names to eight characters (excluding the three-character file extension) and no spaces. To convert a long file or directory name to this format, remove all spaces from the name, use the first six characters of what remains, and then add a tilde character (~) followed by a number indicating which number file or directory this is, if more than one entry in this location could be matched by the first six characters you specified. It may take some experimenting with DIR and CD commands at a DOS prompt to find the right 8.3 format name. As an example, the modern filename of

L 7-7

```
P:\Data\OCP Forms 6i\OCP Demo Form 1
```

converts into the following 8.3 format name:

L 7-8

```
P:\Data\OCPFor~1\OCPDem~1
```

Compile the button and close the PL/SQL Editor. Add similar triggers to the sound and image buttons to open their respective form modules. For the Exit button, create a trigger containing the command **exit_form;** to close the START_SCREEN module. Save your form with a name of **START_SCREEN**, and then run it. In the Forms Runtime program, click the first three buttons in your START_SCREEN application to load and open the other form modules. Execute a query with each module, and position them on your screen so their layout suits your taste. Your screen will end up looking similar to Figure 7-3. When you are done experimenting with your multiple forms, close them all and return to Form Builder.

If you wish to invoke a form module without immediately passing control to it, you can do so by including the NO_ACTIVATE option in the OPEN_FORM built-in command, like this:

L 7-9

```
OPEN_FORM('SOUND_MODULE', NO_ACTIVATE);
```

You can also elect to have a new form opened with its own database connection, separate from whatever database connection is already running on that client computer. The benefit of doing this is that each form will have independent **commit** processing. When multiple forms are opened without this option, and therefore are using the same database connection, a **commit** in any form causes data in all forms to be saved. If the forms do not have a functional relationship, for instance, if one is a sales application and the other is a scheduler, you do not want records in one form to be saved just because records in another are. That is a situation where opening the forms with their own database connections makes sense. To do this, include the SESSION option in the second form's OPEN_FORM built-in command, as shown:

L 7-10

```
OPEN_FORM('SOUND_MODULE', SESSION);
```

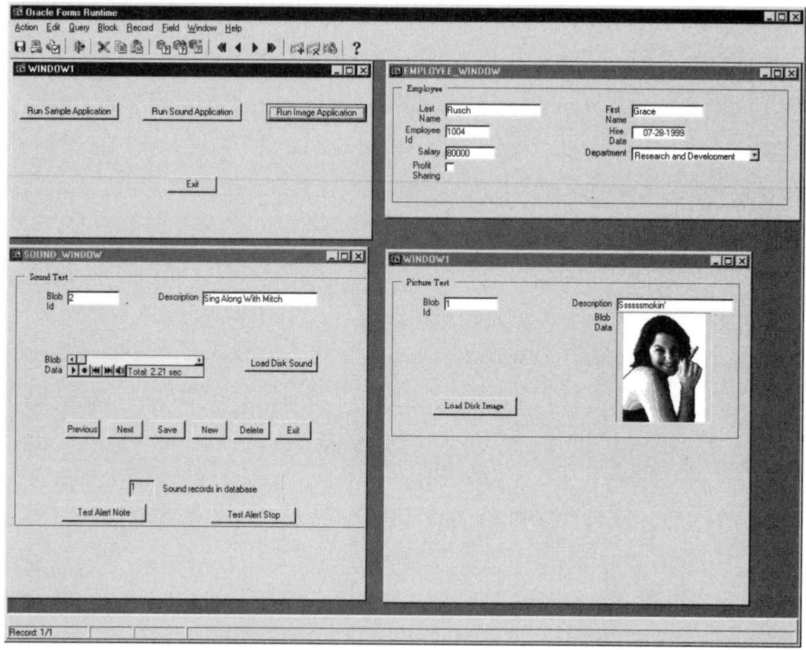

FIGURE 7-3. *Multiple forms running simultaneously*

For this to work, the Forms Runtime program must have its Session option set to TRUE. You can do that by starting the Forms Runtime program with the SESSION=YES option on its command line, like this:

L 7-11

```
IFRUN60.EXE MODULE=module_name USERID=user/password SESSION=YES
```

Another option is invoking a form and having the calling form close automatically, thereby releasing the memory it consumed. The NEW_FORM built-in performs this task. An example of this built-in is as follows:

L 7-12

```
NEW_FORM('module_name');
```

The NEW_FORM built-in has optional parameters enabling you to control what happens to unsaved changes in the parent form before it closes, whether to open the new form in query-only mode, whether to have the new form share library data with other forms, and what parameters will be passed from the calling form to the new form.

To navigate between open forms, the user can simply click on the desired form or use the Forms Runtime program's **Window** command to select a form if it is not in view. You can also control navigation between forms programmatically. The GO_FORM built-in moves focus to a form identified either by name or by internal ID, using the syntax **go_form('*module_name*');**. If you know the order in which forms were loaded, you can also employ the built-ins NEXT_FORM; and PREVIOUS_FORM; to move to the next or prior forms in the form stack.

Table 7-5 offers a reference table of form-related built-ins.

Built-In Name	Purpose
CALL_FORM	Runs a form with options to select whether the calling form maintains the focus, whether the two forms share library data, and whether the called form is to be run only in query mode
CLEAR_FORM	Flushes records from current form
CLOSE_FORM	Closes indicated form
COMMIT_FORM	Saves current form's records to database
EXIT_FORM	Closes current form
FIND_FORM	Returns internal ID of form module with a given name
GO_FORM	Moves focus to the indicated form
NEW_FORM	Enters the indicated form, exiting and closing the current form
NEXT_FORM	Moves focus to next form
OPEN_FORM	Opens indicated form with options to select whether the called form gets focus, shares library data with other forms, and gets its own database connection if required
PREVIOUS_FORM	Moves focus to prior form

TABLE 7-5. *Form Builder Built-Ins for Multiple-Form Applications*

Exercises

1. **Which built-in would you use to cause a form to run another form? Which would you use if you did not want to move focus to the new form immediately? Which would you use to run a form with its own database connection?**
2. **Why would you want to open a second form with its own database connection?**
3. **How can you cause your application to navigate between open forms?**

Chapter Summary

This chapter covered a lot of ground in the area of form programming. You read explanations and did exercises focusing on writing flexible code, sharing objects and code, and creating multiple-form applications. The subjects covered in this chapter represent about 12 percent of the material tested on *OCP Exam 3*.

You started by learning about writing flexible code, which is code that can be used by a variety of objects, in a variety of modules, without modifying the code. Code flexibility comes both from the way code is written and from its availability for use by applications other than the one for which it was originally written. One technique that makes code substantially more flexible is giving it the ability to refer to objects and values with generic names that are evaluated at runtime. Form Builder comes with many system variables to provide this ability, such as SYSTEM.CURRENT_FORM, SYSTEM.CURRENT_BLOCK, SYSTEM.CURSOR_RECORD, and SYSTEM.CURRENT_ITEM. In addition, there are dozens of built-ins to assist in writing flexible code by reading and writing object properties during runtime; their names follow a pattern of GET_*objecttype*_PROPERTY and SET_*objecttype*_PROPERTY. Form Builder also offers a handful of other built-ins that are useful when you are writing flexible code, including ADD_GROUP_COLUMN, ADD_GROUP_ROW, ADD_LIST_ELEMENT, ADD_PARAMETER, COPY, DEFAULT_VALUE, DISPLAY_ITEM, NAME_IN, and SHOW_LOV. The most unusual of these is SHOW_LOV, because it both displays an object (an LOV) and returns a Boolean value indicating whether or not the user selected a value from the object.

Another technique that can increase the flexibility of your code is referencing objects by their internal ID rather than by name. Using internal IDs minimizes the number of places where you have to change hard-coded names, and it allows you to run multiple instances of a single form simultaneously. As an added benefit, it speeds up your code because object names only need to be correlated with their internal IDs once. You can obtain an object's ID by employing one of several FIND_ built-in functions. Each object class has a matching FIND_ built-in; for instance, FIND_WINDOW, FIND_BLOCK, and FIND_LOV. If you want your form module to be able to access values in form items, parameters, and system and global variables in other form, menu, or library modules, you can use the NAME_IN and COPY built-ins to read and write values, respectively, in other modules. These items are called form bind variables, and the technique is known as *indirect referencing*.

The next subject you delved into was sharing objects and code. Reusing objects and code saves time and money, reduces rewriting errors, and ensures uniform appearance and functionality with minimal effort. The Form Builder features that support reusing objects and code include property classes, object groups, object libraries, and PL/SQL libraries. A property class is an object that holds a collection of properties, property values, and triggers that can be inherited by other objects, thereby ensuring that new objects can quickly take on the characteristics you have deemed important. An added benefit of using a property class is that if you need to change a property later, the change is automatically propagated throughout your application. A property class can hold any number of properties, including properties that apply to different object types. Once you apply a property class to an object, you can still decide which property-class properties are inherited from the property class and which are overridden.

Performing a slightly different service are object groups. An object group is a logical container into which you place pointers to other objects in a module, thereby allowing you to group related objects—even objects of different types—so they can be easily copied to, or subclassed within, another module. Object libraries, which are separate files you can create and then attach to a form as needed, provide a more powerful version of this functionality. An object library offers better subclassing features and lets you divide the objects visually into tab pages so you can locate the ones you want more quickly. Object libraries are a powerful way to make objects available to other applications, as well as to enforce standards across an organization's applications.

To facilitate reusing code in multiple modules, Form Builder offers PL/SQL libraries. These allow you to store client-side program units and make them available to any form, menu, or library module. A PL/SQL library stores subprograms, including functions, procedures, and packages. Once attached to a module, a PL/SQL library's program units can be called from your own routines, triggers, and menu item commands. You can attach multiple PL/SQL libraries to a single module, and many modules can attach to the same PL/SQL library. Because a PL/SQL library only loads its program units as an application needs them, it minimizes the demand for client-computer memory. PL/SQL libraries are created and modified under Form Builder's PL/SQL Libraries node. To use a PL/SQL library in a module, you attach it under the Attached Libraries node within the appropriate module; the attached library is read-only.

You then moved on to the subject of multiple-form applications. To create multiple-form applications, you write PL/SQL code incorporating built-ins that invoke other forms. The additional forms only consume client memory when they are called, so this is a good way to minimize your application's memory "footprint." Form Builder gives you plenty of options related to running multiple forms. A newly opened form can run simultaneously with the one that called it, or the new form can replace the old one, causing the calling form to close. Multiple instances of the same form can be run. A form can be opened but kept in the background. And multiple forms can either share the same database connection or they can have multiple independent database connections, as if they were running on separate client computers. The OPEN_FORM built-in opens a form and offers options to select whether the called form gets focus, shares library data with other forms, and gets its own database connection. The CALL_FORM built-in opens a form with options determining whether the calling form maintains the focus, whether the two forms share library data, and whether the called form is to be run only in query mode. The NEW_FORM built-in enters the called form and closes the calling form. The GO_FORM built-in moves focus to a specified form, and the EXIT_FORM built-in closes a form.

Two-Minute Drill

- You can get information about the current form, block, and item using the SYSTEM.CURRENT_FORM, SYSTEM.CURRENT_BLOCK, and SYSTEM.CURRENT_ITEM system variables, all of which return the name of the specified item. To determine the current record—remembering that records do not have names—you must use the SYSTEM.CURSOR_RECORD system variable, which returns the number of the record within its block.
- The difference between the $$DATE$$ and $$DBDATE$$ system variables is that the former gets its information from the client computer's operating system, while the latter gets it from the database.
- You can tell whether an item is visible using the GET_ITEM_PROPERTY(*item_name*, VISIBLE) system variable.
- The DEFAULT_VALUE built-in, whose primary job is to copy a value into variable if the variable is currently NULL, creates the destination variable if it is an undefined global variable.
- The SHOW_LOV built-in displays an LOV and returns a Boolean value to the calling program indicating whether or not the user selected a value from the LOV.
- The benefits of referencing objects by ID instead of by name are faster execution of code that references the object more than once and improved code flexibility and maintainability.

- You can determine an object's ID by employing the FIND_*object_type* built-in.
- The benefits of writing code that references objects indirectly are flexibility (because you can write routines that have no item names hard-coded) and the ability to share data across separate form, menu, and library modules.
- You use the NAME_IN built-in to read a value from an indirectly referenced object, and the COPY built-in to place a value into an indirectly referenced object.
- The benefits of using property classes are reduced development time due to being able to inherit customized settings for similar object types, more uniform appearance and behavior, and greater ease of propagating property changes throughout a system.
- In a Property Palette, a property whose value is unchanged from the default is marked with a small circle. Properties whose values have been changed manually are marked with a slightly larger square. Properties displaying inherited values are marked with an arrow pointing to the right. Properties whose inherited values have been manually overridden are marked with an inheritance arrow whose point is replaced with a red "X."
- Object groups enable you to group together pointers to related objects and then copy or subclass the entire group of related items to other modules in one step.
- The benefits of using an object library include increased productivity due to reusing objects and standardization by having application objects subclassed under a central library.
- Object groups are designed to gather related objects of any type into one easy-to-copy group. An object library, on the other hand, is best at making objects available for subclassing into form and menu modules. The optimal blend of the two features is to group relevant items into an object group and then copy that object group to an object library to make it available to other modules.
- PL/SQL libraries work exclusively with client-side code.
- PL/SQL libraries offer dynamic loading so that program units are only placed in memory when the application needs them.
- You can open form modules programmatically in the Forms Runtime program by using the OPEN_FORM built-in. If you do not want the new form to receive focus immediately, include the NO_ACTIVATE option. If you want the new form to have its own database connection, include the SESSION option.

- When multiple forms are running simultaneously, a **commit** in one causes all forms to save their records to the database. This is undesirable if the forms are not functionally related. Using the OPEN_FORM built-in with the SESSION option allows a new form to open with its own database connection, and therefore its own **commit** timing.
- You can cause your application to navigate between open forms by using the GO_FORM, NEXT_FORM, and PREVIOUS_FORM built-ins in your code.

Chapter Questions

1. **What built-in can you use to open a second form but keep the first form in control?**

   A. SYSTEM.CURRENT_FORM

   B. SYSTEM.MOUSE_FORM

   C. CALL_FORM

   D. FIND_FORM

   E. NEW_FORM

   F. OPEN_FORM

2. **Which system variable can tell you the record on which the user has placed focus?**

   A. CURRENT_ITEM

   B. CURRENT_RECORD

   C. CURSOR_ITEM

   D. CURSOR_RECORD

3. **Which of the following is not a benefit of referencing objects by internal ID? (Choose all that apply.)**

   A. Faster program execution

   B. More secure code

   C. Greater ease of maintenance

   D. Smaller files

4. **You are modifying a Customer form so that it has the ability to place the contents of the customer's ZIP code into a separate form named Dealer. What built-in will you use?**

   A. WRITE_VALUE

   B. ADD_PARAMETER

   C. COPY

   D. SET_APPLICATION_PROPERTY

   E. NAME_IN

5. **You have added an LOV to a form and now want to add code to determine whether the user has made a choice from the LOV or dismissed it. What built-in will help you?**

   A. GET_LOV_PROPERTY

   B. WHEN-LIST-CHANGED

   C. SHOW_LOV

   D. KEY-LISTVAL

   E. POST-TEXT-ITEM

   F. WHEN-LIST-ACTIVATED

6. **Which of the following allows you to collect objects and easily reuse them in other forms?**

   A. PL/SQL Library

   B. Object package

   C. Object group

   D. Trigger library

   E. Property class

7. **You have created a client-lookup canvas, complete with code and all the necessary objects, that has proven popular enough that others want to use it in their applications. How can you make it available to the other applications from one central source point?**

   A. Copy the canvas, code, and objects into a PL/SQL library.

   B. Copy the canvas, code, and objects into an object library.

- **C.** Copy the form module into a PL/SQL library.
- **D.** Copy the form module into an object library.
- **E.** Place the canvas, code, and objects into an object group that the other developers will reference.

8. You have inherited an application from a developer who left to pursue a career in music. While looking through the SALARY item's Property Palette, you notice that to the left of its Data Type property is an arrow with an "X" at its point. What does this symbol indicate?

- **A.** The setting for this property is invalid.
- **B.** The setting has been derived from a Visual Attributes group.
- **C.** The setting has been derived from a property class.
- **D.** The setting has been derived from a Visual Attributes group, but has been overridden.
- **E.** The setting has been derived from a property class, but has been overridden.

9. You want to read the value in an item on another form and use it in your current form. What built-in will you use?

- **A.** SET_ITEM_PROPERTY
- **B.** GET_ITEM_PROPERTY
- **C.** GET_ITEM_VALUE
- **D.** FIND_ITEM
- **E.** NAME_IN
- **F.** COPY
- **G.** SET_ITEM

10. You create a module with two forms: Employee and Product. The application allows users to have the forms open simultaneously. The users notice that when they save an Employee record, any unsaved Product records are also committed; the reverse is also true. This is not the behavior they want. What can you do to change it?

- **A.** Open the first form using the OPEN_FORM built-in with the SESSION option.

B. Open the second form using the OPEN_FORM built-in with the SESSION option.

C. Open the first form using the OPEN_FORM built-in with the ACTIVATE option.

D. Open the second form using the GO_FORM built-in with the ACTIVATE option.

E. Open the second form using the GO_FORM built-in with the NO_ACTIVATE option.

11. You need a built-in that will copy a value into a global variable and create the variable if it is undefined. What built-in has this ability?

A. DEFAULT_VALUE

B. COPY

C. SET_VAR

D. CREATE_VAR

12. You are writing versatile code that checks whether your Employee form's Salary field is visible. If it is, the code hides it; if it isn't, the code shows it. What built-in can you use to determine which route the code will take?

A. GET_FORM_PROPERTY

B. GET_BLOCK_PROPERTY

C. GET_RECORD_PROPERTY

D. GET_ITEM_PROPERTY

E. GET_VIEW_PROPERTY

F. GET_WINDOW_PROPERTY

13. You want to use a single multipage tab canvas for different purposes. Which built-in lets you set the labels for the pages dynamically when the application is running?

A. SET_CANVAS_PROPERTY

B. SET_TAB_PROPERTY

C. SET_TAB_PAGE_PROPERTY

D. SET_PAGE_PROPERTY

Answers to Chapter Questions

1. F. OPEN_FORM

Explanation The OPEN_FORM built-in includes a NO_ACTIVATE option stipulating that the form being opened should not receive control.

2. D. CURSOR_RECORD

Explanation This is a record-level requirement, so the ITEM variables will not help you. There is no CURRENT_RECORD system variable.

3. B, D. More secure code, Smaller files

Explanation The type of object reference you use in your code does not affect security or guarantee smaller files. It does, however, improve the speed at which the code can run if the reference is used more than once, and it simplifies maintenance by allowing you to change an object's name only once within a code segment.

4. C. COPY

Explanation This question requires the use of form bind variables, which cannot be referenced directly across modules. The built-ins NAME_IN and COPY are used to read and write values across modules with form bind variables. In this case, COPY is the right choice, because you wish to place values in another field, rather than read them from the field.

5. C. SHOW_LOV

Explanation The SHOW_LOV built-in has the ability to display an object (an LOV), and also return a Boolean value to the calling program indicating whether or not the user selected a value from the LOV. If you selected one of the WHEN- or POST- choices, be sure to reread the chapter before the exam—those are triggers, not built-ins.

6. C. Object group

Explanation Review the section "Grouping Related Items for Reuse" if you need a refresher on this topic.

7. B. Copy the canvas, code, and objects into an object library.

Explanation Review the section "Reusing Objects from an Object Library" if you need a refresher on this topic.

8. E. The setting has been derived from a property class, but has been overridden.

Explanation A Data Type property can only be derived from a property class. The arrow indicates that this has been done. The "X" at its point indicates that the setting inherited from the property class has been manually overridden for this item.

9. E. NAME_IN

Explanation Some of the built-in names offered as choices don't exist. Of the ones that do, NAME_IN and COPY are used to read and write values from/to items in other form modules. In this case, NAME_IN is the right choice, because you wish to read a value in another field.

10. B. Open the second form using the OPEN_FORM built-in with the SESSION option.

Explanation Review the section "Calling One Form from Another" if you need a refresher on this topic.

11. A. DEFAULT_VALUE

Explanation Review the section "Built-In Subprograms that Assist Flexible Coding" if you need a refresher on this topic.

12. D. GET_ITEM_PROPERTY

Explanation Visibility is an item-level property, so you would use the GET_ITEM_PROPERTY to determine the current status.

13. C. SET_TAB_PAGE_PROPERTY

Explanation Review the section titled "Built-In Subprograms that Assist Flexible Coding" if you need a refresher on this topic.

PART II

Preparing for OCP Exam 4: Build Internet Applications II

CHAPTER 8

Working with Menu Modules

n this chapter, you will cover the following facets of working with menu modules:

- Creating menu modules
- Managing menu modules

Menus are a fact of life in modern application development. Form Builder has features that make it extremely easy to create custom menus for your applications. In this chapter, you will learn how to create custom menus and toolbars, including context-sensitive pop-up menus. In addition, you will learn to control menus programmatically, including determining which menu is active at a given time and which items within the active menu are available to the user. The contents of this chapter constitute about 13 percent of the material tested on *OCP Exam 4*.

Creating Menu Modules

In this section, you will explore the following points related to creating menu modules:

- Menu components
- Creating, saving, and attaching menu modules
- Setting menu properties using the Property Palette
- Creating menu toolbars
- Creating pop-up menus

This section lays the groundwork of knowledge you need to create your own menus and toolbars. You will start with an introduction to the components of a menu and the Menu Editor. With that as a basis, you will then learn how to create custom horizontal and vertical menus, how to easily generate horizontal and vertical toolbars containing buttons corresponding to items in your menus, and how to create context-sensitive pop-up menus that appear when the user right-clicks on an object.

Menu Components

Form Builder provides a Menu Editor that enables you to design menus graphically. Shown in Figure 8-1, the Menu Editor provides a layout that will be familiar by now: a toolbar of buttons at the top providing quick access to often-used functions, a drop-down list to change which object is being viewed, and a design area where you do your work graphically. In addition, starting the Menu Editor alters Form

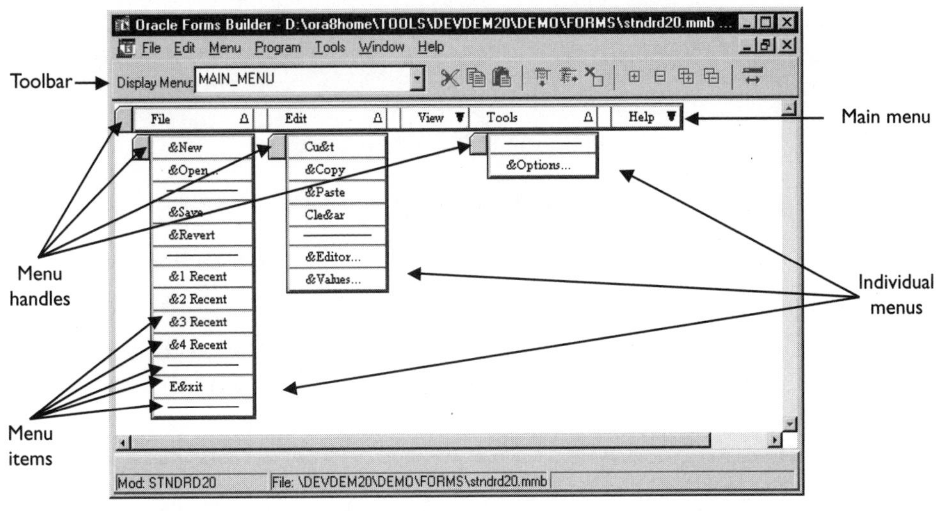

FIGURE 8-1. *Menu Editor sample screen*

Builder's menus, replacing the View and Navigator menu categories with a single Menu category.

When you build a custom menu, the menu itself cannot do any work; it serves only to organize the objects contained within it. The *main menu* organizes *individual menus*. Each individual menu organizes *menu items*, which provide access to the actual functions you build into the menu system. Although all of these different types of objects are stored in a single menu module (**.mmb**) file, they have a hierarchical relationship with each other. This is reflected within the Object Navigator by a traditional tree layout. Figure 8-2 depicts how selecting an item in the Menu Editor causes that item to be selected in the Object Navigator's object tree. The reverse is also true: Select an item in the Object Navigator's object tree and it will be selected in the Menu Editor as well.

In the Menu Editor, individual menus can be expanded or collapsed by clicking on the arrow to the right of each menu name. For instance, in Figure 8-1, the File, Edit, and Tools menus are all open, and to the right of each of their names is a small, hollow, upward-pointing arrow. Clicking on that arrow would cause the items in the individual menu to collapse upward; the items would no longer be visible. Conversely, the View and Help menus are closed, reflected not only by the lack of menu items beneath them, but also by the small, solid, downward-pointing arrow to the right of their names. Clicking on that arrow would cause the menu to expand, exposing its items.

To the left of each menu's top-left corner is a small gray tab. This is the *menu handle*, which enables you to drag the entire menu from place to place.

Exercise

1. **What actions can the main menu object perform?**

Creating, Saving, and Attaching Menu Modules

To create a menu, you start by adding a new menu module to Form Builder. To do this, click on the Form Builder Menus node, followed by the Create button. Change the menu's name to **SOUND_MENU**. Then, double-click on your new menu module to open a Menu Editor for it. The editor will open with a single menu item whose name is MENU1 and whose label says <New_Item>. Change the label to

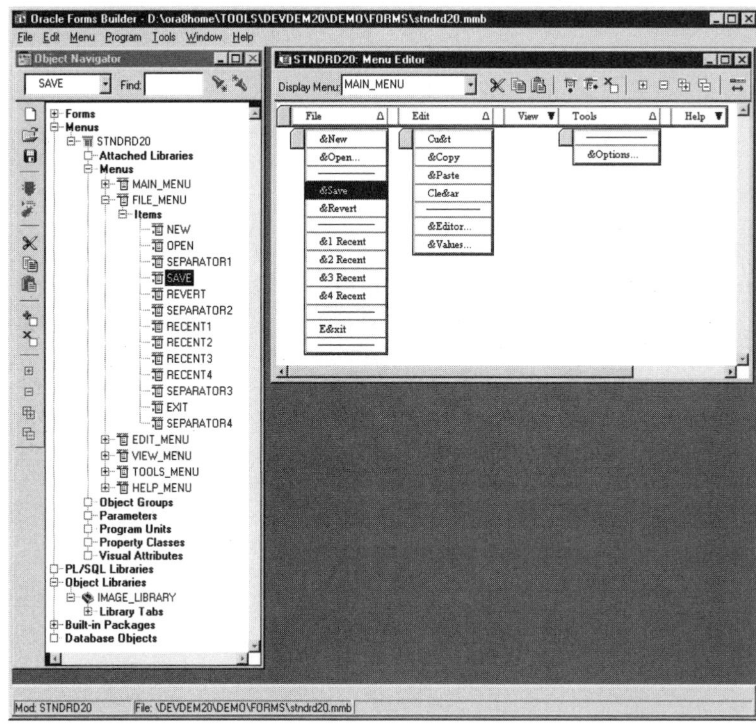

FIGURE 8-2. *Menu item selection coordination*

Action and then click on the Create Right button to create an additional menu item to the right. The Create Right button looks like the following:

Label the new item **Edit**. Use the same technique to create three more menu items named **Record**, **Field**, and **Help**. Then return to the Object Navigator, and change the MENU1 menu's name to **MAIN_MENU**. You now have a main menu.

To create individual menus beneath your main menu, return to the Menu Editor and click on the Action menu item. Then, click on the Create Down button, shown in the following illustration:

This will create a new individual menu whose name will show in the Object Navigator as ACTION_MENU. Change the label of the first item in this menu so that it reads **&Save** (the **&** in front of a character indicates that the character will give one-key access to that menu choice). Click on the Create Down button again, and label the new item **SEPARATOR1**. Add a third item, and label it **E&xit**. Continue this process until your menu structure looks like the one shown in Figure 8-3.

To make the menu items labeled SEPARATOR look like standard separator lines, select them all (using CTRL-clicking), open the Property Palette, and change their Menu Item Type property to Separator. If you want to change the order of items in the menus, you can either drag the items in the Menu Editor and let them go at their new position or perform the same type of drag-and-drop within the Object Navigator. Item order in the Menu Editor and the Object Navigator is inseparably linked.

Now that you have created the menu structure, you need to write the PL/SQL code that each menu item will execute. To do this, select your own menu's Action | Save item and open its Property Palette. Ensure that its Menu Item Type property is set to Plain, and that its Command Type property is set to **PL/SQL**. Then click on the Menu Item Code property's value area, and a More . . . button will appear. Click on that button, and the PL/SQL Editor will open. Enter the following code:

L 8-1

```
DO_KEY('COMMIT_FORM');
```

You can stay in the PL/SQL Editor and enter code for each of the other menu items. Above the PL/SQL Editor's code-entry area is a field labeled Name that gives you

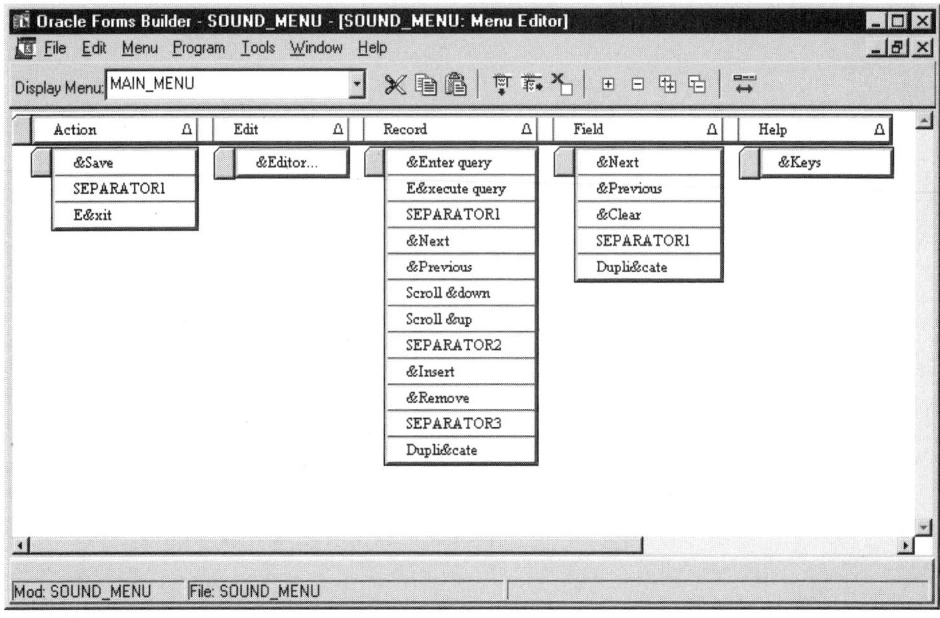

FIGURE 8-3. *Custom menu example*

access to the other menu items in the current menu. To change menus, utilize the field labeled Object. Use these now to enter the code shown in Table 8-1.

You now have a complete, working menu. However, your SOUND_MODULE form module does not yet know about this menu. To attach this menu to the form module, start by saving the menu module with the name **SOUND_MENU.mmb**. Then select its SOUND_MENU menu module object in the Object Navigator and compile it by executing the File | Administration | Compile File command. This will create a SOUND_MENU.mmx file on your disk; this is the file that you will attach to your form. To do this, open the SOUND_MODULE form module (if it is not already open), select its name in the Object Navigator, open the Property Palette, and change its Menu Module property from DEFAULT&SMARTBAR to **SOUND_MENU**. (If you stored the menu module somewhere other than Developer's default path, you will need to enter the entire file path, along with the filename.) Then run your form. In the Forms Runtime program, execute your own menu's Record | Execute menu command to populate the form with data, and then experiment with your other menu items. When you are done, exit from the Forms Runtime program and return to Form Builder.

Menu Item	PL/SQL Code
Action | Save	`DO_KEY('COMMIT_FORM');`
Action | Exit	`DO_KEY('EXIT_FORM');`
Edit | Editor	`DO_KEY('EDIT');`
Record | Enter Query	`DO_KEY('ENTER_QUERY');`
Record | Execute Query	`DO_KEY('EXECUTE_QUERY');`
Record | Next	`DO_KEY('DOWN');`
Record | Previous	`DO_KEY('UP');`
Record | Scroll down	`DO_KEY('SCROLL_DOWN');`
Record | Scroll up	`DO_KEY('SCROLL_UP');`
Record | Insert	`DO_KEY('CREATE_RECORD');`
Record | Remove	`DO_KEY('DELETE_RECORD');`
Record | Duplicate	`DO_KEY('DUPLICATE_RECORD');`
Field | Next	`DO_KEY('NEXT_ITEM');`
Field | Previous	`DO_KEY('PREVIOUS_ITEM');`
Field | Clear	`DO_KEY('CLEAR_ITEM');`
Field |Duplicate	`DO_KEY('DUPLICATE_ITEM');`
Help | Keys	`DO_KEY('SHOW_KEYS');`

TABLE 8-1. *PL/SQL Code for SOUND_MENU Menu*

Exercises

1. **Define the major steps necessary to create a menu module and attach it to a form.**
2. **What is the purpose of the Menu Editor?**
3. **Name two techniques for changing the order of items in a menu.**
4. **What is the most important difference in functionality between a menu and a menu item?**

Setting Menu Properties Using the Property Palette

Numerous menu item properties are worth knowing. Table 8-2 shows these properties, their locations in the Property Palette, and what they do. Some of these properties will only be used when a menu item is created, whereas others are candidates for real-time manipulation using built-ins, which will be covered in a future section.

Exercises

1. **Which menu item property could you manipulate at runtime to gray out an item?**
2. **What type of menu item is best for implementing common functions such as Cut, Paste, and Quit?**

Creating Menu Toolbars

The items you create in menus can also be represented in custom toolbars very easily. All you need to do is enable the Visible In Horizontal Menu Toolbar or Visible In Vertical Menu Toolbar property in the menu item's Property Palette, and specify an icon to depict the item's functionality in the toolbar. To see a quick example of this in action, take the steps on page 294.

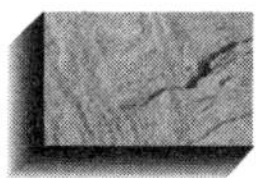

NOTE
*In those steps, you will be directed to associate a graphics file with a menu item. The graphics files used in the following example are provided with Oracle Forms 6*i *and its predecessor, Forms 5 (part of Oracle Developer/2000). The installer for Oracle Forms 6*i *places the files in the directory <oracle_home>*\FORMS60\ORACLE\FORMS\ICONS\, *so place that full path at the beginning of each Icon Filename value that follows. Sometimes the installer for Oracle Forms 6*i *does not install these graphics files; if that occurs, and you have the earlier Forms 5 version, then place the path <oracle_home>*\TOOLS\DEVDEM20\BIN\ICON\ *at the beginning of each Icon Filename value instead.*

Property Node	Property Name	Function
Functional	Enabled	Controls whether item is available or grayed out.
Functional	Menu Item Type	**Plain** Standard menu text item. **Check** Boolean menu item the user checks on or off. **Radio** Boolean item that is one choice within a larger radio menu group of mutually exclusive choices. **Separator** Visual separating line. **Magic** Item that implements predefined properties for Cut, Copy, Paste, Clear, Undo, Quit, Help, About, and Window. Predefined functionality includes item style, position, accelerator, and in the case of Cut, Copy, Paste, Clear, Quit, and Windows, functionality as well (other commands require developer to code PL/SQL commands).
Functional	Visible In Menu	Determines whether menu item appears at all at runtime.
Functional	Visible In Horizontal Menu Bar	Enables you to customize which menu items appear based on whether the menu is display horizontally (the default).
Functional	Visible In Vertical Menu Bar	Enables you to customize which menu items appear based on whether the menu is displayed vertically.
Menu Security	Item Roles	Enables you to implement menu security based on database roles; this will be covered in a future section.
Menu Security	Display Without Privilege	Determines whether menu item appears for users who do not have the privileges necessary to access it.

TABLE 8-2. *Menu Item Properties*

Start by opening your SOUND_MENU menu in the Menu Editor. Select your Action | Save menu item, and then open its Property Palette. Change its Visible In Horizontal Menu Toolbar property to Yes, and its Icon Filename property to **rt_save**. Change the same properties for the Action | Exit menu item, using **rt_exit** as its Icon Filename property. Then, select the Record | Enter Query menu item and instruct it to become part of a vertical toolbar by setting its Visible In Vertical Menu Toolbar property to Yes, and its Icon Filename property to **rt_quer1**. Do the same for the Record | Execute Query menu item, using **rt_quer2** as its Icon Filename property. Then save your menu module, compile it, and run the SOUND_MODULE application. Your screen should look similar to Figure 8-4. The buttons appear in the toolbar in the same order that their commands appear in the menu, so the only way to change the order of toolbar buttons is to change the order of the corresponding commands in the menu.

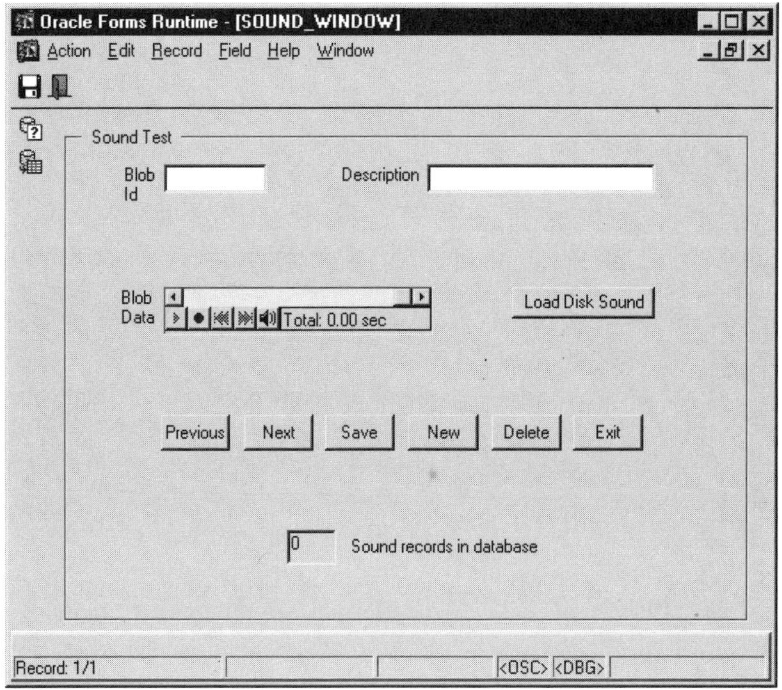

FIGURE 8-4. *Horizontal and vertical toolbars based on custom menu*

Exercises

1. **What steps must you take to make a menu item in a custom menu appear in a toolbar?**
2. **How can you change the order of buttons in a menu toolbar?**

Creating Pop-up Menus

Pop-up menus are context-sensitive minimenus that appear when you right-click on an object. They are intended to include only items relevant to the object they are attached to, so a robust application may have numerous pop-up menus, each of which is attached to many objects of the same type. Unlike the menu modules you just learned about, pop-up menus do not have module files of their own; they are owned by form modules. Look in the Object Navigator now and you will see that one of the nodes beneath your form module is a Pop-up Menus node.

To experiment with making your own pop-up menus, open the SOUND_MODULE form module in the Object Navigator (if it is not already open) and double-click on its Pop-up Menus node to create a new pop-up menu. Change the new pop-up menu's name to **POPUP_TEXT**. Then, double-click on the pop-up menu's name to open it in the Menu Editor. Use the techniques you learned in the previous section to create a menu like the one shown in Figure 8-5. Set the menu items' properties so they match the properties shown in Table 8-3.

Once that is done, you must attach the pop-up menu to the appropriate items. Pop-up menus can be attached to individual items in a data block, or to entire canvases; the latter option is useful if you want the user to be able to click on an

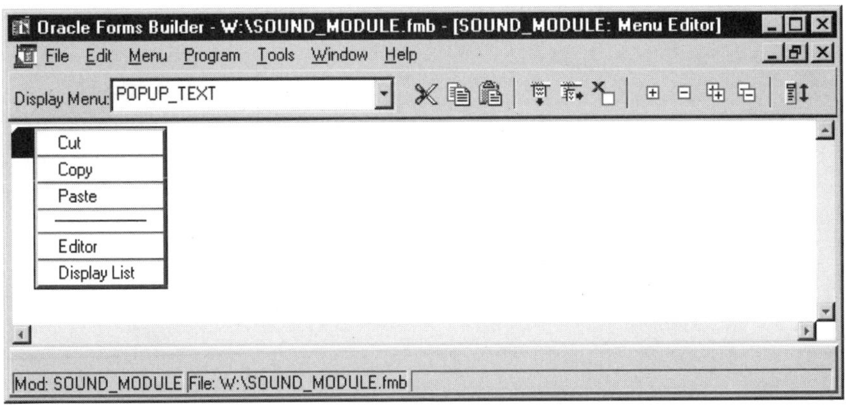

FIGURE 8-5. *Pop-up menu in Menu Editor*

Menu Item	Menu Item Type	Magic Item	Menu Item Code
Cut	Magic	Cut	N/A
Copy	Magic	Copy	N/A
Paste	Magic	Paste	N/A
Editor	Plain	None	`EDIT_FIELD;`
Display List	Plain	None	`DO_KEY('LIST_VALUES');`

TABLE 8-3. *Pop-up Menu Item Properties*

application's background and get a pop-up menu. For this example, you will attach the pop-up menu to data block items. Open the AV_DATA_SOUND data block in the Object Navigator, open its Items node, and select its DESCRIPTION item. Change the item's Pop-up Menu property to **POPUP_TEXT**. Then run your form, populate it, and right-click on the Description field. You should see your pop-up menu appear. Experiment with its functionality, and when you are done, exit from the Forms Runtime program and return to Form Builder.

Exercises

1. **To what level in an application does a pop-up menu belong?**
2. **How many pop-up menus would you need to create to provide identical right-click functionality for 12 text items on 4 different canvases?**

Managing Menu Modules

In this section, you will cover the following points about managing menu modules:

- Controlling the menu programmatically
- Customizing menu modules with substitution parameters
- Implementing menu security

Once you have created a menu, you may find that you need to control its properties dynamically. You can use Form Builder features to modify menu properties when the menu loads, or dynamically while your application is running.

You can also control access to specific menu items, ensuring that users are only able to execute commands appropriate for their work.

Controlling the Menu Programmatically

Form Builder offers a variety of built-ins you can use in your PL/SQL code to control menus programmatically. Table 8-4 lists these built-ins and provides a description of each one.

Exercises

1. **Which menu built-in would let you gray out a menu item programmatically?**
2. **Which menu built-in could you use to determine if the user checked a menu item?**
3. **Which menu built-in enables you to keep specific menu items from showing at all?**

Built-In Name	Description
APPLICATION_ PARAMETER	Displays the current menu's parameters in the Enter Parameter Values dialog box
FIND_MENU_ITEM	Returns the internal ID of a specified menu item
GET_MENU_ITEM_ PROPERTY	Identifies whether a specified menu item is checked, enabled, or visible; can also return the menu item's label
ITEM_ENABLED	Identifies whether a specified menu item is enabled; equivalent to GET_MENU_ITEM_PROPERTY (*menu_item,* ENABLED)
MENU_SHOW_KEYS	Displays runtime Keys screen for a menu module
QUERY_PARAMETER	Displays a Query Parameter dialog box containing current substitution parameters
REPLACE_MENU	Replaces current menu for all windows in an application with specified menu
SET_MENU_ITEM_ PROPERTY	Modifies a menu item's checked, enabled, or visible properties; can also set the menu item's label

TABLE 8-4. *Menu Built-Ins*

Customizing Menu Modules with Substitution Parameters

Form Builder has a feature that enables you to specify code that it will run when a menu module is loaded at runtime. It operates like an ON-NEW-MENU-INSTANCE trigger would, if such a trigger existed. This startup code is useful for initializing *substitution parameters,* which are variables that your menu items' command statements can reference. The menu startup code is also useful for initializing global variables, setting menu items' initial display states, and setting the initial status of check and radio menu items. This is a menu-level property, and can be entered by selecting the menu module in the Object Navigator and double-clicking on the Startup Code property. You can also create your own substitution parameters, if you want. A full treatment of the use of substitution parameters in menu startup code is beyond the scope of this book, so this section will serve as an introduction that you can follow up with on your own if you want.

Form Builder comes with six built-in substitution parameters, which are shown in Table 8-5. All substitution parameter names are two characters long.

Exercises

1. **What is menu startup code? What are the advantages of using it?**
2. **What are substitution parameters?**
3. **What datatype and length are substitution parameter names?**

Substitution Parameter Name	Data Returned
AD	Directory storing current menu's runtime file
LN	Current language preference
PW	Password for current user
SO	Menu item currently selected (stands for "Selected Option")
TT	Terminal type
UN	Name of current user

TABLE 8-5. *Form Builder Built-In Substitution Parameters*

Implementing Menu Security

Any form you build will automatically be limited by whatever security is in place on your Oracle server. In addition, you can also implement your own security in the client application so that certain menu items are grayed out or do not appear at all. This menu security is based on database roles—the group-rights feature built into Oracle server. Once you have roles active in your database, you can identify which roles may use which menu items.

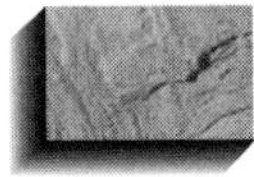

NOTE
*If you are not familiar with database roles, refer to the Oracle documentation on the **create role** and **grant role** commands before continuing with this chapter.*

Menu security is implemented entirely within the menu module. Three steps are required to implement menu security:

1. Enable the security function in the menu module as a whole.
2. Identify the database roles that have access to the entire menu module.
3. Identify which roles have access to each menu item.

For your convenience as a developer, menu-module-wide property that determines whether menu security is implemented. This enables you to disable menu security temporarily for development purposes without having to alter your menu settings on an item-by-item basis. Turning this property on is the first step toward implementing menu security. To see this in action, open your SOUND_MENU menu module in Form Builder. Select the menu module in the Object Navigator and open its Property Palette. Locate the Use Security property under the Menu Security node and set the property to Yes. If you try to run your SOUND_MODULE form now, the form will load, but the menu attached to it will not.

Next, you need to tell the menu module which database roles will be candidates to access its items. To do this, double-click on the Module Roles property. You will be presented with a dialog box in which you will enter the names of the database roles that should be able to access the menu. Form Builder does not have the capability to query the database and present you with a list of roles to choose from; you have to type the role names manually. Enter the **DBA** role now, as well as any other roles you want to add; for instance, clerk, manager, and administrator are common role types. Then click on the OK button to continue.

The last step is identifying which roles may access each menu item. You can do this in either the Object Navigator or the Menu Editor. Whichever method you choose, you can use traditional multiple-selection techniques to set the access roles for multiple menu items simultaneously. To do this from the Object Navigator, open the Menus node, followed by the MAIN_MENU node, and then the Items subnode beneath it. Select all five of the top-level menu items, and then in the Property Palette, double-click on the Item Roles property. You will be presented with the list of role names you established earlier in the menu-level Module Roles property. Select one or more roles to access this menu item and then click on the OK button to continue. Repeat this process for the items within the individual menus, and be sure that at least one menu item is *not* set to give you access, so you have proof at runtime that menu security as a whole is working. When you are done, save your menu module, compile it, and then run your SOUND_MODULE form. When you are done, exit from the Forms Runtime program and return to Form Builder.

Controlling Menu Security Programmatically

Two built-ins are especially useful for implementing menu security. The first is REPLACE_MENU, which changes what menu is displayed. The second is SET_MENU_ITEM_PROPERTY, which lets you control which menu items are enabled or visible in real time. For the SET_MENU_ITEM_PROPERTY built-in to work, you must set each item's Display Without Privilege property to Yes. Although it may seem advantageous to have items not display when the user does not have the privileges to use them, if you do so, you cannot control the items' properties programmatically, and therefore cannot make them visible again. Setting this property to Yes enables you to control an item's properties programmatically, including whether it is visible.

Exercises

1. **What are the three steps to implementing menu security?**
2. **What property turns on the use of security throughout a menu, and at what level is the property set?**
3. **What built-in enables you to change what menu an application is displaying?**
4. **What built-in enables you to control what menu items are visible or enabled at runtime?**

Chapter Summary

This chapter covered a substantial amount of information about working with menu modules. The topics covered included creating menu modules, attaching them to form modules, and controlling the operation of menu modules when they run.

The first area covered was identifying the components of menus and the Menu Editor. The menus you create start with a main menu, which contains one item for each of the individual menus. The individual menus consist of menu items, each of which performs a specific task such as Cut or Copy. The Menu Editor provides a graphical interface through which you can create and modify your menus. It displays a handle adjacent to the top-left corner of each menu; you can drag these handles to move menus from place to place. You can also move the menu items to different locations simply by dragging and dropping them. The menus and menu items are displayed both in the Menu Editor and in the Object Navigator; selecting an object in one selects it in the other at the same time. You can change the order of items from either place. You can add a separator to a menu by adding a menu item and setting its Item Type property to Separator. You can also make individual menu items accessible with a letter of your choosing by preceding the letter with an ampersand character (**&**) in the menu item's Label property.

Once you have created the menu structure, you need to write the PL/SQL code that each menu item will execute. You do this through the menu item's Menu Item Code property, which opens a PL/SQL Editor. Finally, you compile the menu module and then attach it to a form module by setting the form module's Menu Module property to the name of the menu module.

Numerous properties related to menu items are worth knowing. Some of these properties will only be used when a menu item is created, whereas others are candidates for real-time manipulation using built-ins. These properties include Enabled, which controls whether the menu item is available or grayed out; Menu Item Type, which specifies whether the menu item is a standard menu text item, check item, radio group, predefined magic function, or separator; Visible In Menu, which determines whether the menu item appears at all at runtime; the property pair Visible In Horizontal Menu Bar and Visible In Vertical Menu Bar, which enable you to customize which menu items are visible depending on whether the menu is displayed horizontally (the default) or vertically; Item Roles, which enables you to implement menu security based on database roles; and Display Without Privilege, which determines whether a menu item is visible to users who do not have the privileges necessary to access it.

Next, you learned how to create toolbars whose buttons provide shortcuts to menu item functionality. These toolbars can be either horizontal or vertical. To create them, select the desired menu item and enable either the Visible In Horizontal Menu Toolbar or Visible In Vertical Menu Toolbar property in the Property Palette. (You can enable both, although you will rarely have a reason to do so.) You must then specify an icon file to depict the item's functionality in the menu. Menu toolbars created in this way display buttons in the same order that the corresponding commands appear in the menu, so the only way to change the order of toolbar buttons is to change the order of commands in the menu. You can also create pop-up menus, which are context-sensitive minimenus that appear when you right-click on an object. You can also attach a single pop-up menu to many objects, on many canvases, within the form module that owns it.

After establishing the basic premises of creating menu modules, our attention turned to managing them. You can control menus programmatically using a variety of built-ins. These include APPLICATION_PARAMETER, which displays the current menu's parameters in the Enter Parameter Values dialog box; FIND_MENU_ITEM, which returns the internal ID of a specified menu item; GET_MENU_ITEM_PROPERTY, which identifies whether a specified menu item is checked, enabled, or visible, and can also return the menu item's label. Additional built-ins for controlling menus programmatically include ITEM_ENABLED, which identifies whether a specified menu item is enabled; MENU_SHOW_KEYS, which displays a runtime Keys screen for a menu module; QUERY_PARAMETER, which displays a Query Parameter dialog box containing current substitution parameters; REPLACE_MENU, which replaces the current menu for all windows in an application with a specified menu; and SET_MENU_ITEM_PROPERTY, which modifies a menu item's checked, enabled, or visible properties and can also set the menu item's label.

The next topic you covered was customizing menu modules with substitution parameters. Form Builder's menu-level Startup Code property enables you to specify code that will be run when a menu module is loaded at runtime. This startup code is useful for initializing substitution parameters, which are variables that your menu items' command statements can reference. The menu startup code is also useful for initializing global variables, setting menu items' initial display states, and setting the initial status of check and radio menu items. Form Builder comes with six built-in substitution parameters: AD, which returns the directory storing the current menu's runtime file; LN, which returns the current language preference; PW, which returns the password for the current user; SO, which returns the menu item currently selected; TT, which returns the terminal type; and UN, which returns the name of current user. You can also create your own substitution parameters.

The last topic covered was implementing menu security, which enables you to make specific menu items unavailable or keep them from displaying at all based on the database role assigned to the user. Menu security is implemented entirely within the menu module. Three steps are involved to implement menu security: enable the security function in the menu module as a whole, identify the database roles that have access to the menu module, and then identify which roles may access each menu item. You enable menu security using a menu module's Use Security property. Next, you identify which database roles will be candidates to access menu items by typing the role names into a list in the menu module's Module Roles property. Finally, you assign those roles to menu items using the item-level property Item Roles.

Menu security can be controlled programmatically by using two built-ins. REPLACE_MENU enables you to change which menu is displayed, as well as which role the menu should use. SET_MENU_ITEM_PROPERTY lets you control which menu items are enabled or visible in real time. For SET_MENU_ITEM_PROPERTY to work, you must set each item's Display Without Privilege property to Yes; this enables you to control item properties programmatically.

All in all, this chapter comprises about 13 percent of the material tested on *OCP Exam 4*.

Two-Minute Drill

- A main menu object holds other menus, which themselves hold menu items that can perform actions. The menu items do the work; the menus are only organizers and cannot perform any actions on their own.
- The most important difference in functionality between a menu and a menu item is that a menu's only function is to organize items within it, whereas a menu item has the capability to initiate actions by executing PL/SQL code.
- The major steps necessary to create a menu module and attach it to a form (assuming you already have a form module) are creating the menu module, populating it with menu objects and menu items, placing PL/SQL code behind the menu items to define the tasks each item performs, saving and compiling the menu module, and setting the form module's Menu Module property to point to the compiled menu module **.mmx** file.
- The Menu Editor provides you with a graphical area in which to visualize, design, and create your menus.
- To change the order of the items in the menus, you can either drag the items in the Menu Editor and let them go at their new position or perform the same type of drag-and-drop within the Object Navigator. Item order is inseparably linked between the Menu Editor and the Object Navigator.
- The Enabled menu item property controls whether a menu item is available or grayed out.
- The Magic menu item type provides predefined properties for Cut, Copy, Paste, Clear, Undo, Quit, Help, About, and Window menu items. These predefined properties include Font Size, Font Style, and Keyboard Accelerator. Additionally, the actual functionality is predefined for the Cut, Copy, Paste, Clear, Quit, and Windows menu items.
- To make a menu item in a custom menu appear in a toolbar, set its Visible In Horizontal Menu Toolbar or Visible In Vertical Menu Toolbar property to Yes, and provide the name of the icon file to display on the toolbar button for that menu item.

- The only way to change the order of buttons in a menu toolbar is to change the order of the corresponding items in the underlying menu.
- Unlike menu modules, pop-up menus do not have module files of their own; they are owned by form modules. They reside in the Object Navigator in a form module's Pop-up Menus node.
- Pop-up menus can be attached to individual items or to canvases.
- A pop-up menu can be attached to an unlimited number of items in a form module. A single item can only have one pop-up menu.
- You can gray out menu items programmatically using the SET_MENU_ITEM_PROPERTY built-in with the ENABLED parameter.
- You can determine if a menu item was checked by the user by employing the GET_MENU_ITEM_PROPERTY built-in with the CHECKED parameter.
- The SET_MENU_ITEM_PROPERTY built-in also enables you to control what menu items are visible or enabled at runtime.
- Menu startup code is useful for initializing substitution parameters, global variables, menu item display states, and check and radio menu item selection status.
- Substitution parameters are variables that your menu item command statements can reference. The built-in substitution parameters provided with Form Builder return the user's name and password, current menu item, current menu file directory, terminal type, and language preference.
- Form Builder's built-in substitution parameters are AD, which returns the directory storing the current menu's runtime file; LN, which returns the current language preference; PW, which returns the password for current user; SO, which returns the currently selected menu item; TT, which returns the terminal type; and UN, which returns the name of current user.
- The three steps to implementing menu security are enabling the menu module's Use Security property, specifying in the menu module's Module Roles property the role names that may access the menu, and identifying what menu items each role can access by setting each menu item's Item Roles property.
- The Use Security property provides quick access to whether a menu is controlled by database roles, and is set at the menu module level.
- If your application has more than one menu, you can change which menu is displayed by employing the REPLACE_MENU built-in.

Chapter Questions

1. **What actions can a main menu object perform?**
   - **A.** All File, Edit, and Help operations
   - **B.** By default, only File | Exit
   - **C.** All File and Help operations
   - **D.** None of the above

2. **You have created a form module and a custom menu, and now would like to have the menu initialize certain parameters and variables when it starts. What feature will you use to accomplish this?**
   - **A.** SET_MENU_PROPERTY
   - **B.** SET_MENU_ITEM_PROPERTY
   - **C.** WHEN-NEW-MENU-INSTANCE
   - **D.** Menu startup code

3. **You are working in the Menu Editor and would like the order of items to be different from the order shown in the Object Navigator. How can you accomplish this?**
   - **A.** Drag items in the Menu Editor to put them in your preferred order.
   - **B.** Drag objects in the Object Navigator to put them in your preferred order.
   - **C.** Using CTRL-clicking to select the object simultaneously in the Object Navigator and the Menu Editor, set the Property Palette to intersection display mode, and set the Item Order property for each one.
   - **D.** It is not possible for the order of items in the Menu Editor to be different from the order shown in the Object Navigator.

4. **You have created a menu toolbar, but its buttons are not in the order you want. How can you change the order of the menu toolbar buttons?**
   - **A.** Rearrange the order of the items in the menu from which the toolbar is derived.
   - **B.** Open the menu canvas in the Layout Editor and drag the buttons to your preferred positions.

C. Using CTRL-clicking to select the toolbar objects simultaneously in the Object Navigator and the Menu Editor, set the Property Palette to intersection display mode, and set the Item Order property for each one.

D. It is not possible to change the order of buttons in a menu toolbar.

5. **You have created a main menu object in the Menu Editor. What do you need to do to add functionality to it that the user can utilize?**

   A. Open the PL/SQL Editor and add the appropriate code for the functionality you want to provide.

   B. Create an Object Library containing the functionality you want to provide, and attach it to the menu module.

   C. Create a PL/SQL Library containing the functionality you want to provide, and attach it to the menu module.

   D. Add items to the menu, and use the PL/SQL Editor to add the appropriate code for the functionality you want to provide.

6. **You have instituted menu security based on database roles. What is the best way to turn the menu security off temporarily during development without having to modify the security property of every menu item?**

   A. Set the form module's Use Roles property to False.

   B. Set the menu module's Use Roles property to False.

   C. Remove the values from the form's Module Roles property list.

   D. Set the form module's Use Security property to False.

   E. Set the menu module's Use Security property to False.

   F. Remove the values from the menu's Module Roles property list.

7. **Users have asked you to add pop-up menus to your HR application. Under which node in the Object Navigator will you create the pop-up menus?**

   A. Forms

   B. Menus

   C. PL/SQL Libraries

   D. Object Libraries

E. Built-In Packages

F. Database Objects

8. Which menu item property controls whether the user can execute an item he or she sees in a menu?

A. Available

B. Visible

C. Enabled

D. Check

9. You want to add several items to a menu in the fastest way possible. One of the menu items will be an on/off choice; three others will be in a mutually exclusive group; and you have two others. None of the items will provide predefined functionality such as Cut or Copy. What menu item types will you use? (Choose all that apply.)

A. Plain

B. Check

C. Radio

D. Separator

E. Magic

10. What menu item type provides predefined functionality such as Cut and Paste?

A. Plain

B. Check

C. Substitution parameter

D. Enabled

E. Separator

F. Magic

11. **Your SALES application is going out to two different groups of users: salespeople on the road with Windows laptops, and administrators in the central office on UNIX computers. The groups are assigned different database roles, and you have created a different menu for each group. What built-in is the best choice for displaying the correct menu for each group?**

    A. MAIN_MENU

    B. WHERE_DISPLAY

    C. SHOW_MENU

    D. REPLACE_MENU

    E. SET_MENU_ITEM_PROPERTY

12. **Which of the following is *not* a Form Builder built-in substitution parameter? (Choose as many as apply.)**

    A. AD

    B. Add

    C. LN

    D. MM

    E. PW

    F. SO

    G. TT

    H. UID

    I. UN

Answers to Chapter Questions

1. D. None of the above

Explanation A main menu object holds other menus, which themselves hold menu items that can perform actions. The main menu object is an organizer. It cannot perform any actions on its own.

2. D. Menu startup code

Explanation See the section titled "Customizing Menu Modules with Substitution Parameters" for a refresher on this topic.

3. D. It is not possible for the order of items in the Menu Editor to be different from the order shown in the Object Navigator.

Explanation See the section titled "Creating, Saving, and Attaching Menu Modules" for a refresher on this topic.

4. A. Rearrange the order of the items in the menu from which the toolbar is derived.

Explanation Menu toolbars always maintain the item order of the toolbar that generates them.

5. D. Add items to the menu, and use the PL/SQL Editor to add the appropriate code for the functionality you want to provide.

Explanation A menu has no means of providing functionality to the user directly, so you must add items to it before you can do anything else.

6. E. Set the menu module's Use Security property to False.

Explanation The Use Security property is a menu-level property.

7. A. Forms

Explanation Pop-up menus are attached at the Forms level.

8. C. Enabled

Explanation See the section titled "Setting Menu Properties Using the Property Palette" for a refresher on this topic.

9. A, B, C. Plain, Check, Radio

Explanation The on/off menu item calls for a Check item type. The three menu items in a group will be Radio item types. The two remaining menu items will be Plain items because they are not implementing predefined functionality—the realm of the Magic item type. Award yourself an extra half-point if you included Separator items for visual clarity—but don't expect any extra points on the exam for it!

10. F. Magic

Explanation See the section titled "Setting Menu Properties Using the Property Palette" for a refresher on this topic.

11. D. REPLACE_MENU

Explanation MAIN_MENU and WHERE_DISPLAY are present in Form Builder only for compatibility with earlier versions, and will not be supported in future versions, so they should not be used. SHOW_MENU is for use only in character- or block-mode environments, so it is not appropriate for the graphical environments specified. SET_MENU_ITEM_PROPERTY enables you to control individual menu items, not entire menus. That leaves REPLACE_MENU, which fortunately fulfills the specified requirements.

12. B, D, H. Add, MM, UID

Explanation The built-in substitution parameters all have two-character names, which eliminates Add and UID. Of the remaining choices, MM is not a valid Form Builder built-in substitution parameter, but all the other acronyms offered are.

CHAPTER 9

Advanced Forms Programming I

n this chapter, you will explore the following areas:

- Programming function keys
- Responding to mouse events
- Controlling windows and canvases programmatically
- Controlling data block relationships

This chapter and the two that follow it introduce you to the world of advanced Form Builder programming. This chapter begins by explaining how you can reprogram your application's response to function keys pressed by the user. It then explores mouse events, showing how you can create triggers to respond to any mouse action the user performs. Next, you will see how to control windows, and the canvases they display, programmatically. Finally, you will learn about the triggers, program units, and system variables that work together to control data block relationships. The *OCP Exam 4* contains a large number of questions in these subject areas—32 percent of the final score—so you will want to pay special attention to this chapter and study it thoroughly until you know the answers to every one of its exercises and chapter questions. Of course, you have studied every chapter before this just as thoroughly, right?

Programming Function Keys

In this section, you will cover the following points related to programming function keys:

- Redefining function keys
- Determining when KEY-triggers should be used

Most applications currently being written are menu driven, but that doesn't mean the client computer's function keys should be ignored. The Forms Runtime program already has predefined functionality for many of the function keys; you can reprogram that functionality so the keys perform functions related to your application or so they do nothing at all. A complete treatment of this topic is beyond the scope of this book, so this introduction provides the key concepts on what function-key triggers do and when to use them.

Redefining Function Keys

You can easily assign items in custom menus to function keys, as well as create entirely new functionality using KEY-Fn triggers. Form Builder provides ten of these function-key triggers, numbered KEY-F0 through KEY-F9. It also provides a KEY-OTHERS trigger that automatically applies to every key that can have a key trigger associated with it but does not. The KEY-OTHERS trigger is useful for disabling function keys that are not germane to your application. When you use any of these techniques to assign functionality to function keys, the default functionality of the keys is overridden.

Table 9-1 shows the default function key assignments. Table 9-2 shows the triggers available for each of these assignments.

Exercises

1. **What happens to a function key's default functionality when you assign a KEY-Fn trigger to it?**
2. **What happens to a function key's default functionality when you assign a KEY-OTHERS trigger to the form?**

Determining When Key Triggers Should Be Used

Key triggers are especially useful for certain tasks, but cannot be used in certain situations. Key triggers are a good choice when you need to enable and disable function keys dynamically, disable a function key's default behavior, or have a single keystroke perform multiple actions. Disabling default behavior and performing multiple actions are two of the more interesting capabilities because they cannot be duplicated by a menu command like most function key actions can. Regarding their limitations, the KEY-Fn triggers are ignored in Edit mode, and the KEY-OTHERS trigger is ignored while the user is responding to a Forms Runtime prompt or viewing a list of values, the help or Keys screen, or an error screen. Also, certain

	F1	F2	F3	F4	F5	F6	F7	F8	F9	F10
SHIFT-	Display Error	Count Matching Records	Next Primary Key	Clear Record	Clear Block	Delete Record	Clear Form	Print		
CONTROL-	Show Keys									
Normal	Help		Duplicate Field/Item	Duplicate Record	Block Menu	New Record	Enter Query	Execute Query	List of Values	Accept

TABLE 9-1. *Forms Runtime Default Function Key Assignments*

Function Key	Associated Key Trigger
[Accept]	Key-COMMIT
[Block Menu]	Key-MENU
[Clear Block]	Key-CLRBLK
[Clear Form]	Key-CLRFRM
[Clear Record]	Key-CLRREC
[Count Query Hits]	Key-CQUERY
[Delete Record]	Key-DELREC
[Down]	Key-DOWN
[Duplicate Item]	Key-DUP-ITEM
[Duplicate Record]	Key-DUPREC
[Edit]	Key-EDIT
[Enter Query]	Key-ENTQRY
[Execute Query]	Key-EXEQRY
[Exit]	Key-EXIT
[Help]	Key-HELP
[Insert Record]	Key-CREREC
[List of Values]	Key-LISTVAL
[Next Block]	Key-NXTBLK
[Next Item]	Key-NXT-ITEM
[Next Primary Key]	Key-NXTKEY
[Next Record]	Key-NXTREC
[Next Set of Records]	Key-NXTSET
[Previous Block]	Key-PRVBLK
[Previous Item]	Key-PRV-ITEM
[Previous Record]	Key-PRVREC
[Print]	Key-PRINT
[Scroll Down]	Key-SCRDOWN
[Scroll Up]	Key-SCRUP
[Up]	Key-UP

TABLE 9-2. *Forms Runtime Function Keys and Corresponding Triggers*

function keys cannot be redefined because they are often executed by the Forms Runtime program's user-interface management system or the Oracle terminal, rather than by Form Builder. Table 9-3 lists these *static function keys.*

Exercise

1. **What are two features of KEY-triggers that cannot be attained using any existing menu command or toolbar button?**

Responding to Mouse Events

In this section, you will cover the following points about responding to mouse events:

- Introduction to mouse events
- Causing a form module to respond to mouse movement
- Causing a form module to respond to mouse button actions

Everything a user can do with a mouse in an application constitutes an event in Form Builder, and therefore can fire specific event triggers. In this section, you will be introduced to these triggers, learn what causes them to fire, and see how they can be used.

Introduction to Mouse Events

Form Builder comes with a variety of triggers that can fire in response to actions the user takes with the mouse. Table 9-4 lists the mouse triggers available and describes the action that causes each trigger to fire. To assist your programming efforts, Form

[Clear Item]	[First Line]	[Scroll Left]
[Copy]	[Insert Line]	[Scroll Right]
[Cut]	[Last Line]	[Search]
[Delete Character]	[Left]	[Select]
[Delete Line]	[Paste]	[Show Keys]
[Display Error]	[Refresh]	[Toggle Insert/Replace]
[End of Line]	[Right]	[Transmit]

TABLE 9-3. *Static Function Keys*

Mouse Trigger	Is Fired When . . .
WHEN-MOUSE-DOWN	User presses down a mouse button within an item or canvas
WHEN-MOUSE-UP	User releases a mouse button within an item or canvas
WHEN-MOUSE-CLICK	User clicks mouse within an item or canvas
WHEN-MOUSE-DOUBLECLICK	User double-clicks mouse within an item or canvas
WHEN-MOUSE-ENTER	User moves mouse into an item or canvas
WHEN-MOUSE-LEAVE	User moves mouse out of an item or canvas
WHEN-MOUSE-MOVE	User moves mouse within an item or canvas

TABLE 9-4. *Mouse Event Triggers*

Builder also provides a group of system variables appropriate for use in mouse triggers. These variables enable you to determine which mouse button the user pressed, and where the mouse pointer was when the button was pressed. Table 9-5 lists these mouse system variables and describes the data each one returns. When the Forms Runtime program executes the code in a mouse trigger, it initializes and populates any variables in the code just before running the code. Because of this, it is best to use mouse system variables only in mouse trigger code in order to ensure that the contents of the variables are up-to-date when a mouse trigger fires. You will see how to apply these triggers and system variables in the topics that follow.

Exercises

1. **Which mouse event triggers fire when the user presses a mouse button and releases it?**
2. **Which mouse system variables are dedicated to identifying the mouse pointer's location?**
3. **Which mouse system variables tell you what mouse button the user pressed and whether the button was modified with SHIFT, CTRL, or ALT?**

Mouse System Variable	Returns . . .
SYSTEM.MOUSE_BUTTON_PRESSED	Number representing the button the user pressed (1 through 2)
SYSTEM.MOUSE_BUTTON_MODIFIERS	Shift modifier held down while the mouse button was clicked
SYSTEM.MOUSE_CANVAS	Name of canvas mouse is currently in
SYSTEM.MOUSE_ITEM	Name of item mouse is currently in
SYSTEM.MOUSE_RECORD	Number of record mouse is currently in
SYSTEM.MOUSE_RECORD_OFFSET	Offset between first visible record and mouse record
SYSTEM.MOUSE_X_POS	Mouse's X-axis location on canvas or within item
SYSTEM.MOUSE_Y_POS	Mouse's Y-axis location on canvas or within item

TABLE 9-5. *Mouse System Variables*

Causing a Form Module to Respond to Mouse Movement

Three of the Form Builder mouse event triggers fire in response to mouse movement: WHEN-MOUSE-ENTER, WHEN-MOUSE-LEAVE, and WHEN-MOUSE-MOVE. All of these triggers can be defined at the form, block, or item level. When defined at the form level, they are active in any canvas or item in the form. When defined at the block level, they are active in any item in the block. When defined at the item level, they are active only when the mouse enters, leaves, or moves within the item. These triggers fire only in response to mouse movement, so they will *not* fire if the user enters a canvas via menu commands. Similarly, pressing a mouse button will not fire any mouse-movement triggers because pressing a mouse button does not constitute movement. Other triggers can be used to respond to mouse button presses, and they will be explored in the next section.

Exercises

1. **At what levels can mouse movement triggers be defined?**
2. **In what order are the mouse movement triggers likely to fire?**
3. **If a WHEN-MOUSE-ENTER trigger is defined at the form level, will it fire when the user clicks on a field within a canvas? When he or she invokes a pop-up menu? When he or she opens a normal menu?**

Causing a Form Module to Respond to Mouse Button Actions

Four of the Form Builder mouse event triggers fire in response to mouse button presses: WHEN-MOUSE-DOWN, WHEN-MOUSE-UP, WHEN-MOUSE-CLICK, and WHEN-MOUSE-DOUBLECLICK. All of these triggers can be defined at the form, block, or item level. When used in conjunction with the SET_APPLICATION_PROPERTY built-in, the triggers enable you to change your application's cursor in real time. For instance, the following code in a WHEN-MOUSE-DOWN trigger would alter the mouse cursor depending on what mouse button the user has pressed:

L 9-1

```
DECLARE
  v_mouse_button_pressed VARCHAR2(1);
BEGIN
  v_mouse_button_pressed := :SYSTEM.MOUSE_BUTTON_PRESSED;
  IF v_mouse_button_pressed = '1' THEN
    SET_APPLICATION_PROPERTY(CURSOR_STYLE, 'BUSY');
  ELSE
    SET_APPLICATION_PROPERTY(CURSOR_STYLE, 'CROSSHAIR');
  END IF;
END;
```

The action of the WHEN-MOUSE-DOWN trigger could be reversed by the following code in a WHEN-MOUSE-UP trigger:

L 9-2

```
SET_APPLICATION_PROPERTY(CURSOR_STYLE, 'DEFAULT');
```

Exercises

1. **What triggers are available to respond to mouse button actions?**
2. **Which built-in enables you to change a cursor's display style?**

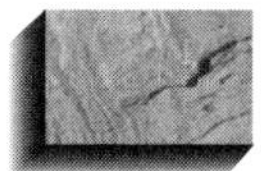

NOTE
Mouse events and mouse triggers are best suited to applications you run using the Forms Runtime program. Don't use them in applications you deploy on the Web!

Controlling Windows and Canvases Programmatically

This section will discuss the following points about controlling windows and canvases programmatically:

- Creating trigger code to interact with windows
- Controlling windows programmatically
- Controlling canvases

Almost by definition, a sophisticated application is likely to consist of multiple canvases and multiple windows. If your application has multiple canvases and multiple windows, you need to be able to control them programmatically. This section will get you started in the right direction, and will cover the topic to the degree necessary to answer the exam questions in this area.

Creating Trigger Code to Interact with Windows

Form Builder offers four different triggers that can fire in response to window-oriented events. The first window trigger, WHEN-WINDOW-ACTIVATED, fires when a window is opened or when an open window receives focus. The second window trigger, WHEN-WINDOW-DEACTIVATED, fires when an open window loses focus. The third window trigger, WHEN-WINDOW-RESIZED, fires when a window's size is changed by the user or programmatically. The last window trigger, WHEN-WINDOW-CLOSED, fires when the user executes the window-close command intrinsic to his or her operating system.

Because windows themselves cannot have triggers, window-oriented triggers are defined at the next higher level in the object hierarchy: the form level.

Exercises

1. **What window-oriented triggers does Form Builder offer?**
2. **At what level in the object hierarchy do you establish window triggers?**
3. **What trigger can help you ensure that a window is always large enough to show its contents, even if the user changes its size?**

Controlling Windows Programmatically

Form Builder provides quite a few built-ins that enable you to control your windows via PL/SQL code. These are shown in Table 9-6. Perhaps the most versatile of these is SET_WINDOW_PROPERTY, which enables you to set any of the properties you

Built-In Name	Description	Data Type Returned
FIND_WINDOW	Returns internal ID of named window	Window
GET_WINDOW_PROPERTY	Retrieves value of properties shown in window's Property Palette	VARCHAR2
HIDE_WINDOW	Hides named window	N/A
ID_NULL	Identifies whether an object created dynamically at runtime (in this case, a window) exists	Boolean
MOVE_WINDOW	Moves named window to X/Y coordinates stated	N/A
RESIZE_WINDOW	Sets named window to width and height stated	N/A
SET_WINDOW_PROPERTY	Sets value of properties shown in window's Property Palette	N/A
SHOW_WINDOW	Displays named window; enables optional X/Y position specification	N/A

TABLE 9-6. *Window Built-Ins*

normally see in a window's Property Palette, such as window size, position, and title. Built-ins are also available to manipulate a window's visual status: SHOW_WINDOW, HIDE_WINDOW, MOVE_WINDOW, and RESIZE_WINDOW.

Exercises

1. **Which three window built-ins have the capability to set a window's position on the screen?**
2. **Which window built-in can you use to change a window's title dynamically at runtime?**
3. **Which window built-in has the capability to speed up operation of the other window built-ins?**

Controlling Canvases

Because Form Builder enables you to assign more than one content canvas to a window, you need some way to specify programmatically which content canvas a window should display. This task is accomplished using the REPLACE_CONTENT_VIEW built-in. Table 9-7 shows this and other built-ins that are useful for controlling canvases via PL/SQL code.

Exercises

1. **What is the purpose of the REPLACE_CONTENT_VIEW built-in?**
2. **What built-in would you use to display a new canvas along with an existing canvas? To retrieve and set canvas properties?**

Controlling Data Block Relationships

This section will cover the following points about controlling data block relationships:

- Definition of block coordination
- Creating and modifying relations
- Characteristics of relation-handling code
- Implementing a coordination-type toggle

Built-In Name	Description	Data Type Returned
REPLACE_CONTENT_VIEW	Display named content canvas, replacing prior canvas	N/A
SHOW_VIEW	Displays named canvas; does not replace prior canvas	N/A
GET_CANVAS_PROPERTY	Retrieves specified property for canvas named	VARCHAR2
SET_CANVAS_PROPERTY	Sets specified property for canvas named	N/A

TABLE 9-7. *Built-Ins for Controlling Canvases*

This section introduces the Form Builder features related to coordinating master and detail data blocks in a master/detail relationship. You can use these techniques to work with non-Oracle databases, control when a detail block queries the database for records, and customize your application in other ways.

Definition of Block Coordination

As you probably know, creating a relationship between two blocks requires that the blocks share one or more columns in common. More specifically, the contents of the master block's primary-key column(s) must be referred to by one or more foreign-key columns in the detail block. When you define a master/detail relationship between such tables, Form Builder ensures that the detail block always displays records related to the current record in the master block, and that new detail records will automatically be assigned to the current master record. This is called *block coordination*, and it relies on triggers and program units. Each time the user does something that causes the master record to change (moving up or down in the master data block, for example, or deleting the current master record), the Forms Runtime program considers it a *coordination-causing event*. Internally, it goes to the detail data block, flushes existing detail records, makes the next master record current, and then repopulates the detail block with a new query.

You can control many facets of this process in order to customize your application's relation-handling capabilities or to augment them with new features. These facets are covered in the following section.

Exercises

1. **Describe block coordination.**
2. **What is a coordination-causing event?**

Creating and Modifying Relations

A *relation* is a logical object in Form Builder that defines how a master data block and a detail data block are related. The relation object is located under the master data block, in a node named Relations. You can create a relation in two ways: with the Data Block Wizard or manually. Not surprisingly, using the Data Block Wizard is much less work. To see this approach, you need to create a new form module and create a relation within it. Start now by creating a new form module and naming it **RELATIONSHIPS**. Then use the Data Block Wizard to create a data block for the DEPARTMENT table. Include all the table's columns as database items. When given the option, elect to *Just create the data block*. Then invoke the Data Block Wizard again to create a second data block, this time for the EMPLOYEE table. Include all the table's columns as database items. When presented with the Wizard's master/detail page, ensure that the *Auto-join data blocks* option is enabled and then click on the Create Relationship button. In the Relationships dialog box that appears, identify the master data block for the relation by selecting the DEPARTMENT data block, and then click the OK button. Back in the Data Block Wizard's dialog screen, open the drop-down list labeled Detail Item and select DEPARTMENT_ID from the available items. Your Data Block Wizard screen should now look like Figure 9-1. Click on the Next button to continue. In the next dialog screen, select the option labeled *Just create the data block* and click on the Finish button. Your screen should now look like Figure 9-2. Notice that in addition to the EMPLOYEE data block, Form Builder created a form-level ON-CLEAR-DETAILS trigger, two block-level ON-triggers under the master data block, a DEPARTMENT_EMPLOYEE relation under the master data block, and three form-level program units. These objects work together to perform block coordination.

To see the properties available for a relation, open the Property Palette for the DEPARTMENT_EMPLOYEE relation. Under the Functional node, you will see that the detail block is specified (you do not need to specify the master block because this relation is owned by the master block), as well as the SQL join condition that synchronizes the blocks. Beneath that you will see the Delete Record Behavior property. This property controls how the Forms Runtime program responds when the user attempts to delete a master record that has related detail records. The first available setting for this property, Cascading, specifies that when a master record is

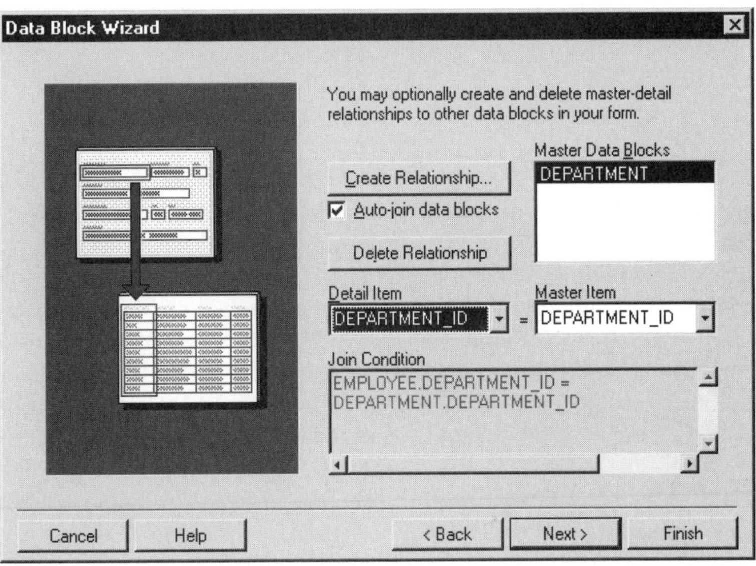

FIGURE 9-1. *Data Block Wizard master/detail page*

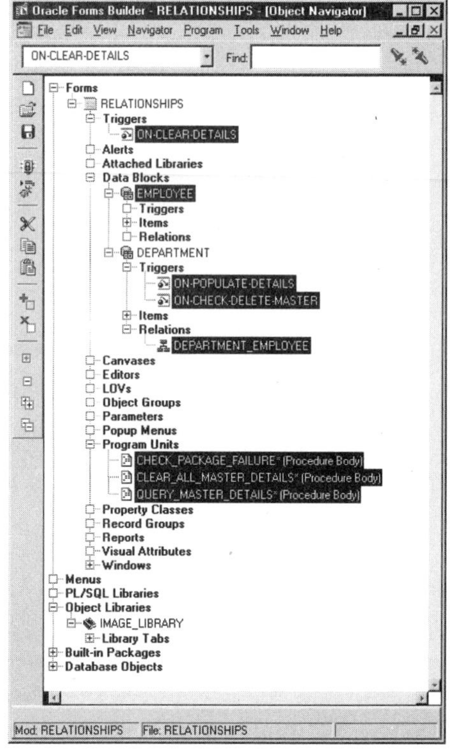

FIGURE 9-2. *Object Navigator with relation-handling objects selected*

deleted, any related detail records will also be deleted when the action is committed to the database. The second available setting, Isolated, enables master records to be deleted without deleting any related detail records, which could result in detail records with invalid values in their foreign-key columns pointing back to the master table. The third available setting, Non Isolated, causes the Forms Runtime program to refuse to delete a master record if it has related detail records. This is the default setting for this property. One fascinating facet of the Delete Record Behavior property is that changing it causes the master data block's triggers to be recreated. Setting the Delete Record Behavior property to Cascading causes Form Builder to generate PRE-DELETE and ON-POPULATE-DETAILS triggers immediately. Setting the property to Isolated causes the PRE-DELETE trigger to disappear, leaving only the ON-POPULATE-DETAILS trigger. Setting the property to Non Isolated causes the generation of an ON-CHECK-DELETE-MASTER trigger to accompany the ON-

POPULATE-DETAILS trigger. The relationship between the settings for this property and the presence of data-block-level triggers is depicted in Table 9-8.

The next property, Prevent Masterless Operations, defines whether the user can insert detail records or query the detail data block when no current master record is available. The next two properties work together to specify when the detail block becomes populated after a coordination-causing event. When the Deferred property is set to No, the detail block is repopulated immediately after any coordination-causing event in the master block. When the Deferred property is set to Yes, the next property, Automatic Query, comes into play. When the Automatic Query property is set to Yes, the detail block will be repopulated as soon as the user navigates into the detail block. This enables the user to change master records often without being subject to potential delays from having the detail block repopulate each time. When the Automatic Query property is set to No, the user must navigate into the detail block *and* execute a query to populate the detail block.

Exercises

1. **What are the three possible settings for a relation's Delete Record Behavior property, and what are the results of each setting?**
2. **What does a relation's Prevent Masterless Operations property do?**
3. **How many usable combinations of the Deferred and the Automatic Query properties can there be? What are the results of each combination? In what conditions would each be useful?**

Characteristics of Relation-Handling Code

At times, you may want to write your own block-coordination code: when you are using non-Oracle data sources, for instance, or when your application has especially long relation chains. Three types of objects are involved in relation handling: triggers, program units, and system variables.

Property Setting	Triggers	
Cascading	ON-POPULATE-DETAILS	PRE-DELETE
Isolated	ON-POPULATE-DETAILS	
Non Isolated	ON-POPULATE-DETAILS	ON-CHECK-DELETE-MASTER

TABLE 9-8. *Triggers Generated by a Relation's Delete Record Behavior Property*

Relation-Handling Triggers

Form Builder automatically generates up to three relation-handling triggers when you set a relation's Delete Record Behavior. An ON-CLEAR-DETAILS trigger is always at the form level, and an ON-POPULATE-DETAILS trigger is at the master block level. In addition, implementing cascading delete requires the use of a PRE-DELETE trigger; this trigger deletes related detail records; this must be accomplished *before* the master record is deleted, which is why a PRE-DELETE trigger is used. If the relation's Delete Record Behavior property is set to Non Isolated, an ON-CHECK-DELETE-MASTER trigger at the master block level is used to check whether detail records exist before a master record is deleted. Table 9-9 shows each of these triggers, what they do, where to use them, and what behavior they produce.

Relation-Handling Program Units

The relation-handling triggers generated by Form Builder rely on the presence of three program units that are also created automatically when you define a relation. In your RELATIONSHIPS form module, you will find them in the form-level node named Program Units. The first program unit, CHECK_PACKAGE_FAILURE, is used by the other two program units to determine whether a PL/SQL statement completed successfully. The second program unit, CLEAR_ALL_MASTER_DETAILS, flushes detail records from the detail block when called by the ON-CLEAR-DETAILS trigger. The third program unit, QUERY_MASTER_DETAILS, fetches a new batch of detail records into the detail block when called by the ON-POPULATE-DETAILS trigger. Table 9-10 lists these program units in an easy-to-reference format.

Relation-Handling System Variables

Three of the system variables available in Form Builder are used in relation-handling code. All three are called by the CLEAR_ALL_MASTER_DETAILS program unit, which itself is called by the ON-CLEAR-DETAILS trigger. The first system variable is SYSTEM.BLOCK_STATUS, which determines whether any of the records in a block are new or changed. For instance, if you wanted to build a trigger that commits records in a block before the block is cleared, you could place the following code in a KEY-CLRBLK trigger:

L 9-3

```
IF :SYSTEM.BLOCK_STATUS = 'NEW' THEN
    COMMIT_FORM;
  ELSIF :SYSTEM.BLOCK_STATUS = 'CHANGED' THEN
    COMMIT_FORM;
END IF;
CLEAR_BLOCK;
```

Trigger Name	Object Level	Purpose	Corresponding Setting of Relation's Delete Record Behavior Property
ON-CHECK-DELETE-MASTER	Master block	Prohibits deletion of master record when detail records exist	Non Isolated
ON-CLEAR-DETAILS	Form	Clears records in a detail block	Cascading Isolated Non Isolated
ON-POPULATE-DETAILS	Master block	Coordinates master and detail blocks	Cascading Isolated Non Isolated
PRE-DELETE	Master block	Executes cascading deletes	Cascading

TABLE 9-9. *Relation-Handling Triggers*

Program Unit Name	Purpose	Called by . . .
CHECK_PACKAGE_FAILURE	Determines whether prior PL/SQL statement executed successfully	ON-POPULATE-DETAILS trigger, CLEAR_ALL_MASTER_DETAILS, and QUERY_MASTER_DETAILS program units
CLEAR_ALL_MASTER_DETAILS	Clears detail records	ON-CLEAR-DETAILS trigger
QUERY_MASTER_DETAILS	Fetches detail records	ON-POPULATE-DETAILS trigger

TABLE 9-10. *Relation-Handling Program Units*

The second system variable is SYSTEM.COORDINATION_OPERATION, which returns one of 20 possible results identifying what type of coordination-causing event fired the ON-CLEAR-DETAILS trigger. It works together with the third system variable, SYSTEM.MASTER_BLOCK, which returns the name of the master block driving the relation. Table 9-11 lists each system variable and identifies where and why each is used.

To use these system variables, you must create local variables in your code and store the values of the system variables into the local variables. An excellent example of this is found in the CLEAR_ALL_MASTER_DETAILS program unit (which is called by the ON-CLEAR-DETAILS trigger). This program unit's code follows, with boldface print used to identify the relevant system variables and the local variables used to store their values:

L 9-4

```
PROCEDURE clear_all_master_details IS
  mastblk  VARCHAR2(30);  -- Initial Master Block Causing Coord
  coordop  VARCHAR2(30);  -- Operation Causing the Coord
  trigblk  VARCHAR2(30);  -- Cur Block On-Clear-Details Fires On
  startitm VARCHAR2(61);  -- Item in which cursor started
  frmstat  VARCHAR2(15);  -- Form Status
  curblk   VARCHAR2(30);  -- Current Block
  currel   VARCHAR2(30);  -- Current Relation
  curdtl   VARCHAR2(30);  -- Current Detail Block
```

System Variable Name	Purpose	Called by . . .
SYSTEM.BLOCK_ STATUS	Reports whether a block's record status is NEW, CHANGED, or QUERY (unchanged since last query)	CLEAR_ALL_MASTER_ DETAILS program unit
SYSTEM. COORDINATION_ OPERATION	Identifies what type of coordination-causing event fired the trigger	CLEAR_ALL_MASTER_ DETAILS program unit
SYSTEM.MASTER_ BLOCK	Returns the name of the driving master block in a coordination event	CLEAR_ALL_MASTER_ DETAILS program unit

TABLE 9-11. *Relation-Handling System Variables*

```
  FUNCTION first_changed_block_below(master VARCHAR2) RETURN VARCHAR2 IS
    curblk VARCHAR2(30);  -- Current Block
    currel VARCHAR2(30);  -- Current Relation
    retblk VARCHAR2(30);  -- Return Block
  BEGIN
    curblk := Master;
    currel := GET_BLOCK_PROPERTY(curblk,  FIRST_MASTER_RELATION);
    WHILE currel IS NOT NULL LOOP
      curblk := GET_RELATION_PROPERTY(currel, DETAIL_NAME);
      IF ( GET_BLOCK_PROPERTY(curblk, STATUS) = 'CHANGED' ) THEN
        RETURN curblk;
      ELSE
        retblk := first_changed_block_below(curblk);
        IF retblk IS NOT NULL THEN
          RETURN retblk;
        ELSE
          currel := GET_RELATION_PROPERTY(currel, NEXT_MASTER_RELATION);
        END IF;
      END IF;
    END LOOP;

  RETURN NULL;
END first_changed_block_below;

BEGIN
  mastblk  := :System.Master_Block;
  coordop  := :System.Coordination_Operation;
  trigblk  := :System.Trigger_Block;
  startitm := :System.Cursor_Item;
  frmstat  := :System.Form_Status;

  IF coordop NOT IN ('CLEAR_RECORD', 'SYNCHRONIZE_BLOCKS') THEN
    IF mastblk = trigblk THEN
      IF frmstat = 'CHANGED' THEN
        curblk := first_changed_block_below(mastblk);
        IF curblk IS NOT NULL THEN
          GO_BLOCK(curblk);
          CHECK_PACKAGE_FAILURE;
          CLEAR_BLOCK(ASK_COMMIT);
          IF NOT ( :SYSTEM.FORM_STATUS = 'QUERY'
                   OR :SYSTEM.BLOCK_STATUS = 'NEW' ) THEN
            RAISE FORM_TRIGGER_FAILURE;
          END IF;
        END IF;
      END IF;
```

```
    END IF;
  END IF;

  currel := GET_BLOCK_PROPERTY(trigblk, FIRST_MASTER_RELATION);
  WHILE currel IS NOT NULL LOOP
    curdtl := GET_RELATION_PROPERTY(currel, DETAIL_NAME);
    IF GET_BLOCK_PROPERTY(curdtl, STATUS) <> 'NEW'  THEN
      GO_BLOCK(curdtl);
      CHECK_PACKAGE_FAILURE;
      CLEAR_BLOCK(NO_VALIDATE);
      IF :SYSTEM.BLOCK_STATUS <> 'NEW' THEN
        RAISE FORM_TRIGGER_FAILURE;
      END IF;
    END IF;
    currel := GET_RELATION_PROPERTY(currel, NEXT_MASTER_RELATION);
  END LOOP;

  IF :SYSTEM.CURSOR_ITEM <> startitm THEN
    GO_ITEM(startitm);
    CHECK_PACKAGE_FAILURE;
  END IF;

EXCEPTION
  WHEN FORM_TRIGGER_FAILURE THEN
    IF :SYSTEM.CURSOR_ITEM <> startitm THEN
      GO_ITEM(startitm);
    END IF;
    RAISE;

END clear_all_master_details;
```

Exercises

1. **Which trigger is necessary to create a cascading delete? At what level is the trigger defined?**
2. **What are the three relation-handling program units created by Form Builder when you define a relation? Which ones are called when a detail block is populated? When it is cleared?**
3. **Which system variable will identify the type of coordination-causing event that fired a relation-handling trigger? Which system variable will return the name of the master block driving the relation?**

Implementing a Coordination-Type Toggle

Earlier in this section you learned about the relation properties that control when a detail block is populated: Deferred and Automatic Query. Because these settings can affect your application's response time, as well as overall network and database demand, at times, you may want to change the properties dynamically or allow the users to do so. This can be accomplished using the SET_RELATION_PROPERTY built-in. To make a detail block repopulate immediately each time the user changes focus to a new master record, you can implement code like the following:

L 9-5

```
PROCEDURE make_coordination_immediate( relation_name VARCHAR2 ) IS
  relation_id RELATION;
BEGIN
  relation_id := FIND_RELATION(relation_name);
  SET_RELATION_PROPERTY(relation_id, DEFERRED, PROPERTY_FALSE);
  SET_RELATION_PROPERTY(relation_id, AUTOQUERY, PROPERTY_FALSE);
END;
```

Similarly, you could use code like the following to cause the detail block to repopulate only when the user navigates into it:

L 9-6

```
PROCEDURE make_coordination_immediate( relation_name VARCHAR2 ) IS
  relation_id RELATION;
BEGIN
  relation_id := FIND_RELATION(relation_name);
  SET_RELATION_PROPERTY(relation_id, DEFERRED, PROPERTY_TRUE);
  SET_RELATION_PROPERTY(relation_id, AUTOQUERY, PROPERTY_TRUE);
END;
```

The corollary command built-in, GET_RELATION_PROPERTY, can return a variety of useful information, including whether coordination is automatic or deferred, the names of the master and detail blocks, and the names of master and detail relations.

Exercises

1. **What built-in can you use to alter relation coordination behavior in real time?**
2. **What relation properties must be manipulated to affect this change?**

Chapter Summary

In this chapter, you have covered a substantial amount of information on advanced forms programming. The topics covered include programming function keys, responding to mouse events, controlling windows and canvases programmatically, and controlling data block relationships. The material in this chapter comprises about 32 percent of the material tested on *OCP Exam 4*.

The first area of discussion was programming function keys. You can use KEY-Fn triggers to replace the default functionality of individual function keys and the KEY-OTHERS trigger to disable any function key that can have a trigger assigned to it but does not. Key triggers are a good choice when you need to replace a function key's default behavior, enable and disable function keys dynamically, or have a single keystroke perform multiple actions.

The next area covered was responding to mouse events. The triggers that respond to mouse movement are WHEN-MOUSE-ENTER, WHEN-MOUSE-LEAVE, and WHEN-MOUSE-MOVE. These triggers fire only in response to mouse movement; entering a canvas via menu commands will not fire the mouse-movement triggers. They can be defined at the form, block, or item level. When defined at the form level, they are active in any canvas or item in the form. Defined at the block level, they are active in any item in the block. Defined at the item level, they are active when the mouse enters, leaves, or moves within the item. Triggers are also available that respond to presses of the mouse buttons: WHEN-MOUSE-DOWN, WHEN-MOUSE-UP, WHEN-MOUSE-CLICK, and WHEN-MOUSE-DOUBLECLICK. These can also be defined at the form, block, or item level. When used in conjunction with the SET_APPLICATION_PROPERTY built-in, the mouse-button triggers enable you to change your application's cursor in real time. Form Builder also provides a collection of mouse-oriented system variables enabling your code to determine which mouse button the user pressed and where the mouse pointer was when the button was pressed. The system variables that return information about the mouse's location are SYSTEM.MOUSE_CANVAS, SYSTEM.MOUSE_ITEM, SYSTEM.MOUSE_RECORD, SYSTEM.MOUSE_RECORD_OFFSET, SYSTEM.MOUSE_X_POS, and SYSTEM.MOUSE_Y_POS. The system variables that return information about what mouse button was pressed are SYSTEM.MOUSE_BUTTON_PRESSED and SYSTEM.MOUSE_BUTTON_MODIFIERS.

Next we explored controlling windows and canvases programmatically. Form Builder offers four triggers that can fire in response to window-oriented events: WHEN-WINDOW-ACTIVATED, which fires when a window is opened or receives focus; WHEN-WINDOW-DEACTIVATED, which fires when an open window loses focus; WHEN-WINDOW-RESIZED, which fires when a window's size is changed by the user or programmatically; and WHEN-WINDOW-CLOSED, which fires when the user executes the window-close command intrinsic to his or her operating system. Because windows themselves cannot have triggers, window-oriented triggers are defined at the next higher level in the object hierarchy: the form level. Form Builder also provides quite a few built-ins enabling you to control your windows, including FIND_WINDOW, SHOW_WINDOW, HIDE_WINDOW, MOVE_WINDOW, RESIZE_WINDOW, GET_WINDOW_PROPERTY, and SET_WINDOW_PROPERTY. The SET_WINDOW_PROPERTY built-in enables you to set window properties such as window size, position, and title. For controlling canvases, Form Builder offers another group of built-ins: GET_CANVAS_PROPERTY, SET_CANVAS_PROPERTY, SHOW_VIEW, and REPLACE_CONTENT_VIEW. The REPLACE_CONTENT_VIEW and SHOW_VIEW built-ins enable you to select a window's current content canvas programmatically; the former built-in replaces the prior canvas, whereas the latter lets the prior canvas to remain.

The final area this chapter covered was controlling data block relationships. This began with an explanation of block coordination, which is the process Form Builder uses to ensure that a detail block always displays records related to the current record in the master block, and that new detail records are automatically assigned to the current master record. Block coordination occurs when the user moves to a next or prior record in the master data block or deletes a master record; these actions are called coordination-causing events.

A master data block is connected to its detail blocks with logical objects called relations. A relation defines how one master data block and one detail data block are related. The relation object is owned by the master data block. Once created, a relation's Delete Record Behavior property enables you to control how the Forms Runtime program responds when the user attempts to delete a master record that has related detail records. The options are Cascading, which causes any related detail records to be deleted before a master record is deleted; Isolated, which enables master records to be deleted without deleting any related detail records; and Non Isolated, which causes the Forms Runtime program to refuse to delete a master record if it has related detail records. Changing this property's setting causes Form Builder to recreate the master data block's triggers because the triggers enforce the settings when the application is run. The next relation property is Prevent Masterless Operations, which defines whether the user can insert detail records or query the detail data block when no current master record is available. The timing of block coordination is controlled by the next two properties: Deferred and Automatic Query. The Deferred property can be considered the more extensive of the two properties because it determines whether population of the detail block is deferred at all. If set to Yes, then the Automatic Query button specifies whether the detail block will be populated automatically when the user enters it, or only after the user enters it and executes a query within it. You can set these properties programmatically using the SET_RELATION_PROPERTY built-in.

If your application requires that you write your own relation-handling code, you will utilize specific triggers, program units, and system variables. In the area of triggers, an ON-CLEAR-DETAILS trigger will always be at the form level to clear detail-block records, along with an ON-POPULATE_DETAILS trigger owned by the master data block. In addition, you can use an ON-CHECK-DELETE-MASTER trigger at the master block level to check whether detail records exist before a master record is deleted, or a PRE-DELETE trigger to implement a cascading delete from master records down to detail records. The relation-handling triggers created by Form Builder rely on the presence of three program units that are also generated automatically when you create a relation. The first, CHECK_PACKAGE_FAILURE, is used by the other two program units to determine whether a PL/SQL statement completed successfully. The second, CLEAR_ALL_MASTER_DETAILS, flushes detail records from the detail block when called by the ON-CLEAR-DETAILS trigger. The third, QUERY_MASTER_DETAILS, fetches a new batch of detail records into the detail block when called by the ON-POPULATE-DETAILS trigger. The CLEAR_ALL_MASTER_DETAILS program unit employs a number of relation-oriented system variables: SYSTEM.BLOCK_STATUS, which determines whether any of the records in a block are new or changed; SYSTEM.COORDINATION_OPERATION, which identifies what type of coordination-causing event fired the coordination trigger; and SYSTEM.MASTER_BLOCK, which returns the name of the master block driving the relation.

Two-Minute Drill

- A KEY-Fn trigger replaces the default functionality of whatever function key it is assigned to.
- A KEY-OTHERS trigger replaces the default functionality of any key that can have a key trigger associated with it but does not.
- KEY-triggers perform two functions that cannot be attained using any existing menu command or toolbar button: replacing the default functionality of all undefined triggerable keys and executing multistep PL/SQL instructions.
- The mouse event triggers that fire when the user presses a mouse button and releases it are WHEN-MOUSE-DOWN, WHEN-MOUSE-UP, WHEN-MOUSE-CLICK, and WHEN-MOUSE-DOUBLE-CLICK.
- The mouse event triggers that fire when the user moves the mouse are WHEN-MOUSE-ENTER, WHEN-MOUSE-LEAVE, and WHEN-MOUSE-MOVE.
- Mouse triggers can be defined at the form, block, or item level.

- A WHEN-MOUSE-ENTER trigger can fire whenever the user moves mouse into an item or a canvas.
- The mouse system variables dedicated to identifying the mouse pointer's location are SYSTEM.MOUSE_CANVAS, SYSTEM.MOUSE_ITEM, SYSTEM.MOUSE_RECORD, SYSTEM.MOUSE_RECORD_OFFSET, SYSTEM.MOUSE_X_POS, and SYSTEM.MOUSE_Y_POS.
- The SYSTEM.MOUSE_BUTTON_PRESSED mouse system variable tells you what mouse button the user pressed. The SYSTEM.MOUSE_BUTTON_MODIFIERS mouse system variable identifies whether the button was modified with SHIFT, CTRL, or ALT.
- The SET_APPLICATION_PROPERTY built-in lets you change a cursor's display style to BUSY, CROSSHAIR, DEFAULT (the default, of course), HELP, or INSERTION.
- Form Builder's window triggers are WHEN-WINDOW-ACTIVATED, WHEN-WINDOW-DEACTIVATED, WHEN-WINDOW-RESIZED, and WHEN-WINDOW-CLOSED.
- Because windows cannot have triggers attached to them directly, you must establish window triggers at the next higher level in object hierarchy: the form level.
- The window built-ins that have the capability to set a window's position on the screen are MOVE_WINDOW, SET_WINDOW_PROPERTY, and SHOW_WINDOW.
- You can change use the SET_WINDOW_PROPERTY built-in to alter window properties such as size, position, and title dynamically at runtime.
- The FIND_WINDOW built-in has the capability to speed up operation of the other window built-ins by providing the internal Oracle ID of a named window.
- The REPLACE_CONTENT_VIEW built-in causes the current window to display a different content canvas.
- The SHOW_VIEW built-in displays a specified canvas along with an existing canvas. GET_CANVAS_PROPERTY and SET_CANVAS_PROPERTY built-ins enable you to retrieve and set specific canvas properties.
- Block coordination is the process of ensuring that the detail block in a master/detail relationship always displays only the records related to the currently selected master record.

- A coordination-causing event is any action in the master record block that changes the current record. This can include adding, deleting, or moving among master block records.
- A relation's Delete Record Behavior property has three possible settings: Cascading, which specifies that when a master record is deleted, any related detail records will also be deleted; Isolated, which enables master records to be deleted without deleting any related detail records; and Non Isolated, which causes the Forms Runtime program to refuse to delete a master record if it has related detail records. This is the default setting for this property.
- A relation's Prevent Masterless Operations property controls whether the user can insert records or query records in a detail data block when no master record is selected.
- A relation's Deferred and Automatic Query properties work together to specify when the detail block becomes populated. When the Deferred property is set to No, the detail block is repopulated immediately after any coordination-causing event in the master block. When the Deferred property is set to Yes and the Automatic Query property is set to Yes, the detail block will be repopulated when the user navigates into the detail block. When the Deferred property is set to Yes and the Automatic Query property is set to No, the user must navigate into the detail block *and* execute a query to populate the detail block.
- Cascading deletes between master and detail blocks are executed by a PRE-DELETE trigger attached to the master block in the relation.
- The three relation-handling program units created by Form Builder when you define a relation are CHECK_PACKAGE_FAILURE, CLEAR_ALL_MASTER_DETAILS, and QUERY_MASTER_DETAILS. Populating a detail block involves the QUERY_MASTER_DETAILS program unit, which also calls CHECK_PACKAGE_FAILURE. Clearing a detail block involves the CLEAR_ALL_MASTER_DETAILS program unit, which also calls CHECK_PACKAGE_FAILURE.
- The SYSTEM.COORDINATION_OPERATION system variable identifies the type of coordination-causing event that fired a relation-handling trigger. The SYSTEM.MASTER_BLOCK system variable returns the name of the master block driving a relation.
- You can alter a relation's coordination behavior dynamically using the SET_RELATION_PROPERTY built-in. Deferred and Automatic Query are the relation properties that control coordination behavior.

Chapter Questions

1. **Which of the following functions can be accomplished only with the use of key triggers? (Choose all that apply.)**

   A. Navigating between blocks

   B. Disabling function keys

   C. Validating data

   D. Modifying data before it is committed

   E. Changing function keys' default functionality

   F. Controlling menu access

2. **Which built-in enables you to change window properties dynamically while the application is running?**

   A. SET_WINDOW_PROPERTY

   B. SET_CANVAS_PROPERTY

   C. SET_VIEW_PROPERTY

   D. GET_WINDOW_PROPERTY

   E. GET_CANVAS_PROPERTY

   F. GET_VIEW_PROPERTY

3. **At what object level do you place WHEN-WINDOW-triggers?**

   A. Form

   B. Canvas

   C. Window

   D. Block

4. **What happens to a function key's default functionality when you define a key trigger for the function key?**

   A. The default functionality is augmented by whatever code is contained in the key trigger.

   B. The default functionality is replaced by whatever code is contained in the key trigger.

C. The default functionality overrides whatever code is contained in the key trigger.

D. Forms determines each time the function key is pressed whether it should execute the default functionality or the key trigger.

5. **Which of the following actions constitute mouse-movement events? (Choose all that apply.)**

A. Clicking on a form field

B. Using the TAB key to leave a form field

C. Entering a new canvas

D. Clicking on a menu to open it

E. Executing a pushbutton

6. **What program units does Form Builder create automatically when you define a relation? (Choose all that apply.)**

A. CHECK_ALL_MASTER_DETAILS

B. CLEAR_ALL_MASTER_DETAILS

C. QUERY_ALL_MASTER_DETAILS

D. CHECK_MASTER_DETAILS

E. CLEAR_MASTER_DETAILS

F. QUERY_MASTER_DETAILS

G. CHECK_PACKAGE_FAILURE

H. CLEAR_PACKAGE_FAILURE

I. QUERY_PACKAGE_FAILURE

7. **Which property and setting will prohibit the user from deleting a master record if related detail records exist?**

A. Master block property Delete Record Behavior set to Cascading

B. Master block property Delete Record Behavior set to Isolated

C. Master block property Delete Record Behavior set to Non Isolated

D. Relation property Delete Record Behavior set to Cascading

E. Relation property Delete Record Behavior set to Isolated

F. Relation property Delete Record Behavior set to Non Isolated

G. Master block property Prevent Masterless Operations set to Yes

H. Master block property Prevent Masterless Operations set to No

8. What trigger can institute a default functionality, or no functionality, for every function key that does not have an explicit trigger?

A. KEY-FUNCTION

B. KEY-NONE

C. KEY-Fn

D. KEY-OTHERS

E. KEY-ELSE

9. Which of the following properties can be set by the SET_WINDOW_PROPERTY built-in? (Choose all that apply.)

A. Height

B. Width

C. Position

D. Title

E. Visible

F. Canvas

10. What built-in gives you the ability to change the cursor's appearance dynamically?

A. SET_APPLICATION_PROPERTY

B. SET_CANVAS_PROPERTY

C. SET_CONTEXT

D. SET_FORM_PROPERTY

E. SET_ITEM_PROPERTY

F. SET_VIEW_PROPERTY

G. SET_WINDOW_PROPERTY

11. **When you define a master/detail relation between two tables, Form Builder automatically creates ON-CLEAR-DETAILS and ON-POPULATE-DETAILS triggers. It also creates three program units, two of which are called by the ON-POPULATE-DETAILS trigger. Which two?**

    A. CHECK_PACKAGE_FAILURE

    B. CLEAR_ALL_MASTER_DETAILS

    C. QUERY_MASTER_DETAILS

12. **What built-in enables you to dynamically control when a detail block is populated?**

    A. SET_BLOCK_PROPERTY

    B. SET_ITEM_PROPERTY

    C. SET_RELATION_PROPERTY

    D. SET_WINDOW_PROPERTY

13. **What trigger is necessary for implementing a cascading delete in a master/detail relation?**

    A. PRE-CASCADE

    B. POST-CASCADE

    C. PRE-DELETE

    D. PRE-POST

    E. PRE-UPDATE

Answers to Chapter Questions

1. B, E. Disabling function keys, Changing function keys' default functionality

Explanation The KEY-Fn and KEY-OTHERS triggers are the only ways to change what happens in your application when a function key is pressed.

2. A. SET_WINDOW_PROPERTY

Explanation See the section titled "Controlling Windows Programmatically" for a refresher on this topic.

3. A. Form

Explanation Windows do not have the capability to hold triggers, so you need to define a WHEN-WINDOWS- trigger one level higher in the object hierarchy: the form level.

4. B. The default functionality is replaced by whatever code is contained in the key trigger.

Explanation See the section titled "Redefining Function Keys" for a refresher on this topic.

5. A. Clicking on a form field

Explanation The only mouse-movement triggers are WHEN-MOUSE-ENTER, WHEN-MOUSE-LEAVE, and WHEN-MOUSE-MOVE, and they only work in relation to an item or canvas. Clicking on a form field would fire the WHEN-MOUSE-CLICKED trigger. Moving out of the field with the TAB key would not because the change in focus was done with a key instead of the mouse. Entering a new canvas would qualify if it were done with a mouse, but that is not specified in the question. The same is true of executing a pushbutton. Clicking on a menu doesn't qualify because it is not a form item or canvas.

6. B, F, G. CLEAR_ALL_MASTER_DETAILS, QUERY_MASTER_DETAILS, CHECK_PACKAGE_FAILURE

Explanation See the section titled "Characteristics of Relation-Handling Code" for a refresher on this topic.

7. F. Relation property Delete Record Behavior set to Non Isolated

Explanation See the section titled "Creating and Modifying Relations" for a refresher on this topic.

8. D. KEY-OTHERS

Explanation The purpose of the KEY-OTHERS command is to replace the functionality of any key that can have a trigger assigned to it but does not.

9. A, B, C, D, E. Height, Width, Position, Title, Visible

Explanation See the section titled "Controlling Windows Programmatically" for a refresher on this topic.

10. A. SET_APPLICATION_PROPERTY

Explanation See the section titled "Causing a Form Module to Respond to Mouse Button Actions" for a refresher on this topic.

11. A, C. CHECK_PACKAGE_FAILURE, QUERY_MASTER_DETAILS

Explanation See the section titled "Characteristics of Relation-Handling Code" for a refresher on this topic.

12. C. SET_RELATION_PROPERTY

Explanation See the section titled "Implementing a Coordination-Type Toggle" for a refresher on this topic.

13. C. PRE-DELETE

Explanation The PRE-DELETE trigger is the only one that has the capability to intercept a master-record deletion, check to determine if related detail records exist, and delete those detail records before proceeding to delete the master record. A PRE-CASCADE, POST-CASCADE, or PRE-POST trigger do not exist.

CHAPTER 10

Advanced Forms Programming

n this chapter, you will cover the following areas of advanced forms programming:

- Building multiple-form applications
- Defining data sources
- Working with record groups

This chapter introduces you to some exciting areas of the Form Builder design process. It starts by describing a variety of different ways to produce multiple-form applications, and explaining how to pass data between forms when they are opened. It then proceeds to a discussion of alternative data sources that you can use to create a data block. The last section is on record groups—tabular data structures you can use not only to feed List of Values (LOV), but also to pass data to other forms, as well as to graphs. Overall, the contents of this chapter comprise about 27 percent of the material tested on *OCP Exam 4*.

Building Multiple-Form Applications

This section covers the following points related to building multiple-form applications:

- Different ways to invoke forms
- Building robust multiple-form transactions
- Passing data between forms using parameter lists

In Chapter 7, you were introduced to the concept of multiple-form applications. The section you are about to read provides much more detailed information about the features and options that are available when you create multiple-form applications. You will explore different ways to invoke additional forms, learn how to move between forms with confidence, and see how to pass information from one form to another when a new form is opened.

Different Ways to Invoke Forms

Form Builder provides three separate built-ins that are capable of invoking forms: CALL_FORM, NEW_FORM, and OPEN_FORM. OPEN_FORM is the standard built-in used for most multiple-form work. Its syntax is shown in the following example, with each available option included and set to its default value:

L 10-1

```
OPEN_FORM ('form_name',
           ACTIVATE,
           NO_SESSION,
           NO_SHARE_LIBRARY_DATA,
           paramlist_id
           )
;
```

The first option, ACTIVATE, specifies that the newly opened form will immediately receive focus. The second option, NO_SESSION, specifies that the newly opened form will share the database connection used by the calling form, as opposed to opening its own database connection. The NO_SHARE_LIBRARY_DATA option specifies that any libraries attached to the newly opened form will not share data with matching libraries attached to other open forms. The last argument specifies the internal ID (or the name) of the parameter list you want to pass to the opened form.

If your application requires that you open a new form modally so that it is the only form that can receive focus until it is closed, use the built-in CALL_FORM. Its syntax is shown in the following example, with each available option included and set to its default value:

L 10-2

```
CALL_FORM ('form_name',
           HIDE,
           NO_REPLACE,
           NO_QUERY_ONLY,
           NO_SHARE_LIBRARY_DATA,
           paramlist_id

           )
;
```

The first option, HIDE, causes the Forms Runtime program to make the calling form invisible to the user while the called form is active. The second option, NO_REPLACE, tells the Forms Runtime program to continue using the default menu module of the calling form, even if the called form has a default menu module of its own. The third option, NO_QUERY_ONLY, specifies that users should be able to insert, update, and delete records in the called form, as opposed to only being able to fetch them.

If you want to open a new form and close the one that was active, use the built-in NEW_FORM. Its syntax is shown in L 10-3, with each available option included and set to its default value.

L 10-3

```
NEW_FORM ('form_name',
          TO_SAVEPOINT,
          NO_QUERY_ONLY,
          NO_SHARE_LIBRARY_DATA
          )
;
```

The first option, TO_SAVEPOINT, specifies that changes that have not been committed will be rolled back to the calling form's last savepoint.

Table 10-1 compares the salient characteristics of each approach to opening forms. As Table 10-1 shows, the most versatile of these built-ins is OPEN_FORM because it enables you to freely navigate between multiple forms just by clicking on the form you want.

When one form opens another and the calling form has pending transactions that have not been posted, the called form is opened in *post-only mode*. This means that the calling form cannot **commit** any transactions or perform a **rollback**; it can only **post** to the database whatever changes the user makes while in the called form. If the user makes changes in the called form and then exits, the Forms Runtime program displays an alert asking if he or she wants to **post** his or her changes before returning to the calling form.

Exercises

1. **Which built-in is the most commonly used for opening forms in a multiple-form application?**
2. **Which built-in enables you to open a form modally?**
3. **Which built-in opens a new form and closes the form that called it?**
4. **When does post-only mode occur, and what are its characteristics?**

Building Robust Multiple-Form Transactions

When you create the ability to open multiple forms, you will soon be faced with a new array of needs: navigating between forms in controlled ways, determining within code what form is active and what form called it, and creating additional database connections without again asking the user for his or her logon information, for instance. This topic explores Form Builder features that satisfy those needs.

Three built-ins enable you to move between open forms: GO_FORM, NEXT_FORM, and PREVIOUS_FORM. The most versatile is GO_FORM because it enables you to jump to any form, not just the next or previous one. L 10-4 shows its syntax.

Built-In	CALL_FORM	NEW_FORM	OPEN_FORM
Purpose	Opens additional form as modal window	Closes calling form and opens new form	Standard built-in used for multiple-form applications
Parameters	HIDE / NO_HIDE, DO_REPLACE / NO_REPLACE, QUERY_ONLY / NO_QUERY_ONLY, SHARE_LIBRARY_DATA / NO_SHARE_LIBRARY_DATA	NO_ROLLBACK / FULL_ROLLBACK / TO_SAVEPOINT, QUERY_ONLY / NO_QUERY_ONLY, SHARE_LIBRARY_DATA / NO_SHARE_LIBRARY_DATA	ACTIVATE / NO_ACTIVATE, SESSION / NO_SESSION, SHARE_LIBRARY_DATA / NO_SHARE_LIBRARY_DATA
Calling Form Remains Open?	Yes	No	Yes
Calling Form Remains Accessible While Called Form Is Open?	No	N/A	Yes
Calling Form Remains Visible?	Yes	N/A	Yes
Allows Separate DB Session?	No	N/A	Yes
Restricted Procedure?	No	Yes	Yes

TABLE 10-1. *Comparison of Built-Ins that Open Forms*

L 10-4

```
GO_FORM('form_name');
```

To support applications in which multiple instances of the same form are opened, you can specify the destination form using its internal Oracle ID, instead of its (now nonunique) name.

To supply your PL/SQL code with information about the application's environment, you can use the GET_APPLICATION_PROPERTY built-in. To see an example of this, open a form module of your choosing, display a canvas in the Layout Editor, add a pushbutton to it, and enter the following code for its WHEN-BUTTON-PRESSED trigger:

L 10-5

```
DECLARE
  v_form_name VARCHAR2(80);
BEGIN
  v_form_name := GET_APPLICATION_PROPERTY(CURRENT_FORM_NAME);
  MESSAGE ('Form: ' || v_form_name);
END;
```

You can also use the GET_APPLICATION_PROPERTY built-in to provide a wealth of other system information. Table 10-2 lists the most relevant of these items.

Exercises

1. **What three built-ins give you the ability to change focus from one form to another?**
2. **What built-in enables you to determine the name and password of the current user? What parameters cause the built-in to return these data items? What parameter would cause the built-in to return the current form name? The current form filename?**

Passing Data Between Forms Using Parameter Lists

Using Form Builder, you can have one form module call another and pass parameters to the called form. You can do this in two ways: Create the parameters under the Parameters nodes in both form modules, or create the parameters in just the called form, and write PL/SQL code in the calling form that constructs the parameter list and then calls the second form. Either way, the called form must have the parameters defined already, so they must be established in the called form at design time.

To create parameters in either the calling form or the called form, click on its Parameters node and then click on the Create button. Give the new parameter a descriptive name; set its datatype and maximum length; and in the calling form, establish an initial value if the parameter is going to have a fixed value such as the name of the calling form. The parameter name, datatype, and length properties must be identical in both the calling form and the called form.

Parameter Name	Data Returned
CALLING_FORM	If current form was invoked with CALL_FORM, returns name of calling form
CURRENT_FORM	Disk filename of currently active form
CURRENT_FORM_NAME	Name of currently active form
DATASOURCE	Type of current database: DB2, NCR/3600/NCR/3700, NONSTOP, NULL, ORACLE, SQLSERVER, or TERADATA
DISPLAY_HEIGHT	Height of display
DISPLAY_WIDTH	Width of display
OPERATING_SYSTEM	Name of current OS: HP-UX, MACINTOSH, MSWINDOWS, MSWINDOWS32, SunOS, UNIX, VMS, or WIN32COMMON
USER_INTERFACE	Type of current user interface: BLOCKMODE, CHARMODE, MACINTOSH, MOTIF, MSWINDOWS, MSWINDOWS32, PM, UNKNOWN, WEB, WIN32COMMON, or X
PASSWORD	Current operator's password
USERNAME	Current operator's username
USER_NLS_LANG	Current value of NLS_LANG environment variable

TABLE 10-2. *GET_APPLICATION_PROPERTY Built-In Parameters*

To create a parameter list dynamically in the calling form, use the CREATE_PARAMETER_LIST built-in. Invoking this built-in returns a numeric value that is the internal ID for the parameter list created; this internal ID can be used in further references to the parameter list. Once the empty parameter list is created, you add parameters to it using the ADD_PARAMETER built-in. Finally, you invoke the called form and include the parameter list's internal ID as the final command argument. The following is a sample bit of code showing how these built-ins work together (remember that you would replace the portions in italics with your own values):

L 10-6

```
DECLARE
  param_list_id PARAMLIST;
```

```
BEGIN
  param_list_id := CREATE_PARAMETER_LIST('list_name');
  ADD_PARAMETER(param_list_id,
                'parameter_name',
                TEXT_PARAMETER,
                'parameter_value'
                )
  ;
  OPEN_FORM('form_name', param_list_id);
END;
```

Note that the ADD_PARAMETER built-in includes the argument **text_parameter**. This tells Form Builder that the value being passed is a VARCHAR2 text string; these have a maximum length of 255 characters. The alternative argument is **data_parameter**, which is a VARCHAR2 string containing the name of a record group in the calling form. This is useful for providing data when calling the Graphics Runtime program, a subject that will be addressed later in the chapter.

If you choose to establish parameters in the calling program permanently by adding them under the Parameters node, those parameters will become part of a parameter list named DEFAULT that is kept internally by all form modules. To send this parameter list to a called form, include its name in the calling command, as shown in the following example:

L 10-7

```
OPEN_FORM('form_name', 'default');
```

Exercises

1. **When can you define parameters to pass from a calling form?**
2. **When must you define parameters that will be received by the called form?**

Defining Data Sources

This section covers the following points about defining data sources:

- Introduction to diverse data source types
- Selecting appropriate data sources for data blocks

This section also provides a comparison of the features and shortcomings of each data source type, along with tips for selecting the appropriate data source for different application needs. These criteria will help you when the time comes to decide what data source type to explore further—after you have passed your certification exam.

Introduction to Diverse Data Source Types

So far in this book, every form data block you have created has been based on a database table. You can also create data blocks based on a database view, a FROM clause query, a stored procedure, or a transactional trigger. In the case of the stored procedure, two options are available for how the data is provided: Data is returned to the data block either in the form of a *ref cursor,* which is a pointer to a server-side cursor that is populated by a **select** statement; or as a *table of records,* which is an array-like structure sent to the client computer containing every record returned by the procedure.

The most common source for a data block is still a database table. However, other data source types have definite advantages such as increased performance, reduced network traffic, increased control and security, and shifting of processing burden to the database server. It is easy to use an alternative data source. For instance, if you have a stored procedure that you would like to use as the basis for a data block, you can simply select Stored Procedure in the Data Block Wizard's Type screen, identify the procedure in the following Procedure screen, and then select columns as you would from a database table. These steps are shown in Figures 10-1 and 10-2.

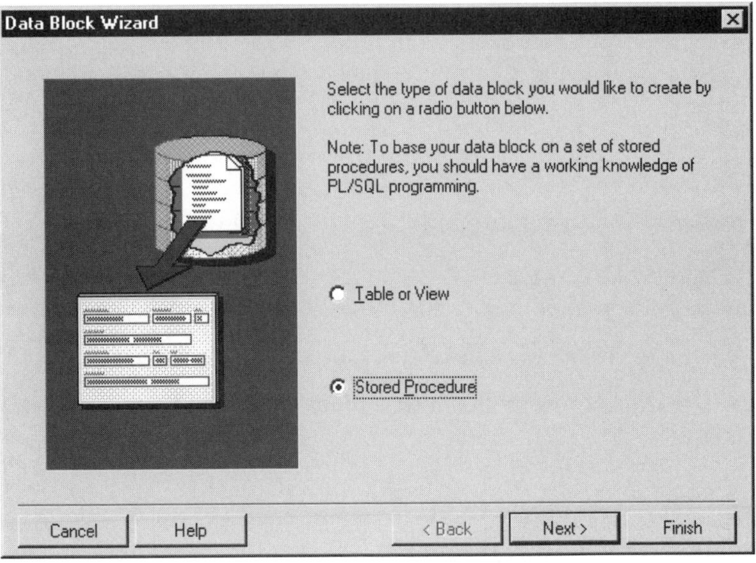

FIGURE 10-1. *Specifying a stored procedure as a data block source*

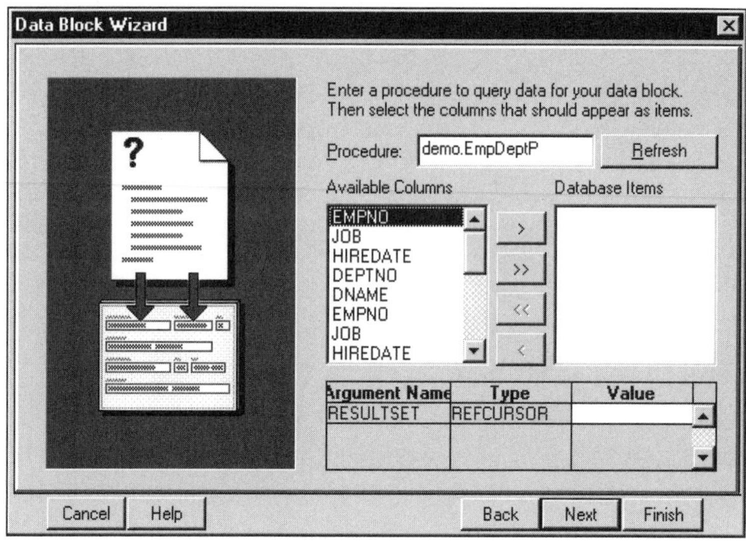

FIGURE 10-2. *Identifying the procedure name and selecting columns*

Selecting a **FROM** clause query as a data source type is almost as easy. You create a new data block manually, set its Query Data Source Type property to *FROM clause query*, and place the appropriate **select** statement in its Query Data Source Name property.

Exercises

1. **Name six types of data block sources.**
2. **What are the two types of data block sources that use stored procedures? What is the main difference between them?**
3. **What choices of data source types are offered by the Data Block Wizard?**
4. **Where do you specify that a data block should be based on a FROM clause query?**

Selecting Appropriate Data Sources for Data Blocks

You should consider many factors when deciding which data source type to use for a data block. Take a look at Table 10-3, which provides a comprehensive

<table>
<tr><th>Data Source</th><th>DML?</th><th>Array Processing?</th><th>QBE?</th><th>Advantages</th><th>Shortcomings</th></tr>
<tr><td>Table</td><td>Yes</td><td>Yes</td><td>Yes</td><td>Simple to implement, standard technique, versatile.</td><td>Can be slow on large transactions.</td></tr>
<tr><td>View</td><td>Yes</td><td>Yes</td><td>Yes</td><td>Simple to implement.</td><td>View must be created beforehand.</td></tr>
<tr><td>FROM clause query</td><td>No</td><td>Yes</td><td>No</td><td>Can perform multiple-table joins, lookups, and calculations without having the DBA create a view on the server.</td><td>Query only; no DML.</td></tr>
<tr><td>Procedure | Ref Cursor</td><td>No</td><td>Yes</td><td>No</td><td>■ Can provide better performance than table data source.
■ Increased control and security.
■ Can query and update multiple tables.
■ Can perform complex computations.
■ Can perform validation on the server.
■ Encapsulates logic with in a subprogram.</td><td>■ Query only; no DML.
■ If used to populate a detail block in a master/detail relationship, allows only the Isolated delete option.
■ Disables any Count Query Hits calculation.
■ Cannot receive a where or order by clause at runtime.
■ Does not support Update Changed Columns Only property.</td></tr>
</table>

TABLE 10-3. *Data Source Type Comparison* (continued)

<table>
<tr><th>Data Source</th><th>DML?</th><th>Array Processing?</th><th>QBE?</th><th>Advantages</th><th>Shortcomings</th></tr>
<tr><td>Procedure | Table of Records</td><td>Yes</td><td>No</td><td>No</td><td>■ Creates very little network traffic. Requires only two network trips: one to execute the stored procedure, and the other to retrieve the entire set of returned records.
■ Increased control and security.
■ Can query and update multiple tables.
■ Can perform complex computations.
■ Can perform validation and DML on the server.
■ Encapsulates logic within a subprogram.</td><td>■ Cannot use array processing.
■ Disables any Count Query Hits calculation.
■ Cannot receive a where or order by clause at runtime.
■ Does not support Update Changed Columns Only property.</td></tr>
<tr><td>Transactional trigger</td><td>Yes</td><td>No</td><td>No</td><td>Useful when running an application with a non-Oracle database.</td><td>Cannot use array processing.</td></tr>
</table>

TABLE 10-3. *Data Source Type Comparison* (continued)

comparison of each data source type's advantages and shortcomings, and you will get an idea of the number of decisions that go into selecting the right data-block source type.

You can simplify the selection process and narrow your choices quickly by asking a few key questions about the reason you are considering other source types and the data block's requirements. For instance, if you want to minimize the network traffic required to fetch large numbers of records, a stored procedure returning a table of records would be your first choice because it reduces network transactions to the bare minimum. If you need to get data from multiple data blocks and don't want to have the DBA (or yourself) create any new objects on the server, a FROM clause query is the way to go. If your users will need to update the records in the data block, your choices are limited to data source types of table, view, or stored procedure returning a table of records. If you are interacting with a non-Oracle database, a transactional trigger is likely to be your best choice. If the data block needs query by example (QBE) capabilities, your choice of data source types is restricted to table or view. If you want to implement array processing, you will limit your data source selection to table, view, FROM clause query, or a stored procedure returning a ref cursor.

Study Table 10-3 until you know it inside and out, and it will serve you well on your exam.

Exercises

1. **Which data source type enables you to join tables, perform lookups, and create calculations without having to create any new objects on the server?**
2. **Which data source type has the greatest potential for reducing network traffic?**
3. **Which data source types produce record sets that can be changed by the user?**

Working with Record Groups

This section covers the following points about working with record groups:

- Creating record groups at design time
- Creating and modifying record groups programmatically
- Building dynamic list items by using record groups
- Applying record groups in other useful ways
- Using a global record group to communicate between forms

A record group is a Form Builder object that makes tabular (column/row) data available to your application. By default, a record group is specific to the form module in which it is defined. You have worked with a record group already when you created a DEPARTMENT_LOV list earlier in the book. Now it is time to learn more about record groups and what they can do for you. Three types of record groups are available:

- **Query** A record group that is based on a SQL **select** statement. This provides a functionality similar to a database view, with two added benefits: The **select** statement that produces the record group can be dynamically created at runtime, and you don't need to add a view to the database.
- **Nonquery** A record group that can also be created and populated dynamically at runtime but has no underlying **select** statement.
- **Static** A record group whose structure and contents are defined at design time and cannot change as the application runs.

Creating Record Groups at Design Time

To create a query record group, open the sample form you have used throughout this book. Click on the Record Groups node and then click on the Create button. You will see the New Record Group dialog box, as shown in Figure 10-3.

Ensure that the option labeled *Based on the Query below . . .* is selected, and then enter the SQL **select** statement in L 10-8.

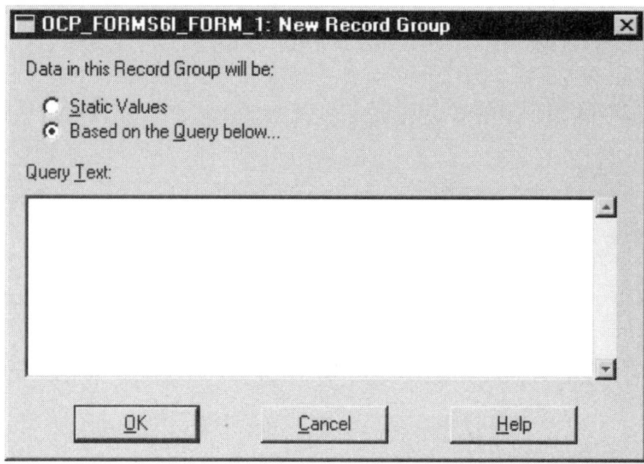

FIGURE 10-3. *New Record Group dialog box*

L 10-8

```
SELECT   d.department_name,
         e.last_name,
         e.first_name,
         e.salary
FROM     department d,
         employee   e
WHERE    d.department_id = e.department_id
ORDER BY d.department_name,
         e.salary
;
```

Then click on the OK button to continue. You will see a new record group added beneath the Record Groups node. Change the record group's name to **DEPT_EMP_SALARY**. The record group is not currently populated; it can be populated at runtime using the POPULATE_GROUP built-in, as shown in the following example:

L 10-9

```
POPULATE_GROUP ('group_name');
```

To create a static record group, click on the Record Groups node and then click on the Create button. Select the *Static Values* option and then click on the OK button. You will be presented with a dialog box similar to Figure 10-4, asking you to define the names, datatypes, lengths, and values for your static record group. For this example, create a sample STATE record group, as depicted in Figure 10-5. Then click on the OK button to complete the process. Change the name of the new record group to **STATE**.

Exercise

1. **What are the three types of record groups? What are the differences between them?**

Creating and Modifying Record Groups Programmatically

Two types of record groups can be created programmatically: query record groups and nonquery record groups. Two built-ins create record groups: CREATE_GROUP and CREATE_GROUP_FROM_QUERY. The syntax of these commands will be covered later; what you need to know to pass this portion of the certification exam is which built-in to use for a specific task.

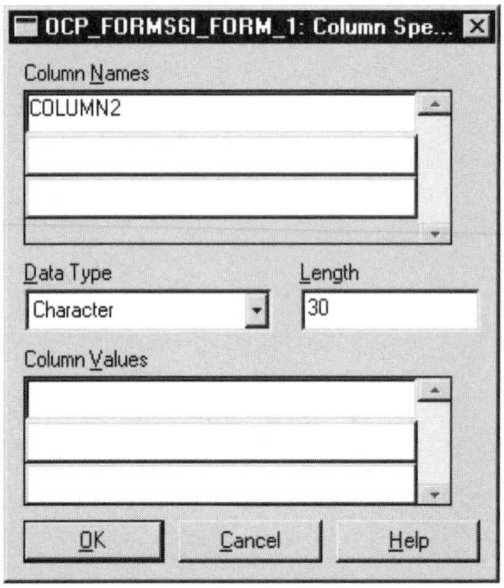

FIGURE 10-4. *Static Record Group column specifications dialog box*

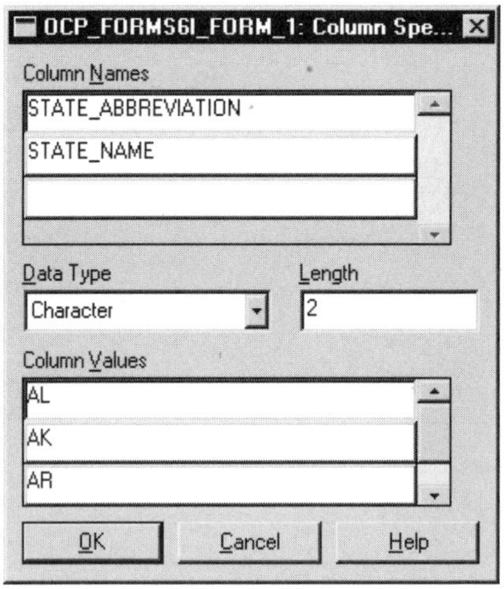

FIGURE 10-5. *Static record group example entries*

The CREATE_GROUP built-in creates nonquery record groups. Because a nonquery record group has no **select** statement to provide it with column information, you must tell it what columns to use and what to populate them with.

You can do this in two ways. If your data is coming from a queryable data source, you can use the POPULATE_GROUP_WITH_QUERY built-in to specify a **select** statement that will define the record group's structure and contents. Populating the record group in this way essentially turns the nonquery record group into a query record group. This is a useful trick when you have a record group you thought wasn't going to change during the application's lifetime and—surprise!—it is going to change after all. If the values for the record group are going to be generated programmatically, the process of populating the record group is, of course, more involved. You first define the record group's columns using one ADD_GROUP_COLUMN built-in for each column. You then add and populate rows using one ADD_GROUP_ROW built-in for each row, along with one SET_GROUP_CHAR_CELL or SET_GROUP_NUMBER_CELL built-in for each item in the row you want to populate.

The CREATE_GROUP_FROM_QUERY built-in creates query record groups. Once created, this type of group can be populated by simply executing the POPULATE_GROUP built-in. If you find you need to dynamically change the **select** statement that underlies an existing query record group, you can do so programmatically with the POPULATE_GROUP_WITH_QUERY built-in. This replaces the record group's **select** statement for the duration of that runtime session. This replacement works as long as the new **select** statement returns records with the same structure as the original **select** statement, and varies only in the content of the records returned.

Exercises

1. **Which built-in will create a query record group? A nonquery record group?**
2. **What is the simplest way to populate a nonquery record group?**
3. **What built-in will let you change the select statement underlying a query record group?**

Building Dynamic List Items by Using Record Groups

When you experimented with creating a LOV earlier in this book, a record group was automatically created to feed data to the LOV. Every LOV needs a record group. However, you can create record groups without creating LOVs, and then later create an LOV to view the records in an existing record group. The LOV can be considered a viewing portal into the record group's rows; each time the LOV is opened, the attached record group is populated automatically. You can also change the contents of the LOV dynamically, or even make the list show an entirely different record group.

To create an LOV based on an existing record group, click on the LOV's node in the form module and then click on the Create button. Select the Existing Record Group choice and then click on the Select button to choose the record group on which to base the LOV. Then click on the OK button to dismiss the Select dialog box and click on the next OK button to complete the process. Finally, rename the LOV so its name reflects its purpose.

To populate an LOV with values from a two-column record group created at runtime, use the POPULATE_LIST built-in. Its syntax is

L 10-10

```
POPULATE_LIST('list_name', 'record_group_name');
```

If you want to modify an LOV so it shows values from a record group that wasn't necessarily created at runtime, or that has more than two columns, use the SET_LOV_PROPERTY built-in. Its syntax is

L 10-11

```
SET_LOV_PROPERTY('lov_name', GROUP_NAME, 'record_group_name');
```

Exercise

1. **What are the two methods for changing the record group associated with an LOV? What are the differences between them?**

Using a Global Record Group to Communicate Between Forms

Generally, record groups remain within the scope of the form module that owns them. You can, however, specify global scope for a record group, so that it is visible to all forms in an application. You can even make the contents of a record group available to other products, such as Graphics Builder. This gives you the ability to alter the contents of a graphic element at runtime.

To make a record group available to all form modules, include the GLOBAL_SCOPE parameter in the built-in that creates the group. Thus, the syntax would be

L 10-12

```
CREATE_GROUP('record_group_name', GLOBAL_SCOPE, array_fetch_size);
```

or

L 10-13

```
CREATE_GROUP_FROM_QUERY('record_group_name',
                        'query_text',
                        GLOBAL_SCOPE,
                        array_fetch_size
                        )
;
```

To pass a record group to a graph, use the RUN_PRODUCT built-in. To do this, the record group must have the same data structure as the query on which the graph is already based.

L 10-14

```
RUN_PRODUCT(GRAPHICS,
            'graph_module_name',
            SYNCHRONOUS,
            RUNTIME,
            FILESYSTEM,
            parameter_list_id,
            'graph_block.graph_item'
            )
;
```

An example of the code to realize this function follows. The example passes data from a record group called GRAPH_RECS to a graph named DPTGRAPH.

L 10-15

```
PROCEDURE run_department_graph IS
  param_list_id PARAMLIST;

BEGIN
  --Check to see if the 'graph_data' parameter list exists.
  param_list_id := GET_PARAMETER_LIST('graph_data');
  -- If parameter list exists, delete it to ensure it contains
  -- only the parameters we want.
  IF NOT ID_NULL(param_list_id) THEN
    DESTROY_PARAMETER_LIST(param_list_id);
  END IF;
  -- Create the 'graph_data' parameter list.
  param_list_id := CREATE_PARAMETER_LIST('graph_data');
  -- Populate the parameter list with a data parameter whose key is
  -- the name of the query currently driving the graph, and whose
  -- value is the name of the record group to pass from this form.
  ADD_PARAMETER(param_list_id,
```

```
                   'GRAPH_QUERY',
                   DATA_PARAMETER,
                   'GRAPH_RECS'
                   )
  ;
  -- Run graph and pass it the parameter list
  RUN_PRODUCT(GRAPHICS,
                'DPTGRAPH',
                SYNCHRONOUS,
                RUNTIME,
                FILEYSTEM,
                param_list_id,
                NULL
                )
  ;
END;
```

Exercises

1. **How can you make a record group visible to all forms in your application?**
2. **What built-in can you use to pass a record group's data to other Forms 6*i* applications?**

Chapter Summary

This chapter covered some fascinating information on advanced forms programming. The topics included building multiple-form applications, defining data sources, and working with record groups. The contents of this chapter represent about 27 percent of the material tested on *OCP Exam 4*.

The first area covered was building multiple-form applications. Form Builder provides three separate built-ins that are capable of invoking forms: CALL_FORM, NEW_FORM, and OPEN_FORM. The standard built-in used for most multiple-form work is OPEN_FORM. If you need to open a new form modally, use the built-in CALL_FORM. If you want to open a new form and close the one that was active, use the built-in NEW_FORM. When one form opens another and the calling form has pending transactions that have not been posted, the called form is opened in post-only mode, which means that the calling form cannot commit any transactions or perform a rollback; it can only post to the database whatever changes the user makes while in the called form. Three built-ins enable you to move between open forms: GO_FORM, NEXT_FORM, and PREVIOUS_FORM. The most versatile is GO_FORM because it enables you to jump to any form, not just the next or previous one.

To supply your PL/SQL code with information about the application's environment, you can use the GET_APPLICATION_PROPERTY built-in. This built-in can return the name of the current form, calling form, and current form filename; the type of data source, operating system, and user interface on the client computer; the display's height and width; the user's name and password; and the language in which the application is operating.

You can pass data between forms using parameter lists whenever one form module calls another. You can do this in two ways: create the parameters under the Parameters nodes in both form modules, or create the parameters in just the called form and write PL/SQL code in the calling form that constructs the parameter list and then calls the second form. Either way, the called form must have the parameters defined already, so they must be established in the called form at design time.

After establishing the basic premises of building multiple-form applications, our attention turned to defining data sources. You can create data blocks based on a database table, database view, FROM clause query, stored procedure, or transactional trigger. In the case of the stored procedure, two options are available for how the data is provided: data is returned to the data block either in the form of a ref cursor, which is a pointer to a server-side cursor that is populated by a **select** statement; or as a table of records, which is an array-like structure sent to the client computer containing every record returned by the procedure. Although a database table is still the most common source for a data block, other data source types offer advantages in specific situations. If you want to minimize the network traffic required to fetch large numbers of records, a stored procedure returning a table of records would be your first choice. If you need to get data from multiple data blocks and don't want to create any new objects on the server, a FROM clause query is the way to go. If your users will need to update the records in the data block, you would look at data source types of table, view, or stored procedure returning a table of records. If you are interacting with a non-Oracle database, a transactional trigger is likely to be your best choice.

The final area covered in this chapter was working with record groups. A record group is a Form Builder object that makes tabular data available to your application. Record groups are the basis for all LOVs. Three types of record groups are available: query, nonquery, and static. A query record group is based on a SQL **select** statement, and it provides a functionality similar to a database view, with two added benefits: The **select** statement that produces the record group can be dynamically created at runtime, and you don't need to add a view to the database. A nonquery record group does not have an underlying **select** statement, and so it must be populated explicitly each time it is used. A static record group's structure and contents are defined at design time and cannot change as the application runs. Query record groups and nonquery record groups can be created programmatically.

To create a nonquery record group, you use the CREATE_GROUP built-in, and populate it either with the POPULATE_GROUP_WITH_QUERY built-in or with a series of ADD_GROUP_COLUMN, ADD_GROUP_ROW, SET_GROUP_CHAR_CELL, and SET_GROUP_NUMBER_CELL built-ins. To create a query record group, you use the CREATE_GROUP_FROM_QUERY built-in, followed by a POPULATE_GROUP built-in to populate it. If you find you need to dynamically change the **select** statement that underlies an existing query record group, you can do so programmatically with the POPULATE_GROUP_WITH_QUERY built-in, which replaces the record group's **select** statement for the duration of that runtime session.

An LOV acts as a viewing portal into the record group's rows; each time the LOV is opened, the attached record group is populated automatically. You can change the contents of the LOV dynamically or make the list show an entirely different record group. To populate an LOV with values from a two-column record group created at runtime, use the POPULATE_LIST built-in. If you want to modify an LOV so it shows values from a record group that wasn't necessarily created at runtime, or that has more than two columns, use the SET_LOV_PROPERTY built-in.

If you want to make a record group visible to all forms in an application, include the GLOBAL_SCOPE parameter in the built-in that creates the group. If you want to make the contents of a record group available to other Forms 6*i* products, such as Graphics Builder, you can do so using the RUN_PRODUCT built-in.

Two-Minute Drill

- The OPEN_FORM built-in is the most commonly used built-in for opening forms in a multiple-form application.
- The CALL_FORM built-in enables you to open a form modally.
- The NEW_FORM built-in opens a new form and closes the calling form.
- Post-only mode occurs when a user opens a new form from a form that has uncommitted changes. While in post-only mode, the calling form cannot commit any transactions or perform a rollback; it can only post to the database whatever changes the user makes while in the called form. If the user makes changes in the called form and then exits, the Forms Runtime program displays an alert asking if he or she wants to post his or her changes before returning to the calling form.
- The GO_FORM, NEXT_FORM, and PREVIOUS_FORM built-ins give you the ability to change focus from one form to another.
- The GET_APPLICATION_PROPERTY enables you to determine an application's current user and password, current form and form disk name,

calling form, database type, display height and width, operating system and user interface type, and language settings.

- You can pass values to a called form when it is opened by creating and using a parameter list.
- The calling form, which sends out the parameters, can define them either at design time by adding them to the Parameters node or at runtime by creating them with the CREATE_PARAMETER_LIST and ADD_PARAMETER built-ins.
- The called form, in contrast, can only accept passed values if the parameters were previously defined in the called form at design time.
- The six types of data block sources are table, view, FROM clause query, stored procedure returning a ref cursor, stored procedure returning a table of records, and transactional triggers.
- The main difference between the two types of data block sources using stored procedures is that one returns a ref cursor pointing to an array of returned records still on the server, whereas the other returns a table of records to the client computer containing all records returned by the procedure.
- The types of data sources made available by the Data Block Wizard are table, view, and stored procedure.
- You specify that a data block should be based on a FROM clause query by setting the data block's Query Data Source Type to FROM clause query.
- The data source type *FROM clause query* enables you to join tables, perform lookups, and create calculations without having to create any new objects on the server.
- The data source type *Stored Procedure Returning a Table of Records* has the greatest potential of reducing network traffic.
- The data source types that produce record sets that can be changed by the user are *Table, View, Stored Procedure Returning a Table of Records,* and *Transactional Triggers.*
- A record group is a two-dimensional table that provides data to a form module. Three types of record groups are available: query, nonquery, and static.
- A query record group is based on a SQL **select** statement. It provides a functionality similar to a database view, with two added benefits: The **select**

statement that produces the record group can be dynamically created at runtime, and you don't need to add a view to the database.

- A nonquery record group can also be created and populated dynamically at runtime, but it has no underlying **select** statement.
- A static record group is defined at design time, and its structure and content do not change when the application runs.
- Nonquery record groups are created with CREATE_GROUP. They are populated either with the POPULATE_GROUP_WITH_QUERY built-in, which essentially turns the nonquery record group into a query record group, or with a series of ADD_GROUP_COLUMN, ADD_GROUP_ROW, SET_GROUP_CHAR_CELL, and SET_GROUP_NUMBER_CELL built-ins.
- Query record groups are created with the CREATE_GROUP_FROM_QUERY built-in. They are populated with the POPULATE_GROUP built-in. As an alternative, you can populate a query record group with a different set of data using the POPULATE_GROUP_WITH_QUERY built-in, as long as the new **select** statement returns records with the same structure as the original **select** statement.
- The two methods for changing the record group associated with an LOV are POPULATE_LIST and SET_LOV_PROPERTY. POPULATE_LIST requires that the new record group be created at runtime and contain exactly two columns. SET_LOV_PROPERTY works with any type of record group, with any number of columns.
- You make a record group visible to all forms in your application by including the GLOBAL_SCOPE parameter in the CREATE_GROUP or CREATE_GROUP_FROM_QUERY built-in that creates the record group.
- You can pass a record group's data to other Forms 6*i* applications using the RUN_PRODUCT built-in.

Chapter Questions

1. You need to add a display item to a form. The item will display a calculated total summarizing data from several different tables. You do not want to create any new objects in the database. What is the best course of action to take?

A. Using the Data Block Wizard, create a block with a stored procedure as its data source type.

B. Using the Data Block Wizard, create a block with a view as its data source type.

C. After creating a data block manually, set its Query Data Source Type to FROM clause query, and write the appropriate **select** command in its Query Data Source Name property.

D. After creating a data block manually, set its Query Data Source Columns property to the desired columns and write the appropriate **select** command in its Query Data Source Arguments property.

2. **What built-in enables you to replace the query associated with a record group?**

   A. ADD_GROUP_ROW

   B. CREATE_GROUP

   C. POPULATE_GROUP_WITH_QUERY

   D. SET_GROUP_QUERY

3. **What built-in can you use to open a second form modally?**

   A. CALL_FORM

   B. NEW_FORM

   C. OPEN_FORM

   D. RUN_PRODUCT

4. **What built-in can provide the name of the current form?**

   A. GET_APPLICATION_PROPERTY

   B. GET_BLOCK_PROPERTY

   C. GET_FORM_PROPERTY

   D. GET_WINDOW_PROPERTY

5. **What built-in can populate a dynamic list item on a form with values from a record group?**

   A. SET_LIST_VALUES

   B. POPULATE_LIST

   C. POPULATE_LIST_WITH_QUERY

   D. RETRIEVE_LIST

6. **What built-in enables you to change a nonquery record group into a query record group?**

   A. CREATE_GROUP_FROM_QUERY

   B. POPULATE_GROUP

   C. POPULATE_GROUP_WITH_QUERY

   D. POPULATE_LIST_WITH_QUERY

7. **How can you base a data block on a stored procedure that uses a ref cursor?**

   A. Using the Data Block Wizard, specify a data source type of table.

   B. Using the Data Block Wizard, specify a data source type of stored procedure.

   C. After creating a data block manually, set the Query Data Source Name property to the appropriate stored procedure.

   D. After creating a data block manually, set the Query Data Source Columns property to the appropriate stored procedure.

8. **Name a benefit of using a FROM clause query as the basis for a data block.**

   A. Can utilize any PL/SQL code

   B. Can include user-defined parameters

   C. Can perform server joins, calculations, and lookups without needing specific access rights to tables

   D. Can perform server joins, calculations, and lookups without needing to create a view

9. **What built-in enables you to populate a record group with data that can be filtered dynamically at runtime?**

   A. CREATE_GROUP_FROM_PARAMETER

   B. SET_GROUP_FILTER

   C. POPULATE_LIST

   D. POPULATE_GROUP

10. You have created a sales application that uses one form for the sales ticket and a second form to list the items being purchased. When the second form is called, the sales ticket is still open and has pending changes. What mode will the second form be opened in?

A. Commit mode

B. Enter-query mode

C. Open-transaction mode

D. Post-only mode

11. What built-in enables you to change the contents of a static record group at runtime?

A. POPULATE_GROUP_FROM_QUERY

B. POPULATE_GROUP

C. ADD_GROUP_ROW

D. You cannot change the contents of a static record group at runtime.

12. What built-in enables you to pass data from a record group to a separate Oracle graph?

A. OPEN_REPORT_WITH_GROUP

B. PASS_GROUP

C. RUN_PRODUCT

D. PASS_GROUP_DATA

13. When you need to design a pair of forms in which one passes values to the other, when and where should you define the parameters that will accept the values?

A. In the calling form, at design time

B. In the calling form, at runtime

C. In the called form, at design time

D. In the called form, at runtime

Answers to Chapter Questions

1. C. After creating a data block manually, set its Query Data Source Type to FROM clause query and write the appropriate **select** command in its Query Data Source Name property.

Explanation You cannot use a stored procedure or a view because both of these require adding a new item to the database. The correct approach is using a FROM clause query.

2. C. POPULATE_GROUP_WITH_QUERY

Explanation See the section titled "Creating and Modifying Record Groups Programmatically" for a refresher on this topic.

3. A. CALL_FORM

Explanation CALL_FORM is the built-in that opens forms in a modal window.

4. A. GET_APPLICATION_PROPERTY

Explanation See the section titled "Building Robust Multiple-Form Transations" for a refresher on this topic.

5. B. POPULATE_LIST

Explanation See the section titled "Building Dynamic List Items by Using Record Groups" for a refresher on this topic.

6. C. POPULATE_GROUP_WITH_QUERY

Explanation The purpose of the POPULATE_GROUP_WITH_QUERY built-in is to fill a record group with data based on a given query, even if the record group was originally a nonquery group.

7. B. Using the Data Block Wizard, specify a data source type of stored procedure.

Explanation The options detailing the creation of a data block manually specify using the name of the stored procedure in properties not designed to hold a procedure name. Using the Data Block Wizard, you do not have to specify a data source type of table when you also have the option for stored procedure.

8. D. Can perform server joins, calculations, and lookups without needing to create a view

Explanation The essence of the FROM clause query is its capability to nest SQL **select** statements in subqueries that perform lookups, table joins, and calculations without relying on a database view.

9. D. POPULATE_GROUP

Explanation See the section titled "Creating Record Groups at Design Time" for a refresher on this topic.

10. D. Post-only mode

Explanation See the section titled "Different Ways to Invoke Forms" for a refresher on this topic.

11. D. You cannot change the contents of a static record group at runtime.

Explanation The definition of a *static group* is one whose contents cannot be changed at runtime.

12. C. RUN_PRODUCT

Explanation The RUN_PRODUCT built-in is designed to open other forms of graphics in their respective runtime programs.

13. C. In the called form, at design time

Explanation A parameter that is to be received must be defined at design time, and of course, it must be defined in the called form. See the section titled "Passing Data Between Forms Using Parameter Lists" for a refresher on this topic.

CHAPTER 11

Advanced Forms Programming III

n this chapter, you will understand and demonstrate knowledge in the following areas:

- Including charts in forms
- Applying timers to form objects
- Utilizing reusable components
- Using server features in Form Builder

You're in the home stretch now on the Forms exams! This chapter covers an assortment of interesting features related to advanced Form Builder programming. You will start by learning how to add graphic charts to your application's forms. Next, you will create an experimental form showing how you can use multiple timers in your applications. Finally, an overview of the reusable components supplied with Form Builder is provided, followed by tips on how to use server features more fully in your applications.

The test questions in this subject area are worth 20 percent of the final score of *OCP Exam 4*.

Including Charts in Forms

This section covers the following point related to including charts in forms:

- Using the Chart Wizard to embed charts in a form

In this section, you will get a taste of how to create visual output from your data. You will see how to create charts based on your application's data and how to place those charts on your forms.

Using the Chart Wizard to Embed Charts in a Form

It's simple to create charts that display on your application's forms. Form Builder provides a Chart Wizard that leads you through the process. In order to see how this works, you will create a new form module and build a form within it that displays the total salaries allocated to each department. To provide data for the form and the chart, you will start by creating a database view that sums salaries by department. Using SQL*Plus or your favorite SQL editor, enter the following code:

L 11-1

```
CREATE VIEW department_salaries AS (
  SELECT department_name,
```

```
        SUM(salary)        total_salary
  FROM  (SELECT d.department_name,
                e.salary
         FROM   department d,
                employee   e
         WHERE  d.department_id = e.department_id
        )
  GROUP BY department_name
);
```

Create a new form module and name it **GRAPH**. Then create a new data block based on the view you just built. (Note that this will require enabling the Views option in the Data Block Wizard's Tables dialog box so it will include the DEPARTMENT_SALARIES view in the list of available data sources.) Add all of the view's items to the data block, and then proceed to the next dialog screen. Select the option labeled *Just Create the Data Block*. Then right-click on the name of the new data block in the Object Navigator, and select the Layout Wizard from the context menu that appears.

Use the Layout Wizard to create a form that shows both of the view's columns in a Tabular layout, displaying five records at a time. When the Layout Editor opens, click on the canvas's background to select the canvas and change the canvas's Name property to **DEPARTMENT_SALARIES**.

To start the process of creating a chart item, click on the Chart Item button shown in the following illustration:

Then drag the mouse on the canvas to create a rectangular area that will hold the chart and its labels. This will cause a dialog box to appear that asks whether or not to use the Chart Wizard to create the chart. Select the *Use the Chart Wizard* option and click on the dialog's OK button. In the Chart Wizard's Chart Title page, leave the Title field empty, select a chart type of Pie, a Chart Subtype of Plain, and then click on the Next button. The next dialog page asks which of the form's data blocks should drive the pie chart. Because the form only has one data block, select DEPARTMENT_SALARIES and then click on the Next button to continue.

The next wizard page asks which item from the data block should produce the pie chart's X-axis labels. Ensure that the DEPARTMENT_NAME field is selected, click on the Right Arrow button to move it to the Category Axis area, and then click on the Next button to continue. The next wizard page wants to know which data block item will provide the values for the pie slices. Select the TOTAL_SALARY item, click on the Right Arrow button to move it into the Value Axis area, and then click on the

Next button. In the final wizard page, change the graph file's name to **DEPT_SAL.OGD** and click on the Finish button to complete the process of creating your chart item.

At this point, you will see somewhat of a mess—a pie chart will appear with four rectangular areas beneath it representing additional copies of the chart for each of the five records your data block displays on this form. To solve this, click on the pie chart to select it, open its Property Palette, and change its Number Of Items Displayed property to **1**. While in the Property Palette, change the Background Color property to **gray**. Then save and run your form. Once it opens in the Forms Runtime program, populate the form by clicking on the Execute Query button. Your form should now look similar to Figure 11-1.

In the exercise you just completed, you created a graphics file named **DEPT_SAL.OGD**. This file is separate from the form module and is called by a chart item on a canvas within the form module. You can use this or any other preexisting graphics file in canvasses other than the ones in which they were created. To incorporate an existing graphics display into a form, you still start by using the Chart Item button in the Layout Editor. When the New Chart Object dialog box appears, select the Build a New Chart Manually option and click on the OK button. The .ogd

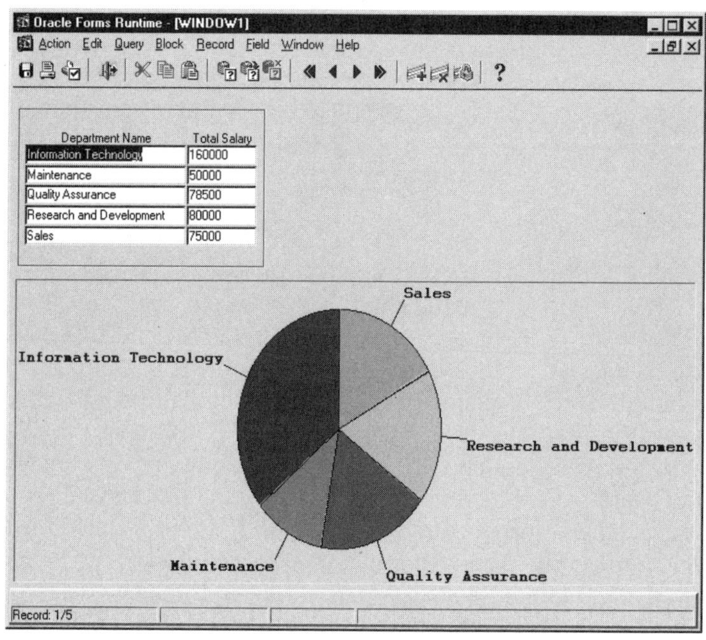

FIGURE 11-1. *Pie chart example*

file will be read by Form Builder, and its settings will be incorporated into the existing form. You then change several of the chart item's properties: the Data Source Data Block, Data Source X Axis, and Data Source Y Axis. Expect to play with this for a while after you have taken your exam because the Oracle documentation on this feature is somewhat sparse.

Exercises

1. **What property controls the relationship between the number of records displayed on your form and the number of chart repetitions displayed?**
2. **If you want to incorporate an existing graphic into a form, should you use the Chart Wizard or build the new chart manually?**

Applying Timers to Form Objects

This section covers the following points about applying timers to form objects:

- Creating a timer and handling timer expiration
- Deleting a timer
- Modifying a timer

A timer is a programmatic construct that catalyzes a defined action in a specified period of time. Timers have many uses in certain types of applications. In this section, you will learn how to create, modify, delete, and respond to timers.

Creating a Timer

A timer's duration is set in milliseconds; 1,000 milliseconds constitutes one second. With a valid range of 1 to 2,147,483,647 milliseconds, you can create a timer that waits almost 25 days before it expires. When you create a timer, you can specify whether or not it repeats after it expires.

The timer itself does not actually execute an action when it expires. That is the job of a WHEN-TIMER-EXPIRED trigger. Each form module can have only one WHEN-TIMER-EXPIRED trigger. The trigger may be fired by more than one timer, so if the form contains more than one timer, the trigger will have to identify what timer fired it—a technique you will learn soon.

To see how timers work, you will create a canvas that lets you run a few of them simultaneously. Start by creating a new form module named **TIMERS**. Create a new data block manually, change its name to **TIMER_CONTROL**, and change its Database Data Block property to **No**. Then create a new canvas object, change its name to **TIMER_CANVAS**, and open it in the Layout Editor. In the editor's toolbar, click on the Display Item button and then draw a display item that is approximately 1 inch tall and 1 1/2 inches wide in the middle of your canvas. Name the display item **DISPLAY_1** and set its Initial Value property to **0**, its Database Item property to **No**, and its Font Size property to **48**. Now place a pushbutton just above the display item and change its name to **TIMER_1_PUSHBUTTON**. Change its Label property to **Start Timer 1** and set its Font Size property to **12**. Then create a WHEN-BUTTON-PRESSED trigger for the pushbutton and enter the following code for the trigger:

L 11-2

```
DECLARE
  v_timer_1 TIMER;
BEGIN
  v_timer_1 := CREATE_TIMER('ONE_SECOND_TIMER', 1000, REPEAT);
END;
```

Close the Layout Editor and return to the Object Navigator. Double-click on the TIMERS module's Triggers node to create a new trigger, and select the WHEN-TIMER-EXPIRED trigger. In the PL/SQL Editor, enter the following code:

L 11-3

```
:timer_control.display_1 := :timer_control.display_1 +1 ;
```

Save your form and then run it. When it opens in the Forms Runtime program, click on the Start Timer 1 button. You will see your display item begin to increment in intervals of approximately one second. When you have been sufficiently entertained, close the Forms Runtime program and return to Form Builder.

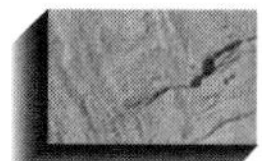

TIP
A number of things in the Forms Runtime environment take precedence over timer execution. Timer expiration will not necessarily occur at exactly the number of milliseconds you state.

Your application could have multiple timers operating simultaneously. Because only one WHEN-TIMER-EXPIRED trigger covers an entire form module, the trigger code needs a way to determine which timer fired. The GET_APPLICATION_PROPERTY built-in has the capability to identify the most recently fired timer. To see how it works, you will modify your TIMER form module so it has two timers running concurrently. Start by opening the TIMER_CANVAS canvas in the Layout Editor. Click on the Display Item button and draw a second display item next to the first one. Name the second display item **DISPLAY_2**, set its Initial Value property to **0**, its Database Item property to **No**, and its Font Size property to **48**. Click on the first pushbutton to set its size as the current default, and then click on the Button toolbar button to create a second pushbutton. Position the new pushbutton above the new display item, and change its name to **TIMER_2_PUSHBUTTON**. Change its Label property to **Start Timer 2**. Then create a WHEN-BUTTON-PRESSED trigger for the pushbutton, and enter the following code for the trigger:

L 11-4

```
DECLARE
  v_timer_2 TIMER;
BEGIN
  v_timer_2 := CREATE_TIMER('HALF_SECOND_TIMER', 500, REPEAT);
END;
```

Close the Layout Editor and return to the Object Navigator. Open the form-level WHEN-TIMER-EXPIRED trigger in the PL/SQL Editor and modify its code to match the following:

L 11-5

```
DECLARE
  last_timer_expired CHAR(20);
BEGIN
  last_timer_expired := GET_APPLICATION_PROPERTY(TIMER_NAME);
  IF last_timer_expired = 'ONE_SECOND_TIMER'
    THEN :timer_control.display_1 := :timer_control.display_1 +1 ;
  ELSIF last_timer_expired = 'HALF_SECOND_TIMER'
    THEN :timer_control.display_2 := :timer_control.display_2 +1 ;
  END IF;
END;
```

Run your form, and when it opens in the Forms Runtime program, click on your Start Timer 1 and Start Timer 2 buttons. You will see both of your display items begin to increment at the time intervals you specified. After you have seen this, close the Forms Runtime program and return to Form Builder.

Exercises

1. **What built-in would you use to make a timer that expires at one-minute intervals?**
2. **What object performs an action when a timer expires? At what level is this object usually defined?**
3. **What built-in can identify the timer that most recently expired? Why is this necessary in form modules with multiple timers?**

Deleting a Timer

At times, you may want a timer to execute a certain number of times and then stop. This can be handled using the DELETE_TIMER built-in. To see how this works, modify the code of your form-level WHEN-TIMER-EXPIRED trigger to match the following:

L 11-6

```
DECLARE
  last_timer_expired CHAR(20);
  last_timer_expired_id TIMER;
BEGIN
  last_timer_expired := GET_APPLICATION_PROPERTY(TIMER_NAME);
  last_timer_expired_id := FIND_TIMER(last_timer_expired);

  IF last_timer_expired = 'ONE_SECOND_TIMER'
    THEN
      IF :timer_control.display_1 < 10
        THEN :timer_control.display_1 := :timer_control.display_1 +1 ;
      ELSE DELETE_TIMER(last_timer_expired_id);
      END IF;
  ELSIF last_timer_expired = 'HALF_SECOND_TIMER'
    THEN
      IF :timer_control.display_2 < 10
        THEN :timer_control.display_2 := :timer_control.display_2 +1 ;
      ELSE DELETE_TIMER(last_timer_expired_id);
      END IF;
  END IF;
END;
```

This code incorporates two new built-ins: FIND_TIMER and DELETE_TIMER. The FIND_TIMER built-in returns the internal ID number of whatever timer name is used as an argument. As you no doubt recall, using the ID number can speed up processing when the object will be referred to multiple times in a routine. The FIND_TIMER built-in can work together with the DELETE_TIMER built-in to identify which timer to delete. To see all of this in action, run your form, and when it opens in the Forms Runtime program, click on your Start Timer 1 and Start Timer 2 buttons. You will see both of your display items begin to increment at the time intervals you specified, and then they will each stop after reaching the value of 10, as shown in Figure 11-2. After you have seen this, close the Forms Runtime program and return to Form Builder.

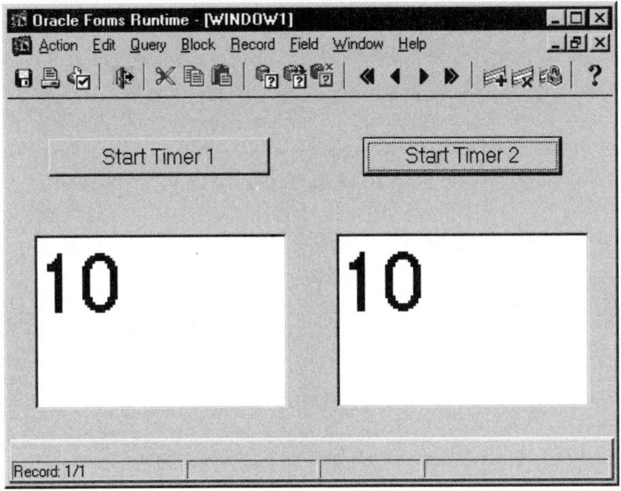

FIGURE 11-2. *Multiple timers*

Exercises

1. **What is the purpose of the FIND_TIMER built-in?**
2. **Which built-in enables you to remove a timer?**

Modifying a Timer

You can modify a timer in other ways besides just deleting it. The SET_TIMER built-in enables you to change a timer's duration or iteration setting. The syntax of this built-in is as follows:

L 11-7

```
SET_TIMER('timer_name', duration, iteration);
```

or

L 11-8

```
SET_TIMER(timer_id, duration, iteration);
```

If you want to change a timer's duration but leave its iteration setting alone, or vice versa, you can specify NO_CHANGE for the value of the parameter you don't want to change. For example, the following code would set the HYPER_TIMER to expire every tenth of a second, without changing its iteration status:

L 11-9

```
SET_TIMER('HYPER_TIMER', 100, NO_CHANGE);
```

Timers can be used to poll values on a regular basis, automatically save data, or perform other periodic actions. Timers are best used in applications designed to run in the Forms Runtime program; they are not a good choice for Web-based applications.

Exercises

1. **What built-in enables you to modify an existing timer?**
2. **What parameters of an existing timer can you change? How do you avoid changing parameters you want to leave alone?**

Utilizing Reusable Components

This section covers the following points about utilizing reusable components:

- Introduction to reusable components
- Using the Calendar class in an application

Reusability is the essence of object-oriented design. This section identifies the reusable components provided with Form Builder and gives an overview of how to utilize one common component, a calendar, in your own applications.

Introduction to the Reusable Components

Form Builder comes with an assortment of reusable components that can provide valuable functionality to your applications. In addition to giving you useful features requiring very little work to implement, reusing components makes it easier to standardize the look and feel of your application. Table 11-1 lists Form Builder's reusable components and describes the functionality each component offers.

Reusable Component	Purpose
ActiveX control	Enables augmenting of forms with predefined ActiveX control objects providing features such as word processing, spreadsheets, and handling of video clips.
Calendar class	Makes it possible to easily add a calendar or date List of Value (LOV) to your application.
Navigator class	Enables you to add an Explorer-type interface to your application, much like the Object Navigator in Form Builder.
Picklist class	Enables you to include a picklist in your applications.
Standard Object library	Contains a collection of predefined alerts, buttons, form input items, layouts, visual attribute groups, and the Calendar, Navigator, Picklist, and Wizard components. This can be extended or modified by the developer, and its objects can be set as standard or customized SmartClasses.
Wizard class	Enables you to create customized wizards for your applications.

TABLE 11-1. *Form Builder Reusable Components*

Exercises

1. **Which reusable component enables you to use third-party commercial objects to augment your application?**
2. **Which reusable component enables you to customize SmartClasses?**
3. **Which reusable component could you use to give your application's users access to other modules in an interface that looks like the Object Navigator?**
4. **Which reusable component can help you lead users through complicated procedures?**

Using the Calendar Class in an Application

The certification exam will not require that you attach the Calendar class to an application, but you will be expected to understand the process involved in doing so. This involves four steps:

1. Create your form module, data block, and canvas.
2. Attach the Standard Object library file stndrd20.olb. Copy or subclass the Calendar class from the resultant STANDARDS object library into your form module. This will add a variety of relevant objects to your application.
3. Attach the PL/SQL library file calendar.pll in order to gain access to the DATE_LOV package it contains.
4. To trigger the calendar from the appropriate date item in your form, create a KEY-LISTVAL trigger on the item. Place code in the trigger employing the DATE_LOV package to show the calendar.

The key to making these steps work is the triggering device: the KEY-LISTVAL trigger. Without that trigger, none of the functionality from the Standard Object library or the Calendar PL/SQL library will ever be used.

Exercises

1. **What object library will you attach when adding a calendar object to your application? What PL/SQL library?**
2. **How can you allow the user to invoke a calendar from a date field that has an LOV attached?**

Using Server Features in Form Builder

This section covers the following points about using server features in Form Builder:

- Introduction to Oracle Server features in Form Builder
- Partitioning PL/SQL program units
- Recognizing the PL/SQL8 features supported in Forms 6*i*
- Handling errors raised by the Oracle Server
- Performing Data Definition Language (DDL) commands

In this section, you will read about the capabilities that Forms 6*i* offers to move a substantial amount of your application's processing to the server. More work done on the server means more potential for server errors, so you will also review how to handle database errors. This section and the chapter wrap up with examples showing how you can make your application generate and execute SQL Data Definition Language (DDL) commands dynamically at runtime.

Introduction to Oracle Server Features in Form Builder

Form Builder provides features that enable you to easily create multitier applications. You can partition your application's program units, PL/SQL libraries, and triggers by simply dragging the objects into the Object Navigator's Database Objects node. Doing so can yield substantial rewards in system performance, data integrity, ease of maintaining standard objects, and simplicity. Performance can improve because record-oriented actions occur on the server, close to the data, thereby reducing network traffic and resultant delays. Data integrity benefits because anything you have defined to ensure data integrity is stored with the data tables, and will thus be available for action no matter what application is accessing the data. Standards benefit because often-used routines can reside on the server, where they are easy to locate and maintain.

When a program unit is placed on the database server, it is called a *stored program unit*. Form Builder lets you create stored program units containing a procedure, function, package spec, or package body. These are stored in specific schema areas on the database server. You can also attach a database trigger directly to a table, thereby ensuring that the trigger will fire at the appropriate times regardless of the front-end application used to access the data.

This is not the same as storing the application itself on the server (a feature offered by Form Builder). This feature relates to where the application is stored for retrieval by users, and the options are the database server or a standard file system available to the user. The choice between these two options does not affect how the application partitions its operations once it is loaded into the client computer's memory.

Exercises

1. **What object types can you store on the server to partition an application's functionality?**
2. **What are three benefits that can result from placing part of an application's functionality on the server?**

Partitioning PL/SQL Program Units

To see how to create program units on the server, open the Database Objects node in the Object Navigator. Beneath that node, you will see each schema available via your current database connection. Open a schema, and you will see subnodes for Stored Program Units, PL/SQL Libraries, Tables, and Views. Double-click on the Stored Program Units node, and you will be given the opportunity to create a new procedure, function, package spec, or package body directly on the server. You can also copy program units from an existing client-side PL/SQL library into the Stored Program Units node of a schema simply by dragging the program units in the Object Navigator and dropping them on the appropriate Stored Program Units node.

When a procedure or function is created on the server, it can be called in exactly the same way as a procedure or function residing on the client computer. Stored procedures have some limitations, however. They cannot refer to bind variables: form items, global variables, or system variables. If you need to pass values to a stored procedure, you must do it using parameters. In addition, all form processing pauses when a stored procedure or function is called; the form waits until the procedure or function completes. So you will want to consider the performance of your server and network when deciding what parts of your application to store on the server.

Exercises

1. **What is the hard-and-fast rule about partitioning applications for best performance? (Note: this is another trick question.)**
2. **What limitations exist for procedures and functions stored on the server?**

Recognizing the PL/SQL8 Features Supported in Forms 6*i*

A number of the features that have been added to Oracle 8 are of interest when designing forms. This section gives an overview of the features supported in Forms 6*i*. Those features include

- External procedures
- Object types
- Collections
- LOB types
- NLS types

You will not be expected to know how to implement these features for the exam, but you will need to be able to look at a list of features and know which ones are new for Oracle 8.

External Procedures

External procedure refers to code written in a language other than PL/SQL. Oracle Forms 6*i* can use routines written in third-generation languages as long as they are within a dynamic link library (.dll) file.

Object Types

An object type consists of a data structure and the functions or procedures used to work with the data in the structure. Oracle 8's object types relate directly to classes used in object-oriented languages such as C++. You can create a PL/SQL object type by executing the **create type** command.

Collections

A collection is a group of elements that all share the same type. Forms 6*i* supports the TABLE collection type (for storing nested tables), as well as the VARRAY collection type (for variable-size arrays). Oracle 8*i* enables a collection to be an attribute of an object type and also to store instances of an object type. Because collections can be passed as parameters, they enable you to move columnar sets of data between tables, stored procedures, and applications.

LOB Types

Oracle 8 provides a variety of new datatypes for storing and manipulating unstructured Large OBjects (LOBs) containing binary data such as audio or video files, as well as large chunks of text. These new datatypes are easier to work with than the LONG and LONG RAW datatypes offered in Oracle 7, and they can store twice as much data too: up to 4GB per object. In addition, you can have more than one LOB column in a table (unlike its LONG predecessor), and you can access data within a LOB randomly, (unlike the LONG datatypes, which only accepted sequential access). Forms 6*i* supports the following LOB datatypes:

BLOB	Binary Large Object
CLOB	Character Large Object
NCLOB	Multibyte NCHAR Large Object
BFILE	Path to operating system file outside the database

The first three of these datatypes store the LOB data within a database table. The fourth datatype, BFILE, stores pointers to separate disk files that reside outside the Oracle database. You work with the LOB data through an Oracle package called DBMS_LOB.

NLS Types

Oracle 8 supports multinational databases by providing extended National Language Support (NLS) in two ways. First, PL/SQL has been augmented to support both the original database character set specified by your DBA and a national character set for NLS data. Using a national character set enables the formats of date and number fields to change based on a given user's session settings. Second, for text fields, Oracle 8 adds the NCHAR and NVARCHAR2 datatypes, which enable you to use the national character set in text strings.

All of these new features—external procedures, object types, collections, LOB types, and NLS types—are available to program units stored on the server. Program units running on the client computer can use all of these features *except* those related to objects.

Exercises

1. **What new Oracle 8 features are supported in Forms 6*i* client-side program units?**
2. **What additional Oracle 8 features are available to server-side program units?**

Handling Errors Raised by the Oracle Server

As discussed in Chapter 6, you can trap errors returned by the Oracle server. This becomes especially important as you move more of your application's processing onto the server. Chapter 6 introduced one of the two ways to trap server error messages: the DBMS_ERROR_TEXT built-in, which returns the message text of the most recent Oracle database error. The following is an example of its use:

L 11-10

```
DECLARE
  dberr_num  NUMBER       := DBMS_ERROR_CODE;
  dberr_txt  VARCHAR2(80) := DBMS_ERROR_TEXT;
  error_type VARCHAR2(3)  := ERROR_TYPE;
BEGIN
    IF dberr_num = -1 THEN
      MESSAGE('Primary key for new record already exists.');
    ELSE
      MESSAGE('Cannot insert this record...reason undetermined.');
    END IF;
  ELSE
    MESSAGE(error_type || '-' || TO_CHAR(dberr_num) || ': ' || dberr_txt);
  END IF;
END;
```

Exercise

1. What built-in returns the text of the most recent database error message?

Performing DDL Commands

You can write PL/SQL code in Form Builder that dynamically generates and executes DDL commands while the application is running. Based on the FORMS_DDL built-in, this very cool feature affords you a lot of flexible control over the database while your application is running. For instance, if you want to store posted records in a temporary database table until they are committed, you can have your application build the temporary table dynamically and then drop it when it is no longer needed. The following is a simple example of how to do this:

L 11-11

```
BEGIN
  FORMS_DDL('CREATE TABLE t1 (c1 VARCHAR2(20), c2 NUMBER) ');
  IF FORM_SUCCESS THEN
    MESSAGE ('Temporary table successfully created.');
  ELSE
    MESSAGE ('Temporary table could NOT be created.');
  END IF;
END;
```

Note that in this example, the SQL DDL statement did *not* have its own terminating semicolon. For multiple-line SQL statements, you should include semicolons in the standard places, with the exception of the last, terminating semicolon. The contents of the SQL DDL command itself can be constructed dynamically at runtime. One simple application of this is demonstrated in the following code, which is adapted from a clever example in the Oracle documentation:

L 11-12

```
PROCEDURE create_n_column_number_table (n NUMBER) IS
  v_sql_string VARCHAR2(2000);
BEGIN
  v_sql_string := 'CREATE TABLE tmp (c1 NUMBER';
  FOR i IN 2..n LOOP
    v_sql_string := v_sql_string || ',c' || TO_CHAR(i) || ' NUMBER';
  END LOOP;
  v_sql_string := v_sql_string || ')';

  FORMS_DDL(v_sql_string);
  IF FORM_SUCCESS THEN
```

```
    MESSAGE ('Table successfully created.');
  ELSE
    MESSAGE ('Table could NOT be created.');
  END IF;
END;
```

Exercise

1. **What is the purpose of the FORMS_DDL built-in?**

Chapter Summary

This chapter covered some powerful concepts regarding advanced forms programming. It included several topics such as embedding charts into your forms, utilizing timers in your applications, incorporating reusable components, and using server features more fully in your applications.

The first area covered was embedding charts into your forms. To add a chart to a Form Builder form, you only need to make sure the form module has a data block that provides the data the chart needs, and then use the Chart Wizard to create the chart. The Chart Wizard generates a separate graphics file with a file type of .ogd, and then generates a chart item on your form to display the chart. That same graphics file can be used by other canvasses as well by creating a chart item and setting its Data Source Data Block, Data Source X Axis, and Data Source Y Axis properties.

The next section explored timers. A timer is a programmatic construct that catalyzes a defined action in a specified period of time. A timer's duration is set in milliseconds (one-thousandths of a second). With a valid duration of 1 to 2,147,483,647 milliseconds, you can create a timer that waits almost 25 days before it expires. When you create a timer, you can specify whether or not it repeats after it expires. The timer itself does not execute code when it expires. That is the job of a WHEN-TIMER-EXPIRED trigger, which you define at the form level. Your application can have multiple timers operating simultaneously. Because all timers will cause the same WHEN-TIMER-EXPIRED trigger to fire, the trigger needs a way to determine what trigger within the timer fired it. The GET_APPLICATION_PROPERTY built-in enables you to determine the name of the most recently fired timer in an application, which you can use as the argument in an **if** statement within the trigger to determine what action to take based on which timer expired. You can delete a timer by using the DELETE_TIMER built-in. You can determine a timer's internal ID with the FIND_TIMER built-in. You can modify an existing timer using the SET_TIMER built-in, which enables you to change a timer's duration or iteration setting.

After working with timers, you were introduced to the reusable components supplied with Form Builder. These include the ActiveX control, Calendar class, Navigator class, Picklist class, Standard Object library, and Wizard class. The ActiveX control enables augmenting your forms with predefined ActiveX control objects providing features such as word processing, spreadsheets, and handling of video clips. The Calendar class makes it possible to easily add a calendar or date LOV to your application. The Navigator class enables you to add an Explorer-type interface to your application, much like the Object Navigator in Form Builder. The Picklist class enables you to include a picklist in your applications. The Standard Object library contains a collection of predefined alerts, buttons, form input items, layouts, visual attribute groups, and the Calendar, Navigator, Picklist, and Wizard components. It can be extended or modified by the developer, and its objects can be set as standard or customized SmartClasses. Finally, the Wizard class enables you to create customized wizards for your applications. You still have to do a little bit of work to use these classes; for instance, to use a Calendar class after all the pieces have been attached, you can create a KEY-LISTVAL trigger for your LOV field.

The last topic was the server features you can use in your Form Builder applications. Form Builder provides features that enable you to easily create multitier applications by partitioning your application's program units, PL/SQL libraries, and triggers between the client computer and the database server. You can move program units, PL/SQL libraries, and triggers to the server by dragging the objects into the Object Navigator's Database Objects node. When a program unit is placed on the server, it is called a stored program unit. You can also create new stored program units directly from within Form Builder. To catch and handle errors returned by the server when it executes stored program units, use the DBMS_ERROR_TEXT built-in, which returns the message text of the most recent Oracle database error. If you need to have your application dynamically generate and execute DDL commands at runtime, you can do so using the FORMS_DDL built-in.

Forms 6*i* supports a number of the features added to Oracle 8. It accommodates third-party external procedures within .dll files; provides a **create type** command for creating your own class-oriented object types containing a data structure along with the functions or procedures to use them; it can manipulate data collections using the TABLE type (for storing nested tables) and the VARRAY type (for variable-size arrays); it supports extended NLS data with NCHAR and NVARCHAR2 datatypes; and it provides larger, easier-to-use LOB capabilities via the BLOB, CLOB, NCLOB, and BFILE datatypes.

All in all, this chapter comprises about 20 percent of the material tested on *OCP Exam 4.*

Two-Minute Drill

- When adding a chart to a canvas, use the Chart Wizard to create and add a new chart display. Create the chart item manually if you are incorporating an existing chart display.
- The CREATE_TIMER built-in generates timers.
- Timers do not perform actions. That is the province of the WHEN-TIMER-EXPIRED trigger. You want to define this trigger at the form level and you can only define one per form. The WHEN-TIMER-EXPIRED trigger fires when any timer within the form module expires.
- The WHEN-TIMER-EXPIRED trigger can determine which timer expired by getting the timer's name with the GET_APPLICATION_PROPERTY (TIMER_NAME) built-in. It can also determine the ID of a timer using the FIND_TIMER built-in.
- A timer can be removed using the DELETE_TIMER built-in.
- A timer can be modified using the SET_TIMER built-in. You can change the timer's duration, its iteration status, or both. To leave one of the parameters as it is, use the constant NO_CHANGE for that parameter.
- Form Builder comes with several reusable components: ActiveX control, Calendar class, Navigator class, Picklist class, Standard Object library, and Wizard class.
- The ActiveX control enables adding predefined ActiveX control objects to augment your forms with features such as word processing, spreadsheets, and video clips.
- The Calendar class makes it possible to easily add a calendar or date LOV to your application.
- The Navigator class enables you to add an Explorer-type interface to your application, much like the Object Navigator in Form Builder.
- The Picklist class enables you to include a picklist in your applications.
- The Standard Object library contains a collection of predefined alerts, buttons, form input items, layouts, visual attribute groups, and the Calendar, Navigator, Picklist, and Wizard components. It can be extended or modified by the developer, and its objects can be set as standard or customized SmartClasses.
- The Wizard class enables you to create customized wizards for your applications.

- When adding a Calendar class object to your application, you attach the Standard Object library to obtain an assortment of relevant objects, classes, and settings, and then attach the Calendar PL/SQL file to gain access to the DATE_LOV package. To invoke a calendar from a form, you can use a KEY-LISTVAL trigger.
- When partitioning an application's functionality between the client computer and the server, you can store program units, PL/SQL libraries, and triggers on the server.
- The benefits of partitioning an application between client and server computers include faster performance due to reduced network traffic and record-oriented procedures executing closer to the relevant data tables; improved data integrity from locating integrity-oriented triggers directly on the tables they protect; and easier maintenance and standardization by having commonly used objects located in one central location.
- The decision about what parts of your application to place on your server depends on a variety of variables: the size of your organization, the amount of code that is used by more than one application, the speed of the server and client computers, and the speed of the network.
- Stored procedures and functions have a number of limitations. They cannot refer to bind variables: form items, global variables, or system variables. If you need to pass values to a stored procedure, you must do it using parameters. In addition, all form processing pauses when a stored procedure or function is called.
- When an error occurs, the DBMS_ERROR_TEXT built-in can provide you with the text of the most recent DBMS error message.
- The FORMS_DDL built-in enables you to have your application generate and execute SQL DDL commands dynamically at runtime.
- Forms 6*i* accommodates third-party external procedures within .dll files.
- You can create your own class-oriented object types containing a data structure along with the functions or procedures to use them by using the **create type** command.
- Forms 6*i* can manipulate data collections using the TABLE type (for storing nested tables) and the VARRAY type (for variable-size arrays).
- You can build extended NLS support into your application by employing the NCHAR and NVARCHAR2 datatypes.
- Forms 6*i* can use Oracle 8's full set of new LOB capabilities: random access, size up to 4GB, and multiple LOB columns per table. The datatypes are BLOB, CLOB, NCLOB, and BFILE.

Chapter Questions

1. **What reusable component enables you to lead your users through complicated processes?**

   A. ActiveX controls

   B. Calendar class

   C. Navigator class

   D. Picklist class

   E. Standard Object library

   F. Wizard class

2. **What reusable component enables you to create an Object Navigator-like interface for your own applications?**

   A. ActiveX controls

   B. Calendar class

   C. Navigator class

   D. Picklist class

   E. Standard Object library

   F. Wizard class

3. **What Form Builder built-ins enable you to set the duration of a timer? (Choose all that apply.)**

   A. CREATE_TIMER

   B. FIND_TIMER

   C. SET_TIMER

   D. SET_TIMER_PROPERTY

   E. WHEN-TIMER-EXPIRED

4. **What built-in enables you to find the internal ID of a timer?**

   A. CREATE_TIMER

   B. FIND_TIMER

   C. SET_TIMER

D. SET_TIMER_PROPERTY

E. WHEN-TIMER-EXPIRED

5. **What reusable component enables you to create a customized SmartClass?**

   A. ActiveX controls

   B. Calendar class

   C. Navigator class

   D. Picklist class

   E. Standard Object library

   F. Wizard class

6. **What built-in enables you to eliminate a timer?**

   A. DELETE_TIMER

   B. FIND_TIMER

   C. REMOVE_TIMER

   D. SET_TIMER

   E. SET_TIMER_PROPERTY

   F. WHEN-TIMER-EXPIRED

7. **You moved a number of your application's program units over to the server and started experiencing DBMS errors. What built-in can you use to capture these errors and the information they return?**

   A. DBMS_ERROR

   B. DBMS_ERROR_NUM

   C. DBMS_ERROR_STRING

   D. DBMS_ERROR_TEXT

8. **What trigger is used to respond to timers, and at what level is it most commonly defined?**

   A. ON-TIMER-BEGIN at the block level

   B. ON-TIMER-EXPIRE at the form level

   C. ON-TIMER at the window level

D. WHEN-TIMER-BEGINS at the block level

E. WHEN-TIMER-BEGINS at the form level

F. WHEN-TIMER-BEGINS at the window level

G. WHEN-TIMER-EXPIRED at the form level

H. WHEN-TIMER-EXPIRED at the window level

9. **What trigger should you use to activate a calendar when the user presses the List of Values (LOV) function key while in a date field?**

   A. ON-LIST-OPEN

   B. KEY-LIST-OPEN

   C. ON-LISTVAL

   D. KEY-LISTVAL

   E. WHEN-LOV-OPEN

10. **What are the steps for embedding an existing chart on a form that is open in the Layout Editor?**

    A. Invoke the Chart Wizard, identify the chart file, and move the resulting chart to the correct position on the canvas.

    B. Execute the File | Import menu command, identify the chart file, and move the resulting chart to the correct position on the canvas.

    C. Create a chart item manually using the Chart Item button, identify the chart file in the item's Property Palette, and move the resulting chart to the correct position on the canvas.

11. **What built-in enables you to manipulate table structures at runtime?**

    A. RUNTIME_DDL

    B. FORMS_RUNTIME

    C. FORMS_DDL

    D. DDL_FORMS

    E. DDL_RUNTIME

12. What built-in enables you to determine which timer fired a WHEN-TIMER-EXPIRED trigger?

A. SYSTEM.TIMER

B. GET_TIMER_PROPERTY

C. GET_APPLICATION_PROPERTY

D. FIND_TIMER

13. What file format must a third-party external procedure be in for Forms 6*i* to use it?

A. PL/SQL8

B. C++

C. DLL

D. Structured Query Language

14. Which of the following can be components of an object type? (Choose as many as apply.)

A. C++

B. Data

C. Data structure

D. Functions

E. Procedures

15. When a national character set is implemented in a Forms 6*i* system, which datatypes can reflect changes in their display format based on the character set's settings? (Choose as many as apply.)

A. CHAR

B. DATE

C. LOB

D. NCHAR

E. NUMBER

F. NVARCHAR2

G. VARCHAR2

16. Which of the following datatypes were added to Oracle 8? (Choose all that apply.)

A. LOB

B. BLOB

C. CLOB

D. NCLOB

E. BFILE

F. GLOB

G. CFILE

H. LONG

I. LONG RAW

Answers to Chapter Questions

1. F. Wizard class

Explanation The Wizard class enables you to create your own custom wizards, which can lead users through complicated processes.

2. C. Navigator class

Explanation The Navigator class contains objects that make it easy to implement a Navigator interface in your own applications.

3. A, C. CREATE_TIMER, SET_TIMER

Explanation CREATE_TIMER generates a new timer with the duration specified. SET_TIMER alters the duration of an existing timer. If you included WHEN-TIMER-EXPIRED in your answer, take care to read the questions more carefully—this question asked for built-ins, and WHEN-TIMER-EXPIRED is a trigger.

4. B. FIND_TIMER

Explanation The FIND_TIMER built-in returns the internal ID of whatever timer's name is provided as an argument.

5. E. Standard Object library

Explanation See the section titled "Introduction to the Reusable Components" for a refresher on this topic.

6. A. DELETE_TIMER

Explanation The DELETE_TIMER built-in's sole purpose is to deactivate and eliminate timers. A REMOVE_TIMER built-in does not exist.

7. D. DBMS_ERROR_TEXT

Explanation The DBMS_ERROR_TEXT built-in is designed specifically to return the text of error messages sent back by the database server.

8. G. WHEN-TIMER-EXPIRED at the form level

Explanation See the section titled "Creating a Timer" for a refresher on this topic.

9. D. KEY-LISTVAL

Explanation The KEY-LISTVAL trigger fires whenever the user presses the LOV function key.

10. C. Create a chart item manually using the Chart Item button, identify the chart file in the item's Property Palette, and move the resulting chart to the correct position on the canvas.

Explanation The Chart Wizard is only useful for creating new charts, so it is not a correct answer because the question specifies that you are dealing with an existing chart. The command File | Import does not exist in Form Builder. When dealing with an existing chart file, you bypass the Chart Wizard, create a new chart item manually, and alter the new item's properties to use the existing chart file.

11. C. FORMS_DDL

Explanation The FORMS_DDL built-in gives you the ability to execute SQL commands during runtime. All other potential answers to this question were made up (FORMS_RUNTIME is a program, not a built-in).

12. C. GET_APPLICATION_PROPERTY

Explanation See the section titled "Creating a Timer" for a refresher on this topic.

13. C. DLL

Explanation An external procedure can be written in a variety of third-party languages, but it must be stored in the .dll format in order for Forms 6*i* to use it.

14. C, D, E. Data structure, Functions, Procedures

Explanation An object type consists of a data structure, along with the code necessary to move data in and out of that structure properly (functions and/or procedures).

15. B, D, E, F. DATE, NCHAR, NUMBER, NVARCHAR2

Explanation See the section titled "Recognizing the PL/SQL8 Features Supported in Forms 6*i*" for a refresher on this topic.

16. B, C, D, E. BLOB, CLOB, NCLOB, BFILE

Explanation The BLOB datatype stores raw data such as images and sound files; CLOB store large selections of text; NCLOB stores large text incorporating NLS characters; and BFILE stores pointers to operating-system files stored outside the database. Choice A (LOB) is a group name for all of these, but is not itself a datatype. GLOB and CFILE are not valid datatype names. LONG and LONG RAW are Oracle 7 datatypes.

Congratulations! You have made it through the entire book! Now practice building your own applications for a while. When you feel you are ready, sign up for the Forms exams. Study and practice like crazy before you go in to take the exams. After taking the exam, you will receive a printout showing how many questions were in each subject area and how many you got right. If you pass on the first try, fantastic! If not, just focus on whatever subject areas the printout shows need a little extra work. Then go back in and pass that exam in style!

Index

G

H

I

J–L

M

N

O

S

T

U

V

W

INTERNATIONAL CONTACT INFORMATION

AUSTRALIA
McGraw-Hill Book Company Australia Pty. Ltd.
TEL +61-2-9417-9899
FAX +61-2-9417-5687
http://www.mcgraw-hill.com.au
books-it_sydney@mcgraw-hill.com

CANADA
McGraw-Hill Ryerson Ltd.
TEL +905-430-5000
FAX +905-430-5020
http://www.mcgrawhill.ca

GREECE, MIDDLE EAST, NORTHERN AFRICA
McGraw-Hill Hellas
TEL +30-1-656-0990-3-4
FAX +30-1-654-5525

MEXICO (Also serving Latin America)
McGraw-Hill Interamericana Editores S.A. de C.V.
TEL +525-117-1583
FAX +525-117-1589
http://www.mcgraw-hill.com.mx
fernando_castellanos@mcgraw-hill.com

SINGAPORE (Serving Asia)
McGraw-Hill Book Company
TEL +65-863-1580
FAX +65-862-3354
http://www.mcgraw-hill.com.sg
mghasia@mcgraw-hill.com

SOUTH AFRICA
McGraw-Hill South Africa
TEL +27-11-622-7512
FAX +27-11-622-9045
robyn_swanepoel@mcgraw-hill.com

UNITED KINGDOM & EUROPE (Excluding Southern Europe)
McGraw-Hill Publishing Company
TEL +44-1-628-502500
FAX +44-1-628-770224
http://www.mcgraw-hill.co.uk
computing_neurope@mcgraw-hill.com

ALL OTHER INQUIRIES Contact:
Osborne/McGraw-Hill
TEL +1-510-549-6600
FAX +1-510-883-7600
http://www.osborne.com
omg_international@mcgraw-hill.com

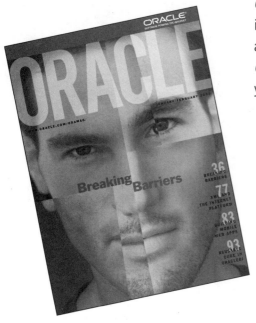

☐ YES! Please send me a FREE subscription to *Oracle Magazine*. ☐ NO

To receive a free bimonthly subscription to *Oracle Magazine*, you must fill out the entire card, sign it, and date it (incomplete cards cannot be processed or acknowledged). You can also fax your application to **+1.847.647.9735. Or subscribe at our Web site at www.oracle.com/oramag**

SIGNATURE (REQUIRED) X ______ **DATE** ______

NAME ______ TITLE ______

COMPANY ______ TELEPHONE ______

ADDRESS ______ FAX NUMBER ______

CITY ______ STATE ______ POSTAL CODE/ZIP CODE ______

COUNTRY ______ E-MAIL ADDRESS ______

☐ From time to time, Oracle Publishing allows our partners exclusive access to our e-mail addresses for special promotions and announcements. To be included in this program, please check this box.

You must answer all eight questions below

1 What is the primary business activity of your firm at this location? *(check only one)*

- ☐ 03 Communications
- ☐ 04 Consulting, Training
- ☐ 06 Data Processing
- ☐ 07 Education
- ☐ 08 Engineering
- ☐ 09 Financial Services
- ☐ 10 Government—Federal, Local, State, Other
- ☐ 11 Government—Military
- ☐ 12 Health Care
- ☐ 13 Manufacturing—Aerospace, Defense
- ☐ 14 Manufacturing—Computer Hardware
- ☐ 15 Manufacturing—Noncomputer Products
- ☐ 17 Research & Development
- ☐ 19 Retailing, Wholesaling, Distribution
- ☐ 20 Software Development
- ☐ 21 Systems Integration, VAR, VAD, OEM
- ☐ 22 Transportation
- ☐ 23 Utilities (Electric, Gas, Sanitation)
- ☐ 98 Other Business and Services ______

2 Which of the following best describes your job function? *(check only one)*

CORPORATE MANAGEMENT/STAFF

- ☐ 01 Executive Management (President, Chair, CEO, CFO, Owner, Partner, Principal)
- ☐ 02 Finance/Administrative Management (VP/Director/ Manager/Controller, Purchasing, Administration)
- ☐ 03 Sales/Marketing Management (VP/Director/Manager)
- ☐ 04 Computer Systems/Operations Management (CIO/VP/Director/ Manager MIS, Operations)

IS/IT STAFF

- ☐ 07 Systems Development/ Programming Management
- ☐ 08 Systems Development/ Programming Staff
- ☐ 09 Consulting
- ☐ 10 DBA/Systems Administrator
- ☐ 11 Education/Training
- ☐ 14 Technical Support Director/ Manager
- ☐ 16 Other Technical Management/Staff
- ☐ 98 Other ______

3 What is your current primary operating platform? *(check all that apply)*

- ☐ 01 DEC UNIX
- ☐ 02 DEC VAX VMS
- ☐ 03 Java
- ☐ 04 HP UNIX
- ☐ 05 IBM AIX
- ☐ 06 IBM UNIX
- ☐ 07 Macintosh
- ☐ 09 MS-DOS
- ☐ 10 MVS
- ☐ 11 NetWare
- ☐ 12 Network Computing
- ☐ 13 OpenVMS
- ☐ 14 SCO UNIX
- ☐ 24 Sequent DYNIX/ptx
- ☐ 15 Sun Solaris/SunOS
- ☐ 16 SVR4
- ☐ 18 UnixWare
- ☐ 20 Windows
- ☐ 21 Windows NT
- ☐ 23 Other UNIX ______
- ☐ 98 Other ______
- 99 ☐ **None of the above**

4 Do you evaluate, specify, recommend, or authorize the purchase of any of the following? *(check all that apply)*

- ☐ 01 Hardware
- ☐ 02 Software
- ☐ 03 Application Development Tools
- ☐ 04 Database Products
- ☐ 05 Internet or Intranet Products
- 99 ☐ **None of the above**

5 In your job, do you use or plan to purchase any of the following products or services? *(check all that apply)*

SOFTWARE

- ☐ 01 Business Graphics
- ☐ 02 CAD/CAE/CAM
- ☐ 03 CASE
- ☐ 05 Communications
- ☐ 06 Database Management
- ☐ 07 File Management
- ☐ 08 Finance
- ☐ 09 Java
- ☐ 10 Materials Resource Planning
- ☐ 11 Multimedia Authoring
- ☐ 12 Networking
- ☐ 13 Office Automation
- ☐ 14 Order Entry/Inventory Control
- ☐ 15 Programming
- ☐ 16 Project Management
- ☐ 17 Scientific and Engineering
- ☐ 18 Spreadsheets
- ☐ 19 Systems Management
- ☐ 20 Workflow

HARDWARE

- ☐ 21 Macintosh
- ☐ 22 Mainframe
- ☐ 23 Massively Parallel Processing
- ☐ 24 Minicomputer
- ☐ 25 PC
- ☐ 26 Network Computer
- ☐ 28 Symmetric Multiprocessing
- ☐ 29 Workstation

PERIPHERALS

- ☐ 30 Bridges/Routers/Hubs/Gateways
- ☐ 31 CD-ROM Drives
- ☐ 32 Disk Drives/Subsystems
- ☐ 33 Modems
- ☐ 34 Tape Drives/Subsystems
- ☐ 35 Video Boards/Multimedia

SERVICES

- ☐ 37 Consulting
- ☐ 38 Education/Training
- ☐ 39 Maintenance
- ☐ 40 Online Database Services
- ☐ 41 Support
- ☐ 36 Technology-Based Training
- ☐ 98 Other ______
- 99 ☐ **None of the above**

6 What Oracle products are in use at your site? *(check all that apply)*

SERVER/SOFTWARE

- ☐ 01 Oracle8
- ☐ 30 Oracle8*i*
- ☐ 31 Oracle8*i* Lite
- ☐ 02 Oracle7
- ☐ 03 Oracle Application Server
- ☐ 04 Oracle Data Mart Suites
- ☐ 05 Oracle Internet Commerce Server
- ☐ 32 Oracle *inter*Media
- ☐ 33 Oracle JServer
- ☐ 07 Oracle Lite
- ☐ 08 Oracle Payment Server
- ☐ 11 Oracle Video Server

TOOLS

- ☐ 13 Oracle Designer
- ☐ 14 Oracle Developer
- ☐ 54 Oracle Discoverer
- ☐ 53 Oracle Express
- ☐ 51 Oracle JDeveloper
- ☐ 52 Oracle Reports
- ☐ 50 Oracle WebDB
- ☐ 55 Oracle Workflow

ORACLE APPLICATIONS

- ☐ 17 Oracle Automotive
- ☐ 35 Oracle Business Intelligence System
- ☐ 19 Oracle Consumer Packaged Goods
- ☐ 39 Oracle E-Commerce
- ☐ 18 Oracle Energy
- ☐ 20 Oracle Financials
- ☐ 28 Oracle Front Office
- ☐ 21 Oracle Human Resources
- ☐ 37 Oracle Internet Procurement
- ☐ 22 Oracle Manufacturing
- ☐ 40 Oracle Process Manufacturing
- ☐ 23 Oracle Projects
- ☐ 34 Oracle Retail
- ☐ 29 Oracle Self-Service Web Applications
- ☐ 38 Oracle Strategic Enterprise Management
- ☐ 25 Oracle Supply Chain Management
- ☐ 36 Oracle Tutor
- ☐ 41 Oracle Travel Management

ORACLE SERVICES

- ☐ 61 Oracle Consulting
- ☐ 62 Oracle Education
- ☐ 60 Oracle Support
- ☐ 98 Other ______
- 99 ☐ **None of the above**

7 What other database products are in use at your site? *(check all that apply)*

- ☐ 01 Access
- ☐ 02 Baan
- ☐ 03 dbase
- ☐ 04 Gupta
- ☐ 05 IBM DB2
- ☐ 06 Informix
- ☐ 07 Ingres
- ☐ 08 Microsoft Access
- ☐ 09 Microsoft SQL Server
- ☐ 10 PeopleSoft
- ☐ 11 Progress
- ☐ 12 SAP
- ☐ 13 Sybase
- ☐ 14 VSAM
- ☐ 98 Other ______
- 99 ☐ **None of the above**

8 During the next 12 months, how much do you anticipate your organization will spend on computer hardware, software, peripherals, and services for your location? *(check only one)*

- ☐ 01 Less than $10,000
- ☐ 02 $10,000 to $49,999
- ☐ 03 $50,000 to $99,999
- ☐ 04 $100,000 to $499,999
- ☐ 05 $500,000 to $999,999
- ☐ 06 $1,000,000 and over

If there are other Oracle users at your location who would like to receive a free subscription to *Oracle Magazine*, please photocopy this form and pass it along, or contact Customer Service at +1.847.647.9630

Form 5

OPRESS

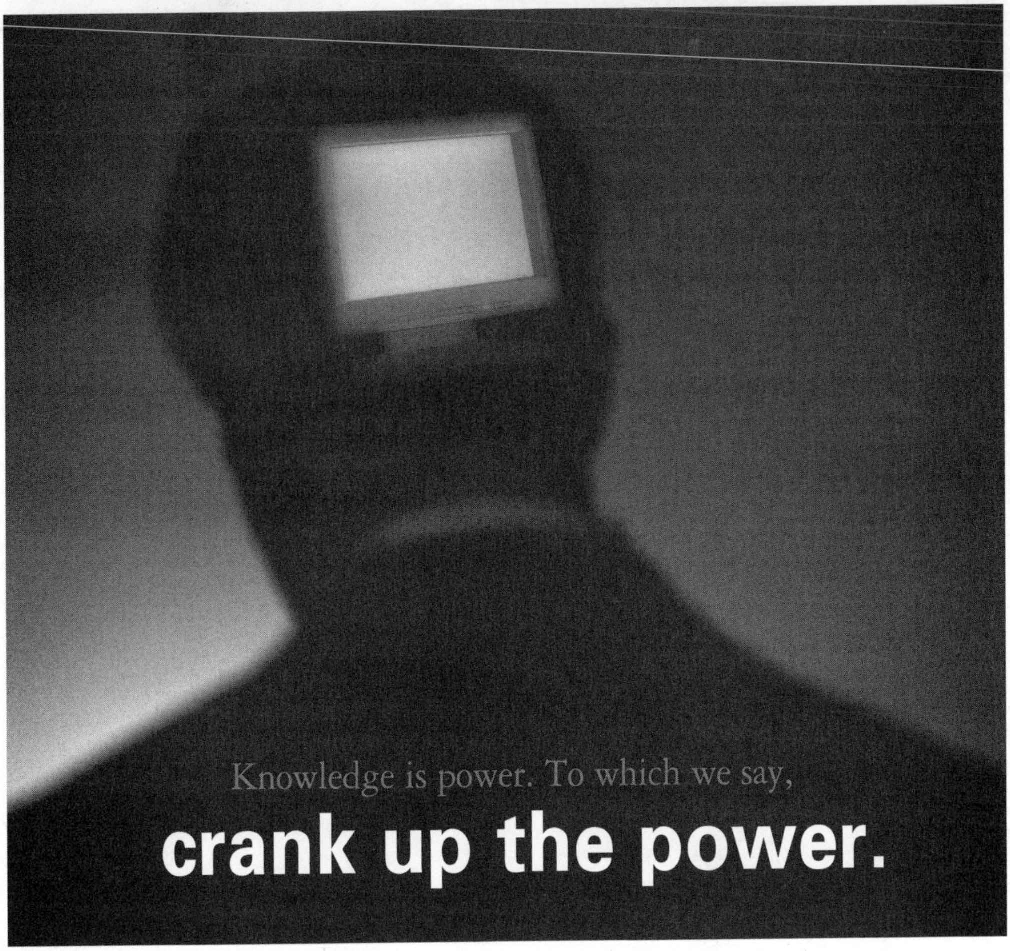

About the BeachFrontQuizzer™ CD-ROM

BeachFrontQuizzer provides interactive certification exams to help you prepare for certification. With the enclosed CD, you can test your knowledge of the topics covered in this book with more than 175 multiple choice questions.

Installation

To install BeachFrontQuizzer:

1. **Insert the CD-ROM in your CD-ROM drive.**
2. **Follow the Setup steps in the displayed Installation Wizard. (When the Setup is finished, you may immediately begin using BeachFrontQuizzer.)**
3. **To begin using BeachFrontQuizzer, enter the 12-digit license key number of the exam you want to take:**

   Building Internet Applications I 380429273697

   Building Internet Applications II 389528292736

Study Sessions

BeachFrontQuizzer tests your knowledge as you learn about new subjects through interactive quiz sessions. Study Session Questions are selected from a single database for each session, dependent on the subcategory selected and the number of times each question has been previously answered correctly. In this way, questions you have answered correctly are not repeated until you have answered all the new questions. Questions that you have missed previously will reappear in later sessions and keep coming back to haunt you until you get the question correct. In addition, you can track your progress by displaying the number of questions you have answered with the Historical Analysis option. You can reset the progress tracking by clicking on the Clear History button. Each time a question is presented the answers are randomized so you will memorize a pattern or letter that goes with the question. You will start to memorize the correct answer that goes with the question concept.

Practice Exams

For advanced users, BeachFrontQuizzer also provides Simulated and Adaptive certification exams. Questions are chosen at random from the database. The Simulated Exam presents a specific number of questions directly related to the real exam. After you finish the exam, BeachFrontQuizzer displays your score and the passing score required for the test. You may display the exam results of this specific exam from this menu. You may review each question and display the correct answer.

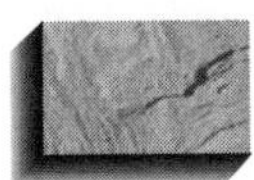

NOTE

For further details of the feature functionality of this BeachFrontQuizzer software, consult the online instructions by choosing Contents from the BeachFrontQuizzer Help menu.

Technical Support

If you experience technical difficulties please call (888) 992-3131. Outside the U.S. call (281) 992-3131. Or, you may e-mail **bfquiz@swbell.net**.

THIS PRODUCT (THE "PRODUCT") CONTAINS PROPRIETARY SOFTWARE, DATA AND INFORMATION (INCLUDING DOCUMENTATION) OWNED BY THE McGRAW-HILL COMPANIES, INC. ("McGRAW-HILL") AND ITS LICENSORS. YOUR RIGHT TO USE THE PRODUCT IS GOVERNED BY THE TERMS AND CONDITIONS OF THIS AGREEMENT.

LICENSE: Throughout this License Agreement, "you" shall mean either the individual or the entity whose agent opens this package. You are granted a non-exclusive and non-transferable license to use the Product subject to the following terms:

(i) If you have licensed a single user version of the Product, the Product may only be used on a single computer (i.e., a single CPU). If you licensed and paid the fee applicable to a local area network or wide area network version of the Product, you are subject to the terms of the following subparagraph (ii).

(ii) If you have licensed a local area network version, you may use the Product on unlimited workstations located in one single building selected by you that is served by such local area network. If you have licensed a wide area network version, you may use the Product on unlimited workstations located in multiple buildings on the same site selected by you that is served by such wide area network; provided, however, that any building will not be considered located in the same site if it is more than five (5) miles away from any building included in such site. In addition, you may only use a local area or wide area network version of the Product on one single server. If you wish to use the Product on more than one server, you must obtain written authorization from McGraw-Hill and pay additional fees.

(iii) You may make one copy of the Product for back-up purposes only and you must maintain an accurate record as to the location of the back-up at all times.

COPYRIGHT; RESTRICTIONS ON USE AND TRANSFER: All rights (including copyright) in and to the Product are owned by McGraw-Hill and its licensors. You are the owner of the enclosed disc on which the Product is recorded. You may not use, copy, decompile, disassemble, reverse engineer, modify, reproduce, create derivative works, transmit, distribute, sublicense, store in a database or retrieval system of any kind, rent or transfer the Product, or any portion thereof, in any form or by any means (including electronically or otherwise) except as expressly provided for in this License Agreement. You must reproduce the copyright notices, trademark notices, legends and logos of McGraw-Hill and its licensors that appear on the Product on the back-up copy of the Product which you are permitted to make hereunder. All rights in the Product not expressly granted herein are reserved by McGraw-Hill and its licensors.

TERM: This License Agreement is effective until terminated. It will terminate if you fail to comply with any term or condition of this License Agreement. Upon termination, you are obligated to return to McGraw-Hill the Product together with all copies thereof and to purge all copies of the Product included in any and all servers and computer facilities.

DISCLAIMER OF WARRANTY: THE PRODUCT AND THE BACK-UP COPY ARE LICENSED "AS IS." McGRAW-HILL, ITS LICENSORS AND THE AUTHORS MAKE NO WARRANTIES, EXPRESS OR IMPLIED, AS TO THE RESULTS TO BE OBTAINED BY ANY PERSON OR ENTITY FROM USE OF THE PRODUCT, ANY INFORMATION OR DATA INCLUDED THEREIN AND/OR ANY TECHNICAL SUPPORT SERVICES PROVIDED HEREUNDER, IF ANY ("TECHNICAL SUPPORT SERVICES"). McGRAW-HILL, ITS LICENSORS AND THE AUTHORS MAKE NO EXPRESS OR IMPLIED WARRANTIES OF MERCHANTABILITY OR FITNESS FOR A PARTICULAR PURPOSE OR USE WITH RESPECT TO THE PRODUCT. McGRAW-HILL, ITS LICENSORS, AND THE AUTHORS MAKE NO GUARANTEE THAT YOU WILL PASS ANY CERTIFICATION EXAM WHATSOEVER BY USING THIS PRODUCT. NEITHER McGRAW-HILL, ANY OF ITS LICENSORS NOR THE AUTHORS WARRANT THAT THE FUNCTIONS CONTAINED IN THE PRODUCT WILL MEET YOUR REQUIREMENTS OR THAT THE OPERATION OF THE PRODUCT WILL BE UNINTERRUPTED OR ERROR FREE. YOU ASSUME THE ENTIRE RISK WITH RESPECT TO THE QUALITY AND PERFORMANCE OF THE PRODUCT.

LIMITED WARRANTY FOR DISC: To the original licensee only, McGraw-Hill warrants that the enclosed disc on which the Product is recorded is free from defects in materials and workmanship under normal use and service for a period of ninety (90) days from the date of purchase. In the event of a defect in the disc covered by the foregoing warranty, McGraw-Hill will replace the disc.

LIMITATION OF LIABILITY: NEITHER McGRAW-HILL, ITS LICENSORS NOR THE AUTHORS SHALL BE LIABLE FOR ANY INDIRECT, SPECIAL OR CONSEQUENTIAL DAMAGES, SUCH AS BUT NOT LIMITED TO, LOSS OF ANTICIPATED PROFITS OR BENEFITS, RESULTING FROM THE USE OR INABILITY TO USE THE PRODUCT EVEN IF ANY OF THEM HAS BEEN ADVISED OF THE POSSIBILITY OF SUCH DAMAGES. THIS LIMITATION OF LIABILITY SHALL APPLY TO ANY CLAIM OR CAUSE WHATSOEVER WHETHER SUCH CLAIM OR CAUSE ARISES IN CONTRACT, TORT, OR OTHERWISE. Some states do not allow the exclusion or limitation of indirect, special or consequential damages, so the above limitation may not apply to you.

U.S. GOVERNMENT RESTRICTED RIGHTS: Any software included in the Product is provided with restricted rights subject to subparagraphs (c), (1) and (2) of the Commercial Computer Software-Restricted Rights clause at 48 C.F.R. 52.227-19. The terms of this Agreement applicable to the use of the data in the Product are those under which the data are generally made available to the general public by McGraw-Hill. Except as provided herein, no reproduction, use, or disclosure rights are granted with respect to the data included in the Product and no right to modify or create derivative works from any such data is hereby granted.

GENERAL: This License Agreement constitutes the entire agreement between the parties relating to the Product. The terms of any Purchase Order shall have no effect on the terms of this License Agreement. Failure of McGraw-Hill to insist at any time on strict compliance with this License Agreement shall not constitute a waiver of any rights under this License Agreement. This License Agreement shall be construed and governed in accordance with the laws of the State of New York. If any provision of this License Agreement is held to be contrary to law, that provision will be enforced to the maximum extent permissible and the remaining provisions will remain in full force and effect.